Cuba Today and Tomorrow

CONTEMPORARY

CUBA

Florida A&M University, Tallahassee
Florida Atlantic University, Boca Raton
Florida Gulf Coast University, Ft. Myers
Florida International University, Miami
Florida State University, Tallahassee
University of Central Florida, Orlando
University of Florida, Gainesville
University of North Florida, Jacksonville
University of South Florida, Tampa
University of West Florida, Pensacola

Contemporary Cuba
Edited by John M. Kirk

A multidisciplinary series focusing on balanced, current, and provocative aspects of Cuban history, culture, society, and politics. Of special interest are works that examine the dramatic changes in Cuba since 1959, such as the role of the military, the nature of economic reforms, and the impact of foreign investments, human rights treaties, and tourism on the island.

Afro-Cuban Voices: On Race and Identity in Contemporary Cuba, by Pedro Pérez-Sarduy and Jean Stubbs (2000)

Cuba, the United States, and the Helms-Burton Doctrine: International Reactions, by Joaquín Roy (2000)

Cuba Today and Tomorrow: Reinventing Socialism, by Max Azicri (2000)

Foreign Relations in a Post-Soviet World, by H. Michael Erisman (2000)

Cuba Today and Tomorrow

Reinventing Socialism

Max Azicri

University Press of Florida

Gainesville · Tallahassee · Tampa · Boca Raton

Pensacola · Orlando · Miami · Jacksonville · Ft. Myers

Copyright 2000 by the Board of Regents of the State of Florida
Printed in the United States of America on acid-free paper
All rights reserved
First cloth printing, 2000
First paperback printing, 2001

06   05   04   03   02   01   C   7   6   5   4   3   2

06   05   04   03   02   01   P   6   5   4   3   2   1

Library of Congress Cataloging-in-Publication Data
Azicri, Max.
Cuba today and tomorrow : reinventing socialism / Max Azicri.
p. cm. — (Contemporary Cuba)
Includes bibliographical references and index.
ISBN 0-8130-1756-4 (alk. paper)—cloth
ISBN 0-8130-2448-X (alk. paper)—paperback
1. Cuba—Politics and government—1959–. 2. Post-communism—Cuba. 3. Cuba—
Economic conditions—1990–. 4. Cuba—Social conditions—1959–. 5. Cuba—Foreign
relations—United States—Foreign relations—Cuba. I. Title. II. Series.
F1788.A93 2000
972.9106'4—dc21   00-044712

The University Press of Florida is the scholarly publishing agency for the State
University System of Florida, comprising Florida A&M University, Florida Atlantic
University, Florida Gulf Coast University, Florida International University, Florida State
University, University of Central Florida, University of Florida, University of North
Florida, University of South Florida, and University of West Florida.

University Press of Florida
15 Northwest 15th Street
Gainesville, FL 32611–2079
http://www.upf.com

For Nickie, David, Danielle, and Fanny Rachel

CONTENTS

List of Figures   ix
List of Tables   xi
Foreword by John M. Kirk   xiii
Preface   xv
List of Abbreviations   xvii

I. An Overview

1. Introduction   3
2. The Impact of the Demise of European Socialism   20

II. The Domestic Environment

3. Rectifying the Revolution's Mistakes   49
4. The Quality of Life under Severe Austerity and Scarcity   69
5. Political Reform under the Special Period   100
6. Economic Reform under the Special Period: Part I   129
7. Economic Reform under the Special Period: Part II   153

III. The External Environment

8. Cuban-U.S. Relations under President Clinton: Part I   179
9. Cuban-U.S. Relations under President Clinton: Part II   197
10. Building New Bridges to the World   225
11. The Pope's Cuban Pilgrimage   251

IV. Looking Forward

12. Reinventing Cuban Socialism   277

Appendices   309
Notes   321
Index   382

FIGURES

2.1. Soviet Sugar Imports, 1978–1989 28
2.2. Market Economies Trade, 1965–1989 32
2.3. Selected Latin American Countries' Real GNP, 1991 39
2.4. Comparison of Adult Literacy Rates, 1992 41
2.5. Average Number of Years of Education Achieved, 1992 41
2.6. Average Life Expectancy, 1992 41
2.7. Average Daily Intake of Required Calories, 1988–1990 42
2.8. Under Age Five Mortality Annually per 1,000 People, 1992 42
2.9. Population per Physician, 1990 42
3.1. Budget Deficits, 1983–1989 56
3.2. Minibrigades' Output, 1986–1987 64
3.3. Contingents' Output, 1987–1989 65
4.1. Countries' Performance According to Social Indicators 70
4.2. Comparison of National and Provincial Social Indicator Rates 72
4.3. Women's Enrollment in Education, 1978–1989 87
4.4. Women's Labor and Civil Status, 1970–1981 88
4.5. Daily Distribution of Time, 1979 89
4.6. Students' Opinions of Quality of Teaching Cuban History 94
4.7. Students' Description of Deficient Teaching Methods 95
4.8. Students' Ability to Remember Historic Events 95
5.1. Women's Legislative Power, 1976–1993 125
7.1. Tourist Industry's Gross Revenues, 1996–1998 157
7.2. Sugar Production, 1995–1998 168

TABLES

2.1. Cuban Trade with Former European Socialist Countries, 1989–1996 37

2.2. Cuban Trade with China, 1991–1996 38

2.3. Cuba's 11 Top Trading Partners, 1996 38

4.1. Share by Country Groups of the World's GDP and Population 73

4.2. Comparison of Seven Countries' Life Expectancy, Infant Mortality Rate, Contraceptive Use among Married Women of Reproductive Age, Maternal Mortality Ratios, 1970–1995 83

5.1. Comparison of the Cuban Political System to Other Regimes 120

5.2. 1995 Opinion Poll on Freedom of Expression 121

5.3. Public Confidence in the Sustainability of Social Equality Levels 121

6.1. Structural Changes in the Cuban Economy 130

6.2. Annual Tax Scale 151

7.1. Foreign Investment by Country, 1988–1995 154

7.2. Foreign Investment by Economic Sector, 1988–1995 155

7.3. Cubanacán's Leading Hotels, 1997 156

7.4. Cuban Military Expenditures, Armed Forces, Population, ME/GNP Percentage, 1985–1995 163

7.5. Economic Performance, 1995–1996 165

7.6. Gross Domestic Product by Economic Sector, 1995–1996 166

7.7. Increases of Selected Sectors' Output, 1995–1996 167

7.8. Foreign Debt in Convertible Currency, Assorted Years 171

7.9. Cuba and U.S. Reports on Cuban Foreign Trade Deficit, 1991–1997 164

8.1. The Cuban-American Lobby: Top Recipients of Money and Major Donors, Jan. 1, 1979–Oct. 16, 1996   182

9.1. Ten Largest U.S. Certified Claims in Cuba   209

10.1. United Nations Resolutions Condemning U.S. Embargo Against Cuba, 1992–1998   226

10.2. Diplomatic Relations between Cuba and Latin America under the Revolution   229

10.3. Cuba and Canada: Import-Export Selected Items and Total Trade, 1989–1996   236

12.1. U.N. Human Rights Commission Vote on U.S. Resolutions Condemning Cuba, 1992–1999   291

FOREWORD

As the 1990s started, it was obvious that growing problems in the Soviet Union would have a major impact upon its close allies. Cuba depended upon Soviet subsidies; its major source of both raw materials and spare parts was the USSR; and this area was also the major purchaser of Cuba's largest single export, sugar. The two economies were so closely intertwined that any problems in Moscow would cause major reverberations in Havana.

The collapse of the Soviet Union, the internecine fighting that broke out in some Soviet republics and Eastern Europe, and widespread political instability in Russia all augured poorly for revolutionary Cuba's survival. Indeed bumper stickers were sold in Miami predicting that Cuban exiles would soon be spending Christmas in Havana. Yet the Cuban government did not fall, and albeit with major problems, the tattered Cuban economy hung on desperately to survive. This survival clearly defied logic and has perplexed specialists the world over.

Max Azicri seeks to provide a framework to address this question. He does so by examining the manner in which the revolutionary government has sought to "reinvent socialism" during the past decade. There are two central sections to develop his arguments: the impact of what Fidel Castro has termed the "special period" upon the domestic environment, and Cuban strategies to build new political and trade alliances in the wake of the USSR´s collapse. In both, Azicri offers useful insights into revolutionary Cuba's ability to withstand these pressures.

It is clear that the Castro government has undertaken extraordinary measures to revive the ailing economy, while at the same time attempting to ensure social gains (principally education and health care). In essence he has introduced a series of (controlled) capitalist measures to ensure the survival of a socialist system. It is not an orthodox model, and it is one that has produced mixed results. Nevertheless, the revolution has survived.

The government has also been obliged to court new international relationships, in both commercial and political terms, so necessary since Soviet largesse and markets disappeared virtually overnight. Havana has stated its willingness to negotiate with Washington, although unfortunately little real progress has been made. Significantly, though, this patchwork quilt of economic reform (more significant than is widely thought in U.S. circles), the maintenance of social programs, and development of different trade and political alliances have succeeded in keeping the revolutionary process alive. To mix metaphors, the ship of state may be a creaky one, with several major leaks and little remaining ballast, but it remains afloat.

In this process of survival the Cuban revolution, bloody but unbowed, has defied the odds for almost a decade. If we are to understand how this has come about (despite enormous obstacles), and what to expect in the future, we need to know the mindset in Havana. This book by longtime Cuba watcher Max Azicri makes a major contribution toward this goal. His thesis—that the revolutionary government has been pragmatic—is well developed, and he further suggests that the government will continue to "reinvent socialism" in the new millennium.

John M. Kirk, Dalhousie University

PREFACE

Cuba's troubled but courageous life in the 1990s and beyond is the subject of this book. Years of firsthand experience have allowed me to write it. After leaving Cuba in 1960, I returned to Havana, my birthplace, for the first time eighteen years later. On many visits since, I witnessed the work of the revolution before and during the present special period in peacetime.

Cubans welcomed me amicably and helped me in my research. I would like to express my gratitude to them, especially to José Luis Rodríguez, Esteban Morales Domínguez, Jorge Hernández Martínez, Alfredo Guevara, Roberto Fernández Retamar, Milagros Martínez, Gabriel Molina Franchossi, Alfredo Viñas, Carmen Villar, José (Pepín) Ortiz, Carlos Batista, Fernando Martínez Heredia, Aurelio Alonso, Rafael Hernández, Juan Valdés Paz, Carlos Tablada, Julio Carranza, Eugenio R. Balari, Jesús Arboleya, Mercedes Arce, Raul Comín Becquer, Alberto Adato, Reinaldo Peñalver, José Massip, Mario González, and the late Tomás Gutiérrez Alea. Good friends have also helped me in the United States, especially Professors Roger H. Harrell, Félix Masud-Piloto, José A. Moreno, Enrique Sacerio-Gari, Richard Dello Buono, Nelson P. Valdés, and, while I attended the University of Southern California, Paul E. Hadley and Joseph Nyomarkay. Also, my thanks go to Professors John M. Kirk and Sinan Koont—the latter reviewed the manuscript for the University Press of Florida—as well as to the reviewer who chose to remain anonymous.

At Edinboro University of Pennsylvania, my thank are due for the President's Scholarly Research Grant reducing my teaching load in 1998 and for the support I have received from so many colleagues, especially former acting Dean of Liberal Arts Donald Dilmore and Professors Roy Brant, Steven Nachman, Donald Swift, Michael Hannah, James Drane,

Thomas E. Gay, Judith Gramley, and Mark Fetkewicz. Special thanks is due Professor Elsie Deal for the editorial assistance she provided on this project. And last but not least, to my wife Nickie and my nine-year-old twins David and Danielle, my apologies for having spent so many hours away from them and my gratitude for their not having deserted me.

ABBREVIATIONS

AAWH	American Association of World Health
ACS	Association of Caribbean States
ANAP	National Association of Small (Private) Farmers
ASCE	Association for the Study of the Cuban Economy
BNC	Cuban National Bank
BPA	Banco Popular (Popular Savings Bank)
BTTR	Brothers to the Rescue
CANF	Cuban American National Foundation
CARICOM	Caribbean Community
CARIFORUM	Association of Caribbean States
CC	Concilio Cubano
CDA	Cuban Democracy Act
CDC	Cuban Committee for Democracy
CDR	Committees for the Defense of the Revolution
CEA	Center for the Study of the Americas
CEE	Center for the Study of Europe
CEJ	Center for Youth Studies
CEPAL	Latin American Economic Council
CIA	Central Intelligence Agency
CIESPAL	International Center of Higher Journalism Studies for Latin America
CIMEX	Department of Convertible Currency
CMEA	Council of Mutual Economic Assistance
CNN	Cable News Network
CNSDE	National Commission for the Direction of the Economic System
COPPAL	Permanent Conference of Latin American Political Parties

CTC	Cuban Confederation of Workers
DR	Revolutionary Directorate, Havana University
ECLAC	United Nations Commission for Latin America and the Caribbean
EU	European Union
EXPOCUBA	National and International Fairs and Exhibits, Cuba
FAO	United Nations Food and Agriculture Organization
FAR	Revolutionary Armed Forces
FEU	Federation of University Students, Havana University
FLACSO	Social Science Latin American Faculty
FMC	Cuban Federation of Women
GDP	Gross Domestic Product
GNP	Gross National Product
GSP	Global Social Product
ICAO	International Civil Aviation Organization
IPC	Consumer Price Index
IPS	International Press Service
ITT	International Telephone and Telegraph
JUCEI	Coordination and Inspection Board
JUCEPLAN	Central Planning Board
MAI	Multilateral Agreement on Investment
MC	Convertible Currency Department
MFN	Most Favored Nation
MININT	Ministry of the Interior
NAFTA	North American Free Trade Agreement
NAM	National Association of Manufacturers (U.S.)
NGO	Nongovernmental Organization
OAS	Organization of American States
OFAC	Office of Foreign Assets Control, U.S. Treasury Department
ONAT	National Office of Tax Administration
OPP	Organs of People's Power
ORI	Integrated Revolutionary Organization
OSPAAAL	Tricontinental: Solidarity Organization with the Peoples of Africa, Asia, and Latin America
PA	Food Program
PCC	Cuban Communist Party
PP	Popular Party (Spain)
PPP	Purchasing Power Parity

PRI	Institutional Revolutionary Party (Mexico)
PSP	Popular Socialist Party
PURS	United Party of the Socialist Revolution
RP	Rectification of Errors and Negative Tendencies Process
SDPE	System of Direction and Planning of the Economy
SELA	Latin American Economic System
STET	Societa Finanziara Telefonica
UBPC	Basic Units of Cooperative Production
UJC	Union of Communist Youth
UNDP	United Nations Development Program
UNEAC	Artists and Writers Union
VENAMCHAM	Venezuelan-American Chamber of Commerce
WHO	World Health Organization
WTO	World Trade Organization

I

An Overview

1

Introduction

This book covers an important period of social transformation in Cuba under extremely difficult conditions. Against the backdrop of Cuban-Soviet relations and the rectification policies of the late 1980s, beginning with the time when, according to many economic and political analysts, the Castro regime seemed incapable of surviving the crisis of European socialism, I examine the hardships the country is enduring and the modest triumphs it is achieving under the current special period in peacetime. I cover the political, social, and economic changes implemented and when and how the decision to resist the impact of the downfall of the Soviet bloc started to pay off modestly and unsteadily.

The study involves examination of the interaction that took place between the international environment of the 1990s and the Cuban regime, with analysis of how the former compelled the latter to undergo reforms aimed at adaptation to a new world reality. It also covers the impact that economic hardship and internal socioeconomic and political reforms have had and are having on the island's domestic environment. As a political system interacting with both domestic and external environments, the revolutionary regime effected changes in a wide area of governmental decision-making capabilities, including extractive, distributive, regulatory, symbolic, and external relations functions. The study covers too the history-making five-day visit in January 1998 by Pope John Paul II to the island and the effect it had on the country.

I distinguish between those parts of the political system that Havana identifies as central and not open for negotiation and others that, despite their relative importance, are subject to change. The pope's visit contributed to reinforcing and advancing the changes in church-state relations and toleration of religious practice that had started in 1992. Looking at some of Havana's newly adopted policies, some of which were previously rejected or not seriously considered, I examine how they have altered the regime's social fabric and ideological system. The study also includes the effect of recently modified social relations, many of which were not anticipated or welcomed, even though to some degree they were instrumental in sustaining the revolution in power at such a difficult time.

The Cuban revolution is always worthy of scholarly attention and study. Havana's resilience and sustaining power in the face of such colossal adversity demands scholarly analysis. It is important to understand the reasons behind the regime's capacity to undergo such a difficult recovery process, to find such inner resources at the worst of times. Numerous defections of high-positioned cadres, internationally known baseball players, and many others have provided evidence of increased dissatisfaction. Yet somehow, Cuba has mustered the capacity to reshape itself and exercise enough staying power to overcome today's misfortune even as it is being sanctioned by the United States. In this book I seek to explain the level of support the revolution seemingly enjoys after years of severe deprivation and scarcity under the special period. I examine the people's affirmation of the revolution's achievements, their determination to safeguard the nation's sovereignty and independence while at the same time loudly voicing dissatisfaction and frustration at their deteriorated living conditions.[1]

Answering the riddle of the revolution's survival could determine whether support for a well-entrenched charismatic leadership, increased governmental control using police methods, or a mix of these and other elements account for such endurance and social forbearance. And yet, some of the answers provided here may not satisfy those who have a preconceived notion of Cuban affairs, especially as they have unfolded in the difficult fourth decade of revolutionary rule.

However, the importance of answering such questions goes beyond an academic concern. Washington's Cuba policy, fueled by conservative Cuban-American and American political forces, is based on the assumption that authoritarian control is the reason for the regime's prolonged life. While social and political control have always existed and are now enforced more diligently than before, repressive police techniques alone could not have saved Cuban socialism from a fate similar to that of European socialism. As social scientists suggest, to have resisted the adversity and undertaken the systemic transformation that has occurred in Cuba in recent years, it is necessary for the government at least to have enjoyed a relatively satisfactory level of sustained legitimacy and not just to be benefiting from widespread inertia and resigned acquiescence.[2]

Voluntary work campaigns, minibrigade construction projects, the

Communist Party and mass organizations–sponsored political mobilization, outward expressions of social cohesion and support for the government, and other such activities must emanate from inner resources and lingering convictions, not from externally applied coercion alone. By its very nature, repression runs contrary to people's revolutionary *conciencia* (consciousness) and could not elicit genuine support and concern for the regime's viability, especially to the degree that it is necessary and expected in today's Cuba—notwithstanding the numerous manifestations of discontent that have taken place in the 1990s.

The Cuban revolution has always provoked passion and controversy, and today's special period is no exception. By enforcing socially equitable policies at a time of acute scarcity because those policies mitigate the hardships of the current economic crisis, Havana made possible a fairer distribution of goods and services among the population—in a way rarely seen among Western societies, which usually support a lopsided distribution of income favoring the wealthy. Cuba's commitment to social equity and welfare, in spite of the special period, is particularly relevant to developing nations, including Mexico, one of the three members of NAFTA.[3]

The underlying theme pursued here is that Cuba is undergoing another radical social transformation under the revolution, different from what was experienced before. The fact that today's social change process is not a matter of choice has no bearing on its relevancy and complexity. While Cubans are currently engaged in the ambitious and difficult task of reinventing (remaking) their socialist system, and while the economy continues rebounding modestly and unsteadily, saving the achievements of the last three decades should keep them busy tomorrow and for years to come.

Organization of the Study

The book is divided into four parts. Part I, the overview, includes this introduction and chapter 2, "The Impact of the Demise of European Socialism." Cuba was one of the countries outside Europe most affected by the events in the Soviet bloc and the former Soviet Union. Even though Castro was one of the world leaders who anticipated the possible demise of the Soviet Union under Mikhail Gorbachev, the collapse of European socialism still found Cuba severely unprepared. The complex web of relations established among Cuba, the USSR, and other European socialist regimes had made Cuba almost totally dependent on the Soviet bloc.

Collapse of the Soviet Bloc

It could be argued that the dependence Cuba had upon the Soviet bloc was qualitatively different from the dependence it had upon the United States. American investments were paramount in Cuba before the revolution. After 1959, no sugar mills, factories, hotels, banks, utilities, or any other economic investment belonged to Soviet bloc countries. But in spite of its very different nature, the dependence upon the USSR proved to be extremely costly in the long run. Precisely because it involved almost every aspect of the country's life and apparently satisfied most of its basic needs, the dependent relationship turned out to be rather exacting once the partnership that had sustained it ceased to exist. In this sense, the fact that the collapse of European socialism was not Cuba's fault makes no difference. And yet, the all-embracing scope of the dependent relationship with the Soviet bloc makes it even more remarkable that Cuba could replace it almost overnight, however unsatisfactorily thus far.

An interesting development of Cuban international trade in the 1990s is that Russia has again become Cuba's leading trade partner, though under very different conditions from those that ruled their trade before. It is their mutual economic interest that prevails in their commercial exchange; ideological links no longer bind them.

Part II, "The Domestic Environment," includes chapters 3–7: "Rectifying the Revolution's Mistakes"; "The Quality of Life under Severe Austerity and Scarcity"; "Political Reform under the Special Period"; "Economic Reform under the Special Period: Part I"; and "Economic Reform under the Special Period: Part II."

Rectifying Internal Mistakes

Chapter 3 examines the process started in 1986 of rectification of errors and negative tendencies. The shortcomings of the rectification process notwithstanding, it appears that the country would have been in worse shape to withstand the collapse of European socialism without it. As in most important events in Cuba, Castro's leadership was a major factor in undertaking this campaign, in which practically all spheres of social and economic life came under scrutiny, including the Communist Party.

Focusing on policy contradictions and uncertainties in the course of the revolution, some Cuba watchers have argued that the campaign of rectifying errors was not in itself new but in reality was the rectification of an earlier rectification. Policies that had been adopted at a given time and heralded as the solution to some serious problems had to be abandoned later for their proven ineffectiveness. Principled critical thinking allowed the regime to identify some of its own mistakes and attempt to correct them, even if imperfectly.

Social Impact of the Economic Downfall

Chapter 4 covers the devastating effect of the downfall of the nation's economy. After three decades of sustained social growth, the revolutionary regime witnessed how Cuban society could collapse. The return of *jineterismo* (prostitution) was a low point for a social revolution that had proudly eradicated it. While the social division caused by the dollarization of the economy in 1993 solved acute survival problems for some, it created two distinct societies depending on whether one had access to dollars or not. Buying in dollars-only stores became a very different shopping experience from using national *pesos*. Those whose access was limited to pesos resented those who had dollars to spend, especially when the dollars came from relatives living in the United States.

The national standard of living seemed at some point to undergo an endless fall, which was partly balanced by inventive policy making, grassroots ingenuity, and vital national character resources that pulled the country together, allowing it to move haltingly against all odds.

Political Reform

Particularly important to Cuba watchers, chapter 5 deals with the controversial subject of political reform. The regime has been charged with acting so slowly that its actions amount almost to no reform. While there have been some changes, the main features of the political system have remained in place: the single party system—the Communist Party—and the Organs of People's Power (OPP), the administrative and legislative national political structure. The new electoral system has introduced direct voting to elect National Assembly deputies and provincial delegates but still lacks electoral competition. (However, at the municipal level several candidates compete for the same office.) As expected, the official slate electoral system has been criticized outside the island and by dissidents from within.

The Fifth Congress of the Cuban Communist Party (PCC) was held October 10–12, 1997, and the elections for OPP delegates at the local level followed a week later. Completing the electoral cycle, the provincial and National Assembly elections were held on January 11, 1998. The government heralded the election returns as a triumph for the revolution, given the very high number of unified votes accepting the official slate of candidates (94.39 percent) and the towering voter turnout (98.35 percent).[4]

Still, the number of ballots left blank and/or purposely damaged signaled a level of political dissatisfaction higher than in earlier periods of revolutionary rule.

Another major event took place in October 1997. After thirty years, the remains of Ernesto Che Guevara and six other revolutionary fighters who fell in Bolivia in 1967 were returned to Cuban soil. A week of ceremonies honored them, while tens of thousands of Cubans formed long lines in the Plaza of the Revolution to file past the small, flag-draped caskets. Guevara's and his comrades' remains were later transported to Santa Clara, where they lay in a newly built mausoleum featuring an impressive statue of Guevara, rifle in hand. Standing next to Defense Minister Raúl Castro, and facing family members, surviving guerrilla comrades, and a crowd of thousands, President Castro praised Guevara, saying: "Honest people of this planet, despite their social origin, admire him. Che is waging and winning more battles than ever."[5]

The thirtieth anniversary of Che Guevara's death also provoked a worldwide celebration that included films, biographies, scholarly studies, testimonial narratives, poetry, videos, conferences, on-line websites, art exhibits, memorial monuments, and newspaper and magazine articles examining the Cuban leader's life and accomplishments. The revolutionary guerrilla with a gifted intellect, who had renounced his hard-gained position in the Cuban government to pursue the Latin American revolution and who was finally ambushed and executed close to his native Argentina, was a source of curiosity and admiration to a world needing to cling to romanticized inspirational lives and memories.

Whether Castro was going to accept another five-year term as the country's president had been a matter of speculation—and he finally did. He had told ABC reporter Diane Sawyer on *Prime Time* in 1993: "I hope that my *compañeros* will not demand from me in five years that I again become a candidate to deputy of the National Assembly [a necessary condition to be elected head of the Council of State, which by making him president of the Council of Ministers would make him the country's president]." Asked if he would like to retire if the embargo were over and Cuba were advancing economically, he said: "More or less. I cannot say exactly what I think about this. One is not free, and I am not here for pleasure. I am a soldier in the struggle at this difficult moment, and it would be cowardice to retire. It is not a promise . . . I am not a man that likes to make promises. I am just thinking aloud. I am telling you how I feel."[6]

In the January 1998 parliamentary elections held just before the pope's visit, President Castro was reelected to the National Assembly, and the following month he was elected to continue as head of the Council of State and of the Council of Ministers.[7] This paved the way for another five-year term that would extend his tenure as president until the year 2003, when he will be seventy-six years old.[8] Seeking undisturbed political continuity, Castro set up an orderly succession transition at the Fifth Communist Party Congress in October 1997, when he selected his brother Raúl to be his eventual successor. Raúl Castro will be seventy-two years old by the end of President Castro's current five-year term.[9] However, shortly after his 1998 reelection, Castro denied having chosen his brother as his successor, arguing that he has no authority to do so. It is unlikely that Castro changed his mind about Raúl becoming his eventual successor, so he was probably reacting to critical comments made abroad, and at home by dissidents, for having chosen his own successor.[10] (See Appendices A and B.)

Probably the most effective way to look at political reform is as a prolonged process that—while not yielding great transformations—will not stop in the near future. As long as the government remains cautious in carrying out political change, the process of change is likely to continue at a slow pace. But slow change is preferable to no change and safer (to the regime) than rapid change. Besides examining what has been done, the political analyst can also speculate on the direction future reform might take. Furthermore, the revival of religious life in Cuba before, during, and after the pope's visit in January 1998 is part of an ongoing process with long-term implications, which at this stage are hard to assess fully.

Economic Reform

Chapters 6 and 7 cover economic reform. The changes implemented since 1990 have proven to be a turning point for a system that for three decades aimed at nearly total economic socialism. The line dividing private and public areas of the economy determines the nature and physiognomy of the new system. The usual explanation is that the former is represented by foreign capital and the latter by the state. But that is not quite accurate. The amount of self-employment and the new agricultural cooperative units established during the special period have allowed economic modalities representing private or nonstate enterprise across the country. The scope and nature of foreign capital investment has been changed and expanded, and the number of joint ventures has increased and will continue to grow in the future. The opening of free zones (two in Havana already) and industrial parks offering new business options received almost immediate positive response from foreign investors.[11]

In addition to newly established foreign banks, the national banking system has undergone significant changes. It has been upgrading its resources to provide the kind of services that are expected under the country's new economic practices, including cash-dispensing machines, which are now found in Havana. The Popular Savings Bank de Ahorro (BPA), where half of the nation's liquidity is currently deposited, has expanded its services, too, including peso and dollar savings accounts available to customers residing on the island or overseas. Family remittances from abroad can now be made through a network of bank correspondents in third countries and can also be deposited in the relative's bank account at home.[12]

Probably the most serious problem confronting Cuba's economic recovery in the 1990s was the difficulty encountered in financing the sugar harvest and the economy in general. The prices paid for available short-term credit were exorbitant and usually insufficient, resulting in lower sugar harvests than planned and needed. (This happened again with the 1998 sugar harvest.) However, the 1998 agreement with Japan, rescheduling the long-term debt that had reduced sharply trade between the two countries for over a decade, offered a new opportunity for similar agreements with other creditors that could provide future financing under better terms. Still, under this agreement Cuba was assuming a burdensome responsibility of making principal and interest payments for old debts at a time of serious economic decline and restructuring.

Part III, "The External Environment," includes chapters 8–11: "Cuban–U.S. Relations under President Clinton: Part I"; "Cuban–U.S. Relations under President Clinton: Part II"; "Building New Bridges to the World"; and "The Pope's Cuban Pilgrimage."

Heating Up the Cold War

As discussed in chapters 8 and 9, relations between Cuba and the United States under the Clinton Administration changed mostly for the worse, though some improvement signals have come from Washington since the pope's visit to Cuba in early 1998. Even though Clinton's support for the Torricelli-Graham Bill when he was a presidential candidate in 1992 was a preview of things to come, there were expectations early in his first term that movement toward normalization of relations between Havana and Washington would soon be in the offing. All in all, this proved to be wrong.

The regrettable 1996 downing of two Brothers to the Rescue (BTTR) planes by the Cuban Air Force followed by the signing of the punitive

Helms-Burton Act took the United States to an across-the-board campaign against Cuba (military operations excepted). Clinton's Cuba policy forced Washington to interfere with the trade practices of its closest allies and other countries, potentially endangering the World Trade Organization's work.

In hindsight, Cuba and the United States acted so imprudently that they put themselves in an untenable position: Washington's repeated interference in Cuban domestic affairs was unacceptable to Havana, while the shooting down of the two BTTR airplanes was equally unacceptable to Washington. Each side had unwisely crossed the line that had kept the long-held U.S.-Cuba problematic within acceptable confrontational limits.

The powerful right-wing sector of the southern Florida Cuban-American community, the domestic political ambitions of presidential candidate Clinton in 1992, and later the reelection campaign needs of President Clinton in 1996 played a mutually reinforcing political game that resulted in Washington's Cuba policy being handled ineptly.

Cuban-American sociologist Lisandro Pérez, director of the Cuban Studies and Research Program at Florida International University, chronicles the meeting at the White House between President Clinton and influential leaders of the Cuban-American community (including the controversial leader of the Cuban American National Foundation, the late Jorge Más Canosa)[13] on August 21, 1994, and its political aftermath:

[The meeting] was centered on imposing additional severe sanctions on the Cuban government on the account that Castro had to be punished for the 1994 *balseros* [rafters] crisis . . . *Más Canosa insisted that the President stop family remittances entirely.* The President agreed to do it. By the end of the meeting the Miami group had achieved imposing measures reinforcing the embargo . . . The meeting . . . made clear to the President that the community's political influence would not be used to defend immigration rights. Therefore, by the end the outstanding and unique status conferred upon Cuban immigrants [immediate political asylum upon entering U.S. territory] was a victim of the common and ordinary considerations that have decided the fate of most immigrant groups, not only in the U.S. but all over the world, *domestic politics.*[14] [Emphasis added.]

After the ensuing immigration accords between Havana and Washington, Cuban *balseros* have been returned to Havana by the U.S. Coast Guard. It was a radical about-face, but more incredible was that the political work of some of the most radical anti-Castro Cuban-American leaders made it possible.

As far as Cuba policy is concerned, the Clinton Administration might come to be known for its inadequate handling of a complex international issue, more so than Republican administrations. While it would not be the first time that domestic politics interfered with foreign policy, here domestic electoral considerations decided the nation's foreign policy on the same issue and by the same president twice (1992 and 1996).

By 1999 opposing signals were coming from Washington regarding its Cuba policy. President Clinton suspended Title III of the Helms-Burton Act for the seventh time, justifying his action to a conservative Republican-dominated Congress by saying: "We are making real progress in strengthening the international effort to bring democracy to Cuba." At a Democratic fund-raising gathering in New York City he stated that he was prepared to "develop bilateral relations with Cuba if it respects democratic principles and ensures human rights." Clinton also noted that the pope's visit to Cuba was of "great value" and that he "welcome[d] it."[15]

After an initial refusal to have the pope's visit influence U.S. Cuba policy, the White House announced easing some of the sanctions imposed on the Castro regime. Two of the sanctions had been established by President Clinton since coming to office in response to Cuba's actions. However, the limited extent of the policy changes made and the anti-Castro rhetoric Secretary of State Madeleine Albright used while explaining the reasons behind curbing such sanctions underscored the White House's confrontational Cold War–style approach against Castro. It also made evident the reduced scope of authority left to the president to make changes in Cuba policy after the Helms-Burton Act was signed into law in March 1996. During her talk to reporters at the State Department, Albright tried to assuage right-wing Cuban Americans' objections, and those of their allies in Congress, by admitting that there had been no real change in U.S. Cuba policy and that both the almost four-decades-old economic embargo and the Helms-Burton Act would remain in place.[16] Secretary Albright recognized that besides responding to the pope's plea for help in carrying out religious and humanitarian relief activities in Cuba, a major reason for ameliorating U.S. punitive measures was to look at Cuba "beyond Fidel Castro," so there would be no rapprochement with the Cuban government as long as Castro remained in power. It was also a way of demonstrating American humanitarian concerns and the administration's desire to improve the living conditions of the Cuban people—especially in the wake of the pope's call for the "world to open itself to Cuba."

Implicit in the official justification for lifting some of the restrictions on aid to Cuba (especially facilitating the licensing to send medicines and medical equipment) was the charge made against President Clinton (and against other presidents before him) by critics of U.S. policy that American sanctions were hurting the people more than the government. In a cautious manner, noting that he had to learn the details of Clinton's decision before making a final judgment, Castro characterized it as positive and constructive.

Clinton's Cuba policy had caused some confusion in November 1997 when the then head of the U.S. interests section in Havana, Michael Kozak, and the CIA's chief Cuba analyst met in Havana with a Cuban foreign ministry official, Carlos Fernández de Cossio, and told him that President Clinton wanted "to mend relations if the island embrace[d] reform." But, denying that a shift in Clinton's policy was in the making, Washington later rejected that a "special message" had been delivered to Castro and reiterated that U.S. Cuba policy remained the same: "if [Cuba is] prepared to take substantial, fundamental steps . . ., we are prepared to make positive responses."[17]

In mid-1997, with the blessings of the State Department, the Italian Societa Finanziara Telefonica (STET) had come to a compensation agreement with ITT in the amount of $25 million for the right to use ITT's Cuban properties that had been nationalized by the Castro government more than thirty years before. But Cuban-American Representative Ileana Ros-Lehtinen (R-Fla.) had "stunned Caribbean ambassadors attending a meeting in Washington with her proposal to end preferential trade status and U.S. assistance to Caribbean nations that support Cuba's entry into their free trade zone."[18] Representatives of the Cuban-American lobby in Congress seemed determined to put pressure on any country in their anti-Castro efforts, which included preventing any policy change that could take Washington away from its long-held hard-line Cuba stance.

An Active Foreign Policy

Chapter 9, "Building New Bridges to the World," is an examination of Cuba's foreign policy in the 1990s. Before 1959 Cuba had diplomatic relations with fifty countries; today it has multiplied its diplomatic relations three times over. This is representative of the kind of foreign policy Cuba has pursued under the special period. Havana has opened itself to the world in search of relations, connections, friends, partners, and associates. Altogether, the effect of the new diplomatic activism has been favorable to Havana. Rather than allowing itself to become isolated from the outside world as Washington would like it to be, Cuba has established a rich network of new and old diplomatic relations at the worst of times in the country's recent history.

A primary area of Cuba's diplomatic activism seeking acceptance and reintegration has been neighboring Latin America and the Caribbean. No interference in any country's domestic affairs is the new mantra guiding the regime's foreign policy, especially in Latin America. By mid-1999 four regional countries still did not hold diplomatic relations with Cuba: Costa Rica, El Salvador, Honduras, and Paraguay (though the latter established consular relations in 1996).

The Ibero-American summits, which include representatives from Spain, Portugal, and Latin America, have been an important arena for high-level diplomacy, with heads of state talking directly to one another. Besides the controversy surrounding the commitment to political pluralism at Viña del Mar, Chile (1996), and its follow-up at Isla Margarita, Venezuela (1997), and Oporto, Portugal (1998), and how its application to Cuba should proceed since Castro signed both final declarations, there have been attempts to curtail Cuba's diplomatic gains at different international events. Nevertheless, the 1999 Ibero-American summit was held in Havana.

While Havana's new foreign policy has done wonders in overcoming international isolation, there still are exceptions, most notably the conservative José María Aznar administration in Spain and the way it was able to modify the European Union's stance on Cuba to a position less palatable to Havana. But Canada seems to have made up for this and other losses. The 1998 visit to Havana by Prime Minister Jean Chrétien (preceded in 1997 by the visit of Canadian foreign minister Lloyd Axworthy) and the different agreements approved by both countries reinforce the high level of Canadian investment in the island. Mexico continues to be a close friend and partner, as it has always been. Both Canada and Mexico have opposed the Helms-Burton Act and have approved antidote legislation to combat its effects.

Castro and the Pope Meet at the Vatican

In chapter 10 I discuss the pontiff's five-day visit to the island. In retrospect, it seems clear that President Castro's journey to Italy in the fall of 1996 was destined to be a historic one. Traveling amidst widespread speculation of when, how, and if Pope John Paul II would visit Cuba,

Castro addressed the delegates gathered in Rome for the World Food Summit of the United Nations Food and Agriculture Organization (FAO). Articulating a forceful message, he became a self-appointed spokesman for millions of poor and hungry people the world over, alerting everyone to the perils to come if the current path is not modified: "Hunger, the inseparable companion of the poor, is the result of the unequal distribution of wealth and of the injustices of the world. The rich do not know hunger. What bandages are we to apply so that within 20 years there are 400 million, instead of 800 million, starving people? These goals, if only for their modesty, are shameful. Why is there fierce competition to sell arms to underdeveloped countries, since they won't make them stronger in the defense of their independence and since hunger is what we must kill? Let truth reign, not hypocrisy and lies. Let us be conscious of the fact that in this world, hegemony, arrogance and selfishness must cease. The bells that toll today for those who die of hunger each day, will toll tomorrow for all of humanity if it doesn't try to save itself, doesn't know how to save itself, or is not wise enough to save itself."[19]

People's reaction in Rome to Castro's presence followed a pattern that has been repeated in practically every city and every country he has visited anywhere in the world, and there have been many in recent years. This is the way a journalist describes it: "Banners wave in the streets, declaring: `Welcome, Comandante.' Admirers follow him, shouting 'Viva Cuba.' And on Monday, government leaders trekked one by one over to the Holiday Inn to pay homage. Fidel Castro—the man Italians call 'Maximum Leader'—is holding court. Castro's revolutionary spirit still evokes respect and passion here, and Italians have been giving him an enthusiastic reception since he arrived Saturday. At the U.N. World Food Summit, delegates flocked around him, taking photographs and begging for autographs. On Sunday, he dined at the home of Gianni Agnelli, Fiat automobile mogul and one of the nation's richest men."[20]

Notwithstanding his appearance at the World Food Summit and the meeting with Italy's President Oscar Luigi Scalfaro, Prime Minister Romano Prodi, and Foreign Minister Lamberto Dini, the personal audience with the pope in the anteroom of the library in the Vatican overshadowed all the other important activities Castro carried out while in Rome. The Western Hemisphere champion of revolutionary Marxism conversed amicably in Spanish for thirty-five minutes with the same pope who had inspired the anti-Soviet rebellion in his native Poland, which ultimately brought down the European socialist regimes.

By the time they met on November 19 at the Vatican, the pope and

Castro had taken similar stands on some controversial issues of mutual concern at the FAO summit. They denounced the industrialized nations' practice of abusing poor nations and of worsening their plight rather than helping them. In his address to the FAO summit, "John Paul II was not short of words censuring how 800 million people in the world are condemned to hunger and even death because of the unfair distribution of wealth and generalized poverty." He also "demanded clearly that the external debt suffocating poor countries should be canceled, and did not abstain from expressing his opposition to unilateral measures of one country against another."[21] Besides treasuring the fact that he and the pope had touched upon the summit's issues with similar perspectives, Castro expressed his gratitude to the pope during their meeting for having earlier condemned the Helms-Burton Act and for having made in his FAO address condemnatory references to the Cuba policy of the United States.

With humility and perhaps with some sense of piety (he was educated by Jesuits), Castro reextended the invitation originally issued in 1979 for the pope to visit Cuba. His Holiness accepted. Reportedly, "among the conditions for the papal visit, the Vatican insisted on greater liberty for the church in Cuba, including permission for foreign priests to aid the island's 200 clergymen."[22] Such permission had been granted by the time the pope arrived in Havana, as had some wider liberty—though not to the entire satisfaction of the Church hierarchy in Rome and Havana. The pope's visit was to include traveling to four major Cuban cities from January 21 to 25, 1998, and conducting mass in each. This also occurred.

Remaking Cuban Socialism

Part IV, "Looking Forward," is a single chapter about reinventing Cuban socialism, centering on the changes Cuban socialism has undergone and the changes that might take place. The crisis of European socialism had more than an economic impact and a political and social sequel; it also provoked reflection and discussion across the country at the theoretical and ideological level. Cuban Marxist thinkers engaged in lively arguments about the role that Marxism should still play in Cuba and the world over. The chapter includes the ideas of members of the faculty of the Philosophy Institute of Havana University, the contributors to a special issue of *Temas*, and other Marxist thinkers in the country. It is noteworthy that besides expressing conceptual differences among themselves, the authors agree that dogmatic thinking should be rejected and that critical and creative ideas—not an inflexible official line disguised as rightful doctrine—should be the bedrock of a revolutionary Marxist ideology.

Fidel Castro's political thought and leadership are central to the Cuban revolution. His imprint on Cuba is so vast and deep that the revolution has been identified as his own. Historically, Castro is a salient contemporary example of a tradition of radical political thought and action in Cuba. There is a historic progression starting in the nineteenth century that culminates in the 1959 revolution. Nationalism, socialism, anti-imperialism, and social justice were political and social objectives sought after and cherished before Castro, but it was he who knew how to make them happen, bringing them into reality through a successful revolution. He also knew how to safeguard revolutionary rule from its enemies. Under Castro's leadership, the Cuban revolution became the most radical social and political transformation that any country has ever experienced in the Western Hemisphere.

The human rights debate has been a sore point for Cuba. The United States had been successful in making political moves against Havana on the human rights question until this practice finally backfired in Geneva in 1998 when an alignment of nations voted to defeat the same American motion denouncing Cuban human rights violations that had prevailed so many times before. However, the human rights vote was reversed against Havana in 1999.

Yet, as a human rights conference attended by American and Cuban delegations indicates, the distinct views of the two countries are not that far apart on some fundamental issues. Many of the remaining differences stem from profound philosophical distinctions. One critical point is Cuba's stance that social rights are a central component of human rights and that political rights should not be prioritized above social rights. To Havana all human rights should be treated equally. Also, Havana claims that the United States has politicized the human rights issue, using it in a campaign against the Cuban revolution while ignoring flagrant human rights violations by other countries.

Under present domestic political conditions, human rights problems would certainly continue to arise. While the recognition and protection of religious rights have become official policy, the government has yet to allow politically independent groups (nongovernmental organizations, for example) to operate freely. Also, despite the obvious risks involved, the sensitive issue of allowing dissident groups to perform the role of "loyal opposition" should be accommodated as part of the ongoing reform process, especially after more than forty years of revolutionary government.

But dissent remains a thorny political question. There seem to be troubling connections between some dissident groups and anti-Castro organizations in Miami and elsewhere, and a recent revival of counter-revolutionary activism has aggravated the situation. In 1997 a series of bombings in Havana hotels and in other cities endangered the tourist industry, which has contributed notably to the economic survival of the country. Luis Posada Carriles's 1998 revelation that Más Canosa and other Cuban American National Foundation leaders have financed his illegal operations—including the 1976 bombing of a Cubana de Aviación airplane, killing seventy-three people—adds to the long list of counter-revolutionary actions.[23]

But rather than assuming counterrevolutionary objectives in all expressions of political dissent, adequate social space could be provided for nonconformist political practices not connected to domestic or foreign seditious intentions. While it might be difficult to differentiate among the groups, the nation's welfare requires that counterrevolutionary groups should not be capable of derailing the exercise of political rights by those who, although disagreeing with official policy, are not bent on undermining the revolution.

While the open practice of religion has been more accepted, Cuba continues to enforce fully the separation of church and state. But the vigorous exercise of religious practice may yet bring unexpected consequences. By reasserting itself within its newly gained social space, the Catholic Church may reach beyond what could be imprecisely defined as the Church's religious domain. The ideological dominance of the revolution could be seriously challenged. The regime would have to confront this dilemma sometime in the future. But by tolerating a diversity of freely competing secular and religious beliefs, the government's definition and practice of human rights could gain more acceptability and recognition abroad.

What will the future of Cuban socialism be? What will the ultimate definition and characteristics of Cuban socialism be? Through the revolution and Cuban socialism, people have fought for their right to exist and to decide freely the final form of their social system. The struggle of the terrible years of the early 1990s is examined in some detail in the following chapters. U.S. punitive policies have served to add more misery to an almost unbearable situation, but they have also served to increase the nation's internal cohesiveness by fostering the people's combative nationalist spirit.

The Cuban people and government and the events of the 1990s have also answered the second question, at least partly. What is essential and cannot be given up has been identified and is held as nonnegotiable: national sovereignty and independence, socialism, a one-party system (one hopes as the party of the Cuban nation), free education and public health care, an interventionist and active state role in the economy and society, central areas of the national economy reserved as public property, among other elements. Broad national economic, political, and social areas remain undefined, so they may still change in the ongoing reform process. Thus, the complete face of Cuba's final socialist modality has not been drawn yet, at least not in its entirety.

Those who today persecute the revolution are not really defeating it, but they do make the reform process agonizingly difficult. Surely, there are many other outstanding problems in Cuba today. Some are acute, almost insurmountable. Pressing problems in the economic area include finding readily available financing for the sugar harvest and lower-priced sources of credit to put the industrial infrastructure back into working order, and overcoming the U.S. embargo and its latest reinforcement, the Helms-Burton Act.

The social impact of such economic problems is disturbing. It includes the social imbalances stemming from the dollarization of the economy; the youth's disappointment with its immediate prospects, given the limited opportunities available; and the number of women (and men) who have prostituted themselves as a means of economic survival but mostly in order to extricate themselves from the doldrums of the special period.

And yet, some facts become clear from the information presented in this book. In spite of the terrible ordeal of the 1990s, the Cuban revolution still appears strong and resilient enough, even though it is no longer the youthful, exuberant social milestone of the 1960s. *Newsweek* reported in 1989 that "during the early years Fidel Castro managed to maintain the revolutionary zeal. But Cuba and Castro are older now, and the revolution is growing tired."[24] The revolution has matured, however, with a government that has been in power for four decades showing no dangerous signs of fatigue. The media could not fathom the test awaiting Cuba in the 1990s and the tireless energy demonstrated during these years.

Perennial shortcomings notwithstanding, the experience accumulated since 1959 provided the know-how that has allowed the revolution to endure the excruciating test of the special period. This fact should be present in a scholarly answer to the riddle of the "Cuban miracle": How could a small island survive such hardships and Washington's enmity? The following chapters are an attempt to answer this and other questions.

The Impact of the
Demise of European Socialism

It took the end of European socialism to prove that contrary to general belief, particularly among U.S. policy makers and Cuba watchers, Havana was not Moscow's satellite. Still, Cuba and the Soviet Union had had a very special although not unique relationship for three decades. Given their unequal resources and development stages, Havana became increasingly dependent on Moscow. Normally, this kind of relationship would lead to a high degree of submissiveness on the part of the weak partner toward its benefactor; but not in the Cuban case—or more exactly, not as it applied to Fidel Castro.

Nonetheless, the literature in Cuban studies characterizes the early 1960s as a period of more independence in decision making, viewing the end of the decade and especially the 1970s as the years when the dependency factor in the relationship took over, with Moscow increasingly exerting its policy priorities and interests over Cuba's. This included Havana's adopting the Soviet political and economic model, which allegedly played a growing influence in the new modalities and structural patterns adopted by the island. The period was characterized as the era of the purposeful structural Sovietization of Cuba. The institutionalization of the revolution in the 1970s was identified by supporters of the Sovietization thesis as primary proof of how Havana had increasingly adopted a Soviet look-alike image and status.[1]

After Castro joined the socialist bloc in the early 1960s, the newly established relationship placed Cuba in a dependency status that largely determined the course of events for years to come. And yet, in spite of providing free of charge more than enough military assistance for the country's defense and of stationing Soviet personnel and troops on Cuban soil, Moscow's commitment never included going to war to defend the island from American military aggression.[2]

Cubans welcomed the Soviet military presence, which became a permanent feature as an outgrowth of the October 1962 missile crisis and the understanding that ensued between President Kennedy and Soviet leader Krushchev. Soviet technical and military personnel stationed on the island were estimated in 1990 to total 7,700 (2,800 military advisors, a military detachment of 2,800—a brigade, and 2,100 electronic technicians assigned to the electronic intelligence gathering station at Lourdes).[3] Three months before the collapse of the Soviet Union, in September 1991, Moscow announced the gradual withdrawal of its military personnel stationed in Cuba.

Havana must have known well the Soviet rationale for a limited commitment to the island's military defense and that Cuba could not make Moscow change this policy, even if it tried. As the island's military capability and readiness developed with time, however, the issue must have lost the urgency it might initially have had for Cuba's national security planners.

Domestic Effect of the Socialist Crisis

Once the limited protective shield and the trade agreements and financial assistance provided by the socialist camp, mostly the Soviet Union, were gone, the revolution's economic and military vulnerability increased substantially. Havana had not anticipated that 87 percent of its international trade—the lifeline of the economy—would collapse almost overnight with the end of the European socialist governments. President Castro had to enforce in peacetime the current special period, a contingency plan conceived for a state of war emergency, when the country would be under military attack and cut off from established supply markets. The plan did not come into effect because of an American military attack, as had been feared for so long, but because of the socialist crisis, an eventuality that should not have caught Cuba as unprepared and exposed as it did.

The country had to tap deftly its domestic resources and expand its newly emerging network of international relations in order to survive the latest ordeal. But it was not an auspicious time to do this—especially in economic terms. The emerging international order of the post–Cold War period ran contrary to revolutionary regimes like Cuba's. Havana had to reassure the international community, especially its Latin American neighbors, that it meant no harm to any government regardless of its political standing. The era of exporting the revolution à la the 1960s had by now been forgotten by the island's policy makers.

Only a handful of non-European socialist regimes had survived the demise of the Soviet bloc, and Marxist political parties and movements and the political left in general were in profound disarray. In Latin America and elsewhere, the left's declining self-reliance in the early 1990s was compounded by its diminished political appeal and eroded legitimacy as well as by its apparent loss of political direction.[4] That Cuba was still alive proved that the political left was not lost altogether. But in order to survive, it had to cast off its former role as patron and center of revolutionary movements in the hemisphere and elsewhere.

Other 1990s events—such as the eruption in Chiapas, Mexico, of a Zapatista rebellion in 1994; the military activity of the Popular Revolutionary Army and other rebel groups in the state of Guerrero and throughout southwestern Mexico;[5] the long-standing struggle of revolutionary movements such as the Shining Path and Tupac Amaru in Peru (notwithstanding the tragic ending of the four-month-long Japanese embassy hostage crisis in Lima in 1996–97); years of guerrilla activity in Colombia—indicated that leftist guerrilla warfare, even if below the level of previous years, was not over in Latin America.

Signifying the West's prevailing euphoria, an American political scientist advanced the notion that as the only remaining ideology and political modality, liberalism would henceforth reign supreme. He also impudently stated that the world had just witnessed "the end of history."[6] In real terms, however, Francis Fukuyama's "end of history" meant not so much the triumph of Western (neo)liberalism as that of the United States as world leader.

For Castro, after the ill-advised downing of two Cuban-American Florida-based airplanes in February 1996 by the Cuban air force, Clinton's resolve to exert his Cuba policy across the world was ominous. President Clinton would not soften his punitive measures until early 1998, following the pope's visit to Cuba, when Clinton announced partial easing of some of the sanctions imposed in 1994 and 1996.

Consequences of Gorbachev's "New Thinking"

Since 1989 Havana's external and internal politics have revolved around the profoundly disruptive effect that the collapse of European socialism has had on the island. The downfall of the central Eastern European socialist regimes, followed shortly by the Soviet Union's, had started with Mikhail Gorbachev's and Soviet Foreign Minister Eduard Shevardnadze's "new thinking" in foreign policy and its unanticipated consequences.[7]

The withdrawal of Soviet troops from Afghanistan was a compelling economic and political, domestic and international imperative for Gorbachev, as was ending the arms race with Washington and the progressive dismantling of American and Soviet nuclear arsenals, to which he and President Ronald Reagan had agreed in the 1980s. For Gorbachev, in addition to the terribly pressing economic problems facing his country, those decisions were motivated by his political new thinking, which had by then become the new Soviet mantra in international politics.

In Gorbachev's own words:

> "What is *perestroika*, or restructuring? Why do we need it? What are its substance and objectives? How is it proceeding and what might be its consequences for the Soviet Union and the world community? . . . perestroika is no whim on the part of some ambitious individuals or a group of leaders . . . perestroika is an urgent necessity . . . Any delay in beginning . . . [it] could have led to an exacerbated internal situation in the near future, which . . . would have been fraught with serious social, economic and political crises.[8]

And on perestroika as it applies to international politics:

> We started perestroika in a situation of growing international tension. The *detente* of the 1970s was, in effect, curtailed. Our calls for peace found no response in the ruling quarters of the West . . . What is the world we all live in like? . . . It is one in which unheard-of possibilities for development and progress lie side by side with abject poverty, backwardness and medievalism . . . An altogether different [way of thinking and acting] has emerged . . . A new dialectic of strength and security follows from the impossibility of a military—that is, nuclear—solution to international differences.[9]

There was a new world outlook in Moscow, and the world was just learning the thrust of this new brand of politics. In a few years, however, everything was going to change in a direction and to an extent unsuspected by even the most experienced political analysts. And the forthcoming events would be disastrous for Cuba.

Enforcing Perestroika beyond the Border

Consistent with policy born of his new thinking, Gorbachev made clear that the Brezhnev doctrine of using military force to safeguard (central Eastern European) socialist regimes would no longer be applied. His action was also bound by the Soviet-Yugoslav Statement of Principles of March 19, 1988, which had laid to rest the "right to intervene militarily to defend socialism from imperialism."[10] The operational shift in the state-client relationship changed drastically the correlation of political forces in Eastern Europe. However unanticipated and unwanted by Gorbachev, the decision to lift the threat of armed intervention served to set in motion the domino effect that rapidly led to the breakdown of the Soviet bloc in 1989 to 1990 and ultimately of the Soviet Union from December 1991 to January 1992.[11]

The so-called Soviet bloc had been built after World War II. It sustained a firmly structured international system operating under Moscow's dominance. Gorbachev ended Moscow's controlling role by not claiming the area as a Soviet sphere of influence. Fueled by long repressed anti-Soviet and anti-socialist sentiment and ideology, the political forces within the Soviet bloc aimed at dismantling the Soviet system whenever possible. Once such forces were allowed to operate somewhat freely in the area neighboring the Soviet Union, it was only a matter of time before their unsettling liberating effect would reach the core of the system itself—Moscow. An event as unexpected as the collapse of one of the two world superpowers was about to take place in an accelerated implosion process.

Gorbachev believed that reforms in the Soviet bloc along the lines of perestroika (as well as glasnost) would improve the quality of socialism as they knew it. In actuality, it accomplished the opposite, destroying the existent socialist structures. When news of what was happening in neighboring regimes reached the Soviet Union, it had an equally disturbing effect. Given the intense flow of communication and the close proximity between the Soviet Union and the members of the socialist camp, changes of the magnitude the latter experienced were bound to have major consequences in the former, too.[12]

Cuba's Reaction to Soviet "New Thinking"

The winds of glasnost (openness, reducing censorship and media control) and perestroika (restructuring, dismantling the centralized economic and political system) also reached Havana. But when the Cuban leaders decided at this critical juncture what policies to enforce, the new Soviet policies were not among them. Gorbachev's reforms were modifying or replacing long-standing Marxist-Leninist values and structures in a way that Cuba was unwilling to do. After having retreated in 1986 from the market reforms instituted in 1976–85 under the System of Direction and Planning of the Economy (SDPE)—reforms that had the unwanted effect of increasing material incentives and consumerism at the expense of revolutionary consciousness—Castro was now opposed to engaging in further market-oriented reforms, which is what Gorbachev was doing in Moscow and was advocating vigorously for other socialist countries.[13]

Castro denied rumors of a Cuban-Soviet discord, insisting that "Soviet-Cuba relations are good but we [Cubans] do things in a different way." The fact that Cuba had chosen its own kind of reform revealed not only the type of remedy found proper for its social ills but also the brand of socialism envisioned for the future. Concerned by 1989 with the turn of events in the Soviet Union, Castro had questioned perestroika, saying, "Why must the so-called reforms be along capitalist lines?"[14] Castro's commitment to conservative socialist modalities was stronger than Gorbachev's; and while he could not help what was happening in Moscow, he could still make his own vision prevail in Cuba.

Gorbachev could not question Cuba's right to make its own decision and follow its own path. Besides, he must have known that even though Castro was under strong international pressure to emulate the Soviet example, the independent-minded leader would ignore it. In addition to revealing Havana's approach to crisis management, the rejection of perestroika (more so than rejection of glasnost) showed Cubans' dismay at repeating what they feared could be a costly, even fatal Soviet mistake. Neither the rationale for nor the ways of enforcing Gorbachev's new thinking made any real headway in Havana from the start. Cubans wondered why they should imitate the Soviet reforms when their past and present conditions and problems were quite different. Speaking before a group of journalists from Ecuador, Castro stressed Cuba's independent decision making: "We were constantly accused in the past of being Soviet satellites and whenever we did something they said it was on the account of the Soviets and now it turns out that we are being accused of not doing what the Soviets are doing. What will it be? How are we going to end up?"[15]

By then, Cuba had already embarked upon its own reform process. The rectification of errors and negative tendencies had been inaugurated at the Third Party Congress in 1986. Among other decisions, it terminated the free peasant markets started a few years earlier, reduced self-employment, and restricted private construction, selling, and renting of houses. On the other hand, it revived revolutionary ideological commitment (consciousness), volunteer work, the minibrigades, and moral incentives as ways of moving away from consumerism, material incentives, and mercantilism.

A Cuban social scientist explained the fact that Havana and Moscow had chosen different kinds of reform, attributing it to their own domestic needs: "Since the mid-1980s, the Soviet Union has entered into a restructuring of its entire society and Cuba has begun a process of rectification of errors and negative tendencies. These processes of change are occurring simultaneously—and in each case in a socialist country—yet they are different. Each responds to extant internal conditions."[16]

He could also have mentioned the differences in what they were willing to transform (and eliminate) and in their ultimate socialist objectives. The Cuban leadership was always painfully aware of the reform process led by Gorbachev and of the way it caused the collapse of the Soviet Union and other European socialist regimes. As Castro put it, not just Gorbachev but the entire Soviet leadership must bear collective responsibility for the country's failure and ultimate destruction. They had mistakenly undermined the political and economic system from within, severely weakening the pillar sustaining it (the Communist Party). The reforms were meant to improve socialism, not to destroy it, stated a frustrated Castro.[17]

With some exceptions, Gorbachev's perestroika, and to a lesser degree glasnost, met serious resistance among Havana's highest officials, who withstood the policies all along. Although Gorbachev was looked upon (at least initially) as a Soviet leader concerned with modifying and/or improving the socialist system, his policies had been received cautiously at first; regarded increasingly with skepticism; and finally rejected altogether.[18] The initial unsettling effect of Gorbachev's policies and the way they finally resulted in the breakdown of the Soviet system led Castro to want to avoid repeating Moscow's ultimate fate at any cost.

The problems Havana encountered with the collapse of its Soviet ally and benefactor had started before December 1991. Dislocation of the Soviet economy brought about by perestroika had also disrupted the Cuban economy; its effects were felt almost immediately. To Cuban chagrin, the internal Soviet problems, rather than diminishing, were escalating. The eruption of feuding nationalities and the newly found assertiveness among separatist movements in several Union republics were making matters worse. But the situation was in flux; there were reasonable expectations that the country would survive the storm. The referendum held on March 17, 1991, to decide whether to preserve the Soviet Union as a "renewed federation of equal sovereign republics" was approved by a majority of Soviet citizens, giving Gorbachev momentary respite in the ongoing crisis. This also was good news to Havana. It was assumed that a Gorbachev stronger at home would be able to resurrect bilateral trade agreements and restore the normal deliveries schedule.

The Bilateral Relationship

Exercising their newly acquired editorial independence under glasnost, some Soviet publications, including *New Times, International Affairs,* and *Pravda,* became particularly critical of Cuba. In criticizing Havana, by implication the Soviet media were also taking a stand against the old policies of the pre-Gorbachev era. Castro responded by banning critical Soviet publications, especially those condemning Cuba's refusal to emulate the ongoing Soviet reforms. This created an unusual situation for Soviet journals in Cuba: they gained new, interested readers, and some even had to circulate as underground literature.[19]

The Soviet media charges leveled at Cuba signified the magnitude of the political and ideological changes taking place in Moscow under Gorbachev. They ranged from accusing Cuba of repeating the mistakes of European socialist regimes by refusing to learn from them to questioning its socioeconomic gains ("not everything is smooth-running"), accusing Cuba of using Soviet economic aid inappropriately, and challenging the need for such a sizable military establishment ("the heavy burden—in view of the smallness of the population—of its defense expenditure"). Also, they criticized Cuba's becoming entrenched in the East-West conflict—which had been fueled, according to an article in *International Affairs* by a high Soviet official in the Ministry of Foreign Affairs, by the "'ossified black-and-white orthodox theory' [that] the USSR had drawn against its own interest."[20]

In spite of the developments limiting Moscow's capacity to continue supporting Cuba, Gorbachev meant to safeguard as much as possible the Soviet relationship with Castro. It had lasted for so long and Moscow had made such massive investments in Cuba that the relationship could not easily be disregarded.

The Soviet Union had also received benefits from Havana. Cuban military successes in Africa in the 1970s, using Soviet military equipment, had increased the prestige of the socialist bloc, particularly in the Third World. The sophisticated electronic intelligence-gathering station at Lourdes allowed Moscow to verify that the United States was carrying out arms control and nuclear disarmament agreements as scheduled. Also, Cuba provided medical care free of charge to 14,083 Soviet children who suffered serious aftereffects from the 1986 Chernobyl nuclear disaster.

The preferential price paid for Cuban sugar by the Soviets has long been a controversial issue. It was repeatedly mentioned as proof of Moscow's heavy subsidizing of the Cuban economy. Cubans point out, however, that Cuban sugar cost the Soviets less than their own domestically produced beet sugar and also saved them hard currency needed for commercial exchanges with market economies. The Soviet need for Cuban sugar was serious. As the largest consumer of sugar in the world (in 1989–90 it consumed 13.7 billion tons), the Soviet Union imported the largest share of Cuban sugar despite its own sugar beet production. Soviet imports had increased from over a fourth of total Cuban sugar exports (27.87 percent) in 1971 to more than half (57.88 percent) by 1987.

Some of the years with the highest imports of Cuban sugar were 1978, 3,797 million tons; 1979, 3,707 million tons; 1982, 4,224 million tons; 1984, 3,508 million tons; 1985, 3,685 million tons; and 1986, 3,861 million tons. In 1988 imports went down to 3,004 million tons, but they rebounded to 3,468 million tons in 1989. Having experienced reduced domestic production of only 9,159 million tons of beet sugar in 1990, the Soviet Union had a deficit of 4,291 million tons, which it supplemented with imports from Cuba.[21] (See fig. 2.1.)

A Treaty of Friendship and Cooperation between Cuba and the Soviet Union was signed on April 4, 1989, committing both countries "to continue developing and enriching their fraternal, bilateral relations on the basis of the traditional principles of nonintervention, mutual respect and equality." Just before the European socialist crisis transformed the international landscape, Moscow's and Havana's common ideological principles and world outlook were still providing a normative foundation for their relationship. Not much later, however, the situation became one of symbolic attempts to put a good face on the rapidly deteriorating circumstances.

A high-level Soviet delegation visiting Havana in December 1990 stated publicly that Soviet support for the island had not faltered in spite of the problems affecting their country and that efforts were being made to

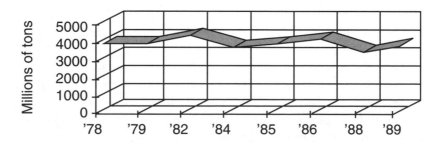

Fig. 2.1. Soviet Sugar Imports, 1978–1989.
SOURCE: Cole Blasier, "The End of the Soviet-Cuban Partnership," in *Cuba after the Cold War*, ed. Carmelo Mesa-Lago, 78–81, Pittsburgh: Pittsburgh University Press, 1993.

avoid hurting the Cuban economy. Havana's media dutifully reported that "the USSR is and always will be at Cuba's side." Soviet officials were still reassuring about their commitments to Cuba, and they probably meant it, but they could not help the ongoing turmoil at home and the increasing delays in making deliveries.

In a triangular ploy, as a way of reducing the burdensome level of trade and aid commitments, Gorbachev promoted the improvement of relations between Havana and Washington. Reducing Cold War antagonism between Cuba and the United States was central to Moscow's international retrenchment under its new thinking in foreign policy. It included switching to a low profile in Latin America (especially de-escalating Soviet involvement in the Central American conflict) and in the Third World in general.[22]

Nevertheless, the beginning of the end of the Cold War had different meanings to Washington and Moscow. Playing to their advantage, Americans were using their improved relations with the Soviets to exert additional pressure to end long-standing Soviet support of Castro. The most favored nation (MFN) status granted by President George Bush to the Soviet Union during the summit meeting he held with Gorbachev in June 1990 had received a cool response from Congress, raising questions about its approval. This meant more American demands to limit—and if possible to end altogether—the Moscow-Havana relationship.

The head of the foreign ministry's Latin American department, Valery Nikolaenko, asked for an end to "tensions, threats, and aggressions directed toward Cuba" and advocated "direct contacts between Cuba and the United States." Meetings like the one held between the Cuban foreign minister and the American secretary of state, discussing in 1990 the Persian Gulf conflict, should continue. Moreover, "the theme [scope] of the conversations [should] widen," he said.[23]

But all the effort was to no avail. Relations between Havana and Washington did not improve. Aggravating Cuba's predicament, the European socialist world so precious to Havana was dying. Former European socialist regimes had started taking adversarial positions to Havana on critical issues. The March 1990 decision by the United Nations Human Rights Commission condemning Cuba's human rights record was promoted by Washington, but it was approved with the support of two former socialist countries, Hungary and Bulgaria, while Poland and Czechoslovakia had issued public statements in favor of condemning Cuba.[24]

The Cuban Interests Section had been housed in the Czech Embassy in

Washington since its formal establishment in 1977, during the Carter Administration. In December 1990 Czechoslovakia refused to continue representing Cuba's diplomatic and consular interests, ending a diplomatic service actually started in 1961. Today, Swiss embassies house the Cuban Section in Washington and the U.S. Section in Havana.

Responding to the Collapse of European Socialism

Among socialist countries outside Europe, Cuba probably was the one most affected by the European socialist crisis. The collapse of European socialism, particularly of the Soviet Union, impacted the country seriously at different levels. The crisis touched the foundation and rationale of the Cuban system, including its legitimacy. But more than that, it meant the loss of Cuba's main supporter and provider and leading political ally in the international arena and the loss of most of its international trade market, including the supplier of practically every imported good necessary to keep the economy and the country running. That Cuba could survive such a crisis is almost a miracle. Indeed, the cost has been very high.

The credit for survival belongs to the Cuban people. In spite of major losses, the people did not hesitate to make and enforce decisions, identifying in the midst of the prevailing confusion what direction to take (and what direction to avoid) and how to find inner resources whenever it seemed that none were left. So they have struggled and sacrificed, enduring shortages of every imaginable necessity. Whether a defense of the country's sovereignty and independence, a belief in the revolution, in nationalism, in socialism, a reaffirmation of long-held Christian values, a basic instinct for survival, some combination of these, or something else has made the people stand firm is open to interpretation.

In the 1990s, however, increasing numbers have deserted (notably high government officials and party members and famous athletes), and countless rafters have risked their lives to escape. While most of the population remains in Cuba, many more would leave the hardships if they could.[25]

Economic Integration and Dependency

The total economic picture showed the magnitude of the crisis Cuba had to face. The degree of integration (and dependency) the Cuban economy had developed with the European socialist economies was a central component of the island's economic development for three decades. According to a Cuban scholar, now minister in charge of the economy and planning, José Luis Rodríguez:

> In attempting to analyze the principal factors that have contributed to revolutionary Cuba's development, it is necessary to take into account a variety of factors, including the insertion of Cuba into the international socialist division of labor and the level of economic collaboration received from the socialist countries . . . Cuba's economic relations with CMEA [Council of Mutual Economic Assistance] members in essence guaranteed it a process of increased production during the last thirty years, assuring the island a stable market and just prices for its exports, as well as the basic supplies needed for its development. Moreover, the financing provided by the socialist countries to assist national development played a decisive role in the process of accumulation since 1959. Of crucial importance in these relations is, without any doubt, the role played by the Soviet Union.[26]

Today, however, the economic activities and trade effort seek to integrate Cuba into the world economy. The process is difficult and complex and cannot replace the relations Cuba had with European socialist countries overnight, if ever. The preferential prices Cuba received for products, coupled with generous developmental and financial aid, most certainly will not be repeated by capitalist trade partners and investors, to whom profit, not ideology or solidarity, is the primary motivation.

Cuba has hurt itself in the process of integration into the world economy by limiting the economic reforms currently under way. Also, the objective of the worldwide campaign (economic war, according to Cuba) that the Clinton Administration launched after the Helms-Burton Act was approved in March 1996—even after the 1992 Torricelli-Graham Act—is to make it difficult for Cuba to make a successful transition into the world economy.

Three Decades of Socialist Economic Growth

The Cuban transition from trading with market economies to closer ties with socialist ones started in the early 1960s, with a decreasing curve with the former and an increasing one with the latter, especially in the late 1980s. Commerce with socialist countries reached 87 percent by 1988, and it averaged 60.3 percent with the Soviet Union between 1959 and 1988 (70.5 percent in 1985). Meanwhile, trade with market economies was still over a fifth of the total trade in 1965 (22.8 percent); it increased to

28.1 percent in 1970, and continued growing to 40.1 percent in 1975. However, it suffered a sharp decline in the mid- and late 1980s—to 13.7 percent in 1985, and 12.9 percent in 1988—rebounding somewhat in 1989 to 16.8 percent.[27] (See fig. 2.2.)

Under the impact of the European socialist crisis, however, between 1989 and 1993 Cuba's imports decreased to less than 30 percent of previous levels, and exports plummeted 70 percent. The national output was cut almost in half, while the overall contraction of the economy came close to 77 percent. During the early 1990s the country had to survive with a small remnant of the economic activity it had had just a few years earlier.[28]

The commercial imbalance between Cuba and the Soviet Union reached 11.5 billion pesos in nineteen years (1963–82). This had favored the island by 136.2 percent. During a twenty-five-year period (1960–85), Havana received 3.8 billion pesos in developmental assistance from Moscow, with 80 percent earmarked for industrial development. By 1986, out of 360 economic projects, 197 were for the industrial sector. At the time, there were 289 projects in process at different stages of completion, and 174 more were expected from the ongoing Moscow assistance programs, 69 of which were for industry. Of the total foreign investment in Cuba between 1959 and 1991, 80 percent came from socialist countries.

Such massive developmental aid produced tangible economic results. Soviet assistance built enterprises and factories generating 15 percent of the country's industrial output, including all cane-harvesting machines, television sets, radios, and sheet metal. Some 90 percent of steel production, 70 percent of the nation's electricity, 60 percent of textiles, and 50 percent of mechanical products came from the same source. The quality of the domestic work force also improved with Moscow's aid. From 1967 to 1987 nearly a quarter of a million specialists were trained in working centers built with Soviet support. Still, based on a partnership that lasted

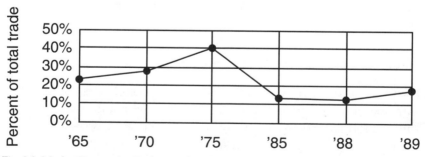

Fig. 2.2. Market Economies Trade, 1965–1989.
Source: Carmelo Mesa-Lago, "The Economic Effects on Cuba of the Downfall of Socialism in the USSR and Eastern Europe," in *Cuba after the Cold War*, ed. Carmelo Mesa-Lago, 133–96, Pittsburgh: Pittsburgh University Press, 1993.

three decades, to some economic analysts the industrial output rate based on Soviet developmental assistance was unsatisfactory.

The European socialist countries also contributed to Cuba's economic development in such fields as agriculture, machine construction, shipbuilding, petroleum production, energy production, the sugar industry, and other industrial projects. Socialist countries assisted in a geological prospecting program that analyzed about half of the promising agricultural zones in the country. Cuba's trade deficit between 1959 and 1988 with Bulgaria, Czechoslovakia, Hungary, Poland, Romania, and the German Democratic Republic came close to 2 billion pesos.[29]

Financial assistance was a central component of socialist aid to Cuba. In almost three decades, European socialist nations granted 13.5 billion pesos in commercial credits. Even though all credits were on favorable terms, the Soviet Union was particularly generous. Moscow never charged interest higher than 4 percent and accepted twelve-year amortization periods and a barter system of payment. It also postponed the payments of up to 100 percent of credits at their face value. Regarding developmental credits, the interest never exceeded 2 percent and had twenty-five-year amortization periods. Similarly to commercial credits, the developmental credits were postponed for up to 100 percent at their face value, and these also included a barter payment system. In 1972 Moscow agreed to the refinancing of all credits on highly favorable terms, granting a thirteen-year grace period for all credits (with no interest payments due) and a twenty-five-year amortization period to start at the end of the grace period. Further, it was agreed in 1984 that the payments due in 1986 would not affect the balance of payment of the five-year exchange period that was planned to start the same year.

Moscow sources have rated the Cuban debt in the early 1990s at 17.2 billion pesos. The total debt to the other members of the former socialist camp was estimated to be much lower. Two-thirds of the Soviet debt stemmed from commercial imbalances incurred in a seventeen-year period (1972–89), with the rest coming from developmental aid. The debt was accumulated in spite of the preferential payments granted to Cuba's exports, which had been indexed since 1976 to the prices of Soviet products to avoid extreme exchange imbalances.

Cuba-Socialist Exchange Grade Report: Mixed Reviews

Some economic reports have claimed that the exchange system had worked to Cuba's disadvantage since 1980, ending in a deteriorating trade system that totaled 28 percent in a ten-year period. If this is correct, argues Rodríguez, approximately two-thirds of the debt to the Soviet Union during the last decade could be attributed to such an imbalance. The Soviet practice of massive subsidies was considered to have had a negative impact on the Cuban economy (the practice was ended after the collapse of the Soviet Union). The quality of European socialist exports—that is, finished industrial products and technology transfer—was also considered to be below the level expected in competitive Western markets.[30]

Another expert estimate found an initial gain for Cuba, followed by a downturn in the Moscow trade relationship. A sample of 39 percent of Cuba's imports and 90 percent of its exports shows a positive improvement from 1968 to 1974, followed by a deterioration in 1975–84. The loss in the early 1980s came to 36 percent (1981–84); however, had the trade been based on world market prices, the losses would have been higher—81 percent.

Cuba depended on Soviet oil to meet more than 90 percent of its needs. While the price of oil in the world market declined in 1986 and thereafter, the Soviet price of crude oil remained unchanged. Oil imports from 1986 to 1990 showed a loss for Cuba of $3.1 billion (in U.S. dollars) in comparison to world market prices.[31] Approximately 12 to 13 million metric tons of Soviet oil were imported into Cuba in 1988, of which 2 million tons were reexported onto the world market. But as Soviet oil exports dwindled rapidly, Cuba's oil reexports were cut in half in 1989, and by 1990 they stopped altogether—the 10 million tons of Soviet oil that had arrived were needed for the domestic market. By the end of 1991 there was a 10 percent shortfall in the 8 million tons (73 million barrels) expected that year, making things worse for the Cuban economy and anticipating the seriousness of the situation in the following years.[32]

Russian economist V. Venediktov calculated that during the 1986–90 period Havana lost 7.2 billion pesos by buying all the oil and oil products it needed from the Soviet Union (Rodríguez estimated Cuba's loss at 5 billion pesos, and the Cuban-American economist C. Mesa-Lago gave it as 4.7 billion pesos). Venediktov also estimated that Cuba had paid twice as much for Soviet machinery and equipment as it would have by world market prices, which totaled losses up to 666 million pesos in a four-year period.[33]

Serious imbalance in the thirty-year long commercial exchange notwithstanding, socialist aid, especially Soviet support, contributed greatly to "the capacity of accumulation and growth generated between 1959 and 1988."[34] In spite of the severity of the special period, Cuba's capacity to survive the effect of the socialist crisis was heightened by the economic infrastructure and the industrial base built in three decades with socialist collaboration. But important projects that would have furthered Havana's position remained unfinished, like the Juraguá nuclear power plant in Cienfuegos.

Additional Exchange Problems

There were additional problems facing Havana's commercial exchange with CMEA countries. Moscow's perestroika and Havana's rectification process were parallel but independent policies that contributed to increasing the level of tension and difficulties while enforcing the exchange agreements. The flow of supplies had become irregular since the mid-1980s, and technical problems and mistakes in planning had increased. The deficiencies were attributed to alterations in the supply process caused by prolonging the foreign investment period and to Cuba's inadequate foreign investment policy before 1985. The commercial exchange deficiencies became more acute in 1989 when CMEA countries started shedding their socialist identity for a capitalist one.

Cuba needed to redefine its commercial exchange with Moscow, which by then had lost its capacity to fulfill deliveries as promised. Havana experimented with new collaboration modalities, like enterprise-to-enterprise agreements and joint Cuban-Soviet enterprises, while searching in vain for long-term solutions. Shortly thereafter, however, it had to devise an entirely new economic and trade strategy: all European socialist countries, including the Soviet Union, had ceased to exist.

Old and New Trade Partners in the 1990s

With the favorable (subsidizing) trade conditions provided by European socialism no longer in place, commercial exchange with former socialist countries continued at a slow pace. The 1989 $742.3 million trade volume was reduced a year later to $410.5 million (a 44.6 percent decrease). The falling off of trade continued the following year, down to $191.8 million (74.1 percent less than in 1989). But in 1992 it improved, when exports to Russia totaled $632.2 million, which elevated total trade with the former Soviet bloc to $774.4 million (a 75.3 percent increase from 1991). However, when commerce with Russia decreased to $436 million in 1993, it lowered the total trade with the region to $527.6 million (a 31.8 percent decrease from the previous year).

Still, commerce increased to $651.7 million in 1994 (19 percent over 1993) when Russian commerce climbed again to $550 million, leaving

Cuba a favorable trade of $52 million. The resurgence of commercial exchange with Moscow was the dominant factor by 1994. It totaled 84.3 percent of total commerce with former Soviet bloc countries. Trade with Moscow continued growing in 1995 ($462 million) and 1996 ($988 million). Russian trade in 1996 surpassed by 56.3 percent the total for 1992 (91.4 percent of commerce with the former Soviet bloc), with a favorable balance to Cuba of $58 million. After practically stopping trade in 1992, Cuba and Russia completed a full cycle by 1993, as they recognized mutual commercial and other interests, even though they were not bound politically as before. (See table 2.1.)

The major export to Russia in 1996 was raw sugar ($503 million), with other goods totaling $20 million. The main imports were fuels ($335 million), machinery ($66 million), semifinished goods ($15 million), transport ($13 million), consumer goods ($4 million), and chemicals ($3 million).

China and the Main Trade Partners

China could not replace the Soviet Union as Cuba's main trade partner, nor was China willing to become Cuba's benefactor. Despite increasingly close political relations, commerce between Cuba and China in 1996 was 43.9 percent lower than in 1991. (See table 2.2.) Between 1990 and 1993, Cuba fell from third to fourth place among Latin American countries trading with China, and by 1996 it was fifth behind Brazil, Peru, Argentina, and Mexico.

Visits to China by President Castro (1995), Raúl Castro (1997), Division General Ulises Rosales del Toro (then army chief of staff and later minister of the sugar industry), Corps General Abelardo Colomé Ibarra (minister of the interior), and others improved the quality and frequency of relations between the countries—both between governments and between communist parties. Relations between the Cuban and the Chinese armed forces are now rated as the best ever. Chinese government and Communist Party leaders and military officers have visited Cuba in reciprocity, including President Jiang Zemin, Deputy Prime Minister Quian Qichen, and Wu Jie, vice president of the State Commission for Economic Restructuring. Government-to-government joint ventures were set up in the medical equipment, tourism, and pharmaceutical sectors, and Beijing extended a soft line credit of $8.1 million and a $3.4 million grant for scientific and technological research. When Cuba adopted the convertible peso mechanism (by which the national currency is convertible to dollar currency) that is now in place, it followed the Chinese currency exchange pattern.[35]

Table 2.1. Cuban Trade with Former European Socialist Countries, 1989–1996 (in millions of U.S. dollars)

	1989	1990	1991	1992	1993	1994	1995	1996	Totals
Cuban Exports									
Belarus[a]				4.0	7.0	1.0			12.0
Czechoslovakia[b]	109.4	40.3	5.0	8.8					163.5
Germany[c]	20.8	23.3	19.0	21.0	14.0	25.0	31.0	22.0	176.1
Hungary	10.7	2.7	1.0	0.2	0.1	0.1			14.8
Poland	15.4	2.3	0.2	1.3	0.5	0.6	1.0		21.3
Romania	117.2	55.0	3.0	5.0	8.0	17.0			205.2
Russia[d]				632.2	436.0	301.0	225.0	523.0	2117.2
Slovenia[e]					5.0	4.0		9.0	
Total Exports	273.5	123.6	28.2	672.5	470.6	348.7	257.0	545.0	2719.1
Cuban Imports									
Belarus				18.0	5.0		3.0		26.0
Czechoslovakia	112.8	75.0	11.6	5.9	2.0				207.3
Germany	124.3	99.9	123.0	59.0	40.0	41.0	70.0	70.0	627.2
Hungary	47.2	29.0	24.0	8.0	2.0	2.0			112.2
Poland	20.1	6.3	4.0	6.0	3.0	2.0	3.0		44.4
Romania	164.4	76.7	1.0	5.0	5.0	9.0			261.1
Russia						249.0	237.0	465.0	951.0
Slovenia									
Total Imports	468.8	286.9	163.6	101.9	57.0	303.0	313.0	535.0	2229.2
Total Trade	742.3	410.5	191.8	774.4	527.6	651.7	570.0	1080.0	4948.3

[a]The Union of Soviet Socialist Republics (USSR) ceased to exist on December 25, 1991 (officially on January 1, 1992). The Byelorussian Soviet Socialist Republic (BSSR), one of the fifteen republics that constituted the USSR, became independent under the name of the Republic of Belarus.

[b]Effective January 1, 1993, Czechoslovakia split into two separate nations: the Czech Republic and the Slovak Republic. Starting in 1993, trade figures correspond to the Czech Republic.

[c]The German Democratic Republic and the Federal Republic of Germany were reunited under a constitutional arrangement known as the Basic Law on October 3, 1990. The last year that Cuba traded with a socialist Germany was 1989.

[d]After the USSR ceased to exist, the Russian Soviet Federated Socialist Republic (RSFSR) became independent under the name of the Russian Federation.

[e]Slovenia (Ljubljana) was one of the six republics that constituted Yugoslavia. It became independent on June 25, 1991, under the name of the Republic of Slovenia.

SOURCE: *Cuba: Handbook of Trade Statistics, 1995* (Washington, D.C.: U.S. Directorate of Intelligence, APLA 95-1001, 1995), pp. 3–16, 92–93; *Cuba: Handbook of Trade Statistics, 1997* (Washington, D.C.: U.S. Directorate of Intelligence, APLA 97-1006, 1997), pp. 1–4, 56–57.

Table 2.2. Cuban Trade with China, 1991–1996 (in millions of U.S. dollars)

	1991	1992	1993	1994	1995	1996	Totals
Cuban Exports	202	183	74	121	214	138	932
Cuban Imports	224	200	177	147	146	101	995
Totals	426	383	251	268	360	239	1927

SOURCE: *Cuba: Handbook of Trade Statistics, 1997* (Washington, D.C.: U.S. Directorate of Intelligence, APLA-10006, 1997), pp. 25–27.

Table 2.3. Cuba's 11 Top Trading Partners, 1996 (in millions of U.S. dollars)

Country	Cuban Main Imports	Cuban Main Exports	Total Trade
Russia	Fuel	Sugar	988
Spain	Semifinished goods	Fish	596
Canada	Foodstuffs	Nickel	491
Mexico	Semifinished goods	Sugar	341
Netherlands	Foodstuffs	Nickel (reexport)	284
France	Wheat	Fish	245
China	Vegetables	Sugar	239
Italy	Machinery	Fish	152
Argentina	Feed and corn	Medicinal products	133
Germany	Machinery	Fruit	92
Japan	Machinery	Sugar, molasses, honey	91
Total			3,652

SOURCE: *Cuba: Handbook of Trade Statistics, 1997* (Washington, D.C.: U.S. Directorate of Intelligence, APLA–10006, 1997), pp. 1–70.

In a six-year period (1991–1996) commerce with China amounted to $1,927 million ($932 million exports, $995 million imports), while in a five-year period (1992–1996) trade with Russia amounted to $3,068 million ($2,117.2 million exports, $951 million imports), or 159.7 percent more than the Cuban-Chinese commercial exchange. In 1996, when Cuba's trade with eleven nations amounted to $3,652 million, Russia already was Cuba's major trade partner ($988 million), surpassing Spain, Canada, Mexico, the Netherlands, France, China, Italy, Argentina, Germany, and Japan. China ranked seventh. (See table 2.3.)

By the time Cuba entered the second half of the 1990s, the economic recovery policy of seeking new trade partners while keeping old ones was paying off. Russia was again Cuba's main trade partner, and commercial exchange was increasing slowly with other nations. The severity of the problems caused by the collapse of European socialism was easing up gradually—but probably too slowly for most people. Limited trade growth alone could not overcome the obstacles hindering the economic recovery. Problems included low production levels, poor quality of exportable goods, economic mismanagement, inflated shipping costs, exorbitant interest rates charged by international financiers, delays in securing credits, lack of profitable exchange markets, and hardships imposed by the U.S. economic embargo.

Low Economic Indicators, High Social Indicators

Comparing selected Latin American countries according to social and economic indicators demonstrates the social advances Cuba made in thirty years and its economic predicament. Applying purchasing power parity (PPP) to measure the (real) gross national product (GNP) or the gross domestic product (GDP) per capita provides an equalizer to countries with serious income imbalance. PPP reflects more accurately people's consumption capacity in developing countries by applying actual purchasing power rather than currency exchange rates as conversion factors. After calculating nine countries' real GNP in 1991 (one year into Cuba's special period) in conjunction with their PPP, Cuba is last, with only $2,000 real GNP. Mexico is at the top with $7,170, and Bolivia is near the bottom with $2,170, slightly higher than Cuba. (See fig. 2.3.)

Using social indicators, however, Cuba occupies first place with only two exceptions, in which it trails Argentina closely. Figures 2.4–2.9 examine comparatively the performance of five Latin American countries—Argentina, Brazil, Chile, Cuba, and Mexico—using six social indicators:

1. Adult literacy rate: 94.5, second to Argentina by 1.
2. Mean years of schooling: 8.0, second to Argentina by 1.2.
3. Life expectancy: first with 75.6.
4. Daily calorie supply as a percentage of required calories in 1988 to 1990: first with 137 percent.

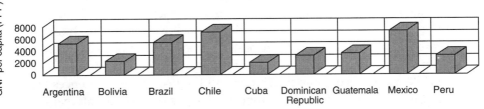

Fig. 2.3. Selected Latin American Countries' Real GNP, According to Their Purchasing Power Parity (PPP) for 1991.
Source: United Nations Development Program (UNDP), *Human Development Report, 1994*, in Manuel Pastor, Jr., and Andrew Zimbalist, "Cuba's Economic Conundrum" *NACLA Report on the Americas* 29 (September–October 1995): 9.

5. Population per physician in 1990: the lowest population per doctor, 270 to 1 (best place).
6. Under five years of age mortality per 1,000 people: the lowest (best place) with 17.[36]

Cuba ranked first in the calorie supply category during the period 1988–90. However, calorie consumption per capita went down as the special period set in, and availability of food decreased sharply thereafter. In March 1994 the U.N. Food and Agriculture Organization (FAO) included Cuba among twenty-four Third World nations where food was "scarce."[37] The food supply did not improve significantly until approximately 1995.

The stark contrast between Cuba's first place in five social-indicator rates and those of four of the most economically advanced Latin American countries is revealing:

1. Cuba's life expectancy (75.6 years) was 1.08 percent higher than Mexico's (69.9 years), with only 27.89 percent of Mexico's real GNP.
2. Cuba had eight times more doctors relative to population (1 doctor per 270 population) than Chile (1 doctor per 2,170 population), with only 28.3 percent of Chile's real GNP.
3. Cuba's mean years of schooling (8) was twice that of Brazil (4), with only 38.16 percent of Brazil's real GNP.
4. Cuba's rate of under five years mortality per 1,000 (17) was around half of Argentina's rate (33), with only 39 percent of Argentina's GNP.
5. Cuba's required daily calorie supply (137 percent) was 0.58 percent higher than Peru's (89 percent), with only 64.3 percent of Peru's GNP.

The economic and social comparison, using figures ranging from 1988 to 1992, is a sign of both triumph and gloom for Cuba. Social policies had created a standard of living with high marks in schooling, medical attention, literacy, life expectancy, and calorie intake, as well as a low mortality rate—conditions rivaling or surpassing those in most of Latin America. But its low GNP underlines the seriousness of its socioeconomic reality. While present economic conditions and their social consequences may not be entirely Cuba's fault—they are largely due to the international socialist crisis—the political, social, and economic effects still are Cuba's main problem.

Under the special period, most aspects of the social fabric were severely affected. The government had to deal urgently with the question of surviving economically, which hinged on making a transition to participation in the world economy. The social programs that had defined and sustained the revolution and had improved the life of the population needed to be safeguarded. Otherwise, the domestic political consequences for the regime could be nearly fatal.

A Fateful Decision, A Collective Ambition

Addressing Cuban nationals living overseas who attended the Nation and the Emigration conference held in Havana in 1994, Carlos Lage, a leading member of the Political Bureau of the Cuban Communist Party

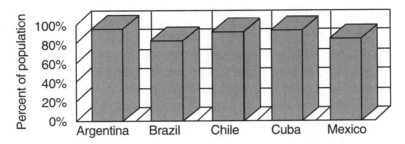

Fig. 2.4. Comparison of Adult Literacy Rates, 1992.

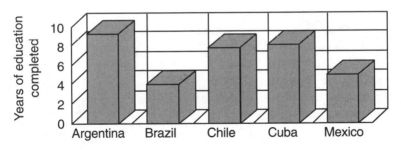

Fig. 2.5. Average Number of Years of Education Achieved, 1992.

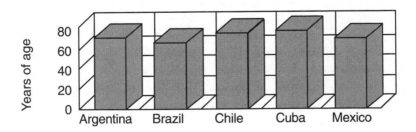

Fig. 2.6. Average Life Expectancy, 1992.

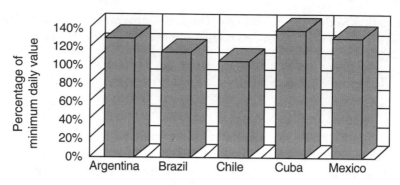

Fig. 2.7. Average Daily Intake, in Percentage, of Required Calories, 1988–1990.

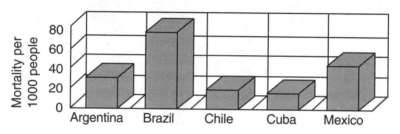

Fig. 2.8. Under Age Five Mortality Annually per 1,000 People, 1992.

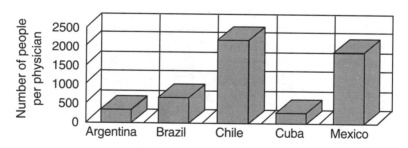

Fig. 2.9. Population per Physician, 1990.
SOURCE: United Nations Development Program (UNDP), *Human Development Report, 1994*, cited in Manuel Pastor, Jr., and Andrew Zimbalist, "Cuba's Economic Conundrum" *NACLA Report on the Americas* 29 (September–October 1995): 9.

(PCC) and secretary of the Executive Committee of the Council of Ministers, recalled how difficult the days of the socialist crisis had been, especially after the Soviet Union collapsed. The central problem facing the regime was deciding whether to resist and move on or to give up in the face of insurmountable losses. The answer coming from the top leadership down was to fight the adversity that had befallen the nation. But carrying the decision out was another matter, as was bringing the economy back to what it had been in the late 1980s.

As Lage noted: *"The first measure [was] the decision to resist;* because when the problems started in the socialist camp, when the Soviet Union and the socialist bloc disappeared, *the will to resist was something unique to our nation,* among those countries. *The situation was so difficult that at the time of the demise of the Soviet Union not even advice would reach us . . .; because the will to resist was not credible for most people in the world."* A few years later, when the situation had started to improve, even if only modestly, Cuba was seen differently by international political actors. Also, said Lage: *"Today there are many friends in the world who sincerely are advising us,* giving ideas, recipes of how to solve our problems, and we are receptive to their advice, we are listening to them, we are studying their ideas, we are also examining the experience of China, Viet Nam and other countries. [But above all] is that in the first years of the special period *the country has achieved a great victory; it has been able to withstand [the problems and difficulties of the special period]"* (emphasis added).[38]

Lage depicted the state of the country as seen from the top. Meanwhile, people at all levels of society were questioning the decisions made to deal with the crisis. A new national obsession, speculating on the nature and extent of the economic malaise and on the solutions applied to solve it, had pervaded the country. While still supporting the revolution, people were disappointed. Expressing anger and frustration about their impoverished living conditions, they mingled together their contradictory feelings and assertions.

Ambrosio Fornet, a well-known writer, literary critic, and screen writer, shared his inner thoughts in an interview in Havana:

I believe that the revolutionary project has to be reformulated. Don't ask me how, I don't know. But I do know that the way we originally conceived of it, the way that popular ideology assimilated it is no longer possible, because it presupposed the existence of a rearguard—the socialist camp in general and the Soviet Union in particular—which guaranteed trade, investment flows, and national security. All of that has disappeared. How are we going to retake what is truly valuable from the project and at the same time make it economically viable? I don't know . . . The mood of the population . . . is one of expectancy. Where are all of these changes going to lead? Nobody knows.[39]

While decisions were made accepting changes that only a few years earlier would have been inconceivable, thinking individuals were digesting what had happened and striving for the best choices for the country under those circumstances. A university professor, author, and director of the Félix Varela nongovernmental organization, Juan Antonio Blanco, like Ambrosio Fornet and other intellectuals, was searching for answers.

In Blanco's words: "A danger exists right now: Cuba depended upon the United States at the time when the revolution began. The conflict with the United States resulted in that country breaking its ties with us and applying an economic embargo. This created an economic vacuum . . . the Soviet Union filled this vacuum. At this moment the vacuum has opened up once again. We don't depend on the United States or the Soviet Union . . . We shouldn't feel sad or pained about this process. A mixed economy is healthier than an exclusively state economy, not because I believe in the sacrosanct virtue of private property but because this is the international and economic reality of the world in which we are living."[40]

Some of the many issues and ideas discussed privately and publicly included reformulating the revolution's project, weighing the reasons for a mixed economy, and seizing the opportunity now that previous states of dependency were gone and for the first time the country was truly independent. Outspoken in nature, Cubans needed to externalize what was burning inside them, which turned into a massive exercise in catharsis and inner healing.

Conclusions

After having positioned itself above neighboring Latin American countries on most social indicators by the late 1980s, Cuba now was at the bottom in economic indicators, with probably the lowest gross national product in the region. Following the collapse of the Soviet bloc, Cuba was thrown into one of its worst economic moments, the special period in peacetime. Sensing the consequences built into Gorbachev's reforms, Havana had refused to apply them. The decision was not internationally supported, but it enabled the island nation to survive the crisis of European socialism. After losing the aid and trade provided by the Soviet bloc, Cuba had to find ways to integrate itself into the world economy. Uplifting the country from the abyss of the 1990s was an oversized task carrying a heavy price tag.

And yet, a hidden paradox was built into the special period: a potential for a new future waited to be tapped. It was a time when a socialist system with the pluses and minuses characteristic of the idiosyncratic *élan vital* of a tropical nation could emerge. The newly emerging socialist system should include accepting religious life, as advocated and practiced by the pope during his visit to the island in 1998.

An intriguing dimension of this historic process is that few seem to know what Cuban socialism will really be like in the end—although some of its characteristics are already visible. Changes in the economy and society have been made slowly, so as not to generate an uncontrollable dynamic.

Despite the potential for troubling consequences, more difficult decisions must be made in the future. The dollarization of the economy solved economic problems but heightened social inequality. While tourism became the most dynamic sector of the economy, it brought back prostitution with a sequel of growing venereal disease. Lifting the limitations on religious practice could presage a serious ideological conflict. The Church's challenge to revolutionary doctrine could threaten the regime's absolute political control. Such risks and others—including further political reform—represent the kind of uncertainties the revolution will confront in the future. However, to keep a socialist democratic polity with a viable economy as a credible objective, those are the kinds of risks the regime cannot avoid taking.

II

The Domestic Environment

Rectifying the Revolution's Mistakes

The national campaign known as the rectification of errors and negative tendencies process (RP) was announced in 1986 at the Third Congress of the Cuban Communist Party (PCC). It happened at a critical juncture for socialism in Cuba and elsewhere. Gorbachev inaugurated his own reforms, glasnost and perestroika, after the RP had already begun.[1] Having launched this reform, Castro began moving away from Soviet policies he thought were counterproductive.[2] The events that followed appeared to vindicate his judgment: Gorbachev's policies were instrumental in bringing down the Soviet bloc. Whether out of insightful intuition or a sense of caution born of experience and maturity, Castro's appraisal favoring his own reform rather than Gorbachev's turned out to be a momentous decision for the Cuban revolution.

Caution has not always been a revolutionary hallmark, however. The regime's first decade exuded idealism and impulsiveness, which accounted for the creativeness of the social engineering process—and for many mistakes as well. The approach was based on the assumption that revolutionary voluntarism, the guerrilla tactic that had been effective in winning the 1956–59 war against President Fulgencio Batista, could also be applied to governing the country. Improvisation and lack of administrative expertise did not seem to matter as long as the new cadres' poor performance was backed by politically correct commitment. While it worked well at times, ideological conviction alone proved to be insufficient to manage the state. It became particularly taxing when, compounded by ongoing social transformation, excessive administrative disarray could have led to utter confusion.

Discerning the revolution's direction was the task for such leaders as Fidel Castro, Che Guevara, Carlos Rafael Rodríguez, and others.[3] They guided the deliberations preceding important decisions.[4] But as inexperienced visionaries (with the exception of Rodríguez, who had held government office before), they also led the government to decisions that would demand correction later. To err by action was still preferable to them than to err by inaction—especially because idleness was contrary to the impetuosity unleashed in the 1960s.

Notwithstanding the regime's penchant for impulsiveness, Havana's record shows that as a rule decisions have been based more on principled pragmatism than on ideological orthodoxy, even though revolutionary values have been used to justify official actions. Regarding policies seen by Washington as radical (like exporting the revolution in the 1960s), there is a logic behind them.

Historically, the RP was not an aberration: Castro had admitted mistakes before, changed direction (even contradicting previous official policy), and amended mistakes. Since the initial transformation from the prerevolutionary social order to the new one, there have been many policy changes.[5] Some policy shifts appear to have followed a linear progression, while others seem contradictory, lacking clearly set objectives.[6]

The three-step process leading to the present Cuban Communist Party was characterized by partisan conflict and constant reorganization. The Integrated Revolutionary Organization (ORI) arranged in 1961–63 combined the extant revolutionary organizations into a single political party: Castro's 26 of July Movement, the Popular Socialist Party (PSP)—the old Communist party—and Havana University students' Revolutionary Directorate (DR). In 1963–65 the ORI was replaced by the United Party of the Socialist Revolution (PURS). Finally, in 1965, the present Cuban Communist Party (PCC) was inaugurated. Anibal Escalante, an old member of the PSP, led a sectarian dispute during the ORI stage, pitting old communists against members of the 26 of July Movement and other revolutionary leaders. Later, in 1967, Escalante was again responsible for another major dispute, the microfaction affair, which had more serious political connotations.

In 1963 Havana abandoned its initial thrust toward industrialization, recognizing that laying a foundation was the best it could do at the time. From 1967 to 1970, the regime immersed itself in an idealistic, phase overlooking such considerations as mercantile and monetary relations in a socialist economy. Castro's mea culpa for failing to fulfill the 10-million-ton campaign promise led to the institutionalization of the revolution in the 1970s. In 1986, in another policy twist that inaugurated the RP, the decade-old market reforms were disregarded. These are past policy reversals and blunders. Today, the regime is engaged in the most drastic changes since the 1960s, dismantling the social order that the revolution created.

The Rectification Process

The rectification process addressed past mistakes and what became known as "negative tendencies." While the former involved policy blunders, the latter addressed the mercantilist mentality created by the market reforms instituted in the mid-1970s. As viewed by a student of Cuban affairs: "The campaign stressed values and organizing principles somewhat akin to those of the late 1960s rapid 'push to communism,' when many of Che Guevara's philosophical ideas were put into practice: moral incentives, an expansion of the state's role in the economy, and collective and voluntary labor. The national leadership argued that the revolution had gone astray and that the Rectification Process (RP) would correct this."[7]

Symbols of the 1960s, like Guevara's economic theories and moral incentive programs, had a revival at the time; but in reality the RP was a complex and comprehensive policy. It mixed action with reflection, evaluating the revolution after the process of building socialism for twenty-seven years. There was much to celebrate and much to regret. Midway through the revolution's third decade, things were not going well, or not as well as they had been expected to go.

Among other pressing issues, besides rectifying blunders, it became necessary to discard some policies and practices that had been copied from European socialism. The regime had to decide which ones to continue, to change, or to dismiss altogether. There was a temptation to return to the mobilization strategies that had gained the people's support in the 1960s but which were not suitable three decades later.

Acknowledging the role objective conditions play in improving productivity, and realizing that subjective means alone are not enough to do it (a blow to the spirit of voluntarism restored in 1986), Castro told a meeting of Havana enterprises that socialism needed better organization to improve economic production. He also admitted that "the capitalists organize production better, have better production methods . . . There are things that should be learned from them," though he added, "not their ideology but their technology." Still, Castro saw no contradiction between the need for better objective conditions to improve the economy and the decision to reverse some of the decentralizing market reforms instituted in the mid-1970s. As he put it, "We do not want people [technocrats] telling us what to do: science and economics are political instruments; they are instruments of the revolution."[8]

To Castro, revolutionary *conciencia* (consciousness) and moral incentives had to be restored at a time when scarce material incentives were failing to increase productivity. Economic needs and the vision of an egalitarian society had informed the decision. In the process, however, the less centralized and less personalized decision-making channels that had been built earlier were dismantled, nullifying the effort to increase productivity. Adding workers' input to the decision-making process, which would have fostered socialist democracy and probably would have improved productivity, was also overlooked.[9]

Evaluating the Rectification Process

While earlier market reforms and the System of Direction and Planning of the Economy (SDPE) were being curtailed, the RP was characterized critically as (1) a "counter-reform," (2) "the rectification of the rectification," and (3) a policy the meaning and content of which "have never been quite clear, even to those involved in it."[10] The first criticism refers to the reversal of market reforms, which were regarded as the real reform, and to the fact that the RP was used to bring back centralized political and economic control, which ran contrary to the decentralization reforms of the mid-1970s. The second critic notes that in 1975 Castro was praising a policy rectifying past mistakes (first rectification) and that in 1986 he was praising the rectification (second rectification) of the 1975 policy. Hence, on both occasions the rectifying policy was praised as the best solution to the problems at hand.[11]

According to the third criticism, the RP has "never been quite clear" (in contrast to the clarity of glasnost and perestroika), so the rectification process could be understood as "a catch-all label for political and economic measures," or "the means by which Fidel could rid himself of those around him—the technocrats—that were bothering him," or "a critical point at which the basic structure and workings of the Revolution would be reexamined."[12]

The view from Cuba was more positive. Comparing the Latin American socioeconomic and political conditions in the 1980s, a Cuban social scientist found the RP quite promising. Fernando Martínez Heredia, senior fellow at Havana's Center for the Study of the Americas, put it this way: "A true revolution within the revolution is the real meaning of the process known as rectification. It signifies the high level of development that the . . . socialist revolution has accomplished in Cuba materially, politically, and spiritually. There is nothing in this process comparable to today's capitalist democratization in Latin America, which faces . . . a terrible crisis, and an even worse combination of exploitative, domineering, marginalizing, and underdeveloped structures."[13]

Cuba had moved to the forefront of Latin America in the social services area, but the 1990s put all its gains to a difficult test. Still, the population's reservoir of goodwill, as noted in Martínez Heredia's statement, provided the regime with the support it needed to cope with the crisis.

Recognizing Mistakes, Justifying Changes

Inasmuch as the RP focused on policy problems, it underscored how ideological rationalization had justified unsavory policy changes. Yet the regime sought to redirect the revolution's course, not to renounce ideology—never mind the negative potential of the policy reversals. Rather than regretting changing policy, the government saw it as another shift in a process ruled by principled pragmatism, even if the approach failed to measure up to proper administrative standards.

José Luis Rodríguez, economy and planning minister, admitted the regime's dilemma while pursuing the revolution's nation- and state-building process:

> Every revolutionary process takes place in the middle of complex conditions in which advances and setbacks, in the search for solutions to the problems encountered in building socialism, are practically inevitable. The conscious participation of every individual in this task is firmly linked to a *developmental process that implies not only economic growth and improvement of basic social services but also the transformation of man as a social being.* The adoption of the measures that would guarantee the fulfillment of such objectives, which presupposes the precise and proper evaluation of numerous factors in a given historic moment, *has not always been accomplished successfully.*[14] (Emphasis added.)

In sum, argues Rodríguez, the Cuban revolution has accomplished significant gains in thirty years but has also had "insufficiencies" and made "mistakes" likely to arise in any normal developmental process. In the Cuban case, however, such deficiencies worsened due to the hostility the revolution has faced given its socialist character.[15]

Searching for Solutions

Political analysts understood the RP as a timely policy reevaluation but also interpreted it as an expeditious political maneuver, seeking to align the top (elite/leadership) and lower (low-income) social strata against the nascent middle sector. To regain control of the economy, internal consumption had to be reduced and industrial export productivity increased, preferably to market economies. The RP also included austerity measures, stopping corruption, and curbing bureaucratic excesses. Rectification sought to avert public discontent with the austerity measures by restraining (penalizing economically) those who had profited from the market reform period that had fostered social inequality.[16]

These were not popular measures, but given his central historic role as leader and chief architect of the revolution, Castro could enforce policies running contrary to people's self-interest. Still, he took pains to explain the need for such sacrifice-laden measures. At such junctures his charismatic leadership came conveniently into play, as he persuasively pointed out the path to follow, even if it was an unpleasant one.

For Petras and Morley, the rectification process meant that the "setting for an understanding of Cuban development in the 1990s [was] the basic shift from dynamic growth [1970–85] to economic stagnation and austerity [1986–89]." Castro was taking a "middle course between raising the question of [external] debt repudiation [by Latin American countries] and practical accommodation with Cuba's foreign bankers, between reaching out to the market externally but cracking down internally, between cutbacks domestically but spreading the burden equally." Still, they said, "it would be a mistake to underestimate Castro's political skills in attempting it."[17]

Recognizing the transitional and complex nature of the mid-1980s, and the need to reform the system further, Zimbalist saw Castro's dilemma in this way: "After a decade of decentralizing reforms [1976–86] a moratorium on further market and private sector liberalization was called in April 1986 . . . As Cuba continues to struggle to find the best balance among material and nonmaterial incentives, market and plan, private and public spheres, the success of its economic system will correlate directly with the introduction of decentralizing and democratizing reforms."[18]

Economic and political reforms were instituted but not until the 1990s, when the regime's survival correlated with its own successful integration into the world market economy. By then, however, Cuba would be blamed for not reforming enough and for not moving away from its socialist system.

There were also problems with the timing of the RP. The regime's external and domestic constraints limited the policy-making scope so that the government had to choose from narrow alternatives a sound, ideologically compatible course of action. The reasons behind the objectives of the RP were mainly domestic, but it assumed that the Soviet bloc would always be there, providing the needed financial support and trade markets for Havana's economic viability. By 1989, however, as the Soviet Union became seriously affected by Gorbachev's reforms, Moscow's economic problems and decreasing productivity were already hurting the bilateral relationship.

In early 1990, addressing the Cuban Trade Unions Congress, Castro said: "Our economic relations with the Soviet Union have not been very [much] affected [yet] . . . [but] it may also happen that problems may occur [to] the Soviet Union . . . [And] any difficulty that the Soviet Union may have . . . must inevitably affect the supplies earmarked for our country . . . we must understand that the stability of the Soviet Union is of the utmost importance for our country."[19] What had appeared as an unlikely scenario—erosion of Moscow's industrial power to the point that it would stop delivering supplies—was already a real possibility.

Due to the impact that Soviet events had on the Cuban economy, the RP had less than four years to produce tangible results.[20] The critical situation confronted in the summer of 1990 worsened rapidly, demanding an emergency program. When the special period in peacetime was declared in effect in August, it moved the RP off center stage. Thus after a short season of rectifying past mistakes and negative tendencies, Cuba had to move on and rapidly devise a strategy for survival under new international arrangements. The relationship Havana had for three decades with European socialism had collapsed altogether. In its aftermath, Cuba was left terribly alone but truly free of any outside political and/or economic influence.[21] The island nation realized that real independence comes in strange ways, and always at a high price.

The Scope and Content of Rectification

Castro unveiled the RP at the Third Congress of the Cuban Communist Party (PCC), on February 4–7, 1986. Due to the national problems confronted at the time, the congress was divided into two separate sessions. The second and closing part was held nine months later, on November 30–December 2. Castro's negative evaluation of most aspects of economic and governmental performance was unexpected. No policy area escaped his critical comments.[22] He blamed the PCC for having developed negative tendencies, and for leaving economic issues to the experts. He accused the government bureaucracy of having assimilated uncritically European socialist political and economic modalities, without considering Cuban idiosyncratic and developmental differences.[23]

Paradoxically, macroeconomic indicators had shown healthy economic growth rates between 1980 and 1985—7.3 percent growth in global social product (GSP) and 8.8 percent in industrial production—while overall economic growth for 1965–84 had been rated at a respectable 6.3 percent. Still, the country was in financial trouble for spending and consuming beyond its means. The state budget deficit had increased 17 percent from 266 million pesos in 1983 to 1,146 million in 1989, totaling 4,162 million pesos for the six-year period.[24] (See fig. 3.1.) What bothered Castro most were both the deficient production of exportable goods and services to market economies and the pressing need to reduce hard currency imports, which contributed to escalating the budget and financial deficit.

According to an April 1986 report by Castro, people's complaints about different problems had surfaced a year earlier. They included deficiencies in public health services, mostly in Havana, lack of control of the income generated by self-employment, violations of salary policy, increasingly lucrative deals made by many since the promulgation of the Housing Law (1984), and irregularities in agricultural cooperatives, especially in connection with the free farmers' markets.[25]

Recognizing the potentially negative political influence of such economic problems and ideological deformations, the regime adopted the RP. As officially reported, the main problems needing rectification were

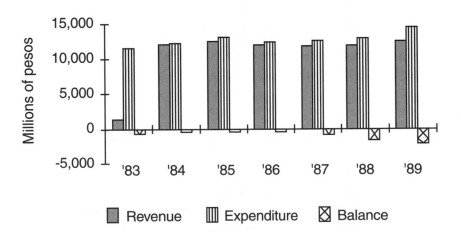

Fig 3.1. Budget Deficits, 1983–1989.

centered on the SDPE, high wages with low productivity, the social services, and revolutionary ideology.

Problems Caused by the SDPE

Under the system of direction and planning of the economy (SDPE), from 1976 to 1985 economic solutions were applied to most problems, and political structures were neglected. This occurred in spite of the 1975 First PCC Congress warnings: "No socialist system could replace ideology and people's consciousness . . . [because] capitalist efficiency is based on factors that cannot be replicated in a socialist society; [under socialism] ideological and moral factors are essential."

Castro stated at the 1986 Second Plenum of the PCC Central Committee: "After all the reforms that [were] instituted, I had expressed on several occasions my concern that issues central to a socialist society should not be ignored, especially in the face of the idealistic errors committed earlier." Also, the implementation of the SDPE was found to be flawed. While material incentives were prioritized with prizes, there were no comparable fines imposed on those failing to fulfill their assigned quota (norm), which had a lasting negative economic effect.[26]

Problems with High Wages and Low Productivity

A serious disparity was arising between the estimated value of economic production and the actual social (use) value available to the population. The enterprises measured their economic effectiveness based on profits and on prioritizing profitable items regardless of their real social value. After a while, the practice caused serious economic distortions, demanding urgent correction.

The principle of compensating according to labor productivity was affected when enterprises used less demanding labor norms, which allowed workers to qualify for higher wages even when their productivity rate did not justify it. In 1984 alone, 77 percent of the work norms used were appraised as lower ones. Overfulfilled labor norms (*normas sobrecumplidas*) reached 110 percent in 1980 (increasing to 117.6 percent in 1986), which led to a 27 percent increment in the average wage in five years, from 148 pesos in 1980 to 188 pesos in 1985. The excessive monetary liquidity in circulation increased to 867 million pesos during the period, affecting the availability of consumer goods and feeding an inflationary black market.

The construction sector had claimed an average value-added growth of 9.3 percent between 1981 and 1985, but in reality 23.8 percent of the construction projects had been classified as investment in 1975–84 and were not completed on time. The unbalanced economic growth of the first half of the 1980s had increased to three times that of the external commercial sector with higher imports than exports. This had a detrimental financial effect by lowering the amount of hard currency reserves left, increasing the external debt, and aggravating the negative impact of having an unbalanced external commerce.

Problems in the Social Services Sector

Social services, including housing and public health, were adversely affected. Between 1980 and 1985 the child-care centers deficit escalated—twenty thousand requests were overdue by 1982—when only twelve child-care centers were built during the period. The problem affected the incorporation of women into the labor force, in spite of the fact that women comprised 56.4 percent of technicians available and 38 percent of the labor force.

The health sector was equally affected, with the index of population per (hospital) bed growing from 175.2 in 1970 to 192.9 in 1985. Havana's situation was even worse: the index escalated from 82.3 to 102.1 during the same period. Notwithstanding population growth, the delay in building new hospital facilities was the main factor impairing the quantity and quality of medical services provided. The traditional housing shortage under the revolution grew even worse. In fourteen years it grew 18 percent, from 754,000 housing units needed in 1971 to 888,000 in 1985. The cities of Havana and Santiago de Cuba were those affected most.

Problems Affecting Revolutionary Ideology

As socially accepted values, individualism was replacing collectivism, and want satisfaction was replacing egalitarianism. This reversal in the value system had serious political implications. The negative effect of mercantilist speculation and the work done by trade intermediaries (emanating largely from the free farmers' market) were blamed for these ideological deviations.

The period's mercantilism also reached enterprise managers, who were more concerned with completing assigned work norms than with real social or economic value. Because labor norms completion rates were used to assess managers' performance, managers wanted to finish projects promptly so that they could receive full credit. Also, the management verification process erroneously disregarded quality and instead concentrated on quantity.

An increasing disregard for the law and socialist property also helped to distance the workers from the notions that national enterprises belonged to them, that they were not just working for their own personal interest, and that higher productivity and better quality were in the national interest as well as their own.

The regime's dissatisfaction with the economic conditions of the mid-1980s was officially attributed to the influence exerted by the economistic tendencies that had appeared in the late 1970s and had spread throughout society in the early 1980s. The government reaction was expressed at the 1986 Second Plenum of the PCC in this manner: "It has become evident that the economist trend of fulfilling production and social service objectives by appealing solely to material incentives—which have been deformed by the wrongful application of extant rules and work norms—is not promoting satisfactory labor conduct, but, contrariwise, is encouraging in labor poor discipline and indifference toward social objectives."[27]

Castro had his mind set on the problems encountered in the 1980s and on engaging in new policies to solve them.[28] The regime enforced the RP, which received the country's attention while the population was being mobilized in a campaign dedicated to correcting the nation's errors and negative tendencies. Predictably, the results did not match official expectations.

The Rectification Process Two Years Later

Two years after the RP became official policy, some of the objectives and issues confronting the country included nine economic problems, three social deformations stemming from the free farmers' markets instituted in 1980 (abolished in 1986), two production problems with negative side effects, five new economic, political, and social measures, and two initiatives to improve media coverage of events, as outlined below:[29]

1. Economic Problems

   Low-productivity workers receiving high wages had their
      performance measured incorrectly.
   Calculating enterprises' efficiency using profit rates did not
      measure cost properly; poor supervision of materials
      allowed their removal for use in marginal production.
   Warehouses did not keep supply inventories, relying wrongly
      on workers' voluntary record keeping.

Due to lack of inventory control and to faulty accounting, a Havana agricultural enterprise reported 117,000 pesos in losses in 1987.

A coastal navigation enterprise was paying workers in dollars without having to leave Cuba's waters.

While all kinds of materials were available on the black market, many state enterprises suffered shortages of needed materials.

Property crimes valued at 19 million pesos were reported in 1987 after 460 audits at state agencies and People's Power institutions.

Illegally appropriated toothbrushes were melted down and used to make earrings, bracelets, hair ornaments, and other knickknacks sold by street vendors.

After eleven years of failing to meet production quotas, textile mills produced 260 million meters of fabric in 1987, but 100 million were of poor quality.

2. Social Problems Caused by the Free Farmers' Markets

After a long chain of go-betweens came into operation many farmers stopped coming to the cities to sell their products.

A surgeon specializing in heart transplants earned 5 percent of the 100,000 pesos a garlic salesman made in a year.

The profit potential of farming an isolated plot of land was making many farmers slow down the setting up of cooperatives.

3. Production Problems with Negative Side Effects

A prolonged drought and local economic problems, combined with lower prices for surplus Soviet oil, damaged sugar and agricultural production.

Errors in domestic production and the low prices of exports impaired servicing the external debt. Since 1985, Cuba had failed to meet its commitment with the Paris Club, an international creditor group independent of the International Monetary Fund.

4. Solutions for Socioeconomic and Political Problems

Bringing back the minibrigade movement (voluntary work) practiced in the 1960s, using workers to build homes and community projects while their coworkers do their regular work.

Increasing the family doctor preventive program, and bringing medical attention closer to the population with young doctors going to isolated parts of the country.

Defending the national standard of living while imports are being cut in half.

Improving the image of the Cuban Communist Party by involving its members in rectifying mistakes and by setting them as models of exemplary behavior.

Making changes in the educational system, including reducing teachers' incentives to collect premiums, and expanding the training period of graduate students.

5. Solutions for Media Coverage Problems

Improving objectivity, avoiding using too many adjectives and apologetic language when public debate is introduced, and having writers contributing to newspapers to improve their literary quality.

Publicizing the rectification of economic mistakes while reporting the debates on economic policy and publishing economic commentaries.

The list includes an array of troublesome problems. But why had such matters as keeping proper inventory of materials in work centers, calculating cost to measure efficiency and productivity, and having the media use objective language while reporting events not been taken care of earlier? Considering the magnitude of problems facing the country, one appreciates that the regime's objective of putting the country back on track while ending policies and practices instituted earlier was worthy but elusive.

While it was important to make the people conscious of the implications the problems affecting them had for the nation's welfare, it seems that it was overly ambitious to think that so many problems could be corrected satisfactorily at once. Still, as a corrective measure the RP implied different objectives. It included a return to revolutionary voluntarism—as evidenced by bringing back the minibrigades and organizing construction contingents—and a reaffirmation of conciencia as central components of people's life. But it also involved downsizing pragmatic decision-making processes, discontinuing market reforms, and diminishing the SDPE.

In a systemic structural overhaul that relied heavily on revolutionary ideology and commitment, the RP was replacing the institutionalized pragmatism of the mid-1970s. Also, by rescuing revolutionary conciencia from partial oblivion, it was resurrecting doctrinal orthodoxy. While observers questioned whether the RP was the proper response to Cuba's unsolved problems, the regime remained committed to enhancing productivity and efficiency following its own logic and methods.

The Rectification Process Record

The RP campaign started with measures correcting deficiencies and improving economic and social programs. In addition, the government started to reorganize itself before the harder economic times looming on the horizon could become real. Decisions were issued in a series from 1986 to 1989 under such titles as "Action Plan against Administrative Irregularities and Mistakes and Weaknesses in the System of Economic Direction" and "Orientations to the State Central Administrative Agencies, and to the Local Organs of Popular Power." Also, a National Commission for the Direction of the Economic System (CNSDE) was established. Areas targeted for reevaluation and rectification included examining working conditions, reviewing and reducing the number of work norms, modifying the salary system, evaluating employment and hiring policy, simplifying administrative procedures and debureaucratizing the system, improving statistical and accounting records, and bettering administrative controls.[30]

Following CNSDE's recommendations, the PCC and the Council of Ministers issued directives and in 1988 modified the system of economic management. This included the direction of the economy, the supervision of economic planning, the structure of economic enterprises, the supply system, economic contractual relations, labor and salary policy, and the system of secondary economic production. The objective was to get to the root of the problems causing deficiencies and irregularities.

In its first year the RP ventured into different areas, modifying the national statistical system and the system of land use by private farmers and restricting self-employment practices. In its second year, the RP suspended the procedure for collecting funds for prizes and awards, and it ended free meals in mess halls and workers' free transportation. In 1988, it instituted new personnel and payroll rules and established the procedures for plastic artists to sell their work. It also reduced the Ministry of Basic Industry's personnel by about 60 percent and adopted a new employment policy nationwide.

The Free Farmers' Market

Elimination of the free farmers' markets in 1986 had a negative social impact. Three main flaws attributed to them had supported closing a useful consumer service. First, the markets had a disruptive effect on the agricultural cooperative program—farmers' high profits worked as a disincentive to joining the cooperative program. Second, the free markets fostered a capitalist mentality contrary to socialist ideology by providing some farmers with the highest income nationwide. Third, these markets promoted a nonproductive class of intermediaries and speculators; the entrepreneurs transporting the farmers' products were selling them for a sizable profit.

By closing the free farmers' markets the government put an end to a valuable experiment in limited individual economic activity. The decision revealed how Castro's vision of a fully egalitarian, socialist society was still an option. But in the 1990s a similar program had to be enforced in order to keep the revolution afloat. While corrective administrative measures could have addressed the conditions affecting the free farmers' markets, the 1986 decision aggravated the consumer, who was left without a viable alternative.

From 1980 to 1986, by favoring those associated with them at the expense of the population, the free farmers' markets had the effect of promoting social inequality. With their inflated income, a relatively small social group could afford what for Cuban standards was an affluent lifestyle. But if the government-operated markets—which used lower subsidized prices—had been more competitive, the free markets would not have been such an economic success for the farmers (and intermediaries).

Notwithstanding the negative ideological impact that the free farmers' markets could have had in a socialist society, the government bungled the opportunity to meet the challenge they posed. Because the state markets failed to provide service comparable to that of the free farmers' markets, the staple food found in the latter was so urgently needed that consumers were willing to pay higher prices for it.

The need for transportation and retail sales service had created the intermediaries and speculators, who were charged with profiteering at the expense of the consumer and the farmers. From the farmers' viewpoint, splitting their profits with someone able to free them from the cumbersome duties of their newly found business was a sound decision. If a state-owned enterprise had provided such services, it would have avoided the intermediaries and speculators altogether and kept the prices lower for the consumer. But the government refused to consider such a possibility. It dreaded putting itself in the position of being a promoter of mercantilism and free enterprise, both anathema to the revolution's value system.

Minibrigades, Contingents, and New Economic Policies

The 1986 revival of the minibrigades was a hallmark of the RP. Concentrating in agriculture and construction (including building day-care centers, health-care facilities, and housing), in four years the minibrigades totaled nearly 1 percent of the entire labor force—40,000 workers out of nearly 4 million in 1990. They had better than average working facilities and equipment but also had highly demanding jobs and worked longer hours.[31]

The minibrigades' contribution was felt soon enough throughout the country. In the first two years they built 111 day-care centers with a capacity for 23,000 children, 16,515 new houses, 1,657 medical facilities for the family/neighborhood doctor program, 9 polyclinics, 8 special schools, 22 bakeries, and the new Havana site for national and international fairs and exhibits, EXPOCUBA. They built a new hospital and expanded others, adding room for three hundred more beds. Later, minibrigades made up of housewives, students, and retired workers were also organized. (See fig. 3.2.)

The Blas Roca Calderío contingent laboring in construction was started in 1987. It included 1,280 workers who worked an average of 13.5 daily hours, who had a productivity rate of 16,004 pesos with a net profit of 23 cents per peso (its average cost was 77 cents per peso), and who received a monthly salary of 315 pesos. In 1988 the contingent achieved productivity 2.12 times higher than the rate achieved by the construction sector three years earlier. That year 61 additional contingents were organized across the country, totaling 20,000 workers by 1989. (See fig. 3.3.)

The RP sought to engage all productive sectors in a campaign to in-

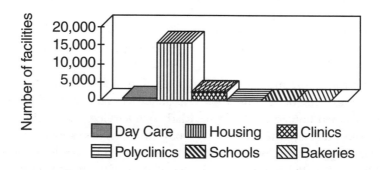

Fig. 3.2. Minibrigades' output, 1986–1987.

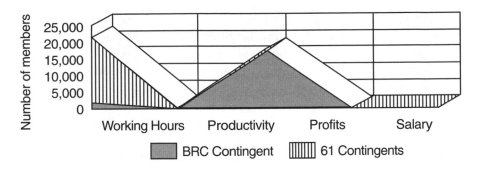

Fig 3.3. Contingents' Output, 1987–1989.

crease their effectiveness. Using cost production to measure economic efficiency, instead of enterprise financial self-sufficiency (given the problems with the price system), was a critical decision made at two meetings of Havana Province and City of Havana enterprises in 1987 and 1988, respectively. Other enterprise meetings held throughout the country reached similar conclusions. Additional streamlining of industrial production in 1988 resulted in 500,000 work norms (production quotas), reduced from 3 million, that affected 65 percent of the occupational tasks and included 14,000 different job descriptions.

Castro claimed progress in important economic areas a year after the RP had started. In comparison with the previous year, exports had increased 8.8 percent and imports had decreased 6.6 percent. Though imports from socialist countries had actually increased by 1.2 percent, the government expected to stay within the 700-million-peso import ceiling it had set for the year. In reality, only 550-million-peso import requirements had been satisfied in the first nine months of 1987.

Salary savings totaled 158 million pesos, inventories were reduced by 332 million pesos (down from previous years), and the recovery of raw materials increased by 4.1 percent. The Ministry of Construction accelerated the construction of new housing with the help of the minibrigade movement. The goal for 1987 was 37,000 new housing units, to which the Ministry of Construction was adding 23,443 under construction, and Havana minibrigades 7,445, for a total of 42,340.[32]

Some economic decisions directly affected social policy. A total of 186,000 workers had their salaries increased to 100 pesos per month in 1987, and other salary increases benefited 13,700 health and bakery workers and 200,000 agricultural workers, while the average salary in the years 1985 to 1988 remained almost 187 pesos per month. By the mid-

1980s, the unemployment rate was steady at 6 percent of the labor force. Pensions were increased in 1987, benefiting 725,000 retirees.

From 1985 to 1988 the budget allocation for basic social services in housing construction and communal services was increased by 7.3 percent and in health care and education by 12.1 percent. A manual for housing distribution among workers (according to their social and labor history) was issued in 1987, and new legislation in 1988 replaced the 1984 housing law. Crime and delinquency were addressed with the 1986 National Commission for [Crime] Prevention and Social Assistance and the 1987 Penal Code, which lowered eighty criminal activities to misdemeanors.[33]

The RP's Balance Sheet

Under the RP the country was engaged in a revival of revolutionary fervor and commitment, the economy improved in some respects, and the nation gained from the sense of purpose that Castro was able to instill in the population. Many of the problems identified as needing rectification were addressed under the RP and were at least partly rectified. But there were drawbacks as well. It was questionable whether the anti-market reforms built into the RP were sound. It was also unclear whether the arrangement to increase economic productivity, based on moral incentives and revolutionary commitment, was sufficient to rescue the nation's economic forces from their doldrums.

Scholarly analysis of the RP's performance includes the following:

Criticism of the RP's Economic Performance

1. The accounting system used made it difficult to measure the actual economic growth attained during the period (using the material balance system, instead of the national accounts system, excluded the value of nonproductive services and included double counting).
2. Austerity measures and limited consumption could not stop the growth of the budget deficit by 279 percent in 1987 (jumping from 188 million pesos to 525 million), after having been reduced the previous year by 26 percent.
3. The deficit in merchandise trading in 1986–87 was 27 percent higher than in 1984.
4. The convertible currency markets export rate for 1987 was 11 percent below that of 1984.

5. International reserves declined 44 percent in 1986–87 from their 1985 level.
6. The hard currency debt more than doubled from 1984 to 1988.
7. Resorting to higher-cost financing through short-term credits became necessary once a moratorium on hard currency debt repayment was declared in 1985.[34]

Criticism of the RP's Political Performance:

1. While the policies were justified by the need to increase hard currency earnings and reduce imports, the values espoused under the RP were contradicted by policies approving foreign capital investment, tourism, and capitalist-like enterprises, which are associated with capitalist societies.
2. Incremental absenteeism in some sectors revealed workers' poor response to RP's appeals to increase productivity and strengthen discipline in the workplace; there were cases of people faking illness to merit a report from the Ministry of (Public) Health.
3. People did not respond gladly to reductions in consumer goods (especially after the farmers' markets were closed down) and cutbacks in earnings and purchasing power.
4. High-level drug trafficking and corruption among civilian and military personnel in 1989 revealed the failure to stop or prevent serious moral decay: General Arnaldo Ochoa, a hero of the Angola war, and three officers were executed and ten others received prison sentences for drug trafficking; and Division General José Abrantes, minister of the interior and previously responsible for Castro's safety, received a stiff sentence for corruption charges and two years later died in prison.
5. There was discontent among political and military leaders (including General Ochoa) for the direction the revolution and the country were taking under the RP and for not following Gorbachev's reforms.
6. The issues raised under the RP were set aside with the enforcement of the special period in peacetime, following the demise of the Soviet Union and the Soviet bloc.[35]
7. The problems with the bureaucracy were not dealt with properly by the RP. In addition to approaching it as a matter

of reducing personnel in state offices, "fundamentally antidemocratic, paternalistic means [were] used to combat antidemocratic [bureaucratic] formations"[36]

Conclusions

In a four-year period the RP could not properly solve the problems confronting the country. Still, the following scenarios are worth considering: (1) the problems affecting Cuba by the mid-1980s could have been worse by 1990 without the RP; (2) the revolution would have not survived if Castro had submitted to pressure and followed Gorbachev's reforms; and (3) without the corrections and changes made under the RP—imperfect as they seemingly were—the Cuban revolution would have been worse off, perhaps even without the option of the special period in peacetime after the demise of European socialism.

It is in the context of such constraints and opposing forces that the RP should be examined. This is not to exonerate the RP, Castro, or the regime for mistakes, wrongdoing, or lack of ingenuity in admitting the limitations, and not to deny the contradictions and the political and economic subtext of the RP, but to study objectively the problems encountered by Cuba and to recognize how formidable they were no matter what solutions were applied.

In retrospect, it could be said that if the changes made in the 1990s had been made in the 1980s, Cuba would be on better economic ground today. But that would be rewriting history. As bad as they were, the conditions of the 1980s scarcely allowed anticipation of the way the Soviet bloc ended. Even though Castro intimated in the 1980s that serious problems were awaiting Moscow, the political and economic context of those years was not conducive to the kind of restructuring Cuba has undertaken in the 1990s. More severe problems demand more drastic solutions, and the RP was not the special period.

However, examining the RP's record shows that building socialism on an island ninety miles away from an antagonistic superpower is an extremely difficult task, one that most likely under different leadership and circumstances would have proven impossible. All in all, the revolution survived and moved on, bolstered by the limited RP achievements and equipped with enough resilience to face the problems that the 1990s were bringing to the embattled island.

4

The Quality of Life under
Severe Austerity and Scarcity

Social Implications of the Special Period

The special period in peacetime began on August 29, 1990, when the crisis of European socialism reached a climax. The demise of the Soviet Union would follow over a year later, in December 1991. For Cuba, losing its trade, financial, and political support (and military hardware supplier) was devastating, provoking a severe decline in the nation's quality of life.

The regime demonstrated determination and ingenuity while managing to survive the crisis and maintain popular support at a respectable level. The special period and its trying social sequel is far from over, but its effect is not as severe as it was during the 1991–94 period. Few developing nations could have endured a similar experience without falling into chaos.

Paradoxically, the government was the victim of its own early success. After the progress achieved in most social areas, reaching levels comparable to those of developed countries, the decline in living conditions and social services caused frustration and hopelessness. The number of defections and the emergence of dissident groups indicated that the revolution was now being questioned as never before.

Besides the political support built through years of social welfare policies and the solutions sought to the economic crisis, the secret of the revolutionary government's staying power lies in the way it approached the hardships of the 1990s. Safeguarding the social equity principle applied in over three decades of developmental policies, the regime distributed the extant meager resources with a sense of fairness. No single social group endured the brunt of the country's predicament. The economic misfortune was largely shared throughout society, while patchwork remedies softened its negative impact.

Development with Social Equity

The regime's approach to social and economic development represents political and normative choices assuming that economic growth should sustain the improvement in the living conditions of all social strata. A Cuban scholar identifies the main objectives of the revolution's development policy as:

Fair (equitable) distribution of wealth;
Erasing the traditional urban-rural difference;
Development understood as an economic and social complex;
Development includes human participation and growth as
    much as economic progress.[1]

While countries like Sri Lanka, Chile, China, and Costa Rica are cited as examples of sustained development with social equity, Cuba is generally ignored, argues Havana University professor Beatriz Díaz. In her view, the political support the revolution has enjoyed has largely been due to the economic development policy based on social equity followed all along. Cuba's social standing in comparison to that in Latin American and developed countries supports Díaz's assertion. Figure 4.1 compares social indicator rates in highly developed countries worldwide, Latin America and the Caribbean, and Cuba by illustrating the extent to which these regions have achieved social goals in four areas: access to medical services, immunization of children under the age of one year, delivery of babies by medical personnel, and attendance in primary school.

The social indicator rates achieved under revolutionary rule carried a

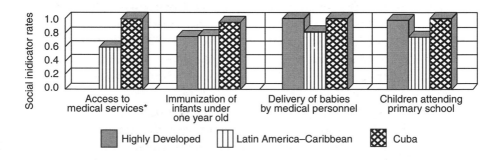

Fig. 4.1. Countries' Performance According to Social Indicators.
*Data not available for developed countries
SOURCE: United Nations Development Program (UNDP), *United Nations Human Development Report, 1992*, cited in Beatriz Díaz, "El Modelo de Desarrollo Equitativo de Cuba," Beatriz Díaz, *Proceedings*, 17th International Latin American Studies Association Congress, Los Angeles, 1992.

price tag higher than the country could afford. They were achieved thanks to the trade and financial and technical assistance provided by the Soviet bloc, especially Moscow. However, gains made in health, education, and other social areas had been social objectives prioritized domestically. Once the Havana-Moscow relationship was over and the quality and scope of social benefits came to an end, the memory of having had better days became a political liability. While people are agreeable to moving up the social benefit ladder, they become irascible after experiencing an unwanted regression.

The gains made under Cuba's social distributive methods are significant, representing social programs that minimize the differences between rural and urban areas and large and small provinces and that refuse to favor the nation's capital at the expense of the country. Before the revolution, some of the areas reaching the highest social rates had traditionally been neglected. The social indicators are representative of the population and the country as a whole. (See fig. 4.2.)

Even after Havana's development approach became untenable, the same principles were used to alleviate the effect of the special period. This policy decision was central to safeguarding the regime's legitimacy and the viability of the revolution. Besides providing historical and ideological continuity, given the unpalatable choices available at the time, equitable social policies proved to be the best possible alternative.

Emerging Social Stratification

The new economic policies created social cleavages, causing resentment and political disaffection among those left out of the new economic opportunities. No matter how equitable the distribution policies alleviating the hardships of the special period were, the injection of capitalist modalities through joint ventures (private foreign investment in partnership with the government) and the legalization of U.S. dollars rapidly stratified new social structures. This moved the country away from the egalitarian social practices that had been followed for three decades. The population was split between those working in the tourist industry or for foreign investors, or receiving dollars from relatives and friends living overseas, and those whose livelihood depended on wages or pensions paid with national currency.

The Social Downside of Neoliberalism

Castro has repeatedly opposed neoliberalism as socioeconomic policy. While his rejection is ideological, it is supported by well-known facts. Neoliberalism's socioeconomic mix, sustaining a free market economy

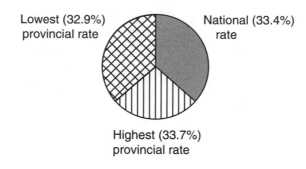

Fig. 4.2. Comparison of National and Provincial Social Indicator Rates. The mean difference between the highest and lowest provincial rates is .8 percent, computed using four social indicators.

Notes: Highest provincial life expectancy (1985–90) rate of 76.01 years is based on six provinces: Villa Clara, Cienfuegos, Sancti Spiritus, Las Tunas, La Habana, Holguin. Infant mortality rate (1991) of 13.2 percent is based on one province, Camaguey. Delivery of babies in medical institutions (1991), at 100 percent, is based on several provinces, including Camaguey, Matanzas, Villa Clara, and Holguin. School attendance rate (1989–90) of 100 percent is for children 6–11 years of age.

Lowest provincial life expectancy rate of 74.21 years is based on three provinces: City of Havana, Santiago de Cuba, Camaguey. Infant mortality rate of 7.4 percent is based on one province, Villa Clara. Delivery of babies in medical institutions, at 99.4 percent, is based on two provinces, Ciego de Ávila and Granma. Primary school attendance rate is 100 percent.

National life expectancy rate is 75.22 years. Infant mortality rate is 10.7 percent. Delivery of babies in medical institutions is 99.8 percent. Primary school attendance rate is 100 percent.

Source: United Nations Development Program (UNDP), *United Nations Human Development Report, 1992*, cited in Beatriz Díaz, "El Modelo de Desarrollo Equitativo de Cuba," Beatriz Díaz, *Proceedings*, 17th International Latin American Studies Association Congress, Los Angeles, 1992.

creating wealth and social inequity, is contrary to revolutionary ideology. While Cuba could explain today's social deprivation and the divisions among the populace caused by the economic reforms as aberrations, it could not justify social inequality with extremes of wealth and poverty as features of a socialist society.

The social and political effects of neoliberalism in developing nations, including Venezuela, Brazil, the Dominican Republic, Jamaica, and others, have been publicized.[2] But the social impact of neoliberalism in highly developed economies is usually overlooked. In 1981, the developed market economies totaled 17.2 percent of the world population and appropriated 71.7 percent of the world's GDP. Their GDP share increased to 74.6 percent in 1993, while their population decreased to 15.3 percent. The United States, Japan, and Germany had the highest GDP share among

Table 4.1. Share by Country Groups of the World's GDP and Population (in percentages)

Country Group	Share of World's GDP		Share of World's Population	
	1981	1993	1981	1993
Developed Market Economies	71.7	74.6	17.2	15.3
U.S., Japan, Germany	44.8	48.1	9.1	8.3
Developing Countries	15.2	18.5	74.3	77.3
Latin America	4.8	4.5	8.2	8.4

SOURCE: *World Social Situation in the 1990s* (New York: United Nations, 1994), 22.

the developed market economies. With 9.1 percent of the world's population, they received 44.8 percent of the world's GDP in 1981. But in 1993, with only 8.3 percent of the world population, the three countries accrued almost half of the world's GDP (48.1 percent). (See table 4.1.)

With the world's largest economy and having benefited from the economic boom of the 1990s, American citizens were assumed to have the world's highest living standard. However, the 1993 United Nations Human Development Index (UNHDI) showed serious maldistribution of wealth. Some population groups were favored over others with a sharp ethnic line separating them.[3]

Based on the UNHDI, the Associated Press reported that "citizens of some developing countries are better off than American blacks or Hispanics, while U.S. whites rank No. 1 in the world on a quality of life index . . . America [is] one country with two nations." Countries (and population groups) were ranked according to an index using a perfect score of 1.0. American whites scored 0.986 (the highest), African Americans 0.881 (next to Trinidad and Tobago, 31st on the list), and Hispanics 0.869 (in between two former Soviet republics, Latvia and Estonia). The report noted that the infant mortality rate for American whites was eight per 1,000 births but more than double this for African Americans, 19 per 1,000 births.[4]

With the second-best economy in the world, Japan scored 0.983 (slightly behind American whites)—but dropped to seventeenth when women were included. The average earning of Japanese women was 51 percent of men's earning, and women held only 7 percent of administrative jobs. As in most developing countries (with the exception of Asian nations), Latin America's living standard decreased from 1981 to 1993. In 1981, with 8.2 percent of the world's population, its GDP share was 4.8 percent. By 1993, the population increased to 8.4 percent but the GDP decreased to 4.5 percent.

Legalizing the U.S. Dollar

The legalization of the U.S. dollar had far-reaching consequences, some of them unexpected. Having direct access to U.S. dollars or not is the great divide in Cuban life, and the workplace has witnessed that dilemma in different ways. Managers of international tourist hotels had to devise a way to pay workers who had "direct" contact with tourists and who received dollar tips (waiters, bellboys) versus those who lacked such contacts but were needed in the hotel business (cooks, chambermaids).[5] Some managers felt that including a gratuity in the price, as European hotels and restaurants do, would remove the workers' incentive to provide better service.

The difference in income becomes even greater when high pesos jobs are compared with those earning dollars. A heart surgeon paid in pesos would have a lower salary and live a more difficult life than a tourism worker, including not only hotel and restaurant managers but lower ranking employees, taxi drivers, etc. A good salary in Cuba could go as high as five hundred to six hundred pesos a month, which would be worth between fourteen and twenty-six dollars. Over a week, four or five one-dollar tips per day could match or even surpass a high pesos salary.

The tourist sector has become a magnet for highly qualified workers. More than a fourth of the three hundred nationals working at the Sol Palmeras hotel have postgraduate degrees, while at the Meliá Varadero hotel over three-quarters of the employees have university degrees. Doctors, teachers, engineers, and other professionals have become bellboys and chambermaids earning dollar tips instead of working in their professions and receiving salaries in pesos.

While today workers in the tourist industry are glad to be earning salaries in U.S. dollars, in the long term this creates serious problems for younger generations. It is now difficult to plan one's own future, to choose a professional career, even though college education remains free. Cuban youth must question the value of higher education if later a profession may be traded for a job in a tourist hotel or restaurant or for driving a taxi to earn dollars.

In spite of more people gaining access to hard currency, such a dichotomous cleavage has led to a social malaise with ideological implications. The country is living in a changing, contradictory, and conflictive social matrix, under austerity conditions worsened by Washington's punitive measures. Even though economic conditions have improved from their low point in the first years of the 1990s, making a living will remain a difficult task for years to come.

Tightening the Nation's Belt

While trade with Eastern European countries was cut in half in 1990 and had ended by 1991, Soviet trade continued at a declining rate—Cuban exports had declined by 9.6 percent and Soviet imports by 13.2 percent.[6] Castro's gloomy report to the nation about the worsening economic situation and faltering Moscow deliveries coincided with the demise of the Soviet Union. Austerity measures were rapidly enforced, and a survival economy emerged as the special period progressed. While hotels, restaurants, and nightclubs catering to international tourists were insulated from the impact of blackouts and other severe actions, few exceptions were allowed to the sacrifices expected from the populace. Life under the special period came to resemble life under war conditions, with the regime appealing to the people's sense of nationalism and revolutionary commitment. While almost everyone survived the first and most difficult years of the crisis, no one was entirely unscathed.

Given the disruptive impact of such a stressful period, the government encouraged stress therapy workshops. José Ramón Ponce Solazábal, a doctoral candidate in psychology, developed an inclusive stress therapy approach that did not rely on pharmacological resources—which were not available by then. Ponce Solazábal argued that pharmacological cures for stress were being discarded by therapists elsewhere, so he favored an integrated approach combining hypnosis, individualized psychotherapy, relaxation, and the analysis of stressful situations. For him, stress treatment should be etiological (looking at the cause) as well as symptomatic (looking at its overt manifestation). Even though the treatment could not eliminate the causes of stress, it helped to provide a way to cope.[7]

The austerity measures of the special period included the following:
Living conditions, social services, and economic production
were seriously affected and/or curtailed.
To conserve energy oil, supply was reduced to the official
sector by 30 percent and to the private by 50 percent.
The 30,000 daily trips on public transportation in the city of
Havana were reduced to fewer than 10,000, and later to even

fewer trips; the only taxis operating were for international tourists.

Electricity was reduced by 10 percent; power was off six to seven hours a day, and blackouts became a daily routine.

No air conditioners or fans were used in workplaces; television was limited to five hours per weekday, nine on Saturday, and fourteen on Sunday; nighttime working hours and sports and entertainment were suspended; hotels, restaurants, and nightclubs for international tourists were exempted.

With less television and night entertainment, many performing artists received permission to work overseas. Writers, artists, and intellectuals followed the same route for similar reasons.

Water shortage became common.

National cement consumption was reduced from 4 million tons per year to just over 1 million.

Production at the nickel plants was stopped or curtailed; work at the Juraguá nuclear plant in Cienfuegos came to a halt; and fuel-inefficient factories were closed or had their working hours reduced. Workers laid off received 60 percent of their salaries while they remained idle.

Lacking pulp and chlorine, the two national paper factories stopped production.

The number of pages and the circulation of the official daily *Granma* and the weekly *Bohemia* were decreased; *Juventud Rebelde* and *Trabajadores*, formerly dailies, became weeklies; with the exception of some textbooks, most other publishing came to a halt.

The educational system suffered due to the shortage of educational materials, including textbooks, notebooks, pencils, etc.

Lacking fuel, tractors became idle, and livestock was used to pull carts and plows.

The rationing system and the ration book (*libreta*) were stepped up, while the official allotments were gradually reduced.

A food self-sufficiency program (Programa Alimentario) was put in place by converting 20,000 hectares of sugarcane field to vegetable production and by organizing new poultry sheds (1,800), dairies (1,000), and fish- and hog-breeding centers (50). Due to the lack of fuel, feed, and fertilizer, the results were disappointing except as regards vegetables and tubers.

Medical personnel levels remained the same (increasing in some areas), but medical services suffered due to the shortage of medicines and imported supplies. Special medical care was available for those seriously ill, but medicines for most common problems, including aspirins, were not available.

The armed forces reduced compulsory military service from three to two years and concentrated on producing food to satisfy their own needs.[8]

Castro's resolve to safeguard the revolution made a difference; his concern that equity should guide the distribution of goods and services was comforting at a time when symbols and gestures were needed. On the downside, the scantiness of goods gave little comfort to a beleaguered population. Organized actions of opposition and rebellion did not materialize, but the spontaneous disturbances in the summer of 1994 in Havana were serious. The people vented their unhappiness with their living conditions by voicing their discontent. As chronicled by a student of Cuban affairs: "Despite the crisis, Castro remained committed to providing social services. He prided himself in speeches for not closing a single school, day-care center, or hospital, and for not leaving a single person destitute. But circumstances led him to call for no expansion of social services and no new housing construction, and to cut food allotments—in quantity and quality—to schools and day-care centers. Said Castro, 'If in five years we don't build housing, if that's the price for saving the revolution, then we'll spend five years without building them'."[9]

Cuba's social fabric started to change, sometimes drastically. At a basic level, people were adjusting to their new environment, finding ways to survive the calamity affecting them. At a higher level, people needed to sort out the events that had followed one after another: the European socialist crisis and its economic impact on the island, the potential for an ideological turning point, and the effect of Washington's renewed antagonism under President Clinton.

Reemergence of Prostitution

Under the combined effects of economic collapse and the presence of foreign tourists, prostitution resumed on a large scale. (Prostitutes are now known as *jineteras*.) This reversed a major achievement of the 1960s, when the prostitution that had been rampant before 1959 was eradicated. Even though the real number of jineteras is not clear, conservative official estimates put it in the thousands in 1995, with six thousand in Havana alone.[10] Rooted in the hardships of the special period, the return of prostitution became an embarrassing social problem.

After publishing the report "Confessions of a Public Woman," *Juventud Rebelde* invited readers to write letters to the editor addressing the problem. The explosion of *jineterismo* was also discussed at the 1996 trade union congress. The president of the Cuban Federation of Women (FMC) and a member of the Council of State, Vilma Espín, denounced the national outbreak of prostitution. She noted that indiscriminate foreign tourism contributed to the problem, affecting society in general and women in particular, although there also are male prostitutes.

Castro agreed with the concern about prostitution and the way international tourism contributed to sustaining and fostering it. Speaking at a 1994 tourism convention, he said: "We don't want the image of a country of gambling, drugs, prostitution . . . We want the image of a country with a high level of culture and ability to welcome visitors, for the world to have the image of an honorable, moral country." As a result of Castro's intervention, a government commission headed by Vilma Espín was charged with finding ways to clean up prostitution and pimping, recognizing that the latter was not only exploiting the former but also promoting its existence.[11]

At the 1996 Fifth Communist Party Plenum Raúl Castro discussed the prostitution dilemma, but available solutions were not especially promising. His report signaled a government offensive against a problem that was escalating out of control. The tourism minister at the time, Osmany Cienfuegos, stated that measures had been taken to reduce the presence of prostitutes in international tourist hotels to "a minimum."[12] The police started to crack down in earnest on prostitutes and those associated with them.[13] But there is no chance to eradicate prostitution while domestic scarcity continues and dollar stores provide consumer goods otherwise unavailable.

The search for dollars underscores the prostitution problem; the jineteras are not after domestic pesos. They pursue international tourists in and around major hotels and in recreational places. In spite of the negative social effect that prostitution entails, the jineteras might constitute an added tourist attraction. Opponents of the regime have charged the government with purposely allowing jineterismo to increase hard currency revenues. Denouncing the media exploitation of prostitution in Cuba, the official newspaper *Granma* stated:

"You will feel yourself being watched by hundreds of available women," announces a recent travel article published in the Spanish magazine *Man*, illustrated with full-color photos of scantily clad models from one of Havana's leading fashion houses. Similar accounts . . . abound in the international press, and given the copious lines of copy dedicated to the theme and the almost delirious tone in which they are written, any intelligent reader would conclude that the basic message is not that there are prostitutes in Cuba, but rather that every woman from one end of the island to the other has suddenly decided to join "the oldest profession in the world."

[T]here has also been a considerable amount of distortion regarding the Cuban tourism industry, often accused of boosting profits by consciously exploiting the sex-trade tourism market. It has almost reached the point where anyone who might want to spend a week relaxing on the sunny beaches of Varadero is instantly suspected of being a sex maniac . . . overlook[ing] the fact that the majority of the one million tourists who come to Cuba each year come with their spouses or families . . . [But] there [have] been unscrupulous individuals . . . promoting sex-trade tourism packages complete with the addresses and phone numbers of beautiful "girls," in clear violation of Cuban legislation prohibiting such transactions.[14]

The problem became critical in the early 1990s, the worst years of the special period. The need for additional consumer goods prompted jineterismo in major cities and in commercial areas developed with foreign investment. Most of the jineteras have a high educational level (above ninth grade) and some hold jobs during regular hours; they are neither starving nor in a state of necessity—no poorer than anybody else. But their regular income in pesos is insufficient to satisfy their needs, which include goods available for dollars and access to dollar hotels, restaurants, and nightclubs.

Again according to *Granma*, from a survey of thirty-three prostitutes, jineteras "appear to be self-confident, assertive young women, for whom prostitution is not necessarily a means of covering their basic needs, but rather an option that provides them with above-average standard of living. It is, essentially, a means of acquiring—with relatively little effort in their view—the trappings of the good life, as they see it: dollars in their pockets, household appliances, fashionable clothes and shoes. In the company of a foreigner, they can go to restaurants and nightclubs, spend the night in a luxury hotel, and perhaps, last but not least, marry a foreigner, and leave the country in search of 'paradise'."[15]

Besides the moral decay involved, it is a dilemma for a regular family to have a relative engaged in jineterismo, and then to have to condone it because the family needs to supplement food and other necessities with what their own jinetera can provide. The special period has had a disturbing effect on the populace, from which society's ethical values could not shield everyone. Yet, according to the official media: "Despite the very difficult economic conditions facing the country today, no Cuban woman genuinely needs to prostitute herself to survive. The vast majority of Cubans—women and men, young and old—somehow manage to cover their basic needs, in terms of food, housing, education and recreation, without sacrificing their ideals, their dignity. *The resurgence of prostitution in Cuba is merely a reflection of a sadly misguided belief, on the part of some members of society, that affluence and ostentation are worthy ends, no matter what the means used to attain them* (emphasis added).[16]

The presence of international tourists (one million in 1996, and nearly two million expected by the end of 2000) and the availability of dollar stores with all kinds of high-priced items brought to the island the kind of consumerism characteristic of developed societies. The living standards of socialist systems, especially in developing countries, are not on par with those in capitalist societies, nor are they intended to be. While an egalitarian, equitable distribution of resources is a hallmark of socialism (guaranteeing minimum consumer standards but limiting their level), structural social inequality is a characteristic of competitive, economically mobile capitalist societies.

An American visiting Havana in November 1997 reflected on the signs of prostitution encountered in the Cuban capital: "Although I had spent only a few days in Havana on my first trip, and all of my time there on this one, I recognized immediately the stark changes: billboards advertising products instead of revolutionary campaigns; markets selling vegetables, meat and tourist items; restaurants, taxis, bookstores, lovely hotels, some nationally owned and some five-star Cuban/Spanish joint ventures; *prostitutes peddling their wares openly. (The latter, and the foreign businessmen hanging on them, are probably the most disturbing sight in Havana today)*" (emphasis added).[17]

Prostitution reemerged due to the economic crisis, but it is a symptom of a deeper predicament. There is no foolproof antidote against prostitution, especially when two very different kinds of lifestyles (socialist vs. capitalist) come together, even if in a limited way. When scarcity and unsatisfied aspirations loom over an entire society, long-held ethical values break down, and self-esteem falls victim of a rationalization justifying the satisfaction of needs by whatever means. Who is there then to judge anyone? Who could be the champion of public morality under such distressing conditions?

Women and Public Health during the Special Period

Among the social effects of prostitution has been an increase in venereal disease to near epidemic proportions. Cases of gonorrhea increased from 174.6 per 100,000 population in 1993 to 377.4 in 1995—41,406 cases nationwide, a 117 percent increase. Syphilis cases increased from 84.8 cases per 100,000 population in 1993 to 136.4 in 1995—15,000 cases altogether, a 62 percent increase. Given such serious health problems and the lack of resources to stop them, the government has resorted to sex education as an alternative to combat the epidemic.[18] Thus prostitution burdens the healthcare system, which is experiencing its most trying period since 1959.

According to a 1997 report issued by the American Association of World Health (AAWH), the "continued inclusion of food and medicine in the U.S. embargo against Cuba has caused a significant increase in suffering—and even deaths, among the ill in Cuba." Moreover, "the licensing procedures imposed by the CDA (the U.S. Cuban Democracy Act of 1992) also have proved so cumbersome and time-consuming as to virtually rule out the sale of medicines to Cuba."[19] Further, local antibiotics are among the most defective of the medicines produced domestically.

According to Cuban and international medical authorities, "Cuba's health care system—once a showcase of the developing world that compared favorably to U.S. and European medical services—is crumbling beneath the pressures of a national economic crisis and a U.S. trade embargo that have left hospitals short of equipment and patients without access to drugs."[20]

A comparison of Cuba's health statistics with those of three advanced Latin American countries (Argentina, Chile, and Mexico) and those of three of the largest economies (the United States, Canada, and Japan) before and during the special period, in 1970–75 and 1990–95, puts to the test the island's health record. (See table 4.2 and figs. 4.1 and 4.2.) The life expectancy at birth indicator for women and men in 1970–75 shows Cuba following Canada (first for women, second for men), Japan (second for women, first for men), and the United States (third for women and men). It shows Cuba ahead of the other three Latin American countries for women but behind Argentina for men—Argentina had higher life expectancy for men than for women. But Cuba has the smallest difference in life expectancy for women and men, three years.

In 1990–95, Cuba was ahead of the three Latin American countries for both women and men—Argentina had a reversal, with life expectancy increasing for women and decreasing for men. Cuba followed Japan, Canada, and the United States in women's life expectancy, while matching Canada, following Japan, and leading the United States under the category for men. Cuba continued to have the smallest difference—four years—between women and men in life expectancy for the period.

In the infant mortality rate per 1,000 live births category in 1970–75, Cuba had a lower rate than any of the Latin American countries but trailed Japan, Canada, and the United States, in that order. In 1990–95, after improving their public health record, the countries followed the same order they had in the previous time period. In the category of married women of reproductive age using modern contraceptive methods, or any other method, Cuba was behind the United States, Canada, and Argentina but ahead of Japan and Mexico for any method used (there are no data for Chile). In modern contraceptive methods, Cuba was behind Canada and the United States but ahead of Japan and Mexico. No data are available for Argentina and Chile.

Due to the economic crisis and the U.S. embargo (including on food and medicines), there were no condoms, birth control pills, intrauterine devices, or injectables available. The kind of contraceptives used is not clear, but based on United Nations data, some contraceptives were made available, or at least information on how to improvise them must have been made public. Finally, the maternity mortality ratio per 100,000 live births in 1990 (when the special period started) positioned Cuba behind Canada, the United States, and Japan but ahead of Mexico, Chile, and Argentina (which has the highest mortality ratio).

Given the gains in social areas, Cuba's leading position in public health in 1970–75 among Latin American countries and its being close behind the industrialized economies was not surprising. What is remarkable is that it sustained its position in 1990–95, as the health system deteriorated and was often in crisis. An explanation for this could be that the period from 1990 to 1995 lumps together the first and advanced years of the special period—data for 1993–95 alone would have indicated better the deterioration of the health system. Still, Cuba moved forward by re-

Table 4.2. Comparison of Seven Countries' Life Expectancy, Infant Mortality Rate, Contraceptive Use among Married Women of Reproductive Age, Maternal Mortality Ratios, 1970–1995

Country	Life Expectancy at Birth 1970–75			Life Expectancy at Birth 1990–95			Infant Mortality Rate (per 1,000 live births)		Contraceptive Use among Married Women of Reproductive Age 1990 (%)		Maternity Mortality Ratio (per 1,000 live births) 1990
	Women	Men	Difference	Women	Men	Difference	1970–75	1990–95	Any Method	Modern Method	
Argentina	71	64	7	75	68	7	49	29	74	—	140
Canada	77	70	7	81	74	7	16	7	73	70	5
Chile	67	60	6	76	69	7	70	17	—	—	67
Cuba	73	69	3	78	74	4	39	14	70	67	32
Japan	76	71	6	82	76	6	12	5	64	57	10
Mexico	65	61	5	74	67	6	68	35	53	45	60
U.S.	75	68	8	79	73	7	18	8	74	69	7

SOURCE: *The World's Women 1995: Trends and Statistics* (New York: United Nations, 1995), 84–87.

ducing the infant mortality rate per 1,000 live births to 7.9 in 1996 and to 7.2 in 1997, almost half the rate reported for 1990–95 and close to Canada's second-lowest rate of 7 deaths per 1,000 in 1990–95.[21]

Vice President Carlos Lage has shed some light on this issue. In his report to the 1997 Sixth International Seminar on Primary Health Care, he said that "Cuba has not reduced spending on health care, but rather has increased the percentage of the budget earmarked for this sector, despite the extreme difficulties faced during recent years, from 6.5 percent in 1989 to 9.3 percent in 1996." Cuba was spending 96 pesos per inhabitant on health care in 1989, and 119 pesos in 1996. By the end of October 1997, he reported, the maternity mortality rate was down to 21 per 100,000 live births.

If such gains were applied to Latin America, said Lage, the rate would mean saving the lives of twenty thousand women who die in childbirth every year. He also reported that only 1 percent of the country's 66,263 hospital beds were dedicated to foreign patients who came to Cuba for its better, less expensive health services, and that the "profits generated by offering [those] services [were] used to buy medications and medical supplies for the [Cuban] population."[22] According to Lage, Cuba was committed to preserving its public health system as best it could no matter the obstacles.

The island's public health record was recognized by the World Health Organization (WHO) during its fiftieth anniversary ceremony in 1998. Castro received in Geneva the Health for All Gold Medal for having fulfilled since 1983 the objectives established by the WHO.

And yet, the combination of food scarcity and a faltering health-care system caused new medical problems. In October 1993, after fifty-one thousand Cubans had been affected with "neuropathy" or optic neuritis, an illness causing eye damage and motor function deterioration, the World Health Organization announced that the epidemic was finally coming to an end. WHO officials reported that the cause of the epidemic was not an infectious agent but a "combination of nutritional deficiency and . . . a toxic substance." Cuban health officials halted the epidemic by distributing 1.5 billion vitamin pills to the population, thus eliminating the symptoms of all but thirteen hundred diagnosed cases.[23]

Also, after the initial contamination brought by soldiers returning from southern Africa, a new wave of AIDS was attributed to northern European tourists in 1993. The quarantine of citizens testing HIV positive would no longer contain the disease, so the government modified its policy. After six months in a sanatorium for AIDS treatment and education, the patient was allowed to live at home and continue treatment as an outpatient.[24]

Testing Women's Achievements under the Revolution

The special period has been hard on Cuban women. In addition to their roles as mothers, wives, daughters, sisters, educators, artists, manual workers, scientists, members of the armed forces, and in many other professions and trades, they endured the brunt of the 1990s crisis. Feeding the family became everybody's obsession, but it remained women's main concern. The reemergence of prostitution underscores the magnitude of the problem. Losing gains made in three decades, women moved backward socially, politically, and economically. After increasing their participation in the labor force from 32.5 to 39.7 percent between 1980 and 1992, they were burdened in the special period with additional domestic and family responsibilities. As noted by two associates of the women's mass organization, the Federation of Cuban Women (FMC): "In 1992, women were more than 61 percent of the middle and upper level technicians, half of the doctors and 40 percent of the executives in the health and education areas. There was a decline of women in the leadership of Poder Popular [the National Assembly] from 34 percent to 28 percent *because of the extra work women had in the home, the difficulties of daily life and the strength of cultural and ideological traditions.* In agriculture there is still a low percentage of women workers—they are one-fifth of the farm workers and one-third of the middle- and upper-level technicians" (emphasis added).[25]

Under the revolution the women's movement did not follow premises akin to Western feminism. Rather than women pitting themselves against men, they pursued their liberation alongside men within the revolution's developmental programs.[26] While women advanced in most social areas, traditional values and mores (*machismo* and others) were not entirely eradicated, so they linger on in the male population and in social practices.

Some changes are noticeable today in the women's movement: "No longer do activists in the *Federación de Mujeres Cubanas (FMC) sharply distinguish themselves from the 'bourgeois feminism' of the women's movement in the United States.*" After interacting in *encuentros* among women in the Caribbean, Latin America, and North America, and having hosted such events themselves, "today they seem more comfortable with feminist approaches to issues."[27] Earlier, Vilma Espín, the FMC founder and president, had differentiated the Cuban women's movement from Western feminism. She noted how the FMC had followed a gender integrationist approach in which women worked alongside men, receiving together the social benefits of the revolution.[28]

Women's progress included many possibilities, from education to labor opportunities and from social to political activism. An indigenous brand of women's liberation started in 1959 and has continued since—notwithstanding the changes and setbacks experienced lately. The regime's approach to feminism and the accomplishments of over three decades have been both applauded and criticized.[29]

The FMC, now a nongovernmental organization, has been charged with enforcing official policy more than with articulating women's needs. The FMC leadership has been accused of representing the founding generation's views and of bypassing those of the new generation. "The criticism raised by some young women points to a generation gap between young *federadas* [FMC members] and the leadership of the FMC. It is felt that 'the Federation isn't on the same wavelength as the younger generation . . . [it] is only [composed] of older women'."[30]

The FMC's magazines *Mujeres* (Women) and *Muchachas* (Teenage Girls) were the target of similar criticism—they stopped publication in the early 1990s.[31] The FMC found *Mujeres* to be "doctrinaire, boring, and too difficult to the average Cuban woman." The magazine failed to portray women's image as "filled with tenderness [and] with a great love of humanity, of truth and beauty, and with profoundly firm political convictions."[32] The FMC's idealization seemed closer to the official image of women (what the regime wanted women to be or become) than to what women really were or wanted to be.

The FMC's place in the system has been difficult, even contradictory, caught between whether to function as a downward transmission belt enforcing official policy or as an upward articulator of women's needs. Its experience has been chronicled this way: "At the beginning there were years of frenetic and innovative activity. Then as the revolution stabilized in the 1970s, innovation was gradually superseded by bureaucracy, routine, and a certain measure of boredom," which also meant that most of the early objectives had been largely achieved. But by the end of the 1980s "a new generation of women . . . did not have the time or inclination for FMC activities. They had outgrown the FMC . . . Ironically, just . . . when the FMC emerged as a more forceful advocate for women, public discussion of disbanding the FMC began to be heard . . . The FMC was becoming moribund and irrelevant because it had neither the freedom to find its own voice and explore varied interests and policies nor sufficient power to pursue them."[33]

The government enforced policies directed at women to facilitate their progress and to incorporate them into the overall developmental programs, so that their gains would be parallel to men's. Women had never had such opportunities before, especially those coming from low-income families. Also, thanks to United Nations support, Havana was able to carry out additional programs benefiting women.

After almost two decades of revolutionary rule, by the end of the 1970s and throughout the 1980s, women's enrollment in education at the primary level remained constant at slightly less than half of primary level students: 1978, 47.5 percent; 1980, 47.5 percent; 1985, 47.3 percent; 1989, 47.4 percent. At the secondary level, however, it was slightly more than half throughout the period: 1978, 50.6 percent; 1980, 50.4 percent; 1985, 50.6 percent; 1989, 51.5 percent. And at the college level, since the mid-1980s, women's enrollment increased from slightly more than half to a solid majority of students: 1978, data not available; 1980, 48.4 percent; 1985, 54 percent; 1989, 57.1 percent. (See fig. 4.3.)

The incorporation of women into the labor force increased from 14 percent in 1960 to 34.8 percent by 1990. The percentage of women becoming economically active between 1970 and 1990 grew by 223.9 percent. The relationship between women's civil status and their joining the labor force in the 1970–81 period sheds some light on this issue—Single: 1970, 21.8 percent; 1981, 25.4 percent; married: 1970, 16.3 percent; 1981, 39.2 percent; cohabiting (living with a mate without being married): 1970, 9.2 percent; 1981, 23.7 percent; divorced: 1970, 41.5 percent; 1981, 61.1 percent; separated: 1970, 7.7 percent; 1981, 43.6 percent; widowed: 1970, 1.3 percent; 1981, 9.3 percent. Widows and separated women experienced the highest increment—over sevenfold and sixfold, respectively—followed by women cohabiting, 2.5 times. The highest percentage in 1981

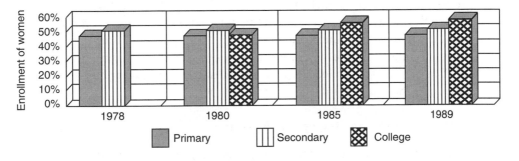

Fig. 4.3. Women's Enrollment in Education, 1978–1989.
SOURCE: *Cuba: Mujeres Latinoamericanas en Cifras* (Santiago, Chile: FLASCO, 1992), 58.

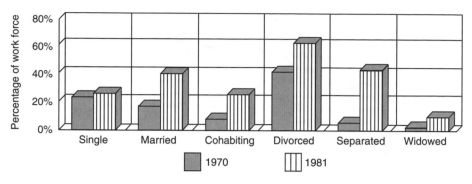

Fig. 4.4. Women's Labor and Civil Status, 1970–1981.
SOURCE: *Cuba: Mujeres Latinoamericanas en Cifras* (Santiago, Chile: FLASCO, 1992), 50.

belonged to women who were divorced (61.1 percent), separated (43.6 percent), married (39.2 percent), or single (25.4 percent). The high number of divorcees joining the labor force reflected the growth in the divorce rate, from 22 percent in 1970 (24,813 divorces) to 37 percent in 1990 (37,646 divorces). (See fig. 4.4.)

The burden imposed on women by the special period can be understood better by comparing the daily distribution of time among working and nonworking women and men during more normal times (1979), years before the current economic crisis. It is noteworthy that men had more free time (5 hours, 23 minutes) than nonworking women (4 hours, 58 minutes) and working women (3 hours, 38 minutes). Working women had the worst compounded daily schedule, with work and house chores time making up 12 hours and 1 minute, while for men these tasks consumed 9 hours and 7 minutes and nonworking women spent 7 hours and 43 minutes on chores at home. (See fig. 4.5.)

Paradoxically, the special period has had an equalizing effect by making household survival an inclusive family affair. Still, the working woman probably carries the lion's share of the newly imposed burden. Women are also being laid off more often than men under current austerity measures and the closing down of work centers, so their traditional double shift has been transformed into an enlarged single shift: taking care of the family in the midst of extreme scarcity.

Children, Youth, and the Special Period

While Cuban youth have been studied before, the problems they confront today have not been properly examined. Children's education under the revolution promoted a life experience that, while relevant before

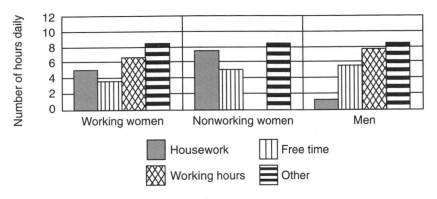

Fig. 4.5. Daily Distribution of Time, 1979.
SOURCE: *Cuba: Mujeras Latinoamericanas en Cifras* (Santiago, Chile: FLASCO, 1992), 50.

the special period, is now difficult to reconcile with the reality surrounding them in the streets and at home. The changes that have taken place in society have brought havoc to the social fabric that emerged after 1959. Social contradictions have been created in the last years that should have been addressed by the government—there is so much to do and time and resources are so limited—but that altogether compose the context surrounding children as they grow up. The end product may very well be some disorientation in defining their lives. Whether to blame Washington, Havana, or both governments for their misery is an open question, the answer depending largely on their parents' loyalty or lack of loyalty to the revolution. As seen by a Cuban-American journalist who visited her homeland while the pope was in Cuba:

> Nowadays, when children come home from . . . [school], they slip on shoes bought with dollars sent by their grandparents in Miami or, in some cases, they work odd jobs catering to American [?] tourists to earn dollars themselves. The contradictions of young . . . lives—hearing one message in school and [sometimes] another, radically different at home—confuses some children. Their teachers want them to fight the Americans; their parents want them to join them or, at least, to get some of their dollars.

> Some parents fear that their children will be ostracized if their teachers know that they live in a nonrevolutionary home. Parents who make a living in what the government considers illegal activities—renting a room or selling cigars without a license—also fear that, if their children talk, the government may confiscate their goods, fine them or, in some cases, jail them.

The burden of living in two distinct realities affects some children in psychological and physical ways. Teresita, a 14 year old ninth grader who lives in Old Havana, said that she had never told her best friend that her parents desperately want to leave the country . . . Her mother rails against President Castro, blaming his Government for the scarcities at home. Two months ago, Teresita began to shed the hairs of her arms and legs. The doctors told her that she lacked some essential vitamins in her diet; the mother thinks it is the result of stress.[34]

Describing a trip to Cuba that took place twenty-seven years after an earlier visit, an American academic attending a 1997 women's conference hosted by Havana University reflected on the impact of cultural influences arising from Western tourism and on how the shortage of children's basic school supplies was displayed on a bulletin board announcing Canadian tourists' activities: "Instead of European and Soviet bureaucrats (the tourists of the 1970s), the hotels of Havana were teeming with European, Latin American, and Canadian businessmen . . . At a lovely resort in the countryside where we stopped for lunch one afternoon, I noted that the bulletin boards were all in English, with directions for Canadian visitors on what time the aerobics class began, where to check out the paddleboats, *and (a particularly Cuban addition) the time the children from the local school would be stopping by to perform and receive their gifts of pencils, books, and school supplies*" (emphasis added).[35]

The problems children confront while growing up under the special period might have a different dimension by the time they become adolescents. Many youngsters have spent their childhood before the special period, but now their aspirations have been cut down to size with lower expectations. The dreams of many teenagers of future career opportunities are dampened by the new reality surrounding them, when they see what has happened to those who received university degrees. Many college graduates have had to give up their professions for menial but paid-in-dollars jobs. And yet, there still are opportunities awaiting Cuban youth today and tomorrow.

It was not the perennial housing shortage that kept Maribel Pérez, a psychology graduate from Havana University, living at home with her parents. As she put it, "As long as I am living in a house where everyone contributes to the family economy, I have no reason to give up practicing my career. But if I lived alone, I don't think I could do much with 198 pesos a month."[36] Her case sums up the predicament of Cuba today, particularly regarding women and youth, the two population groups most affected by unemployment—a problem recognized publicly by the minister of labor, Salvador Valdés Mesa.

While Maribel Pérez attended college free of charge, majored in her chosen field, and now is practicing her profession, she is not being paid a sufficient salary. She must share expenses with her family to survive, though she is already in her twenties. While free college education is available today, being admitted to a university and being able to study in the field of one's choice is more difficult, and finding a job in one's field after graduation is sometimes impossible.

In March 1997, when 18,250 positions in higher education for the next school year were announced, the annual academic competition among college-bound students began. The minister of higher education, Fernando Avecino Alegret, was quoted linking college educational opportunities to ideological commitment, stating that only Cubans "capable of defending the revolution in the realm of ideas and in the streets" would be permitted to study in the universities.[37]

The time when university studies were open to almost anyone interested in a college education has gone; circumstances have changed drastically. Entering a university was difficult and highly competitive in the 1990s.[38] Decreasing opportunities for college graduates and the need to reduce expenditures have forced the regime to limit access to higher education. Still, the number of professionals trained under the revolution produced the ratio of 1,050 researchers per one million inhabitants, a figure comparable to those in industrialized societies.

The government is still able to find jobs for college graduates. The Ministry of Labor placed 47 percent of them in their fields in 1995, and those majoring in education and medicine were placed directly by the agencies in charge. When young professionals specialize in a priority economic sector, like science, tourism, industry, or in work areas favored by foreign investors, the government can guarantee a job in that field. But in economic sectors hit by the lack of imported raw materials—like mining, the chemical industry, and geology—few jobs are available.

During this economic period, working in one's field is not good enough. As a young graduate put it: "I feel somewhat useless after having studied engineering, specializing in automated systems, an area with a lot of potential, but which I have hardly been able to use in the company where I work because of a lack of resources." He added sadly, "The only thing I can do is maintenance and repairs on some of the computer equipment."[39]

Today's bad times and rapid social changes have created a negative attitude among some young people. A 1994–95 study conducted by the Center for Youth Studies (CEJ) is most revealing. There is still a bias favoring professional work due to its social status, but young workers aged twenty-five to thirty feel they are being underused because they are not properly challenged in the jobs they have.

Among unemployed youngsters, 71 percent said that "they felt no economic motivation to work." To them, explains a specialist in work placement at CEJ, "work has lost its value as the fundamental means of livelihood and material well-being." At a time when they should be integrating themselves into society, 79 percent of these young people survive by "being supported by their families or [by] receiv[ing] income from other sources (friends or relatives living abroad)." They feel they are living comfortably this way; only 5.9 percent admitted having a difficult time. The remaining 13.4 percent had found undisclosed forms of employment.[40]

The special period is not the only reason for these problems. They started in the mid-1980s, during the rectification process. But today it seems that people's jobs are no longer their primary source of income. Also, there is a mix of demographic and labor problems: 60 percent of the population is under thirty-four, and 31.1 percent of the work force is between fifteen and twenty-nine years old. Those over twenty-four have shown a strong preference for working in their own field of specialization.[41]

The Union of Communist Youth (UJC) got involved in these matters through its Workers' Front. Reversing the trend of avoiding agriculture and construction work and after a national campaign held in 1996 emphasizing moral incentives, a number of young people started working in the sugar industry. The UJC sought a revision of the Labor Ministry's rules so that unemployed graduates could be hired for posts outside their region. It also requested the enforcement of a UJC resolution asking for the creation of a reserve of skilled labor made up of unemployed graduates. As members of the labor reserve and while remaining unemployed, they would be eligible for a state subsidy.

Youth and Higher Education

Besides graduating professionals that the economy cannot absorb, there are other problems with higher education. According to María Teresa Hechevarria, a chemistry student finishing her fifth and final undergraduate year at Havana University, "the professors are excellent, and I have received great training here, but everyone knows that we need more money to push our research to the next level." She admits that she would like to move on to graduate school for a master's degree and continue her research on altering growth genes in vegetables, particularly potatoes. "Cuba is the only third-world country that has a program as advanced as this one," she says proudly, adding that "the Nobel Prize is what I dream about . . . ; [t]he work I am doing is important for this country."[42]

Havana University Rector (president) Dr. Juan Vela Valdéz, an epidemiologist by training, insists that postsecondary education is free in Cuba, including room and board, transportation, and supplies for some of the two hundred thousand college students. Although the government has not closed a single school, he acknowledges that "there is little money available to purchase new books or other supplies and equipment." The economy is preventing the government from "upgrading materials and equipment at [the country's] 46 higher education institutions, five of them universities."[43]

Scientific studies are popular among the twenty-seven thousand students at Havana University. Among its fifteen schools, biology has the highest enrollment. In support of this trend, Dr. Vela Valdéz states, "It is necessary for Cuba to become a country of scientists." The assistant dean at Havana University's chemistry department, Dr. Georgina Agüero, witnessed three first-year chemistry students showing their research project on "the long-term effect on children of the nuclear accident at Chernobyl [former Soviet Union] 10 years ago" to a science exposition audience. A total of 14,083 children and 2,586 adults from Ukraine and Belarus affected by the nuclear accident were treated in the Tarará medical complex outside Havana, and they were the subject of the study.[44] After the first-year chemistry students presented their findings in Spanish and English, Dr. Agüero said: "It was terrific to see them up on the stage discussing their work in English . . . It was something totally unexpected by everyone in the room." In spite of such educational achievements, students and faculty at Havana University agree on the need to acquire new equipment if the institution is to maintain its present educational level.[45]

Higher education is not doing a good job at teaching students Cuban history. Social science students take courses on Cuban history, including the revolutions from the nineteenth-century anticolonial wars to today, but "students in other fields, including natural and exact sciences, have no contact with such subjects." The reason for these lacunae is typical of college programs: every curriculum has an overload of subjects to cover, and it is assumed that students have had such courses at the primary and secondary level. Responding to a survey conducted by the weekly *Bohemia*, 171 students from nine different academic fields at Havana University, including ninety-six students in the humanities and fifty-one in history, gave worrisome answers concerning the quality of education itself and the possible negative influence on college students' formative years and on society at large, 138 students rating Cuban history instruction "deficient" and only 32 rating it "good." (See fig. 4.6.) The main reasons given for such negative responses were a failure to motivate students (105 students), excessive class rigidity (94 students), and too much memorization (77 students). (See fig. 4.7.)

Subjects central to the revolution's political culture involving nineteenth- and twentieth-century history justifying today's struggle did not register to the extent expected from college students. After more than three decades of perfecting the educational system, the government must have assumed that the teaching of such subjects (indoctrination, in the view of critics of the regime) had a lasting effect on the students. Among the revolution's historic icons are such events as Antonio Maceo's opposition to any compromise in the struggle for the country's independence and the launching of the Baraguá Protest; the death of the founder of the Cuban republic, José Martí; the inauguration of the Cuban republic at the dawn of the twentieth century; the downfall of the Gerardo Machado regime in the 1930s; and the foundation of the Havana University stu-

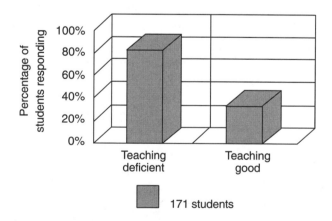

Fig. 4.6. Students' Opinions of Quality of Teaching Cuban History. Data were derived from the responses of 171 Havana University students to a *Bohemia* questionnaire on their experiences at the university.
SOURCE: *Bohemia*, January 8, 1995, B4–7.

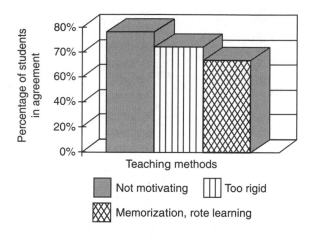

Fig. 4.7. Students' Descriptions of Deficient Teaching Methods.
SOURCE: *Bohemia,* January 8, 1995, B4–7.

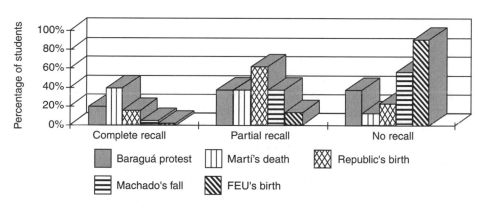

Fig. 4.8. Students' Ability to Remember Historic Events.
SOURCE: *Bohemia,* January 8, 1995, B4–7.

dent association, the Federación Estudiantil Universitaria (FEU). The students' familiarity with these events proved to be from relatively poor to extremely poor. (See fig. 4.8.)

In the words of to the deputy dean of Havana University's philosophy and history school, Dr. Oscar Loyola, "When a student starts his college education he has no patriotic sensibility and is also lacking any motivation for the subject matter, because he sees it as another course he has to pass with no connection to his own problems and objectives." Still, Professor Dolores Breuil affirms that "learning those subjects is important, but it should be a deeply felt, lively history course that provides a patriotic foundation and not something cold and mechanistic, as it happens in many classes." Using materials provided by the Ministry of Education and Hortencia Pichardo's *Documents for a History of Cuba*, "the classes become a cold chronological recitation of facts and dates, with little appeal" for the students. While almost half of the students could identify three or four out of six of Martí's works, when they were asked to relate famous phrases to their authors, more than 10 percent failed to identify Martí's.[46]

The development of universal, free education has been a distinct feature of the revolution. While hard-core scientific disciplines appear to stimulate students to excel, social science subjects, especially courses on Marxism, fall short of what makes a class appealing in the students' eyes. Failing to build a foundation supporting revolutionary rule among the new college-educated generation, as evidenced by these facts, is potentially dangerous for the regime's political future.

Combating Corruption during the Special Period

Acknowledging the pervasive state of corruption in today's society, the Havana provincial committee of the Communist Party held a meeting in March 1997 to study the problem. Members agreed that "a multiple approach confronting crime and corruption should be strengthened," because such problems "cannot be dealt with using coercive police measures alone." The head of the Havana party committee, Esteban Lazo, condemned those who participate directly or indirectly in illicit transactions with merchandise stolen from state enterprises: "We cannot tolerate such behavior . . . present economic and material difficulties cannot be used to condone theft, corruption, and lack of honesty."[47]

As a social phenomenon, a major problem of this so-called wave of corruption during the special period is that it is more a means of individual or collective survival than an intended explosion of criminal behavior. Many of those committing such actions do not see themselves as political enemies of the revolution because of what they are doing, nor do they understand their actions in such terms. They are mainly acting out a survival mechanism that, while selfish and illegal, is taking place at a time when their own livelihood and/or the survival of their family may depend on it.

Still, according to a report published in *Granma*, "criminal and other illegal actions are against the essence of a socialist system, so their ideological-political connotation should not be overlooked." The provincial gathering proposed to keep "a closer internal economic control, as well as a proper accounting system . . . so that circumstances facilitating theft could be avoided." Also, party organizations were asked to "demand a rendition of accounts from those responsible so that all irregularities would come to an end."[48]

Another recent target of the anti-corruption/crime campaign has been some of the fifteen hundred small, private restaurants known as *paladares*, operating in people's houses throughout the country—six hundred in Havana alone. According to Vice President Carlos Lage, many of these paladares "do not respect existent regulations" (they cannot employ salaried workers or serve more than twelve customers at a time), and "when they are inspected, not only violations but also stolen goods are found." Lage insisted that the government was cracking down on thieves, not closing down the paladares.[49] A flea market, set up in two small parks near Havana's central train station and operated by self-employed handicapped individuals, was closed down as part of the remodeling and cleaning of the entire area, which is considered a tourist attraction. Contrary to regulations, unauthorized individuals were taking advantage of the situation and selling stolen goods from the government's warehouses to travelers arriving from the provinces. Some of the goods for sale, such as soap and cooking oil, were rare and in high demand and could not be found even in dollar stores.[50]

Francisco Soberón, president of the National Bank (BNC), became president of the newly formed Central Bank.[51] He stated that special measures have been taken to detect and prevent the illegal flow of capital and money laundering, so that "the international mafia could not use Cuba's banking system." The measures are part of a thorough reform process presently under way in the country's banking system, including training the staff on how to detect and prevent money laundering and other crimes. Soberón claimed that the island's banking system is "totally free of international mafia activities."[52] Presently, there are thirteen foreign banks and ten different government bank entities operating in Cuba.[53]

However, in recognition that corruption has spread dangerously among government officials at different levels of the system, a code of ethics has been promulgated for state cadres. Underscoring its current significance, the code was inaugurated in a ceremony in the Palace of the Revolution presided over by Castro, his brother Raúl, and a legendary fighter of the Sierra Maestra days, Juan Almeida.

The new code of ethics, which "define[d] and systematize[d] the norms that should regulate the life and conduct of state cadres," became effective after the complementary operational guidelines were issued by the Executive Committee of the Council of Ministers.[54] Cases of corruption have occurred with bribes offered to government officials by foreign companies willing to grant favors in pursuance of state contracts. The code appears to address this and related corruption problems, which were not as dangerously widespread and in most cases not as openly discussed before the special period. Exceptions to this were the famous 1989 civilian and military drug-trafficking and corruption cases that made headlines all over the world.

Corruption at the Top

On July 10, 1989, *Granma* reported the court-martial verdict against fourteen officers charged with drug trafficking and other serious crimes. The main defendants, Division General Arnaldo Ochoa, Captain Jorge Martínez Valdés, Major Amado Padrón, and Colonel Antonio De la Guardia, were sentenced to death. Two others, Brigadier General Patricio De la Guardia (twin brother of Antonio, and temporarily released from prison in 1997) and Captain Miguel Ruiz Poó, received thirty-year sentences. Eight other defendants, one woman among them, received prison sentences ranging from ten to thirty years.

In a separate case, the minister of the interior, Division General José Abrantes, was charged with abuse of power, misuse of monies, and neglect of duty, for which he received a twenty-year sentence—he was found guilty of converting pesos into dollars at black market prices. Other top military and civilian officers were fired, including the heads of the Customs Service and the Immigration Department. Personnel from the Ministries of Transportation and the Armed Forces were charged with corruption, and the minister of transportation received a twenty-year sentence.

The case was followed closely in Cuba and abroad. The accused had been held in high esteem, particularly Ochoa. Their fall from grace was not reassuring at a time when the events in socialist Europe were threatening the revolution. Some observers found it difficult to believe that drug trafficking could flourish outside the knowledge of senior officials. "The level of detail Castro gets involved with is nothing short of extraordinary. It really strains the imagination to think he didn't acquiesce to the drug trafficking," said Jacqueline Tillman, former National Security Council advisor. But according to John Fernández, a spokesman for the Federal Drug Administration in Miami, there was "no reason to believe that

Fidel Castro or people [in] the presidential palace were in sympathy with the smugglers."[55]

Charges made in southern Florida asserted that everything had been a Castro-made plot to rid himself of actual or potential enemies, so he purged a popular officer who stood against his involvement in Angola. To a defector living in the United States, Air Force General Rafael del Pino, "Castro had arrested Ochoa to prevent disgruntled officers from carrying out 'an uprising against the regime'."[56]

The trial shocked the country, leaving a bad taste with the public. The Ochoa–De la Guardia affair happened because the network built by the government to escape the U.S. blockade—CIMEX, a Cuban government agency registered in Panama with subsidiaries in other countries and that handled tourism and other businesses, and the Departamento de Moneda Convertible, the Department of Convertible Currency—was illegally used by those in charge. It was an experience that no one wanted to re-live. The government had to invest political capital in unpopular trials and prison and death sentences. It was also the kind of affair asking for polarized interpretations with no room for objectivity. People on either side of the argument were convinced that theirs was the correct version and other explanations were politically motivated rationalizations.

Conclusions

To say that the special period was the worst ever for the Cuban revolution is to state the obvious. After three decades of building a revolutionary society, the regime found that its foundation was far from solid, that it could collapse like the Soviet bloc did. It was a time to pick up the pieces and start anew with no allies and very few friends. The social effect of the special period could be chronicled as years of disaster, disappointment, scarcity, austerity, hunger, prostitution, corruption, defections, ideological confusion, the loss of hard-gained social and economic advances, and other troublesome happenings. But it could also be the period for a new beginning and direction; namely, a redefinition of what the revolutionary socialist project would ultimately be.

The social consequences of these years include dark and bright moments, despair and courage, and the triumph of the quest for survival. Still, the people yearn for better times, for a nicer life to replace today's austere existence. One day the special period and its exigencies will pass, and according to revolutionary leaders and followers, the *patria socialista* (socialist fatherland) will still be there.

5

Political Reform under the Special Period

In 1959 the revolutionary government channeled the nation toward build-ing a new society. Three decades later, recognizing that reforming its own system was unavoidable, a more mature revolution struggled to safe-guard its main achievements. This ongoing transformation will increas-ingly distance the emerging society from what it was before 1990, when the objective was to build a complete socialist system.

The country had to redirect its diplomatic relations, adapting to radi-cally different international conditions. The domestic changes proceeded cautiously, avoiding costly mistakes, but not everyone welcomed a bal-anced approach. Dissidents at home and opponents abroad were not sat-isfied with the paucity of political change.[1] Though economic change was generally welcomed, some critics found it inadequate.[2] Orthodox cadres in the regime took the opposite tack: they believed that the changes had gone too far and could only jeopardize the socialist system, weaken-ing its true nature.[3]

The Scope and Content of Political Change

Castro admitted that the first years of the special period were the most difficult for the revolution. It was quite an admission, given the regime's record. In 1989, when the rectification campaign was still in full swing and the Ochoa–La Guardia affair was shocking the nation, the govern-ment was already struggling to improve the system and to safeguard its moral fiber: "So far, the rectification [process] has accomplished rather serious objectives. But without any doubt we are now entering a more transcendental stage in this process. Perhaps in the future [the 1989] events that have shocked the nation may be seen as the turning point for a *profound institutional, political and moral improvement* (perfeccionamiento) *of the Revolution*" (emphasis added).[4]

A primary concern was to prevent the economic downfall from spilling over and turning into a major political crisis. Political changes were primarily made to safeguard the political consensus and ideology supporting the system. Still, the special period posed a central policy-making dilemma. One policy approach sought to maintain the status quo, opposing any meaningful change. This was not a viable alternative given the severity of the economic crisis. The opposite option, supporting radical change and a multiparty system, was the choice of the regime's opponents. After rejecting both, the government adopted a middle-of-the-road approach that, while helping to overcome the crisis, would not threaten the nation's political and ideological consensus. But even after being carefully managed, changes could still have unforeseen social side effects—like the resurgence of prostitution fueled by growth of international tourism and by legalization of the U.S. dollar.

The transformation process touched upon a broad economic and social area, but the parameters of the political changes were limited. By keeping one-party rule and the socialist system, Havana planned political development within well-defined boundaries. It sought to increase the system's capability to perform effectively under adverse conditions, not to transform it radically or to replace it.

Given the economy's poor standing, the nation's future appeared uncertain to analysts like Jorge Domínguez: a political strategy limited to survival and resistance could only mean "tears, sweat, and perhaps bloodshed."[5] However, this predicament could be improved with some modest political openings. In agreement with the Constitution and a liberalized electoral law, political opponents could be allowed to run in elections for the National Assembly and to challenge the Communist Party's political monopoly. Such a change might not satisfy internal and external opponents, but it would modify the political debate, improving the image of rigidity that characterized the regime.[6]

In the eyes of another Cuba watcher, a post-Castro era could look like any of four possible scenarios: (1) A Mexican model: A hegemonic party controlling elections and exercising power using fraud, pressure, and manipulation. (2) A quasi-Chinese model: Adopting market mechanisms but limiting their effect by denying farmers commercial independence. (3) A Nicaraguan model: A party that relinquished power after losing free elections, but retaining political and social clout by limiting the choices of the succeeding regime. (4) A violent clean sweep: A forceful revolt capable of overthrowing the regime.[7]

Notwithstanding their distinct features, these four prototypes are based on similar premises: the effect of the collapse of European socialism, the island's inability to survive the crisis, and the struggle among factions fighting for their own survival. They are also predicated on the assumption that present change would probably lead to a different outcome than the one pursued by the regime. Hence, especially if the fourth one proves correct, Castro would not be able to decide Cuba's future.[8]

The scope and direction of the change process seem to be based on principled pragmatic decisions. As Castro explained to the leaders of the Latin American left attending the Fourth São Paulo Forum held in Havana in 1993, Cuba had to choose between saving the nation and socialism or, instead, risking the socialist system:

> We had to be able to distinguish between what we had to do to save the nation, the Revolution, and socialism's gains and what we had to do to improve socialism . . . *We shall do whatever is necessary to save the nation, to save the Revolution, to save socialism's principles.* However, whatever we do, we shall do it step by step, because what we want to do is to save not destroy, and if we have to destroy in order to save, we would rather . . . destroy us along with what we have done, along with what we have created . . . I say [socialism's] gains because today we cannot speak of the pure, ideal, perfect socialism we dreamed about, because life forces us to make concessions . . . *[But] we are aiming to save socialism in our country, [we] are aiming to perfect socialism.*[9] [Emphasis added.]

Responding to pressure from the Clinton Administration to embrace liberal democracy, Castro made clear that Cuba had already had its democratic transition in 1959, when the revolution came to power.[10] Speaking at the Union of Communist Youth thirty-fifth anniversary, he regretted that economic reforms had put the country in contact with such "contaminating elements" as the arrival of international tourists, an entrepreneurial self-employed class, and dollar remittances from families living abroad. For Castro, this was "something very difficult to swallow in a country . . . accustomed to equality and even to egalitarianism." Noting that "we could have carried on in our glass urn, but the glass urn was shattered and we ha[d] to learn to live without a glass urn," he surmised that adjusting to prevailing conditions was the price Cuba had to pay.[11]

While nothing guarantees that today's policies will pay off, so far the regime has accrued a viable crisis management record. Examining the changes made in Cuba and Nicaragua in the 1980s, and the chances for managing effectively the problems of the period, I have noted elsewhere: "Paradoxically, a revolutionary regime operating in a political system with a division of powers among the different branches of government, as in Nicaragua, seems less capable of steering the nation along a path of meaningful social transformation than a one-party, organically integrated Marxist-Leninist political system, such as exists in Cuba. This seems to contradict the notion that a decentralized political system is more effective in conducting the affairs of state than a highly centralized (and consequently less democratic) one."[12]

Contrasting the Nicaraguan and Cuban experience sheds some light on Havana's present change process. Pluralism allows interest groups and political parties to seek demand-satisfaction while competing for the government's attention. This is anathema to Castro, who sees in multiparty politics the kind of fragmentation that would provide a window of opportunity for the revolution's enemies. A unified nation under a single political party exemplifies Castro's political mode of choice. He did not have to rely entirely on Marxism-Leninism to take such a stance; he could draw from José Martí's nineteenth-century struggle for Cuba's independence under a single political party, the Cuban Revolutionary Party. According to Arnold August in *Democracy in Cuba and the 1997–98 Elections*:

> There [was] opposition to the divisive effects of [the multiparty] electoral system foreign to the young, but entrenched Cuban heritage arising out of the Guáimaro Constitution. An alternative to [such a] political process, in which Cubans were incited to divide themselves along the lines of one or the other of the political parties each of which fought to attain political power for itself, was also put on the agenda. José Martí and his collaborators, based in the main on . . . workers, revolutionary intellectuals and professionals, small and patriotic sections of the sugar bourgeoisie, were taking carefully calculated organizational steps. Martí combined this with a definite ideology and politics to organize a [single political] party dedicated to the vast majority of Cubans, especially the most humble section from whose ranks the [Partido Revolucionario Cubano] emerged.[13]

Juan Marinello, a Marxist writer and intellectual, noted differences and similarities between Martí's and Lenin's single-party politics: "The fact that in [Martí's] Cuban Revolutionary Party there coincided an array of groups—not of personal affiliations—invited to a free debate, and the existence of a personal power exercised energetically has made some *compañeros* think of similarities with the party thought out and constructed by Lenin's genius. Assessing both of them as equivalent is, of course, not valid, because the thought behind and the nature of their objectives were different; but it is true to say that in both cases traditional patterns used to ignore the popular will and to enforce the hegemony of the powerful were ignored."[14]

Even though their bias against political parties turned out to be misplaced, the case could also be drawn from another experience: the American founding fathers' attitudes and preferences:

> The [American] Constitution makes no mention of political parties, and many of the Founders abhorred them. George Washington sought to avoid partisanship by forming a cabinet composed of the best available talent, including Thomas Jefferson as secretary of state and Alexander Hamilton as secretary of the treasury. The appointment of these two gifted but philosophically opposed individuals reflected Washington's belief that the public would best be served by calling on the nation's wisest and most public-spirited citizens to work together for the public good . . . Unfortunately, Washington's noble attempt to avoid partisan politics ultimately failed.[15]

Still, American political values did not influence Cuban revolutionaries. Their vision was rooted in Cuban traditions, with Martí's political legacy and twentieth-century Marxist revolutionary thought, particularly Lenin's, at its center.[16]

The Communist Party in the 1990s

Displaying political realism, the Cuban Communist Party (PCC) sought to broaden its appeal and support base by abandoning social class distinctions and taking a new identity as the party of the Cuban nation. Religious believers became eligible for party membership. This widened the party ideologically; the PCC was now adding religious beliefs held by new members to Marxism-Leninism and Martí's *ideario* (principles). But despite Castro's remarks welcoming them into the party ranks, the decision encountered opposition in the assemblies held preceding the 1991 Fourth Party Congress.

The pragmatic operational guideline of the 1990s was tested again at the Fifth Party Congress on October 10–12, 1997. The Central Committee had announced early in the year that preparations for another PCC congress during the special period were under way.[17]

The Fourth Party Congress

On October 10, 1991, the Fourth Party Congress was inaugurated with eighteen hundred delegates attending.[18] Controversy surrounded the communist gathering from the time of the *llamamiento* (announcement) months earlier. An eyewitness chronicled the congress this way:

This was the first Congress where not all the votes were unanimous, where debate was heard (on issues like the free farmers' market, crime and its causes, the electoral system and the press). More debate would have hit the floor, especially on the question of religious believers in the Party, if it weren't for the fact that provincial caucuses spent hours wrangling over the point on the eve of the Congress . . . Never has Cuba been under such assault from all sides . . . Yet, this time the response that won out was to open the door to discussion, divergence of opinion, criticism.[19]

The most important decision of the congress was to resist, to keep socialism and the one-party system. It disappointed those expecting major reforms to transform the system. The changes had been cautiously drawn. It was not a time for risky decisions but for policies that would adapt the country to a different world, that would rescue the nation from the economic crisis and still keep socialism alive.

Decisions at the Fourth Party Congress included the following items:

1. Party Internal Rule

Becomes the party "of the whole nation";

Welcomes religious believers in the party;

Encourages "free expression of ideas" and "respect for differences of opinion";

Keeps the party's role as the country's political guide based on its "moral authority" and the "wisdom of its policies";

Recommends strengthening the autonomy of government bodies and other institutions with no party interference.

2. The Party Program

Defends Cuba's freedom of choice and "the independent and socialist course of the revolution";

Declares the 1986 party program to be dated; criticizes past tendencies to copy uncritically from the Soviet Union and Eastern Europe;

Defends the rectification process; reaffirms the superiority of

socialism and the conviction that Cuba will overcome its
difficulties and defeat U.S. aggression.

3. Economic Policy

Recommends that some manufacturers should sell directly
abroad; proposes a revision of international markets and
increasing exports of sugar and derivatives, tobacco, fish,
coffee, nickel, and citrus;

Ratifies a first choice for Latin America and the Caribbean for
foreign investment through joint ventures and other modalities;

Advises increasing savings and productivity to attain cost
efficiency in the economy; advises fighting corruption, lack
of discipline, and negligence; and recommends revising
labor and penal legislation;

Recommends streamlining government agencies and personnel and keeping central economic planning;

Suggests that small private farmers should continue supporting the country's agriculture but decides against the free
farmers' markets [which were approved three years later, in
October 1994];

Recognizes that the economy should sustain health, education,
and social security policies;

Anticipates the need to cut further transportation, electricity,
and other services.

4. Elections and the Organs of People's Power (OPP)

Recommends direct election of candidates for provincial and
national OPP assemblies, reversing indirect election by
municipal delegates;

Supports government procedures eliminating bureaucracy;
recommends increasing public control over elected representatives;

Requests that the National Assembly extend the term of office
of provincial and municipal delegates and review the rights
and obligations of national deputies.

5. Foreign Policy

Expresses a warning on the dangers following the European
socialist crisis and the power exercised by the United States
in a unipolar world;

Notices increasing gap between developed and underdeveloped nations and recommends further integration of Third World economies;

Accepts developing trade and cooperation with market economies;

Rejects the imposition of a single political model in the world, reaffirming Cuba's right to choose its own system;

Asks for an end to Washington's blockade and the return of the territories of the U.S. Naval Base at Guantánamo and recommends solving problems with the United States on the basis of "strict respect for [Cuba's] independence and sovereignty, and equality between [both nations]."

6. New Faculties and Reductions

Recognizes that this is "the most decisive moment in the history of Cuba" and empowers the Central Committee to monitor the special period and take whatever measures necessary to save the country, the revolution, and the socialist system.

Reduces the party's bureaucracy by eliminating its Secretariat (its functions were transferred to the Political Bureau);

Reduces Central Committee membership to 225;

Reduces Central Committee staff by 65 percent and that of the Provincial Committees by 45 percent.[20]

The Fourth Congress set up the framework governing the country under the special period. In 1992 the party's recommendations were adopted by the National Assembly in a constitutional reform law. Later events would force changes beyond those approved by the Fourth Congress—like legalizing possession of U.S. dollars, which was not even considered at the time, and reopening the free farmers' market.

The Communist Party's Centrality

The Fourth Congress directed the party to shed its elite image and to reach the populace, confirming its influence beyond its membership. The party's democratic features needed to be enhanced, while its authoritarian features needed to be curtailed.[21] An American scholar found troubling developments for the party and the leadership. Among other assertions:

1. In spite of defending a "single vanguard party" and a "centralized, state-owned economy," in reality the leader-

ship is "implementing their version of the Chinese/Vietnamese economic model."

2. With "Communist party political control," the leadership hopes "to reactivate [the] economy . . . with the help of foreign investors."

3. The Communist leadership is responding to the crisis in fear that "rapid uncontrolled political (and economic) change might lead to regime collapse."

4. Castro's role is changing and "he no longer controls every significant development in Cuba . . . [but he] still serves to provide a focus for elite unity . . . [and] defines and publicly defends the political formulas of the transition."

5. "The political loyalties, and independent leadership of this emerging elite are a big unknown in the Cuban political equation."[22]

Castro knew he could not repeat Gorbachev's mistake of purposely eroding the authority and centrality of the Soviet Communist Party. The decade between the PCC's founding in 1965 and its 1975 First Congress was a time of institutional weakness to which the Cuban Confederation of Workers (CTC) was not insusceptible. But the fate of Castro and the revolution are today tied to the party's fate. In his interview with Nicaragua's Tomás Borge, Castro noted that Gorbachev's policy undermining the Soviet Communist Party was critical in bringing down the Soviet Union.[23]

Still, Havana studied China's and Vietnam's experiment combining political control with economic liberalization. Castro's visit to both countries after visiting Japan in 1995 provided first-hand knowledge of Asian communist developments. The Chinese reciprocated Castro's visit with six high level political and military missions to Cuba in eight months alone, between 1996 and 1997, leading to the first Sino-Cuba joint ventures in tourism and agriculture.[24]

Preparations for the Fifth Party Congress

Two weeks after the 1997 *convocatoria* calling for the Fifth Party Congress, *Granma* published a Central Committee document reviewing the state of the party, "The Single Party of the Cuban Nation." Party membership had grown in the last five years an average of 46,000 new members per year (59 percent higher than the 27,000 average of the previous decade), and close to a third of the members had joined the party during the special period, from 1991 to 1996. Party membership grew to approximately

780,000 by 1997, of whom 232,000 were exemplary workers recommended by their work centers.

A third of the membership was made up of workers directly involved in production (32.1 percent, increasing to 40 percent if the service sector is included), 22 percent were professionals and technicians and 2.5 percent farmers; these groups together accounted for 65 percent of party members. A total of 13 percent of the nation's labor force belonged to the party; the historic average of 20,000 members lost per year due to death, inactivity, disciplinary expulsion, and other causes had remained the same.[25]

Defending the one-party system, the PCC has stated: "In Cuba we know well the multiparty formula that divided and weakened us . . . We have been exceptional witnesses of what happened in the former European socialist countries, their multiplicity of parties and the painful political, economic and social consequences of their collapse." The PCC held that it was "the guarantee of [the] . . . people's unity, and [that] as the . . . representative of the legitimate interests of the Cuban nation it will never be stopped."[26]

The PCC's *convocatoria* recognized extant difficulties, credited the work accomplished, and encouraged people to join in the tasks awaiting the country. It stated that the Fourth Congress had "alerted properly [the populace] that the country was entering the most difficult period of the Cuban revolutionary process . . . [and that it] had to adopt new working methods given such reality . . . with speedy decisions."

The party was reinvigorated with new membership, but some members had underestimated the seriousness of the problems. The PCC's political and ideological work was made more difficult by the economic reforms, the hardships of the special period, and the hostility of the revolution's enemies. The party readied itself to combat attitudes like selfishness, mercantilism, greed, consumerism, and the loss of revolutionary ethical values.

The party was acknowledging the social and ideological conflict affecting the country. The introduction of capitalist modalities, even if limited to foreign investment and self-employment, was affecting people's expectations both positively (those working in the tourist sector and for foreign corporations) and negatively (those earning pesos and enduring terrible living conditions). The contradictory situation was unlikely to improve until the national economy could restore the nation's living conditions to a satisfactory level.

The convocatoria also called for popular support for the food program and for reducing costs, making production and services cost effective, completing the sugar harvest, building tourist installations, saving electricity, substituting imports, applying the new tax system, and cleaning up the internal financial situation. It credited Cuban women as "the undisputed heroes of the special period."[27]

In May 1997, the PCC published "The Party of Unity, Democracy, and the Human Rights We Defend," a document "charting its course into the twenty-first century." It defended the political system and public health, education, work, housing and the absence of racial and gender discrimination as human rights. As noted by Cuban scholar Aurelio Alonso, "the capitalist world has underestimated the significance of social and economic rights, [only] emphasizing political rights."

The defense of such rights and services was a rebuke to the campaign against the regime's human rights record. The document provided the basis for discussion by party members before the Fifth Congress, but opponents accused the party of failing in its support of political reform. "The government insist[ed] on keeping a neo-Stalinist model," stated dissident Elizardo Sánchez.[28]

The Fifth Party Congress

With 1,482 delegates and 250 guests attending, the gathering of Cuban communists on October 8–10, 1997, was observed intently by friends and foes alike. Recognizing that economic changes were painful but necessary, in a seven-hour opening speech Castro charged Washington with "total economic and political war" against Cuba and stated that the capitalist system "belongs to prehistory and has nothing to offer mankind." Warning against "falling into the clutches of anarchic capitalism" and the "blind laws governing the capitalist market," he nevertheless admitted that some capitalist modalities could be emulated when necessary.[29] José Luis Rodríguez, minister of the economy and planning, stated: "We must study the markets and how they work, how the exchange market operates, and we must be able to predict possible events because we cannot afford to lose foreign currency due to oversight or inexperience."

The objective of the Fifth Party Congress was to preserve the national consensus supporting the revolution through political continuity. It included maintaining the changes made by the Fourth Congress, safeguarding socialism and the one-party system, and agreeing on the eventual succession after Castro of his brother Raúl. Foreign investment in state enterprises, using U.S. dollars domestically, and limited self-employment were endorsed. The Fifth Congress also affirmed the state's central role in directing the economy (reinforced later with new legislation in 1998).

Vice President Carlos Lage summarized the major economic problems affecting the country:

> The deficit from sugarcane- and agricultural-producing units of cooperative production (UBPCs) and food-producing state farms and enterprises.
>
> The improper rise in retail prices and service charges affecting grassroots production entities.
>
> The need to apply the revolutionary armed forces' business experience to the civilian sector.
>
> The need to make the state enterprises and the economy more effective.
>
> The need to adapt administrative techniques proper to a functioning economy.
>
> The need to control wholesale prices and their effect on workers' pocketbooks.
>
> The need to improve workers' social security payments.
>
> The need to remedy shortages of food, medications, housing, and cooking fuel.
>
> The need to continue improving internal finances.
>
> The need to recognize that economic recovery is an irreversible fact.[30]

Concluding that "we have no reason to create millionaires, to create enormous inequalities," Castro spoke against privatization of state enterprises and self-employment growth. But he accepted small family businesses, saying that "our only interest is that these small, privately owned businesses be law abiding and honest," and recognized that private property may play a role in those activities where state intervention is not advisable. Reversing long-standing policy, the regime announced that "the private hiring of workers will be henceforth allowed, albeit under strict state supervision."[31]

It was reasoned elsewhere that Cuba's future direction would be decided by the Politburo members appointed at the Fifth Party Congress, who will oversee the Sixth Party Congress in the year 2002 and the transition to Raúl Castro. When Abel Prieto and Ricardo Alarcón de Quesada were reappointed and others from the ranks of the "middle generation" were added to the Politburo, future flexibility and change were guaranteed (see appendix C). If the *histórico* wing and the military wing, for example, had prevailed, the chances for more conservative policies would have increased.[32] No matter what group prevailed, all plans could fail if the party did not engage the population in remaking the country and to move out of the special period and into the next millennium.

Reforming the Constitution

It took more than seventeen years of revolutionary rule for the first socialist constitution in the Western Hemisphere to become law. After its major revision in an almost equal number of years, the 1976 Constitution is now identified as the 1992 Constitution. The charter institutionalized the revolution in the mid-1970s, and the 1992 changes have embraced limited market reforms. The fundamentals of socialism had remained in place, but the revised constitution made room for present and future reform.[33]

The changes approved in 1991 at the Fourth Communist Party Congress, and others that followed, called for updating the constitution. Not needing a national referendum to revise the charter, the National Assembly approved the constitutional reform on July 13, 1992.[34] Three new chapters were added for a total of fifteen, but the final number of articles in the reformed text was reduced from 141 to 137. Altogether, seventy-seven articles were revised.

The modified chapters and articles of the constitutional text included:

  I.   State Political, Social, and Economic Fundamental Provisions (27 articles, 23 reviewed)
 II.   Citizenship (6 articles, 2 reviewed)
III.   Aliens (1 article, 1 reviewed)
 IV.   Family (4 articles, 1 reviewed)
  V.   Education and Culture (2 articles, 2 reviewed)
 VI.   Equality (4 articles, 3 reviewed)
VII.   Fundamental Rights, Duties, and Guarantees (22 articles, 1 reviewed)
VIII. State of Emergency (1 article, 1 reviewed)
 IX.   Principles of Organization and Functioning of State Organs (1 article, 1 reviewed)
  X.   Higher Organs of People's Power (33 articles, 13 reviewed)
 XI.   Political and Administrative Divisions (1 article, 1 reviewed)
XII.   Local Organs of People's Power (17 articles, 17 reviewed)
XIII. The Courts and Attorney General (11 articles, 8 reviewed)
XIV.   Electoral System (6 articles, 3 reviewed)
 XV.   Constitutional Reform (1 article, 1 reviewed)[35]

The main areas of constitutional reform were (1) political and social fundamental principles; (2) Organs of People's Power; (3) religious regulations; (4) family; (5) education and culture; (6) the judicial system; and (7) the economic system.

Political, Social, and Economic Reforms under the Revised Charter

The revised Constitution established direct elections for deputies of the National Assembly (article 71) and for delegates of the provincial assemblies of the Organs of People's Power (OPP). In order to be elected a National Assembly deputy or a provincial or municipal OPP delegate, a candidate must receive more than half of the votes cast in his or her electoral circumscription (article 136). The procedures determining what to do when no candidate receives a majority of the votes were left to a new electoral law adopted in October 1992. National deputies and provincial delegates are elected every five years, and municipal delegates every two and a half years. The functions and responsibilities of the provincial and municipal assemblies have been structured and differentiated more clearly, including the relationship among themselves and with the National Assembly (chapters XI and XII, articles 102–19). The Popular Councils are organized as entities representing the local OPPs and their communities and are dedicated to improving production and services at the local level (article 104). They are organized by the provincial assemblies upon recommendation from the municipal assemblies (article 105).

The revision made the newly established National Defense Council responsible in any eventual state of war, national emergency, and/or national mobilization (article 101); Castro presides over it. The National Assembly has the authority to declare a state of war in the case of aggression (article 75). The Council of State could declare war against another nation engaged in hostile actions against the country and call for a national mobilization. It could also negotiate peace, ending the hostilities (article 90).

The Soviet Union was omitted from the charter's preamble—anticipating the collapse, the party had recommended the omission two months before the collapse occurred. The nineteenth-century hero and founder of the republic inaugurated seven years after his death in 1895, José Martí, was recognized as the foremost patriot and forefather of the Cuban nation. He was credited for being the guiding force behind "the [revolution's] vanguard . . . [and of the generation that came of age during] the centennial anniversary of [his] birth, [the generation] who imbued with his teachings led . . . to the popular victory of January [1959]." Thus the Constitution upholds Martí's principles and Marxist-Leninist ideology.

The acknowledgment of Martí and his ideas, besides filling a significant gap in the original 1976 Constitution, signals some of the ideological changes taking place. To survive and retain its socialist character, the regime needs to root itself more deeply by using historic national symbols. By ignoring past associations with European socialism, the government is enhancing its legitimacy at a moment of crisis and permitting the development of an autochthonous brand of socialism.

The concept of the entire nation, embracing workers and the people at large, is the leading political force. Broadly defined with no class distinctions, the nation supersedes the dictatorship of the proletariat, the initial stage in building socialism. Also, the defense of the fatherland is entrusted to the nation inclusively defined (articles 1 and 3). There is no reference to democratic centralism (the hierarchical structure of authority) as the operational concept for state organs, which now are "integrated and [develop] their activities based on socialist democracy" (article 68).

Still, reflecting mounting internal pressures under the special period, the Central Committee published an invitation for "greater internal democracy but not at the cost of sacrificing national unity and 'democratic centralism'." While emphasizing the need for "an ever greater democracy within the body of the party," democracy was described as "all the space necessary for the expression of ideas, proposals, opinions, whether they coincide or disagree about any issue, however polemic or complicated." Democratic centralism was now defined as not permitting "tendencies which weaken the discipline and political activity of the party" or new movements that could "threaten the essential unity of our existence as an independent nation." Still, the PCC reiterated its commitment to religious freedom, stating that "religious values, when honestly practiced, are good for the people and therefore for the country."[36]

The independent and sovereign socialist state is made of workers "organized by all and for the good of all . . . united [in a] democratic republic, for the enjoyment of political liberty, social justice, individual and collective well-being, and human solidarity" (article 1).The Communist Party, following Martí's *ideario* and Marxism-Leninism, is recognized as the "highest leading force in society and the state, organizing and directing the common effort for the lofty objective of building socialism and advancing toward a communist society" (article 5).

The social and mass organizations have no state functions (article 7) .

The separation of Church and state, with equal standing for all religions, is established, and religious freedom is guaranteed (article 8). Any form of discrimination, including religious discrimination, is forbidden (article 42). The family is recognized as a social institution responsible for educating and molding new generations (article 35). The state supports workers' involvement in scientific tasks and development and promotes citizens' participation in educational and cultural programs through social and mass organizations (article 39). The judiciary is independent and owes obedience only to the law (article 122). Judges can be recalled only for proper cause and by the organs responsible for their election (article 126). Fostering professionalism among the judiciary, the one-time full-term election replaces the five-year election term.

Economic Reforms under the Revised Charter

> Socialist property. State ownership is limited to the *fundamental* means of production, rather than *all* means (article 14).
>
> New property system. The Council of Ministers and/or its Executive Committee can transfer property and assets to individuals and enterprises to promote social and economic development (broadening Law No. 50 of 1982 creating joint ventures).
>
> New ownership modalities. Articles 14 and 15 expand the forms of ownership, including mixed enterprises (joint ventures) and other associations legally established (article 23).
>
> Economic planning system. The plan for economic and social development was replaced with a less centralized "plan that would guarantee the programmed development of the country" (article 16).[37]

The revision also authorized the creation of autonomous enterprises, which would manage their own finances but under state supervision, thereby facilitating new joint ventures in partnership with the state (article 17). (*Cubanacán*, dedicated to international tourism and operating outside central state planning, was responsible for its finances before the constitutional reform.)[38]

New Electoral Law and Five Election Returns

In October 1992 the new electoral law was approved.[39] The December 20, 1992, and February 24, 1993, elections were the first ones held under the new law. Delegates for the OPP municipal assemblies were elected first, followed by provincial delegates and National Assembly deputies in the second elections.

The elections were rated as a plebiscite attesting to the people's support for the government. The response of the populace, who turned out in massive numbers at the polls, resulted in a political victory at a time when the regime's viability was in doubt. Following the electoral timetable (elections held every two and a half years for municipal delegates and every five years for provincial delegates and National Assembly deputies), municipal elections took place in July 1995. Municipal elections were held on October 17, 1997, and runoff elections a week later for candidates who received no majority of the votes cast. The provincial and national elections on January 11, 1998, completed an electoral cycle ten days before the pope arrived in Havana.

Political forces opposing the electoral process became active again. In a press conference undisturbed by Havana's police, five dissidents forming the Domestic Dissidence Working Group announced an elections boycott. Besides demanding negotiations with the government, they said that "Cuban exiles who send money to relatives on the island" should ask them to "join the peaceful struggle for change." The press conference was held in the home of Vladimiro Roca, the dissident son of the late communist leader and revolutionary Blas Roca, who was arrested and in 1999 sentenced to a five-year prison term.[40]

Of more than 7.5 million voters (8 million plus in 1998), 97.2 percent, 99.6, 97.1, 97.6, and 98.35 percent went to the polls in 1992, 1993, 1995, 1997, and 1998, respectively. The highest number of blank and nullified ballots (noting public discontent) in the 1992 municipal elections was in City of Havana and Havana provinces (where the hardships were felt strongly)—14.73 percent and 12.65 percent, respectively—but nationally only 7.03 percent did not vote. Reports from Miami announced that between 20 and 30 percent of the voters had nullified their ballots.[41] Havana denounced the intense campaign against the elections launched in 1993 using Radio Martí's broadcasts and other means of asking people not to vote.[42]

In reference to the 1993 elections (and to other elections), Castro said that they had been *something quite unprecedented and unmatched in a true election where there wasn't even the slightest trace of fraud . . . [and] in the* conditions that the country [was] going through, in the special period, in the face of such a ferocious anti-election campaign, with slogans from abroad picked up by counterrevolutionary elements within Cuba, encouraging people not to vote, to spoil their ballots, or to leave them blank, [it] is something quite remarkable and unprecedented" (emphasis added).[43]

Among those elected in 1992, from 28,500 candidates for 13,432 delegate posts in 150 municipal assemblies, 16 percent were under thirty years of age, 13.5 percent were women, and 46 percent were reelected municipal delegates. The presidents for the People's Councils had been nominated in special assemblies held throughout the country. In 1993, 1,900 delegates for fourteen provincial assemblies and 589 National Assembly deputies were elected for the first time by direct vote.

For Juan Escalona, then president of the National Assembly, the 1993 elections gave a vote of confidence for the regime: "[The] challenge of the direct vote is one of participation and, in this sense, the process [has] become a kind of plebiscite . . . the voter may not agree and may vote for only one candidate, for five, for all or for none . . . That is what we are striving for." Accepting that opposition candidates did not have a chance to run in the elections, he said that "knowing the idiosyncrasies of our country . . . some of these figures could hardly be nominated." But dissident Elizardo Sánchez said from Havana that what was keeping dissidents from running in the elections was the lack of "signs from the government . . . indicat[ing] sufficient will to make changes."[44]

A total of 274 municipal delegates elected in 1992 became candidates for the National Assembly in 1993. The remaining 315 candidates were provincial and national figures who had been nominated at open meetings in electoral precincts. The government wanted to increase grassroots participation and support for the electoral process, but the nominating system at the provincial and national levels differs from the direct municipal system. After being nominated, candidates for higher level posts have to be confirmed by the Candidacy Commissions (made up of university and intermediate students and mass organizations and headed by trade union representatives) in a final selection under the supervision of the Ministry of Justice National Electoral Commission.

Under the new electoral system there is only one candidate for each provincial or national post. The voter is not choosing from competing candidates but endorsing or rejecting the slate selected at the base and confirmed by the Candidacy Commissions. The voter can vote for one or more candidates, reject them all, or leave the ballot blank, signifying disapproval of the candidates. Only candidates with a majority of the votes cast are declared elected. In 1993, 88.48 percent of the voters supported the entire slate, as the government wanted.

Making the vote secret and direct added political value to the OPP as an institution and to the deputies/delegates as representatives of the people. This improved the responsiveness of the system, and some deputies became full-time legislators (work commissions chairs and similar posts) instead of continuing on a part-time basis. But by allowing a single candidate for each provincial and national post, the new electoral system denied any competition among candidates and failed to give the voter a choice beyond a previously chosen slate. Choosing candidates on the basis of personal merits and political correctness could turn the end product into an electoral meritocracy system.

The regime insisted that a "unity vote" (voting for the entire slate) gave a chance to those with less name recognition and denied incumbents an undue advantage. Only 20 percent of the elected deputies in 1993 were incumbents, and almost half of the 589 National Assembly deputies were initially elected as municipal deputies (two of them were elected to the National Assembly's Council of State).[45] The electoral system allowed unknown citizens to achieve national political status, but with no competing candidates for the National Assembly (and provincial assemblies) it could hardly be seen favorably abroad, where it has received more criticism than praise. Still, the regime avoided two troublesome outcomes: a low turnout rate and a high number of candidates with less than a majority vote, which could have had negative consequences. But victory did not come easily. Castro had to lead a campaign asking voters to mark their ballots with a single vote, supporting the entire slate and therefore the revolution.[46]

In the October 1997 municipal elections, 31,276 candidates nominated in neighborhood assemblies were running for 14,533 local council posts in 169 municipal assemblies. The number voting exceeded 1995's turnout by 250,000, and the turnout at the polls in all provinces stood at over 95 percent (97.59 percent national average). In the City of Havana province 70,000 more votes were cast than in 1995 (95.85 percent of registered voters). From a total of 13,435 elected municipal delegates, almost half were reelected (49.54 percent). It was officially reported that 7.21 percent of the 7 million plus votes cast were left blank or spoiled (3.23 percent blank, 3.98 percent spoiled), but other reports put the number at 11.3 percent—expressing dissatisfaction with the elections and/or the regime.[47]

At the Ibero-American Viña del Mar Summit in 1996 first, and later at Margarita Island in 1997 and at Oporto in 1998, the final declarations committed the signatories to fostering democratization in their own countries, including Castro's Cuba. While condemning Havana, Presidents Carlos Ménem of Argentina and Arnoldo Alemán of Nicaragua "used their opening statements in Margarita Island to urge Cuba to open its doors to democracy." But "Castro appeared unmoved and suggested others should change."[48] President Clinton stated on NBC "that he wanted to develop 'an ongoing relationship with Fidel Castro's Cuba much like the one he has with China, but only after America's communist neighbor moves toward democracy'."[49]

Castro dismissed such criticism as irrelevant and self-serving: "the [political] situation in Cuba contrasts sharply with the United States' and other countries' that have copied U.S. methods, where practically no one turns out to vote, despite the fact that the political parties spend millions of dollars on propaganda and campaigning."[50] Indicating his satisfaction with Cuba's elections, he added that they were "the most democratic ones in the world" and were "not like before the revolution when they amounted to a war among the political parties, and politics belonged exclusively to those with money and power."[51] Even though the slate of candidates had been nominated through a grassroots participatory process, he overlooked the fact that elections are expected to give voters a choice among different candidates (as the municipal elections do).

The regime asked for a unified vote in the 1998 parliamentary elections for 601 delegates to the National Assembly and 1,192 deputies to the Provincial Organs of People's Power. The elections were also rated as a national referendum on the nation's socialist system. As in 1993, the regime claimed electoral victory. Almost all (98.35 percent) of the 8 million plus registered voters went to the polls. Ninety-five percent of the 7,534,008 votes cast were valid, but 130,227 (1.64 percent) were void and 266,379 (3.36 percent) were blank—5 percent of the total ballots signified a lower negative vote than in 1993.

The unified vote totaled 7,111,169 (94.39 percent), while the selective vote (supporting some candidates) amounted to 423,218 (5.26 percent). The province with the highest turnout was Cienfuegos (99.9 percent), while the City of Havana had the lowest (97 percent).[52] Half of the candidates had been nominated by the people's councils, and the remainder were from state institutions and agencies. As reported, "the process of finding and selecting candidates [was] initiated at [the] neighborhood level [where the candidates'] merit, capacity, intelligence, integrity, . . . representativity [and political correctness] were the focus from start to end."[53] As he was leaving the El Cobre polling station in eastern Cuba, Castro responded to an inquiry about his vote: "The vote is secret," but he added, "I voted as a patriot and revolutionary." He then characterized the elections as a "civic *fiesta* of patriotism and democracy."[54]

Measuring Political Attitudes

The government gauged public opinion to learn where people stood on public issues. An opinion poll measuring the people's attitude toward the political system and how they rated it in comparison with other regimes was conducted before the 1998 elections. The response was highly favorable, indicating a wide support margin, even if the regime had inflated the numbers. (See table 5.1.)

A 1995 poll measuring generalized perceptions of freedom of expression showed that respondents rated the local OPP delegates' rendition of accounts (somewhat similar to town meetings), the Cuban Communist Party (PCC), the Committees for the Defense of the Revolution (CDRs), and the Organs of People's Power, in that order, as the arenas where economic, social, or political opinions could be most freely expressed. The Organs of People's Power and the Communist Party received the highest number of "no answer" responses. (See table 5.2.)

Recognizing the overall improvement in economic conditions from the low point reached in 1992–94, public confidence that the regime could preserve the social equality levels established since 1959 increased from 1995 to 1997. Although 57 percent answered affirmatively in 1997, a fourth of the respondents remained doubtful. (See table 5.3.)

The people also showed their support for free education and free public health. Seventy-five percent agreed on keeping free education and 77.9 percent free public health, while 22.1 percent and 19.6 percent agreed to continuing them partly free. Almost 1 percent somewhat disagreed on free education (0.9 percent) and free public health (0.7 percent), while 0.6 percent and 0.3 percent totally disagreed. And 1 percent (free education) and 1.1 percent (free public health) were not sure. The prevailing public opinion of keeping both programs free of charge mirrored the people's increased confidence in the country's future by 1997.

Table 5.1. Comparison of the Cuban Political System to Other Regimes

More democratic	88.8%
Equally democratic	6.5%
Less democratic	2.4%
Not democratic at all	2.1%
Total*	99.8%

*2,554 respondents.
Source: Darío L. Machado Rodríguez, "Democracia Política e Ideología: Una Opinión Después del V Congreso del Partido," Cuba Socialista 9 (1998): 49.

Table 5.2. 1995 Opinion Poll on Freedom of Expression

Political forum	Yes	No	No Answer
OPP delegates' rendition of accounts meetings	78%	16%	7%
Cuban Communist Party	73%	14%	13%
CDR assemblies	72%	20%	8%
Organs of People's Power meetings	68%	17%	15%

SOURCE: Darío L. Machado Rodríguez, "Democracia Política e Ideología: Una Opinión Después del V Congreso del Partido," *Cuba Socialista* 9 (1998): 54.

Table 5.3. Public Confidence in the Sustainability of Social Equality Levels

	1995	1997
Yes	52%	57%
No	17%	13%
Not Sure	24%	25%
No Answer	7%	5%

SOURCE: Darío L. Machado Rodríguez, "Democracia Política e Ideología: Una Opinión Después del V Congreso del Partido," *Cuba Socialista* 9 (1998): 55.

The Organs of People's Power

The Organs of People's Power (OPP) is the highest political body in the nation, representing the people's power and sovereignty, according to the Constitution. It is responsible for administrative duties at the municipal and provincial levels and for legislative and constitutional functions at the national level. The National Assembly's executive office is the Council of State (parallel in rank is the Council of Ministers' Executive Committee). The chairman of the Council of State and of the Executive Committee is the country's President, the office occupied by Fidel Castro since its inception in 1976.[55]

While the PCC stands as the "highest leading force of society and the state" (article 5), the OPP as the supreme organ of the state "represents and expresses the sovereign will of the people" (article 69). The OPP's independence and democratic nature have been questioned, as has the control the PCC exercises over it. It is debatable whether the OPP and PCC could coexist without infringing upon each other and whether a deputy could shed party affiliation and represent his or her constituency in the case of dual membership. Hence, if the OPP stands for democracy, is Cuban socialism truly democratic?[56] No matter how central these questions are to liberal democracy, they are not germane to the organic structure of a socialist political system.

Still, two issues are relevant here: the need to broaden the party base to include the entire nation (putting away the social class notion embedded in the dictatorship of the proletariat) and the need to end the party's policy implementation and administrative functions (limiting its role to policy recommendation). While the party is entrusted with overseeing ideological correctness (a difficult task once religious believers join the party), it should be restrained from making decisions that correspond to government structures like the OPP.

In an organically integrated system, with the single political party playing a central role, dual membership should not be the problem it seems. There should be no question of loyalty or of conflict of interest among members of the PCC and the OPP. The political system works better with a functionally integrated, institutionally based division of labor, as long as the structures have specific functions to perform. The system does not seek confrontation between the PCC and the OPP but political reinforcement. While the party works as the system's political force, the National Assembly deliberates and legislates the party's policy recommendations.

Both institutions should perform their assigned functions in pursuit of the nation's best interest, while the voters should be able to influence the decision making in the system. The regime has claimed that the democratic features of the system have been improved under difficult conditions. But it is debatable how much has actually been done. Also, the reform process might be affected by the relaxation of long-held limitations on religious practice, particularly after the pope's visit in 1998.

Improving the OPP's Performance

The first local government after 1959 was the Coordination and Inspection Board (JUCEI), followed in the mid-1960s by the Local Powers. These served as a framework for such mass organizations as the Committees for the Defense of the Revolution (CDRs, combating the counter-revolution in the neighborhoods) and the Cuban Federation of Women (FMC, the women's organization founded in 1960). The Local Powers were replaced in the mid-1970s by the Organs of People's Power, which established a pyramidal politico-administrative structure running from the local to the national level. The OPP's local objectives included:

Creating a government structure at the local level, with
authority over community issues.

Modernizing the community's roles; instituting election of
officials, scrutiny of office holders (the rendition of accounts
by elected officials), and participation in local affairs.
Creating a local government culture; eliminating corruptive
political and administrative practices.[57]

The local OPP's assembly managed the municipal executive committee and administrative personnel. It controlled health, social security, employment, and other social services as well as the enterprises responsible
for restaurants, cafeterias, construction (buildings, schools, hospitals),
and maintenance and repairs, while the provincial and national levels
supervised economic production. The OPP's performance at the local
level has been scholarly recognized.[58]

A 1990 public opinion poll supported change in the OPP, especially in
the National Assembly. The deputies were trusted by 59.5 percent of the
respondents, while 40.6 percent questioned the OPP's democratic value,
and 51.4 percent believed it lacked authority to solve problems affecting
them. In response to another question, 59.4 percent found the OPP politically irrelevant, and 39.3 percent questioned its role in governing the
country. Still, people were not ready to part with it because 70.5 percent
wanted to make the OPP, especially at the national level, more effective.[59]

More criticism was voiced at a Union of Communist Youth plenum
held in Havana. Given the economic conditions befalling the country,
public opinion became more dissatisfied than before. Not wanting to
wait for the Fourth Party Congress, the regime instituted some reforms.
One hundred of the 496 deputies were turned into full-time legislators,
drawing them closer to the National Assembly's business, rather than
having them attend only the two short yearly legislative sessions. Later,
the OPP's executive committees were replaced with an advisory professional staff, and the line separating the provincial and municipal levels
was more clearly defined.

The Fourth Party Congress acknowledged that the OPP was not performing effectively and was falling short of many of its objectives.[60] As
part of the OPP's overhaul, Ricardo Alarcón (after having served as
ambassador to the United Nations and minister of foreign affairs) was
elected in 1993 to preside over the National Assembly. The discussion
preceding his election was summarized in this way:

Fidel Castro reportedly opposed the move, saying Alarcón was too
valuable where he was, but was finally convinced that only the
Foreign Minister has the requi[red] three characteristics [to be a
new deputy, to be nationally known, and to know parliamentary

procedures], as most others with "national" names had been deputies in the old Assembly. Therefore, while Alarcón moved to a position that previously inferred less status, in reality the post was promoted in importance by his presence in it. Alarcón has a reputation for frankness, efficiency, intelligence and "common sense" within Cuba.[61]

The 458 national deputies elected in 1993 averaged forty-three years old, with 77.7 percent under fifty. Of the legislators, 75 percent had college education, including eighty-three scientists, forty-eight physicians, four college professors and teachers, eighteen artists, eleven journalists, nine athletes, and ten college students. Ten percent were sugar and agricultural workers, 5.24 percent union leaders, 0.43 percent religious leaders, 18.9 percent presidents of popular councils, and 23 percent were women. Also, 8 percent of the initial candidates were PCC or Union of Communist Youth officials; thirteen of the forty government cabinet ministers had been nominated, and 19.2 percent of the deputies had sought reelection.[62]

There had been 27,494 nominating assemblies nationwide for the 1992–93 elections, with 29,505 candidates nominated to the different OPP posts. Of the 14,246 delegates elected (municipal and provincial), 16.6 percent were women. More than 98 percent of the 7,240,039 registered voters voted in the 1993 elections.[63]

The 1992–93 elections were not favorable for women. They reversed the gains of 1986, when women had scored their highest rates since 1976 and 1981, the first elections for national, provincial, and municipal OPP assemblies. The 1993 electoral reversal has been attributed to the special period. Given the scarcity of consumer goods and other hardships in the 1990s, women had to concentrate their efforts on the home front.[64] (See fig. 5.1.)

The Problem of Centralization of Power

Centralization of power as a political problem has existed since 1959. During the *llamamiento* (announcement) to the Fourth Party Congress, "finding the proper balance between centralization and decentralization" was opened for public discussion.

At the center of power is Fidel Castro. How power is personalized in him needs to be understood. His authority is based on his revolutionary history, charismatic leadership, moral standing, and personality traits (not always prone to delegate power). Probably because of his leader-

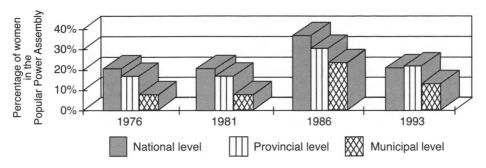

Fig. 5.1. Women's Legislative Power, 1976–1993.
Source: National Electoral Commission, Havana, n.d.

ship, no other leader has emerged to rival or equal his authority. And it is likely that no other leader would have been able to unify the country and lead it through the special period with the effectiveness and conviction that he has exercised.

Cuban scholars have noted that decentralization is not without flaws and that decentralizing objectives could be achieved within a centralized model. The centralized decision-making model practiced since 1959 guaranteed the defense of the revolution, national sovereignty, a democratic order based on equal distribution of wealth and social justice, and wide political participation. For the first fifteen years such a model was at the heart of the political socialization process, with values internalized by those occupying today's decision-making offices. Thus it should not be surprising that a centralized political decision-making model finds support in Cuba.[65]

The Yummies and the New Generations

Castro's succession was established at the Fifth Congress of the Communist Party. While he was ratified as the Central Committee first secretary and his brother Raúl Castro as second in command, the latter was also anointed as Fidel's successor.[66] Still, a new generation that has moved upward in the nation's political structure seems destined to be the country's next rulers—most likely under Raúl's leadership following Fidel's eventual retirement.[67]

The new leaders have been called *yummies* by *Newsweek*—"young upwardly mobile Marxists" who were children when the revolution started and now are in their thirties and early forties, some in their late forties or early fifties, who are "educated and ambitious, [and] hold the key to Cuba's future."[68]

Some already occupy the highest positions in and out of government, like cabinet ministerial posts and as members of the Communist Party's Politburo. They include Roberto Robaina, a mid-forties former head of the Union of Communist Youth and foreign minister until he was surprisingly replaced in mid-1999; Felipe Pérez Roque, the new foreign minister, has been at the center of political power as Castro's close assistant responsible for his personal schedule and was in 1999 only a year older than when Robaina was given the same post in 1993; Carlos Lage Dávila, a forty-six-year-old physician directing the country's economy from his vice presidential post in collaboration with José Luis Rodríguez, minister of the economy and planning, who is in his fifties; Abel Prieto, a forty-seven-year-old former head of the influential Artists and Writers Union (UNEAC) and now minister of culture; Jesús Martínez, a forty-year-old newspaper director who had injected into *Juventud Rebelde* a fresh, lively style appealing to young readers; Concepción Campa, a forty-six-year-old scientist who helped develop a new meningitis vaccine and was placed in charge of the prestigious Finlay Institute.[69] Somewhat older, but the most influential among them, is Ricardo Alarcón, former ambassador to the United Nations and former foreign minister, now president of the National Assembly and in charge of dealing with the United States on immigration and other sensitive matters. These people and others occupying important posts in government, in scientific research institutes, in economic production centers, the media, etc., represent the first generation who came of age following the generation of the revolution's founding fathers.

As inheritors of Castro's mantle, the new generation will be responsible for leading the revolution in the twenty-first century, for defining the ultimate nature of the country's socialist system, and for taking Cuba out of the special period. They have been involved in turning the economy around and resurrecting the nation's quality of life, which started to show progress around 1995. They have been groomed and anointed by Castro, who is positioning the leadership that eventually will replace him. (Castro celebrated his seventieth birthday in 1996.) Recognizing the new generation of leaders when he was foreign minister, Robaina acknowledged the present collective nature of the regime's leadership: "In relation to the issue of what will happen to Cuba once Fidel is no longer among us I have categorically stated that Fidel's work transcends his physical presence and therefore, for a long time now, *Fidel himself has been incorporating everyone into a work system where collective decisions and a collective spirit are the standard*" (emphasis added).[70]

Being highly pragmatic, "the *yummies* want the best of both worlds: the health care and educational advances of Castro's revolution [keeping the socialist system] and a good meal [opening the economy to foreign investment]." Seemingly, "the word 'communist' has disappeared from their vocabulary, but the idea of profitmaking capitalist bosses is repugnant to them. They are nationalists first, ideologues second." Robaina, expressing ideas approved by Castro, said: "There is [not] only one way or one model . . . We're living in extremely complex times for which no one has an exact recipe."[71]

Meanwhile, the armed forces minister and deputy secretary of the Communist Party, Raúl Castro, talked to an even younger generation, keeping them on the right revolutionary track. Speaking to the Federation of Students in Intermediate Education, he put "a strong emphasis on the training of young people for work in agriculture and skilled employment in general." Characterizing the young delegates as showing "responsibility, stoicism and the determination to win," he added that "without the impetus of the youth movement, it would be impossible to emerge from the complex situation which the country suddenly had to face, given the disappearance of the Soviet bloc and the intensification of the U.S. blockade."[72]

Raúl Castro addressed the need for military preparedness, saying that "more mobilization should be carried out to fulfill defense duties," to increase the intermediate students' "understanding of the present need for adequate military training." For him, the fortitude demonstrated by the people during the special period is the country's "richest asset."

Conclusions

Putting pressure on Cuba to democratize the political system is counterproductive—especially if it comes from conservative Americans and Cuban Americans. Nothing could be less legitimate in Cuba than claims made by those who have been enemies of the revolution all along. The dissidents' major problem is the perception that they are Washington's tools and have been entrusted with the task of attacking the revolution from within. But while there is evidence supporting this charge, it is not true in all cases. Freely expressing contrary opinions should be an available option. Since the regime encourages criticism within its own ranks, it should also allow divergent political viewpoints without judging them as troubling expressions. "Everything within the revolution," as Castro told Cuban intellectuals in 1961 in setting up the parameters of permissible expression, becomes increasingly confining as time goes by. The regime's enemies' use of dissidents to foster political change is a mistake too, invariably nullifying any realistic expectation of achieving change.

Today's hardships notwithstanding, some steps have been taken toward political reform. The extant political system needs major improvement and Cubans are the first to recognize this. But they are equally ready to say that it is up to them and no one else to decide when and how to improve and/or change it. A Miami monthly commented on Cuba's achievements during its survival drive of the 1990s: "In spite of the impression of a Cuba in crisis that is forced to make concessions, the truth is that Cuba has triumphed over the challenge of violence, has gained in the ideological field and in the popularity issue, has legitimized its objectives and its possibilities as a chosen model, and in being seen as a stable and permanent phenomenon."[73]

Cuban leaders would go along with such an assessment regarding their share of fortune in a period of acute misfortune. As Carlos Lage, Cuba's vice president in charge of the economy, colloquially put it: "The country's economic recovery cannot be blocked by anything, not by [Hurricane] Lili, [U.S. Senator Jesse] Helms, or [U.S. Congressman Dan] Burton."[74] The minister of the armed forces, General of the Army Raúl Castro, put it in a more contentious fashion: "Socialism is here to stay in this land, defended by the people's guns!"[75]

Yet, a compelling need for political change remains. To divest a single-party system of the nondemocratic notion that liberal democracies associate with it, the PCC needs to open up and democratize itself. Though the Fourth Party Congress broke no extensive new ground, it did recognize the right of religious believers to become party members. Besides the Christian social presence advocated by the pope, there is a political presence as well. A good number of believers among the membership would have Marxists and non-Marxists making party's decisions. By functioning in a democratic fashion, the party would become a true representative of the entire nation. Also, sensible electoral and political reform would reinforce the system as a socialist democracy, while increasing its political legitimacy at home and especially abroad.

6

Economic Reform under the Special Period: Part I

Three Decades of Economic Policy

While the regime's development program was far from complete when the Soviet bloc collapsed, Cuba's prospects for a successful reintegration into the world market economy depended largely on the efficacy of the agenda pursued in 1959–89.[1] Its present economic infrastructure and production capability are largely the result of the policies and objectives—including achievements and failures—of the first three decades of revolutionary rule.

An open economy with limited export-import markets and financing would always have problems in overcoming underdevelopment. To leave underdevelopment behind, it is necessary to expand capital accumulation, yielding economic growth, and to increase and stabilize the production of exportable goods over a prolonged period. Since the 1960s, the transformation of the country's economic structure sought to diversify revenue sources and prioritize exports with higher value added. This led to an industrialization policy that included the sugar industry (and sugar derivatives), mining, metallurgy, electronics, mechanized industry, chemical products, and consumer goods.[2]

The main economic objectives emphasized import substitution, increasing exportable goods, and improving the nation's standard of living. The sugar industry was at the heart of the industrialization drive, since it had the highest export value potential, capable of producing sufficient financial capital that could generate spillover benefits to the national economy. However, the 1970 ten-million-ton campaign was an incorrect application of economic objectives. Maximizing sugar production to generate capital to finance future development backfired. The resulting economic disarray was more harmful than not having reached the production target.

The solution to Cuba's economic needs lay in developing relations with the Soviet bloc and ultimately in integrating its economy into the Council of Mutual Economic Assistance. In return, Havana was assured preferential prices for its exports, which guaranteed a stable trade relationship allowing long-term economic planning, credits and financing, and needed imports, including consumer goods and industrial inputs.

The structural changes from 1961 to 1981 permitted higher productivity in some sectors of the economy. This developed new patterns among different production areas by changing considerably their share of the country's gross domestic product (GDP). (See table 6.1.)

The policy did not generate balanced growth among all industrial sectors, causing some economic realignments. The production of consumer goods (textiles, beverages, tobacco, and sugar-based products) represented 60 percent of the total industrial output, which impacted negatively the production of exportable goods.[3] But it permitted a decline of the sugar sector, from 12.6 to 7.9 percent of GDP (limiting it to 2 percent annual growth), and increases in manufacturing, from 24.4 to 30.7 percent (increasing it to 5.5 percent annual growth), and in capital goods, from 1.6 to 6.6 percent (increasing this sector to 11.5 percent annual growth). Another variable contributing to the economic changes was a 2.9 percent sustained growth in labor productivity between 1959 and 1985, with the highest rate in the 1980–85 period (1960–70: 0.4 percent; 1970–80: 4.3 percent; and 1981–85: 5.2 percent).

The government invested close to 47.3 billion pesos in the nation's economy between 1959 and 1985. Given the long-term nature of some

Table 6.1. Structural Changes in the Cuban Economy

Economic Sector	1961	1970	1981
	Contribution to Gross Domestic Product (GDP) (%)		
Agriculture*	18.2	18.1	12.9
Sugarcane	7.9	9.2	4.9
Other	10.3	8.9	8.0
Industry	31.8	38.4	46.4
Manufacturing	24.4	29.7	30.7
Capital goods	1.6	2.5	6.6
Sugar and derivatives	4.7	4.8	3.0
Construction	5.2	5.7	13.0
Total sugar sector	12.6	14.0	7.9

*Including forestry and fishing.

SOURCE: Claes Brundenius, *Revolutionary Cuba: The Challenge of Economic Growth with Equity* (Boulder, Colo.: Westview Press, 1984), table 3.10.

investments and that there were other problems, the investment did not pay off as expected.[4] During 1975–85, a period of sustained economic growth, investment was a major component behind the economic expansion cycle. Nonetheless, even though the rate of economic growth was more than modest, it was insufficient to transform the underdeveloped economy. Also, the structural features of the pre-1959 economy could not be eradicated entirely.[5]

A critical assessment of the first decade of revolutionary rule identified economic policy and performance this way: "The dismal economic performance of the 1960s, particularly the second half of that decade, was caused by several factors: the rapid and wide collectivization of the means of production . . .; the numerous changes . . . in the model of economic organization and development strategy . . .; the idealistic errors and inefficiency of the Mao-Guevarist stage . . .; the exodus of experienced managerial, technical, and professional personnel and its substitution by loyal but incompetent revolutionaries; the decline of managerial studies; and the predominance of politics and subjective conditions over expertise and objective conditions."[6]

However, C. Mesa-Lago reviewed the 1970s more favorably: "In the current pragmatist stage, economic growth rose from bottom to top priority, and such predominance may continue in the 1980s. This dramatic shift in priorities has been associated with a positive transformation in the Revolution's attitudes toward market mechanisms, cost analysis, training of economists and managers, material incentives, capital efficiency, and labor productivity [some of which were denounced by Castro in 1986 when the rectification process was inaugurated]."[7]

C. Brundenius's analysis of the period's economic performance was more favorable yet:

In contrast to the first Five-Year plan (1976–1980), the second plan (1981–1985) was initiated with a real boom in the economy. In 1981 it was estimated that material production increased by 17 percent (in constant prices), spearheaded by the manufacturing and construction industries increasing by almost 18 percent, but with agriculture following suit not far behind, with an impressive 14 percent. Important in the remarkable increase in agricultural output is that most of it was accounted for by the nonsugar sector . . . During the last years, growth rates have slowed down (particularly in 1982) but the accumulated growth rate as of 1983 indicates that Cuba is very likely to achieve most of its goals set for the target year 1985.[8]

In 1986, Castro's major critical evaluation of economic policy since 1976 led to the rectification of errors and negative tendencies process (RP). The impact of the trade deficit was a major consideration in his negative review. While imports had grown at an annual rate of 8.1 percent between 1959 and 1987, exports increased at a lower rate, 7.1 percent, during the same period. In 1983 imports represented 28 percent of economic accumulation, but by 1987 imports were sustaining practically whatever economic expansion was taking place.

The socialist trading partners absorbed 70 percent of Havana's trade imbalance, but this could not solve what had become a persistent problem under revolutionary rule. And yet, in four more years the collapse of the Soviet bloc would cause the worst crisis ever, which led in turn to the special period and years of extreme hardship.

In some ways, Cuba was properly prepared to meet the challenges of the 1990s, but in other ways it was not. While relations with socialist countries allowed Havana to undertake an ambitious development program, they also helped to create a dangerous state of mind. Complacency resulted from Cuba knowing that the socialist market would always bail it out, and that the Soviet bloc would not put pressure on the island to improve its productivity rate and the quality of exports—particularly since most of Moscow's and Eastern Europe's exports were below Western market criteria.

Such a relationship explains why Cuba, capable of developing areas similar to those in developed economies, still exhibits a productivity and efficiency index associated with poorly developed economies. This has influenced adversely Cuba's chances to compete with market economies. And it is under such conditions that Havana is now struggling to overcome the exigencies of the special period.

The economic conditions Havana faced in the early 1990s were harsh indeed. Imports had decreased approximately 64 percent, from $8.1 billion in 1989 to below $3 billion in 1992. Havana's trade with Moscow had contracted from $5.52 billion in 1989 to less than a third of that by 1991, $1.7 billion.[9] Also, the international sugar price of 13.6 U.S. cents per pound in 1989–90 fell to 9.1 cents per pound in 1990–91. The 1992 sugar harvest was 1.5 million tons less than in 1990 and provided only a fourth of the import resources the country had received from its sugar exports in 1989. From 13.11 million tons in 1989 (the last year of Cuba's normal economy), imported oil decreased to 6 million in 1992.[10]

The 1989 GDP of $20 billion had fallen 35 percent to $12.7 billion in 1993—rising slightly (0.7 percent) to $12.8 billion in 1994, when it started to bottom out; it continued to recover thereafter. The budget deficit stood at $1.4 billion, but from 33.5 percent of the GDP in 1993 the deficit was reduced to 7.3 percent in 1994. The size of the money supply amounted to $12 billion in mid-1994, but a 24 percent reduction a year later brought it down to $9 billion—especially after price increases for goods and services like cigarettes, beer and rum and other alcoholic beverages, gasoline for private consumption, electricity rates based on usage, postal service, intercity bus rates, domestic airfare, and water. The rate of exchange plummeted rapidly from 150 pesos to the dollar in mid-1995 to 18 by late 1996. The peso could not entirely regain its purchasing power because of the scarcity of consumer goods. The excessive growth of money supply aggravated economic and financial conditions and the insufficient amount of goods available, all of which contributed further to the ballooning of the submerged economy (black market).[11]

In Search of a New Economic Model

The first step in a reform process is the decision to abandon the old system. The second is deciding what characteristics the new system should have. So far the economic changes already enforced are indicating what that ultimate economic model will look like. Cubans from all walks of life have contributed their thoughts on the subject. The following are some samples of what nongovernmental and governmental sources had to say on economic reform.

Cuban Economists' Perspectives

For Gerardo González Nuñez, a basic requirement of any new economic model is to include economic, political, and social components envisioning the full use of human resources. Economic production should change its direction for an intensive modality, abandoning the extensive, less competitive mode it has used. In any new industrial plan, exports should remain central. Besides satisfying domestic needs, they represent the best alternative for capital accumulation and economic expansion.[12]

Serious obstacles are affecting Cuba's economic reintegration into the world capitalist markets. Besides facing increased hostility from the United States, Cuba has internal problems demanding solutions if the country is to become reasonably competitive. The industrial sectors should be ranked based on their cost effectiveness, productivity, and market value. Given present conditions, technological modernization must wait. Advancing management efficiency coordinated with the effective use of human resources should have an incremental effect, improving the quality and competitive value of the nation's industrial output and guaranteeing the viability of the system itself.

Notwithstanding the Fourth Party Congress position that no new measures besides those coping with the special period could be enforced at the time, today's economic problems preceded the period. The relationship between planning and market, the existence of mercantile-market mechanisms regulating relations among the different enterprises (state and foreign capital), and the decentralization of economic activity are issues the new system must deal with, according to González Nuñez.

For Julio Carranza Valdés, former deputy director of the Center for the Study of the Americas: "The objective of economic reform is to create the conditions to make the Cuban revolution viable in a much more complex international context and with a more diversified society than before . . . We propose a fundamental transformation of the Cuban economy without giving up its socialist character. Cuba must go from one model of socialism to another model of socialism."[13]

According to Carranza Valdés, Luis Gutiérrez Urdaneta, and Pedro Monreal González, the new socialist model, using different methods, should still satisfy the interests of the population; this time, however, it will include a wide range of economic actors in addition to the state. State enterprises would then be reformed, as would all property ownership modalities. Operating within a decentralized market economy, state and private enterprises should be competing alongside each other with a high level of profit and efficiency.[14]

As a reformed economic actor, the state should retain these characteristics:

> It should keep under its control the fundamental means of production.
> It should be capable of planning national economic development by different available means.
> It should represent the country in any negotiations with foreign capital.
> It should have enough revenue to avoid extreme poverty.

For the revolution to exist, says Carranza Valdés, the system should be able to sustain a social-welfare state. This fundamental component would include universal health care and education. The resources for implementing such a system would come from putting the state economic productivity and redistributive capacity at effective levels. Even though there still might be differences in income, the state could not tolerate extremes, whether they be great accumulation of wealth or dire poverty.

Government Leaders' Perspectives

To some analysts reform has been slow, as if it were made reluctantly. Still, the total reform record is notable, and it assures that the final scope of change will be substantive. Besides President Castro and sometimes Raúl Castro, the spokesmen for the regime's reform program are Carlos Lage, vice president, and José Luis Rodríguez, economy and planning minister. They have articulated the features of the emerging system, including the economic and political assumptions of the reform process. Among other features, they have stressed the following:[15]

> The objective is to perfect socialism, not to move toward capitalism.

> There would be no "transition" in Cuba as in the European socialist countries, which "have had a transition to hell."

> The state can accomplish more when it is organized better and becomes more efficient.

> The state will keep an active, central economic role (ratified in 1998).

> The state will not be limited to supervising social services like health, education, etc. (as in a welfare state).

> The state's economic role represents the interests of the people.

> It matters who holds political power and whose interests are being served.

> State enterprises should and can be efficient and competitive.

> The solution to the external financial deficit lies in the domestic economy.

> The economic improvement is directed to solve fundamental economic problems (i.e., the scarcity of convertible currency reserves).

> We are not afraid of challenges or the market.

> We are not afraid of economic reform creating social imbalances; our people understand the reasons behind them and support them.

> There will be no massive privatization or expansion of private business, which will not solve our problems.

> Large industrial units should solve fundamental problems, not the proliferation of thousands of small private businesses.

> There will be no free contracting of workers or private salaried employment.

> There will be no independent trade unions, but the self-employed may be able to join official unions (still at the experimental stage).

> There will be no independent associations questioning the existence and objectives of the revolution.

Regarding future trends:

> Self-employment will expand and eventually become stable.
>
> Directives concerning small- and medium-sized private business are under study, including state enterprises, cooperatives, and joint ventures between the public and private sectors.
>
> External commerce has been decentralized, from fifty enterprises in 1989 to 150 by 1996 (and has continued growing since).
>
> External commerce with Latin America has grown, from 6 percent in 1989 to 35 percent by 1995 (and has continued growing since).
>
> Exports have grown, 16 percent by 1994—3.5 percent in 1994 alone (and have continued growing since).

The ideological beliefs sustaining such assumptions included:

> There is no future without the homeland, the revolution, and socialism.
>
> We disagree with neoliberalism that state enterprises are inferior to private ones.
>
> A feasible utopia is turning into a reality.

The official position on the reform process appears more doctrinaire than the ideas suggested by Cuban economists. While everybody volunteered to defend socialism, it is the regime's responsibility to apply the concept with practical policies, so it insists on more centralized economic activity. (However, other forms of property ownership and the role of different economic actors are in a state of flux.) The 1997 Fifth Party Congress discussed new directions in the reform process, but it retained the cautious approach that has typified policy making in the 1990s. When changes are measured in retrospect and not daily, the full extent of economic reform can be properly appreciated.

Scholarly Reactions Abroad

Economic analysts have watched the reforms under the special period closely. Traditionally, they have been critical of the policies pursued by the government, particularly its political and economic objectives. Recent comments on issues related to the reform process include the following.

C. Mesa-Lago, on the reform's economic and political issues: "[The reforms] involve a series of conflicts. First, there is a contradiction between the necessity to open the economy to market forces and the desire to keep the process under state control through detailed regulations and restrictions that the government seems increasingly incapable of enforcing. Second, as the private and informal sector expands, the formal state sector contracts, thus creating a trade-off between economic improvement and the loss of state economic power. Third, most of the reforms are facilitating the creation of a new class in Cuba made up of black marketeers, employees of enterprises in the hard currency sector, recipients of dollar remittances from exiled relatives, legal and illegal micro-entrepreneurs, and the self-employed. The majority of this group is critical of the government and would like to see it changed and the market expanded."[16]

J. Pérez-López, on a comparative analysis of economic reform: "Structurally, the Cuban economy is one of the few remaining bastions of central planning, probably putting Cuba in this regard close to pre-reform Czechoslovakia. This means that a reform strategy for the country will have to be very comprehensive, tackling essentially all areas of the economy . . . The Cuban state's control over productive resources is very high, certainly higher than in pre-reform Poland and probably in the range of 90–100 percent state ownership estimated for pre-reform Hungary and Czechoslovakia . . . Over the last three decades, the Cuban government has worked to eliminate—or incapacitate—the market-oriented institutions that were in place at the onset of the revolutionary regime in 1959. A reform strategy for Cuba must include substantial work in the rebuilding of institutions that support the market, including a legal framework that recognizes private ownership, a commercial code, banking regulations, a tax code and a social safety net."[17]

A. R. M. Ritter, on the external debt and compensation to American nationals:

A normalization of Cuba's place in the international financial and trading system requires a resolution of its debt problems and of the issue of compensation for the properties of U.S. nationals seized in 1959–1963 . . . Cuba's convertible currency debt, amounting to $7.8 billion in early 1993, is very high in a Latin American context, and has been in a . . . moratorium since 1988. Cuba's ostensible debt with the Soviet Union and the countries of Eastern Europe likely exceeded $30 billion by 1992, but its status is ambiguous . . . The value of [U.S. nationals' seized] . . . property would be about $6.1 billion as of mid-1993. Cuba may consider a counterclaim for embargo and other damages, but this is unclear. International law on the matter of nationalization and compensations seems widely accepted and relatively unambiguous . . . [But] international law is silent on damages which may be imposed on a large country which imposes economic sanctions or covert destabilization on a small neighbour. Normal ideas of equity and fairness do not support the right of a large country to damage a small neighbour in this way, however.[18]

Mesa-Lago draws a zero-sum game for the regime. It is bad not to reform, but if it does so, the reform will ultimately make the regime lose political support and control. Pérez-López compares Cuba's current stance with the moment preceding the collapse of European socialist nations, indicating hence that an implosion as in Eastern Europe is likely to happen. Ritter gives his own interpretation of international law and debt calculations. Havana would agree with his statement that it is not right for a large country like the United States to damage a small nation like Cuba.

Economic Reforms in the 1990s

On July 26, 1992, while commemorating the attack on the Moncada Barracks, Castro's announcement that new reforms were forthcoming provoked anticipation. People wondered what the new changes would be like. These are some of the special period's economic reforms:

Constitutional reform legalizing associations with foreign
   investors (1992)
Legalizing the U.S. dollar (1993)
Authorizing self-employment (1993)
Creating the Basic Units of Cooperative Production (UBPC,
   1993)
Reducing military expenses (1994)
Reducing/consolidating government agencies (1994)
Penalizing illegal acquisitions and profits (1994)
Increasing prices for goods and services (1994)
Penalizing fiscal delinquency (1994)
Ending gratuities (1994)
Tax law (1994)
Reopening farmers' markets (1994)

Opening industrial markets (1994)

Opening sugar industry and real estate to foreign investment (1994)

Introducing a peso convertible to foreign currency (1995)

Expanding self-employment, legalizing small restaurants (*paladares*, 1995)

New customs system, higher duties imposed (1995)

Registry of travel agencies operating in Cuba (1995)

New law expanding foreign investment (1995)

New Mining Law (1995)

Regulating foreign exchange with foreign firms (1995)

Charging tolls to motorists on Matanzas-Varadero highway (1996)

Procedure to collect income tax (1996)

Selling housing to foreign investors for hard currency (1996)

Antidote (anti–Helms-Burton) Law (1996)

Free Zones and Industrial Parks (1996)

Regulating Labor Code for foreign investment (1996)

National register of subsidiaries of foreign trading companies (1996)

Regulating the fishing sector (1996)

Limiting Havana's population growth (1997)

Restricting housing rentals (1997)

There were mixed reactions to the reforms on the island and elsewhere. In Cuba they meant reordering the lives of people who were this time awaiting improvements. Besides affecting living conditions, the reforms have had a bigger impact at the macro level than at the individual one. Deeply ingrained social values were coming under scrutiny. The notion that the society was based on real equality (with some exceptions) and that now inequality was being accepted was a point of contention. Also, the attitude toward those who migrated after 1959, who were generally seen negatively, had to be reconsidered. Monies sent by relatives living abroad to their family back home had become an important source of national revenue—but such money caused those receiving it to become a privileged social group. U.S. dollar sites (restaurants, hotels, stores, etc.) were off limits to those with no access to hard currency, who found themselves segregated in their own country. These conditions were too hard for many to accept gladly, but so were the hardships of the special period.

Critics of the regime abroad stated that the government was making reforms as a result of internal social dynamics and that it was mostly legalizing a situation that already existed. The careful approach governing the reforms was proof of a split in the leadership between reform supporters and conservative opponents. Arguments held by deputies in National Assembly sessions became evidence of the ongoing controversy the reform process provoked within the regime.[19]

Legalizing U.S. Dollars

The 1993 Decree Law 140 states that "the conditions of the special period and the economic difficulties that the country is experiencing make new regulations and measures necessary regarding the possession of freely convertible currency . . . It is advisable to decriminalize the possession of such currency." The dollar, once made legal, replaced the devalued Cuban peso as the currency of choice guaranteeing one's personal well-being. It also had a social cleavage effect, separating those with access to dollars from the rest of the population. Looking for dollars became an important pursuit among those who directly or indirectly could find access to hard currency.

Moreover, when the prices of goods in dollar stores were doubled following the decision, the black market upsurge that ensued had a negative effect on the national currency, which slipped from 60 to 80 pesos per dollar. All individuals who were imprisoned for holding convertible currency illegally were released.[20] The worst year of the special period was possibly 1993. Not surprisingly, Cubans reflected seriously on the pros and cons of such a radical change and on the decisions that should follow, supplementing it. According to a Cuban political scientist:

> Tens of millions of dollars [were] circulating among the people. While the penalties for having [U.S.] dollars were in force, regular Cubans found ways of shopping, indirectly, in sophisticated shops for tourists and foreign residents, buying for their own families or for the black market . . . This measure would make this situation "honest" and collect hard currency . . . It could stimulate remittances from abroad, especially Miami. It is hard to speculate about the amount of [dollars] . . . but given the peculiarities of Cuban migration they should not amount [to what they have] in other places [in Latin America]. [Also, there are] social effects and political costs. Fidel himself recognized the increment of inequality and called for the revolutionaries to be understanding. [But creating] . . .

a privileged social group based on its relationship with Miami is something difficult to accept by a population that for over three decades has been defined as the antithesis of "those who left." These arguments might suggest that it is a wrong decision [when] the economic benefits do not compensate for the political cost. [Still] there is a powerful reason that justifies it: [we need] to activate our internal economic relations and our ties with the world market, [so] the decision has merits.

However, it would be necessary to relate it to other decisions equally audacious that would connect the incoming dollars with a stimulus to increase production and economic services, even to the extent of privatizing the areas where the state has proven to be ineffective, or becoming a system that puts an end to the myth of a dual economy in which the dynamic sector is linked to foreign investment and the domestic economy is dragging its feet in the midst of scarcity.[21]

For a Cuban economist, a country like Cuba that lost 75 percent of its import supply needed new financial resources to revitalize itself. In that sense, to González Nuñez the legalization of the dollar is correct. Still, by itself it is insufficient because the economic problems are much more complex: "The Cuban economy faces the challenge of having to find its viability because it lost its supply markets. It faces this challenge in an increasingly competitive world market that excludes underdeveloped countries and, in the Cuban case, with no international support and under the impact of U.S. hostility toward the revolution. This demands that Cuba's economy undergo a revitalization based on internal factors, which would guarantee economic development and would also solve the daily crisis confronted by the populace."[22]

Given present conditions, both social scientists agreed that legalizing the dollar was necessary, but they were skeptical that it could solve problems of such magnitude. As part of a reform package, the dollarization of the economy raised concerns with its social implications. Talking to the Federation of Cuban Women in 1995, Castro said that the economic reforms would continue and that "elements of private property, capitalism and market forces" were being considered, while preserving the social welfare gains of the revolution remained always an objective.[23]

The economic reforms included correcting internal finances by reducing money supply growth (reducing inflation); establishing a tax system that included income, self-employment, farmers' markets and industrial markets, and joint ventures with foreign investors; by increasing prices of goods and services; cracking down on the black market; streamlining the size of government; turning state-run agricultural farms into semiprivate cooperatives; and by other means. Even after reversing the downward economic trend, the economic gains were not sufficient to improve living conditions noticeably.

To alleviate hardship and provide incentives to increase production, the regime awarded hard currency vouchers to workers in basic industry, construction, fishing, and the tobacco industry, giving them access to dollar stores. The regime distributed $3 million in incentives in 1994. Those working in the tourist industry and in foreign-trade-related industries also have access to dollars, as do those who are receiving remittances from relatives living abroad. Approximately one-fifth to one-third of the population has gained access to dollars.[24]

According to a 1997 official report, in 1996 dollar stores increased their sales and services 18.3 percent over 1995—$627 million and $530 million, respectively. The number of workers receiving hard currency coupons redeemable in dollar stores increased from 1 to 1.3 million in 1996. This represented 23 percent of the total labor force of 4.5 million (government and cooperatives). In 1995, only 17 percent of the labor force received dollar coupons as part of their salaries. CIMEX, operator of the Pan American stores, was cited as an example to emulate, having increased hard currency collection 85 percent in 1996 over the previous year. In Granma province alone it collected $6 million more than originally planned, and it intended to increase dollar collection in 1997 to $20 million.[25]

Other Economic Reforms

The Farmers' Market

Economic changes were aimed at ameliorating the population's burden under the special period. Favoring the consumer, the farmers' markets were opened again in 1994 with more suppliers than before. After having functioned since the early 1980s, they had been closed in 1986. Now consumers could choose from approximately thirty products in 130 markets across the country. The selection included potatoes, grains, rice, vegetables, rabbit, pork, mutton, and cooked dishes. Prices are lower than in the black market but still high for the average person. The sale of goods produced on state farms (such as milk, tobacco, rice, beef, horse meat, and coffee) is not allowed. Nevertheless, "the presence of the markets meant that the food shortages were over and—perhaps as important—that the *sense* of shortage was over."[26]

The president of the National Association of Small (Private) Farmers (ANAP), Orlando Lugo Fonte, said that opening markets with prices based on supply and demand would "increase production and increase the efficient use of land." The government sought to reduce food shortages and curtail black marketeers' illegal business. Private farmers, cooperatives, and others could sell their surplus products after fulfilling their assigned production quotas. The private farmers could also use intermediaries to transport products and conduct sales. The use of intermediaries and what was seen as their undeserved profit had prompted the closing of the farmers' markets in 1986.

In the first four months of operation (October 1994–January 1995) the farmers' markets sold 600 million pesos' worth of merchandise, paid 60 million pesos in taxes, and distributed 21 percent of the total agricultural production. The most active markets were in Havana, Holguín, and Santiago de Cuba, and the least active in Pinar del Río, Isle of Youth, Cienfuegos and Guantánamo.[27]

Once the farmers' markets were reopened (always operating in pesos) and measures had been taken to improve internal finances (reducing the amount of pesos in circulation and the black market prices), the value and purchasing power of the peso improved. The exchange rate fluctuated between 80 and 140 pesos to the dollar in 1994, but a year later it had dropped to 35 to the dollar, and for a short time it was at 15 and even 10 and 7 to the dollar. Since then, the peso has remained at 20 to 35 to the dollar.

Another factor strengthening the peso was the May 2, 1994, law freezing the saving accounts in the nation's banks, which held 60 percent of the money in circulation. Exchanging government bonds for people's savings should reduce further the budget deficit, which had totaled 4.2 billion pesos in 1994.

The Food Program

A food program (Programa Alimentario, PA) was created in 1988 after the government analyzed the "problems and deficiencies affecting agriculture and cattle production and the food industry." The objective of the PA was to build upon the development programs of 1960 to 1988, when the ratio of cultivated land per capita had increased from 0.39 hectares to

0.41 and unused land per capita had been reduced from 0.21 hectares to 0.08 Under those programs, 1.1 million hectares were transferred from agriculture to industrialization, reforestation, urban development, and other projects, while extensive work improving agriculture was done as well.

In the late 1980s goods like rice, fruit, and potatoes, which had previously been available, became scarce; and corn, beans, vegetables, roots, tubers, and viands became extremely scarce. The food program was integrated with all economic and industrial sectors that were connected with food production. It provided support to independent farmers and agricultural cooperatives in the form of financial and technical assistance.[28] The PA output was short of what was expected. Underscoring the food problem, General of the Army Raúl Castro stated in 1994: "Today, the political, military, and ideological problem of this country is to find food. From all points of view it is the most important task."[29]

The UBPCs

Seeking to increase agricultural production, the Politburo agreed in 1993 to organize the Basic Units of Cooperative Production (UBPCs)—replacing the state-run farms with worker-managed cooperatives. The new structure sought to use agriculture more effectively by encouraging higher production levels at a minimum cost. To function efficiently, the UBPCs were granted:

The right to use the land freely (user rights only).

The right to own their own production (not the land).

The right to sell their production to the state through their own enterprises.

The right to have their own bank accounts.

The right to elect their own leadership (like other cooperatives).

Their responsibilities included:

The duty to provide for their own technical/material resources.

The duty to contribute to the national fiscal expenses.

The regime was deciding the size of sugar and nonsugar crops according to national needs. Some UBPCs were organized to exploit unused lands under government supervision.[30] The UBPC project was started after the food program and agriculture in general had taken a nosedive with the terrible storm of March 1993, which had destroyed portions of export crops. The sugar harvest had sunk to only 4.2 million tons, the lowest since 1963. Sugar Minister Nelson Torres stated that "Cuba will start and finish its 1993–94 sugar harvest early so that the industry can concentrate its efforts and resources upon improving future harvests."[31]

By late 1994, there were 2,879 UBPC units covering 3.2 million hectares, which represented 46.5 percent of all agricultural lands. They were divided between sugarcane and other crops, 1.43 million hectares and 1.45 million hectares, respectively. In late 1995 land distribution followed this pattern: the UBPCs had 46 percent (on lease from the government); government land, 35 percent; cooperative owners, 8 percent; and individual owners, 11 percent. The total number of workers involved was 263,000 (29 percent of the agricultural sector). The UBPCs' production represented one-third of all tubers and vegetables, half of the milk, and about two-fifths of all rice. Three years after they were created, the UBPCs' output was far below expectations. According to government reports, "three out of every five [were] unprofitable."[32]

In 1997 the UBPC sugar producers were also in trouble. Only one in every seventeen UBPCs had made a profit or broken even. The combined loss of 1,286 cooperatives was the equivalent of 4.2 percent of the GDP in 1996 and was estimated as "over one-fifth of the export value of the last three sugar harvests combined." But to a student of Cuban agriculture, it was "simple to understand that the ultimate objective of [the UBPC] reform could not be achieved in the short run; some time is needed to reorganize production under present circumstances to obtain higher yields."[33]

However, according to a study by three Cuban economists: "An important group of UBPC[s] had serious problems from their inception. Further foreseeable problems, such as shortage of all kinds of material resources (quality seeds, fertilizers, pesticides, energy for irrigation systems and agricultural machinery, and other supplies), made evident the poor utilization of resources, the improper management of the labor force and working hours, and the incompetence of the administration."[34]

And yet, Minister of Finance and Prices Manuel Millares reported in 1997 that emergency measures were being taken to correct the situation:

1. Official support was extended under strict production rules.
2. The amortization period for government aid was extended.
3. New credits were granted.
4. A special fund was created to support the 1997–98 harvest.
5. Special loans were offered to cover losses for the 1996–97 harvest.
6. Cooperatives were compensated for erroneous government decisions affecting them.

7. Government paid half the cost of developing new growing areas.

8. Government reimbursed 30 percent of mobilization expenses.

9. The price for goods and services provided to the UBPCs was being reconsidered.

10. The price paid to the cooperatives for sugar was going to be in line with prevailing sugar prices and production costs in the future.[35]

Self-Employment

Authorized on September 8, 1993, by Decree Law 141, self-employment (*trabajo por cuenta propia*) was an important byproduct of the special period. Licenses for small private business and services allowed 135 private trades, which later increased to 157. A fixed monthly fee (tax) ranging from 20 to 80 pesos was levied, depending on the particular trade exercised. The different categories (each one containing several trades) included: transportation and support; housing repairs; agricultural jobs; family and personal needs; home services; and others. New categories like carpentry, gardening, repair of household equipment, animal grooming, and restoration of dolls and other toys were added later. The number of the self-employed grew to over 200,000 and then declined rapidly (it fell from 208,000 at the end of 1995 to 170,000 by early 1997). The government estimated that the number would climb again to become stable at approximately 350,000, but labor leaders estimated in late 1995 that it could climb up to 13 percent of the total work force.

In 1995 the hundreds of paladares—private family-owned restaurants—that had spread throughout the island, especially in Havana and other major cities, were legalized. They were authorized to employ only family members and to serve a maximum of twelve customers at one time. Paladares were required to pay a tax fluctuating from a hundred to four hundred dollars a month.

According to figures released by the Ministry of Labor and published in the economic weekly *Cuban Business*, by early 1998 the nongovernmental sector of the economy had become the number one employment-generating area. Out of 66,300 new jobs created in 1997, 53 percent were nongovernment jobs. The government had generated 15.5 percent of the new jobs, while the emerging mixed economy produced the remaining 32 percent. The unemployment rate, according to official figures, had decreased to 6.9 percent in 1997, but the level for the previous year was not released. Reportedly, more than 200,000 were self-employed in 1996.[36]

The Ministries of Labor, Social Security, and Financing and Prices issued a resolution in early 1996 regulating self-employment. The self-employed were expected to carry out their work "individually and without employing salaried workers." In the case of paladares, "family help" was restricted to the preparation of food and drinks, and each family member involved needed to have a license and pay taxes. They were not allowed to provide services or sell products to state or private companies or joint ventures with foreign investors.[37] Another constraint imposed on self-employment was that those with degrees in the liberal professions were initially excluded from applying for this economic outlet. Later, however, they were allowed to work in areas other than their own professions.[38]

Self-employment was approved when approximately a fourth of the total labor force was estimated to be underemployed. In 1995 unemployment was between 7 and 17 percent of a labor force of 3.5 million. One forecast suggested that 245,000 to 600,000 workers were unemployed later in the year, while another put the labor surplus as high as 1.5 million workers.[39] The secretary-general of the Cuban Confederation of Workers (CTC), Pedro Ross Leal, had recognized during the trade unions' seventeenth congress in 1995 that unemployment stood at 7 percent. Self-employment had allowed a significant portion of the population to become disconnected from the official labor network and to be more self-reliant economically. The possibility that this growing sector might become a political force with its own sectarian agenda is a political concern for the government.

The 1997 restrictions suggest that the regime may fear that creeping capitalism could be encroaching, disguised as self-employment. The self-employed were called "the new rich" and the "stalwart enem[ies] of the economic and social order." Thus arose the need for the regime to limit and regulate self-employment more strictly. The downside may be to discourage it to the extreme of lessening what has been a contribution to the national economy and an alternative that has helped to alleviate people's harsh living conditions.

Housing and Immigration Regulations

Decree Law 171 governing housing rentals and subletting was approved in 1997.[40] It authorized "rentals of housing, rooms with or without private baths, and other spaces considered integral to a housing unit" and stipulated that revenues from rental taxes would be used for housing maintenance.[41]

Strict limitations were established: "Rentals for the purpose of conducting lucrative commercial business are not allowed, nor for industry or services"; and "areas designed as being of interest for tourism are prohibited from engaging in private rental arrangements." The law made it difficult for the self-employed to operate. Often self-employment demanded a place of business (renting a room or part of a house). The Vedado section of Havana, the heart of the city today, is a center of self-employment activity. Many housing and sublet rentals have been negotiated for all kinds of trades, services, and paladares by *cuentapropistas* (the self-employed). And both parties, the self-employed and the house owner, depend on the income generated from the business.

Several concerns are behind the new restrictions. The government had complained that people renting out rooms to other Cubans, and especially to foreign tourists, were not reporting it, which caused a security risk. Though not related to this situation, in May 1997 a new law limited the population in the capital city of Havana, where massive migration from all over the island was taxing the city beyond its capacity to provide needed services. The internal migration law limited the availability of Havana housing to those who had come from other regions of the country to share in the capital's lifestyle. The law caused a surge of requests to legalize residence in Havana. Otherwise, people would be evicted and sent back to their place of origin.[42]

Today's social and economic dislocations have increased migration to Havana. The net incoming migration balance that existed until 1989 was 10,000 to 12,000 persons per year—the difference between those arriving and those leaving for other cities. But the net balance escalated to 29,000 by 1996, when new arrivals numbered 55,000. The capital's population density has been reported at 2,900 persons per square kilometer, but in Old Havana and Centro Habana the numbers go as high as 23,000 and 47,000, respectively.

Under the new regulations, the people learned that "all those who live for some time and fail to register are illegals . . . [and their] presence in the capital is illegal."[43] The president of the National Housing Institute, Mario Cabello, reported that 150 evictions of squatters were carried out in 1997 and that 1,145 tenants had committed irregularities in violation of the new housing statutes. In a period of eighteen months, 2,100 housing units that had been vacated by those fleeing the country were given to needy people, after being confiscated by the government.[44]

According to an official survey, 505,700 residents in the country's capital (23 percent of the city's population) were born somewhere else. These people are popularly known as "Palestinians" for their precarious living conditions. Nearly half of the City of Havana's immigrants come from the eastern provinces. An east-west breakdown of the immigrants' province of origin follows:

Santiago de Cuba: 13.2 percent
Granma: 11.8 percent
Holguín: 10.2 percent
Las Tunas: 4.1 percent
Camagüey: 5.2 percent
Ciego de Ávila: 3.4 percent
Sancti Spiritus: 5 percent
Cienfuegos: 3.4 percent
Villa Clara: 10.1 percent
Matanzas: 7 percent
Havana: 8.5 percent
Pinar del Río: 9.5 percent
Isle of Youth Municipality: 0.5 percent

The number of violations of the immigration and housing regulations in 1997 was significant. After investigating 1,000,350 houses, the CDRs (Committees for the Defense of the Revolution) in charge of the inspections found 218,000 violations or "irregularities"—meaning that one in every five homes was not following the housing regulations. Most of the reported offenses consisted of renting rooms without a permit, sheltering unregistered residents, some kind of illegal construction, or the unregistered (illegal) sale of a home. The first provinces screened for housing violations by mid-1997 were Sancti Spiritus, Santiago de Cuba, Las Tunas, and the Isle of Youth municipality.[45]

Industrial Markets

Decree Law 192 established industrial markets. When it came into effect in 1994, 160 shops opened for business with prices determined by supply and demand. The markets' suppliers included 160,000 self-employed individuals as well as local industries, the Ministry of the Interior, and the state's central administration. The objective of the markets was to give the consumer an accessible shopping alternative to the black market.[46]

The industrial markets were not as successful as the farmers' markets. Not enough producers were participating in the markets, including government-owned and -operated manufacturers. Consumers complained that "there is nothing to buy" and "the prices are far too high." Months later the situation started to improve. The new goods included clothes, shoes, coffee makers, frying pans, hand-forged toasted-sandwich makers, knives, and stove and oven fittings, though at prices still considered too high. Still, good opportunities appeared sometimes: "In two shops in Havana, the most crowded counter was one run by the state electronics producer *Cubaelectrónica*, which was offering a wide selection of electronic parts like resistors and transistors at reasonable *pesos* prices."[47]

In the first months the industrial markets sold 2.5 million pesos worth of goods, and three thousand self-employed artisans sold 1 million pesos' worth of products. In the first six months of 1996 sales increased 127.2 percent, which favored the Consumer Price Index (IPC) and decreased the informal economy 22 percent. Altogether, the IPC had a 4 percent contraction in the same period, most notably in the agricultural sector with 30 percent.[48]

Taxation

Law No. 73 was approved in 1994, establishing an Integral Tax System and reversing a no-tax policy that had lasted for over three decades. The timetable enforcing the tax system was slow and by stages, so that those affected could adjust to their new fiscal responsibilities. The minister of finance and prices approved Resolution No. 21 in 1996, establishing the procedure to collect taxes for national currency income, which were paid in pesos. Income received in U.S. dollars was taxed for the first time in 1996. Even now, the majority of the labor force, up to 75 percent, works for the state and pays no taxes. The main target for this tax are the self-employed private businesses, amounting to 90 percent of taxpayers.

Salaries are included as taxable income, but given their low average (185 pesos per month), they are not being taxed. During the special period "the state paid pensions and retirements on time to more than 1.2 million citizens, besides subsidizing health and educational services, which are free."[49] But given the nation's financial conditions, taxes were inevitable once the different economic reforms were more or less in place.

The taxable transactions in pesos included using labor, public services, special products, land transportation, legal documents, property transfers and inheritance, and exploiting natural resources. Also subject to tax were business profits, personal income, sales, placing advertisements and using commercial publicity, levies to protect the environment, social security payments, airport and port fees, and highway tolls.[50] The established tax scale runs from 10 to 50 percent of the cuentapropistas' net income in pesos. (See table 6.2)

According to the National Office of Tax Administration (ONAT), self-

Table 6.2. Annual Tax Scale

Net Income (in Cuban pesos)*	Taxes (in percentages)
Up to 3,000	5
3,000–6,000	10
6,000–12,000	15
12,000–18,000	20
18,000–24,000	25
24,000–36,000	30
36,000–48,000	35
48,000–60,000	40
Over 60,000	50

*Article 4: Excluded from this tax are the following kinds of income: (1) income with a relevant national connotation; (2) legal organizations' scholarships, traveling, and work missions; (3) pensions and retirement payments; (4) donations to the state by nonprofit organizations; (5) insurance compensation; (6) income by UBPC and Agricultural and Cattle Cooperatives members from state enterprises.

SOURCE: "Impuestos Sobre Ingresos Personales en Moneda Nacional, Resolución No. 21/96," *Correo de Cuba*, vol. 1, no. 2: 30–33.

employed workers paid 120 million pesos in taxes in 1996; cuentapropistas earning convertible currency also were paying taxes. It will take time before the tax system and the economic significance of taxing the self-employed are well understood and accepted by the public.[51]

In 1996 all juridical entities had to subscribe to a national tax register, including state and private companies and any other income-earning association. A register for individual taxpayers was also being set up. The first sworn tax statements were not due until 1997, but cargo and passenger transport services and the resale of agricultural products had been taxed since 1996. License fees for transportation providers ranged from 50 to 300 pesos (sometimes payable in U.S. dollars), while agricultural resellers were taxed 200 pesos monthly.

The 1997 tax report was mixed, tending to the positive side. At the end of the 1996 tax period the collection from personal income amounted to 200 million pesos (up from 106 million pesos in 1995). Most taxpayers (92.5 percent) had paid for the required tax forms, which they have to purchase, and 14 million pesos and $141,000 dollars had been collected from 245,000 sworn declarations (86.7 percent of expected revenues).

The majority of taxpayers (approximately 90 percent) had fulfilled their 1996 income tax payment by the 1997 deadline, but 37,000 were still delinquent. The tax management office extended the deadline, allowing tax evaders to complete their tax returns. While tax returns for individuals and companies stood at over 2 billion pesos, there were almost 490 million pesos of unpaid taxes from 1996, with 12.6 million belonging to companies operating in hard currency. Several transportation enterprises owed 3 million pesos, while surcharges for late payments totaled 88.7 million pesos.

Conclusions

According to ONAT, having 90 percent of income tax returns on file by the deadline was satisfactory. Even an initial return of 72 percent would have been acceptable, considering that taxes were being levied again after thirty years without them.[52] The provinces with the highest rate of returns in 1997 were Havana, Villa Clara, and Cienfuegos (over 90 percent), followed by Matanzas, the City of Havana, Santiago de Cuba, Holguín, and Pinar del Río (over 86 percent).

The new tax policy could contribute to purging the economy of erroneous past practices, forcing economic actors in the public sector to perform more effectively, especially state enterprise managers. In 1997, "for the first time since 1986, the taxes paid by state enterprises surpassed the total amount of the subsidies these enterprises receive from the government—by 750 million pesos"—complying enterprises numbered only six hundred state enterprises, about 18 percent of their total number.[53] The ten-year period included years when the Soviet bloc still existed, and the problems that caused its demise had not yet begun.

The question of whether the economic problems of the special period were due to the collapse of European socialism or were as much induced by domestic error is still relevant. Hence, the complex issue of economic reform under the special period is further examined in the next chapter.

7

Economic Reform under the Special Period: Part II

Foreign Investment

The economic recovery allowed foreign investment in partnership with the regime in joint ventures. Based on Decree Law 50 of 1982 and the constitutional reform of 1992, the Foreign Investment Act of 1995 (Law 77) expanded foreign investment.[1] Enterprises from abroad could own up to 100 percent of a business in some economic areas and could invest in business from agriculture to industry, including real estate. An attractive profit potential, repatriation of earnings, and an educated work force free of labor unrest were offered as incentives to international investors.[2]

The first joint venture was with Spain to build a hotel in Varadero. After 1992, joint ventures increased, but between 1994 and 1995 they almost doubled. In early 1995, 290 projects were under consideration, and by the summer 212 new partnerships were in full operation, increasing to 260 a year later. They were limited initially to ten countries but soon expanded to include fifty-three nations.[3] Investors from Spain, Mexico, Canada, England, France, and Holland led foreign investment in Cuba. (See table 7.1.) The 1996 U.S. Helms-Burton Act sought to stop this essential component of Cuba's economic recovery.

An attractive sector to foreign investors is biotechnology, which has been a priority among Cuban scientific research programs. Approximately two hundred pharmaceuticals, including interferon (used to treat AIDS) and the hepatitis B vaccine, could be profitable exports if properly marketed. Despite its pharmaceutical success, Cuba still needs to import medicines from the United States. According to a 1992 Johns Hopkins University study, without the embargo U.S. medicine exports to Cuba could reach $90 million a year.[4]

Foreign ventures approved by 1995–96 totaled $2.1 billion—up from $1.5 billion in 1994. Projects committed by mid-1996 totaled $5.6 billion, but some experts claimed that it was lower.[5] In 1995, 212 joint ventures

Table 7.1. Foreign Investment by Country, 1988–1995

Country	1988	1990	1991	1992	1993	1994	1995	Total
Spain	1		3	9	10	14	10	47
Mexico		2	3	3	4	1		13
Canada			2	8	16			26
Italy			1	5	4	7		17
France	1		3	5	2	2		13
Holland			1	2	3	3		9
Rest of Latin America		2	3	11	9	4		29
Rest of world	1	4	11	16	22	4		58
Total	1	2	11	33	60	74	31	212

Source: Comisión Económica para la América Latina y el Caribe-CEPAL, *Cuba: Evolución Económica durante 1995* (New York: United Nations, 1996), 22, based on figures provided by the Cuban Ministry of Foreign Investment and Cooperation, May 1995.

covered thirty-four economic sectors in such areas as agriculture, mining, petroleum, industry, tourism, transportation, construction, and communication (see table 7.2). By mid-1996 there was a 22 percent increment in joint ventures over 1995, and 143 projects were under consideration. Of the 260 corporations operating in 1997, 17 percent had started after the 1996 Helms-Burton Act.[6] The foreign investment minister stated that "since the . . . Helms-Burton law, there has been more foreign investment in Cuba than in all of last year . . . investments have not ceased."[7] By early 1998, 332 joint ventures were reported in operation. (Other estimates placed them close to 360.)[8]

In March 1998, Alamar Associates led a few American businessmen to Cancun, Mexico, to attend a Cuban investment opportunities seminar. After presentations by high government officials, the group traveled to Havana as official guests and met with Castro.[9]

In 1995 Mexico's Grupo Domos sold 25 percent of its $700 million Cuban telephone investment to a subsidiary of Italy's state phone company, STET, and by 1997 appeared ready to quit altogether (which it did); but Canada's Sherritt expanded from nickel mining and oil exploration to tourism, real estate, agriculture, sugar, communications, electricity, and finance.[10] In 1998, Sherritt expanded its Cuban investment by approximately $190 million. It acquired 37.5 percent of the cellular telephone company for $38.2 million and planned additional investments totaling $150 million to produce electricity from natural gas. The power project was in partnership with Cuba's Energas and had a twenty-six-month completion schedule in the area of Varadero-Boca, east of Havana. Sherritt

Table 7.2. Foreign Investment by Economic Sector, 1988–1995

Economic Sector	1988	1990	1991	1992	1993	1994	1995	Total
Agriculture			1	1	3	3	2	10
Mining		1		10	17		28	
Petroleum		1	1	11	8	4		25
Industry		5	9	17	12	13	56	
Tourism	1			4	9	16	4	34
Transportation						1	4	5
Construction			2	3	6	10	1	22
Communications		1		1		1		3
Other		1	4	7	10	7	29	
Total	1	2	11	33	60	74	31	212

SOURCE: Comisión Económica para la América Latina y el Caribe-CEPAL, *Cuba: Evolución Económica durante 1995* (New York: United Nation, 1996), 23, based on figures provided by the Cuban Ministry of Foreign Investment and Cooperation, May 1995.

will hold a one-third equity interest in Energas once the gas-to-electricity project is completed. Reducing the cost of producing electricity makes the project central to the recovery program.[11]

Tourism

With thirty-four foreign investments, tourism represented over 16 percent of all joint ventures in 1995. In 1998, the Italian company Siata agreed to construct and manage four new hotels in partnership with Cubanacán. Two hotels will be in Cayo Coco and the other two in Varadero. Siata's president stated that "Cuba's future lies in tourism because it has all the right characteristics: first of all, its people; and second, the confidence which this country inspires."

Founded in 1994, Cubanacán is in charge of managing and marketing numerous hotels and seeking financing for remodeling and construction of others. Cubanacán has developed resorts in isolated areas never exploited commercially and is co-proprietor of some leading hotels. Prior to the Siata agreement, Cubanacán had eight foreign partners from five different countries: Spain, Canada, Jamaica, Germany, and the Netherlands. It now employs over two thousand workers, manages fifty-four hotels with 9,244 rooms, plus 722 bungalows and townhouses, and received 460,000 visitors in 1996. Cubanacán's earnings grew 32.3 percent in 1997 and it is increasing the number of rooms to thirteen thousand by the year 2000 and has representatives in nine branches in Europe, Canada, and Latin America.

Cubanacán's occupancy rate runs from acceptable to excellent: Club Varadero 90 percent, Meliá-Cohiba 72 percent, and Tryp Cayo Coco 65 percent, for example. Among the hotels with lower occupancy rates are four in Santa Lucía Beach with 54 percent (see table 7.3). Other state-run enterprises include Cadena de Hoteles Horizontes, Grupo de Turismo Gaviota (managed by the military), Grupo Hotelero Gran Caribe, and Cadena de Turismo Islazul.[12]

Foreign managers have praised Cuban workers: "They learn fast, they are polite, and their higher cultural level is a plus in their interaction with tourists." Members of the Communist Party are sought after by hotel managers, who prefer them for their "discipline and work ethic." At Sol Palmeras the number of workers belonging to the party or the Union of Communist Youth rose from 30 percent to 50 percent in three years.

Labor costs in Cuban hotels are higher than in Latin America, but lower than in developed nations. In Cuba, labor costs represent 12 percent of total costs, compared to 3 percent in Brazil but 40 percent in the United States and Spain. Still, the state sector has tried to adopt some of the joint ventures' managerial practices. Cuban managers are demanding the flexibility afforded foreign management to hire and fire at will. They requested from the labor ministry an adjustment to working regulations to meet international standards and to become more competitive. Among the government-associated domestic employers, Cubanacán has already moved in that direction.

Table 7.3. Cubanacán's Leading Hotels, 1997

Location	Number of Hotels	Rooms/Bungalows/Town houses*
Havana	9	1,215r, 326b, 70th
Varadero Beach	8	2,799r, 290b
Cayo Coco Beach	2	965r
Santa Lucía Beach	4	1,076r
Guardalavaca Beach	5	981r, 36b
Baconao Park	6	803r
Santiago de Cuba	2	363r
Chivirico	2	232r
Marea del Portillo Beach	2	270r
Total Locations: 9	40	7,735r; 652b; 70th

*r=rooms; b=bungalows; th=town houses.

Source: "Cubanacán at Center of Tourism Boom," *CUBANEWS* 5 (December 1997): 9.

Tourism is the most dynamic sector of the Cuban economy and the main source of hard currency, surpassing even remittances from relatives living abroad, which were estimated by the United Nations Commission for Latin America and the Caribbean (ECLAC) at $800 million per year in 1995. "Since 1990, the tourism industry in Cuba has registered average annual growth of 19.3 percent while the average growth in the rest of the Caribbean has been 4.3 percent."[13] José Luis Rodríguez, minister of the economy and planning, reported that tourism revenues grew in 1997 ($1.5 billion) by approximately 12 percent from 1996 ($1.35 billion). Revenues in 1998 were expected to increase by 22 percent to $1.8 billion. (See fig. 7.1.) The government reported that the cost for each dollar spent by tourists increased from 69 cents to 71 in 1997. Some independent sources have "estimated final net tourism revenues to be in the range of . . . 30 to 40 percent of the annual growth in income."[14]

The number of tourists increased 72.8 percent from 1989 (314,900) to 1993 (544,100) and has continued growing since. There were 617,300 tourists in 1994, 740,000 in 1995, and 1.1 million in 1996. Some 1.2 million tourists were expected in 1997, and close to 2 million by the year 2000. Since 1996, Cuba has become one of few places in the Caribbean area receiving over 1 million tourists a year, the others being Mexico, Puerto Rico, the Dominican Republic, the Bahamas, and Jamaica. With the exception of Cuba, which Washington forbids American tourists to visit, and the Dominican Republic, where Americans constitute only 20 per-

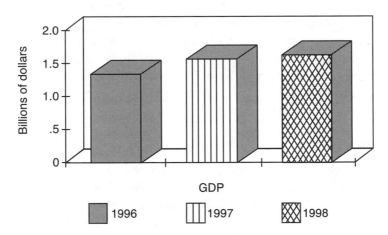

Fig. 7.1. Tourist Industry's Gross Revenues, 1996–1998.
SOURCE: "Economic Report for 1997 Finds GDP Grew 2.5 Percent. Forecast Is Gloomy," in *CUBANEWS*, 8.

cent of tourists, between 65 and 80 percent of all tourists in the region are from the United States.[15]

In 1994 Canada had the highest number of tourists visiting Cuba (109,700), followed by Italy (66,100), Spain (62,000), Germany (60,200), Mexico (48,900), Argentina (36,400), France (33,900), and United Kingdom (25,400). Europe represented the highest group, 300,800 (48.8 percent), followed by the Americas, 268,500 (43.5 percent), Cubans living abroad, 37,200 (6 percent), and Africa, Asia, and Oceania, 10,700 (1.7 percent).[16]

In 1996 the order of nationalities changed somewhat: Italians were number one, followed by Canadians, Spanish, Germans, and French. Also, tourists from Russia and Yugoslavia were being attracted through joint-destination packages with Jamaica. Gross earnings from tourism in 1995 were $1.1 billion, increasing in 1996 to $1.3 billion, or 18 percent. By then one of the main problems affecting tourism was building new rooms to keep pace with the increase in arrivals. Cuba's total hotel room capacity in 1997 was estimated at 27,000, but the government announced that it was planning to build, with foreign investors, fifteen new hotels with more than 6,000 rooms. Analysts speculated correctly that tourism would soon replace sugar as the country's most important source of hard currency.[17]

Forty-eight airlines are now flying to Cuba from twenty-seven countries. Cubana de Aviación, the national airline, carried 30 percent of all passengers in 1996. About half of all tourists arrive in Havana and about a fourth in Varadero beach. Both airports have been expanded in anticipation of larger numbers of tourists arriving in coming years. The Varadero airport, inaugurated in 1989 with capacity to accommodate 700,000 tourists, now has a capacity of two million annual visitors. A new six-lane highway seventeen kilometers long connects the city of Havana with its airport.[18]

Defending Tourism from Saboteurs

A series of terrorist bombings in 1997 in international hotels and restaurants, aimed at disrupting the successful tourist industry, increased the regime's concern for stricter control of house subletting. An explosion in a Havana hotel in June was followed by a deactivated bomb in the resort city of Varadero. These were the first terrorist attacks of this kind since the 1960s. In September three bombs went off within ten minutes at Havana's Tritón, Chateau Miramar, and Copacabana hotels, located in the Miramar residential district, killing an Italian-Canadian tourist, Fabio di Celmo, and causing extensive damage at the three hotels. A bomb exploded in the well-known Havana restaurant La Bodeguita del Medio. In a period of five months nine explosions or attempted bombings were reported in Havana and Varadero.[19]

Though initially silent, after the second bombing the government claimed to have proof that such criminal actions had been directed from the United States in an attempt to sabotage the tourist industry and the country's economic recovery.[20] The bombing spree signaled the resurgence of terrorism by radical anti-Castro Cuban-American groups in southern Florida and elsewhere and called into question the effectiveness of Cuban state security. Certainly, the increasing number of foreign tourists (1.2 million by October 1997) made it more difficult to sustain the security and controls exercised before. The regime's dilemma was that displaying the police excessively to stop further attacks was not attractive to foreign visitors. But given the ongoing terrorist campaign, the security apparatus had to move diligently to protect international tourists and the tourist industry.[21]

A member of the Counterintelligence Division at the interior ministry announced that a "self-confessed mercenary," the Salvadoran national Raúl Ernesto Cruz León, had been arrested and charged with carrying out a half dozen of the recent bomb attacks on hotels and restaurants.[22] Another Salvadoran, Otto René Rodríguez Llerena, was arrested and charged with "setting off a bomb in the upscale Meliá-Cohiba [hotel] and of attempting to import explosives for attacks on historical sites." Following imposition of the death sentence for both Salvadorans by Cuban tribunals in 1999, a campaign ensued in El Salvador and elsewhere seeking to spare their lives.

Supporting Cuba's claim of a terrorist conspiracy behind the bombings, an investigation conducted by the *Miami Herald* concluded:

> A spate of bombings in Cuba this summer was the work of a ring of Salvadoran car thieves and armed robbers directed and financed by Cuban exiles in El Salvador and Miami . . . The ring's leader is Francisco Chávez, son of an arms dealer with close ties to Cuban exiles and a pistol-packing ruffian who apparently was in Havana just hours before the first bomb exploded at the luxury Meliá-Cohiba hotel . . . But the Salvadorans were only delivery boys for the bombs, paid and taught to assemble the explosives by a Cuban exile—a tight-lipped, superbly disciplined man in his 30s who has partici-

pated in several of the anti-Castro operations in Central and South America . . . And it was Luis Posada Carriles, a veteran of the Cuban exiles' secret war against President Fidel Castro and explosive expert in his 60s, who was the key link between El Salvador and the South Florida exiles who raised $15,000 for the operation.[23]

Paradoxically, this was happening when Havana was being renovated to improve its image with international tourists—Havana and Varadero are the main tourist attractions. Besides giving the capital city a facelift, the government provided safer housing for tenants of eighty thousand dilapidated buildings. More than half of the houses in Havana were "in pretty bad shape," admitted a party official. The poor housing conditions added pressure to enforcement of immigration and housing regulations in the nation's capital.

The Army and the Economy

The Revolutionary Armed Forces (FAR) under the direction of the minister of defense, General of the Army Raúl Castro, today play an enlarged role in the economy in tourism, livestock, industry, and agriculture. Besides seeking self-financing to reduce military expenses from the national budget, FAR's economic involvement has the objective of "guaranteeing the availability of weapons in their modern [military] installations."[24]

However, expanding the FAR beyond a military role could result in a diminished readiness to provide for the nation's external and internal security, according to a Miami University North-South Center scholar:

> The challenges posed by the military's expanded participation in the domestic economy since the late 1980s may prove to be the most difficult for the institution to surmount. Unlike its other missions . . . its participation in the economy entails a high profile, pro-active role. Despite the benefits that the FAR may accrue by virtue of its economic role, the limits to gain in productive efficiency suggest that success may not necessarily correlate with the force's preparation and efforts, even though the prestige of the institution may be on the line . . . In addition to the overarching aims of achieving self-sufficiency and self-financing and maintaining combat capabilities, the specific tasks included the FAR's development of fish farming as a renewable food source and of "green medicine" to reduce reliance on foreign imports. Such tasks are assigned in addition to the

FAR's extensive efforts to achieve continuing gains in the production of military industries and agriculture at a time of shrinking resources.[25]

Originating during the 1960s when the Cuban revolution was exported to Latin America and other areas, the long-held fear in some regional capitals that the island's military preparedness signaled a threat to neighboring countries no longer exists. The U.S. military strategic planners have said so publicly, recognizing how much the economic crisis has affected the country's military forces.

General Charles Wilhelm of the U.S. Marines, head of the U.S. southern command, now operating out of Miami after being transferred from Panama, was quoted by the *Miami Herald* in 1998 as saying that the Cuban armed forces had been "dramatically reduced" since the collapse of the Soviet Union in 1991, dropping from about 130,000 well-trained active forces a decade ago to about half that size today. Wilhelm continued:

> The number of reserve troops also has been cut significantly, most of the armed forces' equipment is unusable, and the number of airworthy tactical aircraft is "very small, significantly less than it used to be. [Cuba's military] has no capability whatsoever to project itself beyond [its own borders], so it's really no threat to anyone around it . . . 70 percent of the armed forces' effort is involved in their own self-sustainment, in things like agricultural pursuits . . . it doesn't even begin to resemble the Cuban armed forces we contemplated in the '80s. [Also, there is] no evidence that President Fidel Castro's government tolerates drug smuggling through the island."[26]

Retired marine general John Sheehan, the highest ranking American military man to visit Cuba since 1959, also described the Cuban military after a visit to the island as strictly "defensive" and conveyed publicly "Castro's own vow to do nothing to embarrass President Clinton."[27]

But political pressure by conservative Cuban Americans on issues related to Cuba continued unabated. After requesting a report from Secretary of Defense William Cohen about Cuba's military capabilities, Democratic Senator Bob Graham of Florida requested a revision of the report after it had concluded that there was no military threat to the United States coming from Cuba. Opting against the Defense Intelligence Agency and the Pentagon, Cohen asked for revisions of the report under pressure from "a politically potent constituency in Florida and elsewhere that identifies Cuba as a regional menace years after it lost its Soviet patronage and its economy imploded."[28]

There is a stark contrast between how the economy and the armed forces operated in 1985 and 1995. In 1985 Cuba's GNP was $40,460 million in constant 1995 dollars ($4,014 per capita), and out of a population of 10.1 million, the armed forces numbered 297,000 (29.5 soldiers for every 1,000 citizens)—rather high for the country's size. Also, defense expenditures totaled $1,830 million in constant 1995 dollars ($182 dollars per person and 4.5 percent of GNP). By 1995 the picture was quite different. The GNP stood at $22,550 million (estimate) in constant 1995 dollars ($2,068 per capita), and out of a population of 10.9 million the armed forces numbered 70,000 (6.4 soldiers for every 1,000 citizens)—a proper number for the country. Defense expenditures totaled $350 million (estimate) in constant 1995 dollars ($32 dollars per citizen and 1.6 percent of the GNP).

The size of the armed forces and of defense expenditures mirrored the country's economic reality in 1985 and 1995. In 1985 Cuba had higher military expenditures and larger armed forces even though it could rely on military assistance from the Soviet Union. By contrast, in 1995 national security was safeguarded with military personnel numbering less than a fourth (23.5 percent) of the former total, with less than a fifth (19.1 percent) of former expenditures, and with only 21.6 percent of the rate of soldiers for every 1,000 citizens that it had previously had. Also, the 1995 GNP was 55.7 percent of what it had been ten years earlier, and the GNP per capita was 51.5 percent of the former rate. Thus, after provoking a major crisis in the Cuban economy, the collapse of the Soviet Union helped to bring some proportion to Cuba's defense expenditures. It also enhanced FAR's economic role during the special period without visibly jeopardizing the island's national security. (See table 7.4.)

General Ulises Rosales del Toro, then FAR's chief of staff, was in charge of eight economic directorates, while Division General Julio Casas Regueiro supervised the specialist staff. FAR's commercial structure involves eight directorates, including different enterprises and activities: (1) Gaviota—hotels, tourism, marketing, investments, real estate development; (2) Almacenes Universales—free zones, industrial areas, storage; (3) Construcciones Antex—construction, real estate; (4) Industriales —power projects, telecommunications; (5) Banca Metropolitana—financial operations; (6) Turquino, Manatí Plan, Granjas Integrales, and Ejército Juvenil del Trabajo (EJT, the Youth Working Army)—the agribusiness sector; (7) Tecnotex/Trenoimport—export and import of jobs and services, civilian and military transport; and (8) Tiendas de Recuperación de

Table 7.4. Cuban Military Expenditures, Armed Forces, Population, ME/GNP Percentage, 1985–1995

Year	Military Expenditure (ME)*		Armed Forces	Gross National Product (GNP)		People	ME/GNP	ME per capita	Armed Forces (per 1,000 people)	GNP per capita
	Current[a]	Constant 1995[a]**	Thousands	Current[b]	Constant 1995[b]**	Millions	%	Constant 1995	Soldiers	Constant 1995**
1985	1,335	1,830	297	29,520	40,460	10.1	4.5	182	29.5	4,014
1986	1,307	1,744	297	31,240	41,940	10.2	4.2	172	29.2	4,127
1987	1,306	1,690	297	33,700	43,620	10.2	3.9	165	29.0	4,260
1988	1,350	1,685	297	34,720	43,350	10.3	3.9	163	28.7	4,195
1989	1,377	1,650	297	35,460	42,490	10.4	3.9	158	28.5	4,070
1990	1,400	1,609	297	33,690	38,720	10.5	4.2	153	28.1	3,672
1991	1,160E	1,282E	297	26,950	29,780	10.6	4.3	120	27.9	2,798
1992[c]	NA	NA	175	23,850	25,650	10.7	NA	NA	16.3	2,392
1993	600E	629E	175	21,460	22,500	10.8	2.8	58	16.2	2,086
1994	600E	615E	140	22,000	22,550	10.8	2.7	57	12.9	2,079
1995	350E	350E	70	22,550	22,550	10.9	1.6	32	6.4	2,068

*In millions of dollars.

**In constant 1995 dollars.

[a]The series omits a major share of military expenditures, including most expenditures on arms procurement.

[b]Estimate based on partial or uncertain data.

[c]Most military data unavailable in 1992.

SOURCE: World Military Expenditures and Arms Transfers (Washington, D.C.: U.S. Arms Control and Disarmament Agency, 1997), 67.

Divisas (TRDs)—dollar stores. Concentrating on economic issues in addition to having assigned military high-tech projects, the FAR has been working closely with the Chinese military, which reportedly is a "source of inspiration for the Cuban military and its approaches to economic reform."[29] (National Public Radio's *All Things Considered* reported in 1998 that the ruling Chinese Communist Party accused the Chinese military of corruption practices stemming from its economic enterprises.)

The FAR was able to finance 30 percent of its approximately 750 million-peso budget in 1995, after covering 24 percent in 1994. Continuing the downsizing of government (the military was cut in half), the FAR budget for 1996 was reduced to 701 million.[30] Raúl Castro was credited as "the star of Cuba's reform show," and in 1995 the "Cuban Armed Forces [were recognized as] the axis of transformation, interested in promoting various forms of 'reformed Castroism' while avoiding economic and social collapse, and possible civil war."[31]

Having fewer military resources is helping rather than hurting Cuba's international goals. It adds credibility to diplomatic and commercial outreach initiatives, making them more palatable to neighboring countries. That the Cuban military is being entrusted with civilian tasks reinforces such a notion. Still, the economic role played by the FAR could pose a threat to the nation. If the military proves to be more effective than civilian authorities (in some areas it already has), the temptation of applying military modalities to the civilian sector would be difficult to resist (it happened during the 1970 ten-million-ton campaign). The end product could be a pseudo-militarization of the economy during the special period. This development could adversely affect the nature of Cuban society, and, moreover, the direction of the overall process of social and political change currently under way.

Turning the Economy Around

The Cuban economy performed modestly in 1997 after rebounding vigorously in 1996; before that there had been an unassuming start in 1994, followed by a somewhat better one in 1995. In 1997, Carlos Lage, vice president of the Council of State and secretary of the Executive Committee of the Council of Ministers in charge of the economy, declared that the Cuban economy would complete the year with 2.5 percent GDP growth, as it actually did (down from 7.8 percent a year earlier). The forecast for the 1998 GDP rate, based on government estimates, was between 2.5 and

3.5 percent. In 1996 Lage had been able to give an optimistic economic report (the best for the 1990s) in spite of the Helms-Burton law, the disruptive effect of which was not felt until 1997. After the GDP's 34.8 percent fall in 1990–93 (1993 was the worst year of the special period), Cuban officials could rightly claim an overall 10 percent investment growth in such areas as housing, hotels, roads, and water works.[32]

The Economy's Upward Curve

The economy had started to rebound in 1994 with a modest 0.7 percent growth, followed by 2.5 percent in 1995 and 9.6 percent in the first half of 1996. It was expected to come down to 5 percent by the end of 1996 (the first six months are the most productive) but finally leveled off at 7.8 percent (1995 and 1997 had the same 2.5 percent growth rate). Still, the GDP increases could not sustain the 8 percent consumption increment of oil and lubricants that took place. (See table 7.5.)

The Ministry of Economy and Planning stated: "The economic transformation indicates the [beginning of the] gradual orientation of the Cuban economy toward the conditions of efficiency and competitiveness of the international economy."[33] Though by no means out of the

Table 7.5. Economic Performance, 1995–1996

Selected Economic Indicators	1995	1996
Population*	10.9	11.0
Gross Domestic Product**	13,190.0	14,218.0
Dynamics (%)		
GDP**	2.5	7.8
Labor productivity	2.7	8.5
Investment	4.2	54.0
Exports	20.0	33.0
Imports	21.0	33.3
External Debt in Convertible Currency**	10.5	10.4
Nonofficial Exchange Rate (US$)	32.1	19.2

*Population in millions.
**Gross Domestic Product, GDP, and external debt in convertible currency in billions of pesos.

Source: *Cuba: Informe Económico* (Havana: Ministerio de Economía y Planificación, 1996), 1–8; Central Bank (Havana, 1997).

Table 7.6. Gross Domestic Product by Economic Sector, 1995–1996 (in percentages)

Sectors	1995	1996
Agriculture, hunting, and fishing	4.2	17.3
Manufacturing	6.4	6.8
Construction	7.3	30.8
Tourism	20.0	30.0*

* Preliminary figures.

SOURCE: *Cuba: Informe Económico, 1996* (Havana: Ministerio de Economía y Planificación, 1996), 1–8.

woods, by 1996 Cuba had finally started to move away from the 1991–93 economic conditions, advancing slowly toward a more competitive standing. Foreign investment in joint ventures experienced significant gains, from 4.2 to 54 percent, while exports and imports had their share of gains, 20 to 33 percent and 21.1 to 33.3 percent, respectively; and labor productivity surpassed a threefold improvement, from 2.7 to 8.5 percent, which exceeded increases in median salaries.

The main sectors that contributed to the economic recovery by increasing their 1995 output in 1996 were agriculture and fishing (4.2 to 17.3 percent), manufacturing (6.4 to 7.8 percent), construction (7.3 to 30.8 percent), and tourism (20 to 30 percent). Agriculture, construction, tourism, and labor productivity also surpassed the official expected estimates (see table 7.6).

The Best Economic Year: 1996

The 1996 increase in productivity was not sustained in the following years. While the Food Program (Programa Alimentario) could claim modest results (in vegetables, tubers, rice, and fishing), sugarcane, nickel, oil refining, energy, steel, textiles, and fertilizers had substantial gains. Altogether, 1996 was the first really good year under the special period (see table 7.7).

The price paid for these gains was rather high. Very expensive short-term credits were used to finance production and keep the country's industrial structure running. The level of economic activity left no room for capital accumulation and very little for the resources needed for maintenance and repairs for the following year.

Still, the economy continued the modest recovery started in the mid-1990s. Some economic sectors increased production in 1996, exceeding

Table 7.7. Increases of Selected Sectors' Output, 1995–1996

Sectors	Metric Unit	1996	% Increase, 1996 over 1995
Sugar	MT*	4,446.0	33.6
Nickel	MT	53.6	24.9
Tobacco	MT	33.1	30.1
Rice (consumption)	MT	254.4	55.2
Viands (tubers)	MT	1,568.0	28.6
Vegetables	MT	610.3	29.9
(Gross) fishing	MT	123.9	21.1
Fertilizers	MT	259.0	20.3
Textiles	MMm^{2}**	52.5	18.0
Steel	MT	240.0	17.0
Oil refining	MT	1,863.0	31.2
Electricity	GWatt	12,002.0	5.0

*MT=metric tons
**MMm^{2}=millions of square meters.
SOURCE: *Cuba: Informe Económico, 1996* (Havana: Ministerio de Economía y Planificación, 1996), 1–8.

their already improved 1995 output. The increase in 1996 production over the previous year included such sectors as sugar (33.6 percent), oil refining (31.2 percent), tobacco (30.1 percent), nickel (24.9 percent), and rice (55.2 percent).

The 1995–96 sugar harvest (4.45 million tons) helped to improve the economic outlook. The 1994 *zafra* (sugar harvest) of only 3.3 million tons was surpassed by 33 percent, coming only 55,000 tons short of the 4.5 million target. But the 1996–97 sugar harvest decreased to 4.25 million tons and the forecast for 1997–98 was for between 3.2 and 4 million tons, probably to settle on 3.8 million tons. (See fig. 7.2.)

Besides the economic results of 1996, Lage apprised the public that the economy had shrunk so much since 1989 that it would take years of sustained growth to reach its former level.[34] The 1996–97 sugar harvest was below the previous one due to Hurricane Lili, difficulties in finding short-term financing, the high price of short-term credits available, and other factors. Short-term credits contributed to lowering the sugar harvest output, and relying on them for financing the zafra was harsh indeed. Besides being difficult to find, short-term credits were excessively expensive; interest rates ranged from 14 to 22 percent, sometimes even as high as 30 percent.

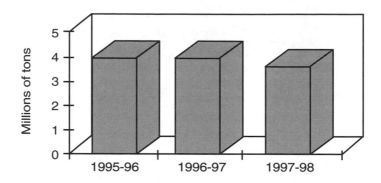

Fig. 7.2. Sugar Production, 1995–1998.
SOURCE: "Economic Report for 1997 Finds GDP Grew 2.5 Percent. Forecast Is Gloomy," in *CUBANEWS,* 7.

Impact of the Helms-Burton Act

In 1997 the Helms-Burton Act made it difficult to find credits. According to Lage, "$200 million worth of financing for the sugar harvest [was] not delivered because of the Helms-Burton law . . . Cuba [had] to pay $1.42 worth of debt to obtain every fresh dollar of credit with which to pay for vital fuel imports." The government admitted that the low 1996–97 sugar production level had practically "crippled the island's capacity to obtain foreign financing."[35]

Economists speculated that poor sugar harvests at high costs were compounding the financial and budgetary deficits afflicting the economy. While the cost of the 1996 sugar harvest was marked at $1,477.31 million, its estimated market value was only $1,202.77 million (a $274.5 million loss, 18.5 percent); likewise, the cost of the 1997 sugar harvest was marked at $1,350.47 million and the estimated market value was $1,011.9 million (a $338.5 million loss, 25 percent). Together these harvests created a combined loss of $613 million (21.6 percent of actual production costs). Low sugarcane yields and costly operations by sugar UBPCs exacerbated the difficult economic conditions. Production figures published in *Trabajadores* revealed the reasons behind the growing concern with the sugar industry: "Cane and sugar cannot result in losses, they cannot keep being a burden [to the economy]."[36]

Washington's economic campaign against Cuba was taking its toll. Economic minister Rodríguez revealed publicly that "the net external financing fell 'notably' . . . [and the Helms-Burton Act was felt] more than expected." The president of the Economic Affairs Committee of the National Assembly recognized that the sugar deficit had delivered a blow to the economy. A self-reinforcing cycle took over sugar production: expensive financial sources lowered production, lower sugar harvest outputs made it more difficult to find better financing, and so on, all of which had the adverse effect of slowing down the economic recovery program.

Still, different financial arrangements were pursued. Sugar barter was one alternative. It involved arrangements usually lasting up to four months and concentrated on oil and grains in return for sugar. This exchange attracted companies like the Swiss-Dutch Vitol, the Anglo-Swiss Glencore, and the French Soufflet. But a larger modality involved making investors responsible for financing all or part of the sugar harvest of an entire province. In 1996, arrangements of this type totaled $190 million, including such investors as ED&F Man, of England, at $50 million; ING Bank, the Netherlands, $30 million; Bilbao Vizcaya Bank, Spain, $30 million; Sucres et Denrées, France, $20 million; Indosuez Bank, France, $20 million; Glencore, Anglo-Swiss, $20 million; Vitol, Swiss-Dutch, $15 million; and an Italian hotel company that loaned the remaining $5 million. Financing the island's sugar industry was a financier's market with the lender dictating the price and other aspects of the arrangement. According to a journalist writing from Paris: "Financiers . . . have significantly more leverage with Havana than previously, and have become much more demanding since Cuba is limited in finding sources of financing . . .Investors are now able to dictate just what parcels of land they want to finance, what quantity of sugar they want to produce, what ports they want to use, and more."[37]

Cuba has had a difficult time negotiating better terms, for compelling reasons. Havana's failure to service its hard currency debt since 1986 created the present financial malaise. Not being a member of the International Monetary Fund and the World Bank was another reason, but its effect was aggravated further by the U.S. economic sanctions, which virtually blocked access to most international lenders. Cuba also had problems shedding its risky investment image, so the financiers willing to do business were taking advantage by charging exorbitant prices.

The External Debt

Foreign debt in convertible currency—not including the debt to the former Soviet Union and Eastern Europe (estimated at $28 billion and $2.7 billion in 1993, respectively)—amounted to $10.4 billion in 1996, a 15.3 percent increase over the $9.1 billion of 1994 but a decrease of 0.3 percent from 1995, when it had totaled $10.5 billion (see table 7.8). The short-term debt category in the suppliers' credits category was reduced by almost $1.2 billion in 1996, from the $2.4 billion it had been a year earlier. Cuba's failure to service the debt since 1986 was a major cause of today's financial difficulties.

In 1996 the external debt was structured under three different categories: bilateral (government to government), 57.7 percent; financial institutions, 25.2 percent; and individual lenders, 11.4 percent (81 percent of the debt belonged to the principal and 19 percent to interests). With 61 percent concentrated in five nations, country creditors followed this order: Japan 15.7 percent, Argentina 12.8 percent, Spain 12.1 percent, France 10.2 percent, the United Kingdom 9.8 percent, Italy 4.9 percent, Mexico 4.4 percent, Switzerland 2.6 percent, Germany 2.2 percent, and Austria 2.1 percent; other countries accounted for 23.2 percent.

The external debt problem started after 1979; before that the nation's financial prospect was quite positive. Havana had received credits from Western market economies satisfactorily during the 1970s, but in 1979 and throughout the 1980s its finances had worsened. In addition to falling sugar prices, the fall in the price of oil affected Cuba badly—profits from reselling Soviet oil that was destined for Cuba but was not used domestically declined sharply. The devaluation of the dollar compounded the predicament, so that profits from reselling Soviet oil plummeted further. Then, besides adverse climatic conditions, Washington's economic embargo and sanctions were reinforced.

After rescheduling convertible currency debt payments in 1984 and 1985, with short-term credits totaling $2.4 billion, Cuba failed to make payments in 1986. When a second round of negotiations rescheduling the debt was rejected by international bankers (after the governments involved had accepted it), Cuba failed to make payments again. This made it extremely difficult to retain the national credit in good standing; after that, Havana practically lost access to short- and long-term credits available to others. The short-term solution had been to increase trade and financial arrangements with the Soviet bloc. However, the demise of European socialism and the lack of trade partners or any financial compensation exposed Cuba to the international markets in the worst possible conditions. An industrial structure based on dated European socialist technology and chronic managerial and labor productivity deficiencies aggravated the problem further. Cuba's falling prey to lenders charging

Table 7.8. Foreign Debt in Convertible Currency, Assorted Years (in billions of dollars)

Year	Debt	Variance	
1982	$2.91		
1993	$7.80	+ $4.9	(167.6 percent)
1994	$9.08	+ $1.3	(16.4 percent)
1995	$10.50	+ $1.4	(15.6 percent)
1996	$10.46	- $39.5	(.3 percent)

SOURCE: Julio Carranza Valdés, "Cuba: Las Finanzas Externas y los Límites del Crecimiento," *Viento Sur* [online, http://www.nodo50.ix.apc.org/viento-sur, February, 1998]; A. R. M. Ritter, "Financial Aspects of Normalizing Cuba's International Relations: The Debt and Compensation Issues," in *Transition in Cuba: New Challenges for U.S. Policy* (Miami: Florida International University, U.S. Department of State, and U.S. Agency for International Development, n.d.), 501–61, esp. 550.

exorbitant prices was not an accident—it was a disaster waiting to happen.

With only short-term financing and import credits available, the amortization of the external debt could be made through debt-for-equity trades or purchasing Cuban goods. In the 1990s the debt with Mexico was reduced in a trade deal exchanging investments in the construction materials and telecommunications sectors for debt reduction. The Mexico-Cuba trading agreement took place around the time when prices in the domestic market had been increased to reduce the money supply growth to improve internal finances and to restore purchasing power to the peso. The effect was positive. It reduced the escalating curve that correlated the external debt with the GDP measured in percentages of actual (consumer goods) prices: 1990, 34 percent; 1991, 52.1 percent; 1992, 58.2 percent; 1993, 47.3 percent; 1994, 48.5 percent; and 1995, 46.5 percent.

Cuba has paid a high price for the economic gains of the 1990s. Lacking domestic capital and having management and labor deficiencies, it has found the shortage of available credits and the high prices they command to be obstacles to uplifting the economy. Still, with characteristic bravado, Cuba made public that it would not accept being treated differently from any other nation. Such hard posturing was sometimes used before starting negotiations, but given Cuba's financial and economic position, it did not improve the terms demanded by lenders.[38] Even after payments were made on time in 1996, interest rates charged in 1997 were still high. (President Castro rated them close to 16.6 percent.) Former sugar minister Nelson Torres announced that $300 million in foreign loans needed to purchase imports like fertilizers for the 1997 sugar harvest had been obtained, but they were $30 million short of the original target.

The most important arrangement dealing with the external debt happened in 1998, when a rescheduling agreement was signed with Japan. The reorganization of the debt ($769 million, involving 182 companies and $1 billion to the government from bilateral trade) unlocked a trade potential that had been suppressed for over a decade. The Havana-Tokyo agreement could serve as a model for rescheduling Cuba's debt with other creditors, which would provide greater access to international lending under better terms.

The Havana-Tokyo agreement divided the debt into two parts of $384 million each, with repayment spread over twenty years. During the first five years, Cuba will only service one half of the debt (paying interest), but after five years it will make payments including interest and principal. Payments for the second half will start in ten years with interest and principal included. Trade between the two countries in 1998 amounted to only $115 million, but in 1975 it had totaled $2.07 billion. Throughout the 1960s and 1970s there was active commercial exchange between Havana and Tokyo, but it declined once Cuba stopped making payments in 1987. The "[Havana-Tokyo] agreement might have emerged from increased contacts between Cuba and Japan as a result of the 1996–1997 hostage crisis at the Japanese ambassador's residence in Lima [Peru]," and from Cuba's offer to play a mediating role to end the hostage crisis.[39]

Granma announced the "bilateral rescheduling of debt with Japan . . . [as] a new step in [the] reactivation of the Cuban economy." The minister of the Central Bank said that "having a normally developing financial and commercial situation with the world's second economy is of great significance for the country."[40] Still, the commitment to make payments for old debts is a burden that only a very well managed economy can afford.

Japan also approved two small aid projects in public health. One plan ($69,300) will provide six thousand units of insulin to children with diabetes, to be distributed through the Catholic organization Caritas. The second project ($9,105) was arranged through the French organization Doctors of the World and will distribute medication to combat sexually transmitted diseases. The deputy minister of foreign investment and economic collaboration thanked the Japanese government for its generosity and the nongovernmental organizations for collaborating in carrying out the humanitarian programs.[41]

Trade: Gains and Deficits

The years 1995 and 1996 were good ones for resuscitating commercial exchanges. There was a turnaround starting in 1994 from the low reached in 1993. The downward trend from 1991 ($7,255 million) to 1993 ($3,315 million) had totaled 45.7 percent. But in 1994 ($3,520 million), trade grew again by 6.1 percent, springing forward in 1995 ($4,430 million) by 25.8 percent, and continuing the upward trend in 1996 ($5,220 million) by 17.8 percent. While trade in 1996 still was $2,035 million below that of 1991 (28 percent), it also was $1,905 million (57 percent) above that of 1993.[42]

The downside of the trade recovery was that trade deficits were building up with imports exceeding exports, which worsened the cash crunch facing the economy. To Minister of the Economy Rodríguez, foreign trade deficits had been accumulating and escalating for several years, with exports repeatedly lower than imports, while "heavy reliance on short-term financing was 'feeding a growing debt'." Looking for solutions to mounting problems, Rodríguez said: "The real solution for our shortage of hard currency will be found in the revenue that we are capable of generating and the costs that we are able to reduce in our own economy [not in borrowing money at exorbitant prices]."[43]

The trade deficit estimate reported by Havana was higher than the Cuban deficit reported by Washington (see table 7.9). While the reports overlap in 1994–96, the U.S. report includes the years 1991–93, which are not included in Havana's report. Cuba includes 1997 but the U.S. tally does not, being usually a year late. Washington reported the trade deficit for 1991–96 in million of dollars as: 1991, -125; 1992, -150; 1993, -665; 1994, -590; 1995, -1,180; and 1996, -1,190 (the deficit for 1996 is 89.5 percent higher than 1991). The Cuban government reported the trade deficit for 1994–96, also in millions of dollars, as: 1994, -686 ($96 million or 13.9 percent more than in the U.S. report); 1995, -$1,140 ($230 million more than U.S. report, 16.4 percent); and 1996, -1,600 ($410 million more than U.S. report, 25.6 percent). Whatever figures are used, the conclusion is the same: accumulating trade deficits obstructs economic recovery.

From 1991 to 1994, fuels represented over a third of all imports—from 33.6 percent to 37.6 percent—but they declined in 1995 and 1996 to 29.7 percent and 30.2 percent, respectively. Even after Russia resumed being a provider of fuel (at market prices), the high cost of energy contributed to the financial problems affecting Cuba today.[44]

An important development with great potential for foreign investment and growth was the inauguration in 1997 of two free trade zones

Table 7.9. Cuba and U.S. Reports on Cuban Foreign Trade Deficit, 1991–1997 (in millions of U.S. dollars)

Cuban Report		U.S. Report			
Year	Trade Deficit	Year	Trade Deficit		
1991	NA	1991	-125		
1992	NA	1992	-150		
1993	NA	1993	-665		
1994	-686	1994	-590	96 less	(13.9%)
1995	-1,400	1995	-1,180	220 less	(15.7 %)
1996	-1,600	1996	-1,190	410 less	(25.6 %)
1997	-2,300	1997	NA		

SOURCE: José Luis Rodríguez, *Report on the Economic Results for 1997*, cited in *CUBANEWS* 6 (January 1998): 6–9; *Cuba: Handbook of Trade Statistics, 1997* (Washington, D.C.: U.S. Directorate of Intelligence, 1997), 1.

near Havana, in Wajay and Berroa, together known as Zona Franca Ciudad Habana (City of Havana Free Trade Zone). Close to one hundred foreign firms have received licenses to operate in them. The foreign trade minister stated that they represent "one more option for foreign investors." Two more free trade zones were scheduled for 1998 in Mariel and Cienfuegos.[45]

Conclusions

Besides some success in stopping the economic downslide, Cuba has learned how difficult it is to extricate itself from the special period. The problems hindering economic recovery include finding adequate sources of credit and financing and reducing imports, which keep increasing the external debt. The Helms-Burton Act is also aggravating the financial situation. "After three years of modest economic growth, problems with [financing] Cuba's sugar harvest, a growing trade deficit and foreign debt [were] making Havana officials worry about a slowdown [by 1997–98]."[46]

Another reason for an economic slowdown is low sugar production, which is caused by the tardiness of financial agreements and the delays in starting the sugar harvest. Low sugar harvests may offset the gains in tourism and other sectors and lead the regime into uncharted territory of economic reform. As stated in the 1997 report of the Economic Commission for Latin America and the Caribbean:

The advances made during the transitional evolution carry with them the need for adopting new forms and instruments to conduct the economy. The market would occupy a major role in coordinating the economy and would gradually replace in different sectors the prevailing quantitative planning modality. Because of this, the development of new state mechanisms of macroeconomic control and distribution should not be delayed. According to this logic—which Cuba has seemingly embraced—initially there would be an attempt to build some kind of socialist economy with market elements that the Cuban government does not identify with the traditional concept of market socialism. At any rate, the future would not be trapped by the traditional dichotomies of classical capitalism or socialism. There are other ways, as proven by the balance made between efficiency, equity and growth in Northern Europe—with Sweden representing such a paradigm—in the Asian Pacific countries from China and Vietnam to the four dragons (Hong Kong, the Chinese province of Taiwan, the Korean Republic and Singapore), or in Costa Rica and Chile, in Latin America.[47]

Havana is evaluating an array of modalities available, looking for its own socialist blueprint. It will have to decide on the extent of self-employment and small or medium-sized private business and the future of foreign investment.[48] Havana should adopt a pricing policy that, coupled with ending subsidies to unprofitable enterprises, could end budgetary deficits. Also, improving managerial performance, labor productivity, and quality production would make exports more competitive in international markets.

Cuba should allow native entrepreneurial talent to flourish in some commercial sectors (beyond today's self-employment), permitting an individualized outlet in areas where government or foreign investors have shown no initiative. It is advantageous for the government to regain full capacity as social services provider (in education, medicines and medical equipment, employment, etc.) rather than letting nongovernmental organizations (like Caritas and others) do it and having their social standing rise at the government's expense. This situation could be more troublesome politically than allowing a few people to have economic independence by making a living outside governmental control.

Similar to the changes enforced in response to the special period, the final features of Cuban socialism would reflect the physiognomy of a country changed by a major revolution. But they would also mirror the contingencies that limited the latitude of change during the 1990s. Cuba has been encircled by internal and external demands and pressures curtailing its political and economic choices, though not to the extent that the final product will be less than a truly democratic socialist system.

British economist Ken Cole, acknowledging the prevalence of politics over economics as well as the intermingling of political and economic policy in Cuba, puts it this way:

> A socialist development strategy for Cuba, while being founded upon a coherent socialist economic strategy, implies a re-activation and extension of political participation through *Poder Popular* [Organs of People's Power]. Socialist participation, and the extension of freedom, is contingent upon an economic surplus, allowing a diminution of "labor determined by expediency and external necessity." The Special Period in Time of Peace, with the emphasis on austerity and sharing shortages, is not a context conducive to socialist development. But, given the rationale of the Rectification Campaign, to reassert the "political" over the "economic," as the economy picks up . . ., increasingly there will be opportunities to extend the process of socialist development, which is fundamentally a political question, although based upon a socialist economic strategy.[49]

III

The External Environment

Cuban-U.S. Relations under
President Clinton: Part I

The Cold War That Never Ends

Russia profited from the end of the Cold War. President Boris Yeltsin attended the 1997 summit of highly industrialized countries as a full member and was invited to join the Paris Club, an international group of lenders.[1] In reciprocity, Yeltsin agreed to have former Soviet bloc members join NATO.[2] Why then has the Havana-Washington conflict worsened? Could it be that while Cuba had been entangled in the East-West conflict, the "Castro problem" was not truly rooted in the Cold War but in America's ambitions to keep the island within its sphere of influence?[3]

A Cuban scholar, Esteban Moralos Domínguez, noted.

The Cuba–United States conflict, or what is known today as the bilateral differential, did not start in 1959. It suffices to examine the thought of Cuba's main independence leaders, José Martí and Antonio Maceo, to realize that the most advanced political ideas since the mid-nineteenth century reflected the extant conditions between a Cuba that struggled to free itself from Spain and remain independent of United States [control], and the latter's actions during the peak of its expansionist period, attempting to turn Cuba into its own new colony . . . As a matter of fact, the United States has never recognized the Cuban nation's sovereignty, which has been precisely the central factor that has united the political forces inside Cuba that fought against colonialism first, and against imperialism later . . . Therefore, to understand the aggressiveness and hostility that have characterized U.S. policy toward revolutionary Cuba for over forty years [it] is necessary to realize that for the United States any Cuban action reaffirming its sovereignty—either domestically or in foreign policy—is an illegitimate action, especially if in order to sustain its sovereignty Cuba has had to stand against American interests . . . How to solve the problem?

. . . If it were possible, it would be convenient for Cuba to forget that the United States [exists].[4]

Was the 1996 phase of the Havana-Washington conflict born of President Clinton's political ambitions? If not, why did Clinton and Castro allow their differences to escalate to such a level, more than under Presidents Reagan and Bush—especially when the initial expectations were that relations would improve under Clinton?

The second Clinton Administration's Cuba policy was more than hostile; it was aggressive and generated conflict the world over. It put the United States on a collision course with close allies and threatened established international trade practices normally supported by Washington. Meanwhile, Cuba was establishing cordial relations with as many nations as possible. In this chapter and the following one I examine this political phenomenon, attempting to shed some light on it.

One Blockade, Two Blockades

Since President Eisenhower canceled the remaining seven hundred thousand tons of the Cuban sugar quota for the American market on July 6, 1960, and on October 19 declared a trade embargo that President Kennedy extended and expanded, Cuba has lived under an embargo enforced by nine American presidents. Castro could neutralize the impact of the embargo with the support he received from the Soviet bloc, but this support ended with the demise of European socialism. Cuba lost more than economic and financial aid and most of its trade relationship. It also lost the source of the industrial and technological infrastructure provided by the Soviet bloc to sustain Cuba's economic integration into the socialist Council of Economic Assistance. Neither most Cuban exports nor Soviet bloc exports were competitive in the international market. But their poor-quality products permitted an exchange relationship among themselves. Still, the predicament following the demise of European socialism prompted Cuba to claim that it was living under two blockades.[5]

The Russian blockade has changed from what it was in the early 1990s. Ricardo Cabrisas Ruiz, Cuban minister of foreign trade, stated in Moscow in 1997 that in two or three years the exchange between the two countries could again reach the level of 1989–90, close to $3.3 billion dollars (with no subsidies involved). In 1996, trade already amounted to $988 million dollars ($523 million Cuban exports, $465 million imports from Russia), which made Russia again Cuba's first trade partner.[6] The current exchange is not limited to Cuban sugar for Russian oil. It includes

Russian machinery, spare parts, and technology. Bilateral discussions were also held about possible ways to pay Cuba's debt, which according to Moscow's Interfax agency totaled $30 billion dollars.[7]

In defiance of Washington's open opposition, Russia seemed ready to resurrect the Juraguá nuclear plant project (it was deferred indefinitely in 1998). Castro had said in 1997 that "there [was] no hope" of completing the nuclear plant in spite of the billion dollars already invested ($750 million were needed to finalize it). The Russian nuclear energy minister announced that an international consortium, under Russian leadership and including Germany, England, and Brazil, was exploring the possibility of having the project restarted. However, the spokesman for the State Department declared then that the United States would recommend to possible investors that "they'd better think twice" before committing themselves to the Juraguá project.[8]

Renewed American Hostility

The realities of the 1990s have affected Cuba adversely on many fronts. Pursuing further Castro's international isolation, Washington implemented new and harsher policies with the Cuban Democracy Act of 1992 (the Torricelli-Graham bill) and the Cuban Liberty and Democratic Solidarity Act of 1996 (the Helms-Burton bill). Clinton, first as a presidential contender against President Bush and later seeking reelection as president, was instrumental in bringing to life two of the harshest American Cuba policies ever. Clinton sought to provoke by economic strangulation an implosion like that of Eastern Europe, as long as Cuba refused to transform itself into a liberal democracy.

Several features of the Helms-Burton law, especially its extraterritorial nature, provoked strong condemnation among America's allies and trade partners. The law codified an array of executive orders, and policies accumulated in three decades by different administrations, which now require congressional action to be modified or reversed. Clinton's approval of this provision of the law amounted to a renunciation of presidential authority in such a thorny foreign policy issue as U.S.-Cuba relations.[9]

Electoral Politics vs. Foreign Policy

Cuba played a different role in the 1992 and 1996 presidential elections than it had before in American politics. President Clinton manipulated the Cuban issue to his own advantage, but at some political cost. Con-

Table 8.1. The Cuban-American Lobby. Top Recipients of Money and Major Donors, Jan. 1, 1979–Oct. 16, 1996

Top Recipients	Trustees*	PAC**	Total
Ileana Ros-Lehtinen, R-Fla .	$116,237	$7,012	$123,249
Robert Torricelli, D-N.J.	92,150	26,750	118,900
Paula Hawkins, R-Fla.	73,800	5,000	78,000
Dante Fascell, D-Fla.	41,436	33,387	74,823
Robert Menéndez, D-N.J.	52,218	20,000	72,218
Connie Mack, D-Fla.	55,252	16,000	71,252
Lincoln Díaz-Balart, D-Fla.	57,233	11,250	68,483
Ernest Hollings, D-S.C.	44,350	21,000	65,350
Jesse Helms, R-N.C.	36,697	25,000	61,697
Claude Pepper, D-Fla.	29,250	20,000	49,250
Bob Graham, D-Fla.	32,550	11,000	43,550
William Gunter, D-Fla.	34,000	5,000	39,000
Dan Burton, R-Ind.	17,900	19,750	37,650
Joseph Lieberman, D-Conn.	24,500	11,989	36,489
Larry Presler, R-S.D.	17,000	15,000	32,000
Neal Smith, D-Iowa	7,900	23,500	31,400
Rudy Boschwitz, R-Minn.	13,550	15,500	29,050
Larry Smith, D-Fla.	12,600	14,500	27,100
Alfonse D'Amato, R-N.Y.	12,000	12,000	24,000
Peter Deutsch, D-Fla.	15,146	8,000	23,246
Edward Kennedy, D-Mass.	21,800	0	21,800
Carrie Meek, D-Fla.	16,800	5,000	21,800
Orrin Hatch, R-Utah	9,020	10,250	19,270
Robert Kasten, R-Wis.	6,000	12,500	18,500
Frank Lautenberg, D-N.J.	4,500	13,600	18,100

Major Donors	Total
Más Canosa family***	$219,920
Domingo Moreira family***	135,881
Manuel Medina family***	43,830
Elena D. Amos	42,550
Pedro Adrian family	36,505
Alberto Hernández	32,750
Diego Suárez	31,000
Francisco Hernández	28,000
Carlos Portes family	27,000

*Money received from trustees of the Cuban American National Foundation (CANF).
**Money received from CANF's Free Cuba Political Action Committees.
***Among the top Cuban-American donors to political parties, besides to individual candidates, are the Más Canosa family, $49,550; Moreira family, $46,435; and Medina family, $31,000.

SOURCE: Center for Public Integrity, Washington, D.C., 1997, as cited in "Cuban American Clout" and Cynthia Corzo, "Debate por Influencia Federal de Fundación," both in *Miami Herald,* January 24, 1997.

gressional aides had labeled the Torricelli-Graham bill (the Cuban Democracy Act) a "dog" and a "throwback to the 1960s." But then-Congressman Robert Torricelli (D-N.J.), chairman of the House Subcommittee on Western Hemisphere Affairs, Senator Bob Graham (D-Fla.), and the Cuban American National Foundation leader at the time, Más Canosa—the real force behind the bill—were committed to having it become law. Torricelli, Graham, and other elected officials benefited from the support by the foundation and its leaders (soft money) for politicians and political parties who would play an anti-Castro role. The list of recipients (see table 8.1) included some unexpected names, like Senator Edward M. Kennedy (D-Mass.). And eighty-five thousand Cuban Americans settled in New Jersey helped Congressman Torricelli to get elected U.S. senator in 1996. He reciprocated by supporting the 1996 Helms-Burton Act and the 1997 legislative initiatives tightening the embargo even further (but not turning it into law) and by attending Más Canosa's funeral in 1997 as President Clinton's representative.

The Bush Administration knew that asking for international support for a Cuban embargo was contrary to American interests. As the deputy assistant secretary of state for inter-American affairs said in testimony before the House Foreign Affairs Committee, "The proposed legislation would remove the focus on Cuba and shift the burden to the United States." He added, "Our attempt would be rejected . . . few [nations] want to impose an embargo against [Cuba]." It was clear that internationalizing a hard-line Cuba policy would carry a high diplomatic cost to the United States.[10]

But in a presidential election year (1992), electoral concerns prevailed over rational decision making, and the Cuban-American lobby was determined to tighten the Cuban embargo. Florida was a big prize in the electoral contest, and Clinton understood the dilemma Bush faced: while he needed to exercise some accountability in conducting foreign policy, Bush also had to please his Cuban-American supporters, especially the influential Más Canosa.

The Road to the White House Takes You to Miami

Clinton attended a political fund-raiser in Miami's Little Havana in 1992 (raising between $125,000 and $250,000), where he came out in support of the Torricelli-Graham bill, saying, "I like it." As the *Miami Herald* put it in an article entitled "How Candidates Were Squeezed on Castro Policy": "With those three words Clinton may have done more for democratic prospects among Cuban-Americans than any previous Democrat."[11] Clinton had started the dilemma that would characterize his Cuba policy and had begun his pattern of giving in to the Cuban-American lobby. Another reason for his anti-Castro politics was that he blamed Castro for his gubernatorial reelection defeat after the rioting on June 1, 1980, by Cuban refugees interned in Fort Chaffee, Arkansas. The Cubans had arrived in the United States in the 1980 Mariel boatlift, and two thousand local residents carrying rifles and clubs had demanded to be allowed into the camp "to bash heads." Three Cubans had been hospitalized after being shot by state troopers.[12]

President Bush also gave in and signed into law the Torricelli-Graham bill just before the 1992 elections, including provisions laying the foundation for future trouble with U.S. trade partners. (Canada, Great Britain, and Mexico approved legislation that would penalize companies complying with the Cuban Democracy Act.) On April 18 Bush implemented two of its measures: "barring foreign vessels that stop at Cuban ports from entering U.S. ports" and "granting permission for people to send humanitarian aid packages directly to the island." The Bush Administration's turnaround was duly noted in the press: "In a policy flip-flop, the Bush administration has dropped its opposition to a proposal that would tighten the embargo against Cuba and penalize countries and U.S. companies abroad that trade with the island. The administration has reached agreement with the Cuban American National Foundation and key House Democrats on the proposed Cuban Democracy Act, sweeping legislation that would bar foreign subsidiaries of U.S. companies from initiating new trade with the Fidel Castro regime . . . The State Department—facing fierce objections from such important U.S. allies as Canada, Great Britain, and Spain, which host U.S. subsidiaries that do hundreds of millions of dollars of business with Cuba—had battled the measure for months."[13]

Yet, while Bush's decision was agreeable to the bill's sponsors, it was not enough to satisfy them. According to *Miami Herald* analyst Tom Fiedler, Más Canosa knew how to outmaneuver the presidential candidates by playing a "game of political one-upmanship" when at "key moments" he "both shaped policy and brilliantly played the politicians off against one another . . . President Bush, who can be quite shameless in trying to cultivate votes among Cuban Americans, [is] terrified that . . . provisions of the Torricelli-Graham bill would offend both allies abroad and several major corporations whose foreign subsidiaries [do] business with Cuba . . . [The bill] would cut off aid to any country that still trades with Cuba, or would strip away tax benefits from any U.S. company that allows its foreign subsidiaries to do so. Bush sees these elements as dangerous meddling in foreign policy." But then "Clinton stepped [in and] "professed to have no qualms about irritating allies or corporations . . . Moreover, by upstaging President Bush, he served notice that he would carry the fight to him, even in his strongest strongholds."[14]

Más Canosa, "who enjoy[ed] ready access to the highest level of power at the State Department and the man who guide[d] Cuban policy, Bernard Aronson," sat with President Bush "at a $1,000-a-plate Bush fundraiser and beamed when the president praised Más Canosa during the speech." They met again to talk about the bill but the word was out that Clinton was going to support it. President Bush was reported to have told Aronson he would "not be upstaged on Cuba by Bill Clinton." However, what Bush did not know was that his friend Más Canosa "had long been working the other side of the street in the effort to get Clinton to endorse the bill."[15]

The foundation's leader had figured out that if Clinton supported the bill publicly, President Bush would have no choice but to sign it into law, as he did. For Más Canosa it was a political triumph to treasure, because he had learned how to tailor America's Cuba policy to his own wishes. Pat Jordan of the *Los Angeles Times* quoted Más Canosa as saying, "I was a political exile . . . not an economic immigrant. I thought I'd return in a few months, in a year or two . . . I love America . . . I would die for it. I'd never have been so successful in Cuba. But people like me need to be fed with more than success. I have all the money I'll ever need. I don't do this for money. I do this because I feel like a tree without roots."[16] The 1992 article described Más Canosa as:

> a sometimes brooding, soft-featured man who sees the world in terms of conspiracies that only he can unravel. He drives a bomb-proof Mercedes-Benz 560 SEL and is known to carry a loaded .357 magnum in his briefcase. He debugs his house every few months. He is not afraid to act physically to defend a real or imagined slight. A few years ago he punched out his younger brother Ricardo over a business matter. Ricardo sued Más for libel and won a judgment of more than a million dollars . . . Más . . . established "a very profitable business" of installing telephone lines for Southern Bell, one that . . . made him a millionaire ten times over. But more important, to him anyway, it [gives] him access to the corridors of power, especially in Washington, where he is known as "the Lone Ranger" . . . Más has a fascination with Israel. Israel was founded by men who were called "terrorists" until they assumed power and, miraculously, became "statesmen." It's a transition that he and other exiles

would like to make in Cuba. He is also fascinated by the subtle way the Israeli lobby in America has pressured this country to support Israel, by linking its survival with American ideals of freedom and democracy. He . . . learned from that lobby that it is more important to have access to congressmen and senators than speedboats and missile launchers. He . . . tried, not always with success, to make that transition himself, from a man of action to a man who wields influence behind the seats of power.[17]

In his characteristic style, Más also denied that the United States would take over Cuba if Castro fell. As he said in an interview with Madrid's *El Pais:* "That is bullshit. [Americans] haven't even been able to take over Miami! If we have kicked them out of here, how could they possibly take over our own country?"[18]

The Torricelli-Graham Bill Becomes Law

The Cuban Democracy Act (Torricelli-Graham bill) was finally signed in Miami by President Bush on October 23, 1992, at a political rally to which Congressman Torricelli was not invited. For all the trouble and scheming that went on, the election results must have been disappointing to President Clinton. President Bush received 75 percent of the Cuban-American vote, Clinton close to 20 percent, and Ross Perot 5 percent. Bush won the state of Florida by a 2 percent margin, eighty thousand votes. As a political analyst said, "You could make an argument that the large amount of [Hispanic votes Bush] won helped him carry the state." Democratic leaders were disappointed; they had expected that Clinton would receive at least 25 percent of the Cuban-American vote.[19]

Sales mostly of food and medicines by American subsidiaries had been tolerated since President Gerald Ford had allowed them in 1975. In 1980–89 trade between Cuba and U.S. subsidiaries totaled $2.6 billion, involving 1,236 U.S. companies in twenty-four countries. In 1989 alone the trade reached $332 million: $169 million in imports by Cuba and $162 million in Cuban exports, mostly naphtha, sugar, tobacco, and molasses.[20] After defeating amendments exempting the sale of food, medicines, and medical equipment, the House approved the Cuban Democracy Act, which included these provisions:

Barring foreign subsidiaries of American companies from
   trading with Cuba and denying parent companies the right
   to claim tax deductions for any trade with the island.
Making ineligible any country providing assistance to Cuba to

receive American aid, debt forgiveness, or free trade arrangements (unless the president would grant an exception).

Fining any American citizen visiting Cuba illegally up to fifty
thousand dollars, in addition to criminal charges (those
engaged in news gathering, research, disseminating information, or religious or human rights activities were exempted).

Barring the sale of medicines and medical equipment unless
the president could verify by "on-site inspections and other
appropriate means" that the items were not resold abroad or
misused; continuing barring the sale of food, with the
exception of private donations.

Authorizing the president to enhance telephone communications and direct mail service with Cuba.[21]

The prohibition against selling medicines and medical supplies appeared to be ending in mid-1997, when reportedly Havana and Washington had agreed that the Roman Catholic relief agency Caritas could
monitor the sale of American medicines and medical supplies, verifying
that they were used for humanitarian purposes. But Havana's approval
of Caritas Cubana as the on-site monitor was not readily issued. By then,
the American Association for World Health had issued a report (March
1997) charging that the U.S. embargo was a major contributor to the deteriorated conditions of health and nutrition in Cuba. While the embargo
on food continued, the Treasury Department's Office of Foreign Assets
Control (OFAC) approved licenses to several American manufacturers to
send representatives to Havana to negotiate sales of medicines and medical supplies. (The prohibitions established by the Torricelli-Graham Act
and later by the Helms-Burton Act remained in place until Clinton partially eased some of the sanctions following the pope's visit to Cuba.)

Supported by Cuban Americans, medical doctors, religious leaders,
and others, a bipartisan group of thirty congressmen sponsored the Cuban Humanitarian Trade Act of 1997: "to make an exception to the United
States embargo on trade with Cuba for the export of food, medicines,
medical instruments, or medical equipment, and for other purposes."[22]
As expected, the three anti-Castro Cuban-American congressmen—Ileana
Ros-Lehtinen (R-Fla.), Lincoln Díaz Balart (R-Fla.), and Robert Menéndez (D-N.J.)—protested the proposed bill.[23] Havana reacted skeptically
but expressed its appreciation for the bill's sponsors' good intentions.
Given the experience Cuba had had with the Administration and Congress, it did not see how the proposed legislation could become law.

Cuban leaders were seriously concerned with the ten amendments to the Helms-Burton Act proposed in Congress to toughen the embargo even further—seven of which had been approved by the House of Representatives.[24]

An outbreak of dengue fever in the province of Santiago de Cuba was reported in June 1997—the first one since 1981 when a dengue epidemic caused 158 deaths, including children. After claiming the ability to control it, the regime reported the outbreak of dengue fever to representatives of the World Health Organization in Havana. According to officials of Caritas, there were confirmed cases of life-threatening hemorrhagic dengue with ten deaths in the initial phase of the epidemic.[25]

Castro: An American Tradition or an Obsession?

American concern over Cuba policy has moved beyond the usual circle of specialists, reaching the media that deals with issues germane to the general public. As journalist William Raspberry noted in his nationally syndicated column: "My American Heritage Dictionary defines obsession as a 'compulsive preoccupation with a fixed idea . . . often accompanied by symptoms of anxiety; a compulsive, often unreasonable, idea or emotion.'. . . The lexicographers might have added: See U.S. Cuba policy . . . The United States said Thursday (Feb. 20) it would boycott a World Trade Organization (WTO) panel formed to judge the legality of Washington's embargo of Cuba . . . Why? The Cuban Obsession."[26]

Still, the foundation and Más Canosa continued playing political hardball, knowing that "visceral anti-Castroism is a fine American tradition . . . and a bipartisan one."[27] After all, "when Más Canosa sa[id] jump, [American] politicians lace[d] up their sneakers."[28] The foundation's leader surmised that the end of the Castro regime was coming, so he seized the moment and used American power to further his own interests. The 1996 Helms-Burton Act and the 1997 proposed reforms hardening it even more were looming on the horizon.

As a seasoned student of Cuban affairs noted: "The prevailing expectation in the United States, and certainly among American political leaders, seem[ed] to be that the end [was] near for Cuban President Fidel Castro and his revolution. Indeed that has been the expectation for some years. In December 1992, shortly after passage of his Cuban Democracy Act, which tightened the embargo against the island, Congressman Robert G. Torricelli (D-N.J.) assured Americans that Castro would fall within weeks. Senator Jesse Helms (R-N.C.), in putting forward legislation . . .

with Congressman Dan Burton (R-Ind.) to further tighten the embargo, said Castro was on the ropes and needed only a final shove. The Helms-Burton bill would prohibit the normalization of relations with any future government that included Castro."[29]

Still, why this American obsession with Castro if the Cold War was effectively over? The question had been answered in 1992 this way: "Why are Americans so fanatically anti-Castro? . . .What makes Castro different [for Americans] is that he has committed all his sins in America's backyard. Violate the Monroe Doctrine and test U.S. containment policy . . . and the result is explosive."[30]

With the Cuban Democracy Act (CDA) in force, Clinton became president in 1993. For the next three years he was cautious while the CDA "two-track" policy was being implemented. While the embargo had been tightened (track one, the stick), at the other end (track two, the carrot) a window was opened facilitating exchange of information and travel by certain individuals. To Havana and some political analysts, under the guise of increased person-to-person relations, Washington's real objective with track two was to undermine the revolution from within: "Let us remember that in the words of its principal architect, then-Rep. Robert Torricelli, the purpose of the Cuban Democracy Act [Torricelli Act], or CDA, was to 'wreak havoc in Cuba' and get rid of the Castro government. Torricelli assured one and all in a debate on Cable News Network in December of 1992 that, as a result of the legislation, the Castro government would fall within weeks!"[31]

The target of track two was Cuba's civil society, the social life and organizations that had vanished under Castro. Washington wanted to rebuild it anew to create an anti-Castro movement. The former minister of culture, Armando Hart, denounced Clinton's track two and explained the government's position on civil society and nongovernmental organizations, indicating which ones were acceptable to and appropriate in Cuban society:

> In the nineteenth century, during the expansion of bourgeois liberalism, the expression *civil society* was coined, and up to this time the concept has been interpreted differently. However, they all cover a similar problem: the relationship between the state and the extant social, economic, labor, professional, community, and cultural institutions of a given society . . . The socialist content of our civil society is determined by the nature of our social system and the character of the state . . . [As happened with other issues], the ideologues that

vulgarized Marxism did not understand the dialectic between form and content; production relations appear in the fundamentals determining the nature of the civil society and the state . . . [but] an oversimplification was made . . . [and consequently] the Party lost its social prestige and vanguard position once its social standing had been lost . . . Taking advantage of such weaknesses, imperialism was able to penetrate the Eastern European societies . . . Now [Washington] is trying to do the same with Cuba, from the outside is attempting to provoke chaos in our society by establishing directly relationships with some individuals, promoting organizational models outside of our political system, seeking to destabilize the democratic order of our society.[32]

Still, the enforcement of the Cuban Democracy Act and its track two continued. After his appointment in 1995 as Clinton's advisor on Cuba, Richard Nuccio, who had taken part in drafting the statute, was responsible for enforcing it. Castro's response to Clinton's interference in Cuban domestic affairs took some time in coming, but when it did on February 24, 1996, it brought Cuban-American relations to one of their lowest moments.

Reelection Politics vs. Foreign Policy

The 1996 presidential elections marked Clinton's second run for president. By then he had rejected any pragmatic approach to dealing with Cuba. The Cuban issue was probably high on the White House operatives' agenda but one to be handled using domestic reelection tactics for short-term political gains. The State Department's concern about the international ramifications of some Cuba policies was not relevant to the White House's election priorities.

The litmus test for any policy dealing with Havana in 1996 was whether it would improve President Clinton's chances of getting the Cuban-American vote. Such an approach distorted the significance of the Cuban problem, especially regarding American global interests and political and commercial concerns, but it made no difference to those responsible for Clinton's reelection campaign.[33] An October 29 poll gave Clinton 41 percent of the Cuban-American vote and an overall advantage in Florida over Senator Robert Dole, the Republican candidate, of 47 percent to 39 percent. On election day, 108,000 Cuban-American votes (36 percent) gave Clinton the edge he needed in Dade County (where Cuban Americans represent 40 percent of the electorate) to win the state by 76,000 popular votes.

That Clinton could split the Cuban-American vote, win Florida, and be reelected president appeared to vindicate his southern Florida strategy. But Cuban Americans were motivated to vote Democratic by their fear that Dole would slash social and economic programs and by the Republican endorsement of English as the official language.[34] In political terms, whether a large segment of the Cuban-American vote in southern Florida was effectively moved from the Republican to the Democratic column or whether the 1996 vote was only a momentary realignment was something that only time would tell.

February 24, 1996, and Its Aftermath

The year 1996 was a difficult one for Cuban-American relations. On February 24 Cuban Air Force MiGs shot down two Cessna airplanes belonging to Brothers to the Rescue (BTTR), the Miami-based Cuban-American anti-Castro organization. Whether it happened over Cuban territorial waters or international waters has not been settled, even though this had major consequences on ensuing events. The prevailing conditions in U.S.-Cuba relations could be traced to before and after the shooting of the airplanes, and each country's stance vis-à-vis the other has been based on its own interpretation of the events of that day.

To understand Havana's action it is necessary to examine the events leading to the shooting of the airplanes. The U.S. position is centered on its own interpretation of what happened on February 24, while the illegal actions leading to that day are dismissed as irrelevant.

Prior to February 24, 1996, Cuba had strongly protested to international authorities and the U.S. government that airplanes departing from southern Florida had purposely violated its territorial air space on nine occasions between May 1994 and January 1996. In May 1994 it had happened four times, and once each in the summer and fall. It happened twice in 1995 and again in January 1996.[35]

Havana saw the aerial violations of its territory as serious, and these were compounded by the dropping of antigovernment leaflets on the island. On July 13, 1995, Havana protested that a Cuban exile flotilla of "eleven vessels, six small aircraft and two helicopters [had] entered Cuban waters and air space" until its advance was stopped by Cuban naval forces. Also, "on January 9 and 13, 1996, intruding airplanes departing from the U.S. had dropped subversive leaflets again." Havana characterized those actions as "irresponsible and criminal attacks against [the] country." The danger posed to international aviation by the aerial incursions had forced the temporary closing of the Giron corridor normally used by civilian aircraft and also affected the operations at Varadero International Airport.[36] The following are excerpts from interviews and reports released by the sources involved in the incident:[37]

Information provided by the Cuban foreign ministry:

Between 3:21 P.M. and 3:28 P.M. of February 24, 1996, two private Cessna planes coming from the airport in Opa-Locka in the state of Florida were downed by planes of our air force while they violated once again air space over Cuban waters at distances between five and eight miles north of Baracoa beach west of Havana.

At 1:21 P.M.: when they came toward Cuba again [airplanes of the same type had penetrated Cuban air space earlier that day] one of those responsible for these incursions was warned by the Havana Air Traffic of the risk they were putting themselves in by penetrating them, to which he answered that it was clear he could not violate the zone but that he was doing it.

At 3:15 P.M.: it was learned from internal communication of one of the pilots that he was [flying] toward Havana. While two of the planes penetrated [Cuban airspace] the leader of the group [José Basulto], in a third plane, stayed outside the 12-mile limit.[38]

Information provided by senior Clinton Administration officials:

3:01 P.M: Three BTTR aircraft begin operating south of the 24th parallel.

3:09 P.M.: One MiG 23 and MiG 29 Cuban fighter aircraft are airborne.

3:22 P.M.: Lead BTTR aircraft penetrates three nautical miles into Cuban airspace.

3:24 P.M.: The MiG 29 pilot requested and received permission to destroy the second aircraft. The pilot quickly noted that the aircraft had been shot down. This occurred approximately five nautical miles north of Cuban airspace.

3:31 P.M.: The MiG pilot noted another aircraft in sight, requested permission, received permission and reported the third aircraft destroyed. This occurred approximately 16 nautical miles of [sic] Cuban airspace.

Reported by the *Miami Herald*:

[Pilot José] Basulto: For your information, Havana Center, our area of operations [is] north of Havana today. So we will be in your area and in contact with you. A cordial greeting from the Brothers to the Rescue and its president, José Basulto, who is speaking to you.

Havana Center: OK. Received, sir. I inform you that the zone north of Havana is active. You run danger by penetrating that side of north 24.

Basulto: We are conscious we are in danger each time we cross the area south of 24, but we are ready to do it. It is our right as free Cubans.

The *New York Times* on Basulto's background:

The combination of harsh talk and nonviolent tactics represents a turnaround for Basulto, a 55-year-old engineer who after training with the CIA for the failed Bay of Pigs Invasion—he escaped by crossing over to the American naval base in Guantánamo—turned to paramilitary groups and other military activities such as aiding the Nicaraguan Contras fighting the Cuban-sponsored Sandinistas.

A Cable News Network interview with Ricardo Alarcón, president of Cuban National Assembly:

Correspondent Lucia Newman: Could you tell me why is Cuba so sure . . . that these planes were shot down over Cuban territory and not international waters?

Alarcón: We know very well where the incident took place. We have some material evidence that it was found on Cuban waters where the U.S. is claiming that the incident occurred elsewhere, but they haven't found anything and they cannot find anything outside of Cuba . . . That was the perception . . . that the State Department had. If not, why did Mr. [Warren] Christopher [U.S. secretary of state] instruct his man in Havana, Mr. Sullivan, to ask permission for the U.S. Coast Guard to enter into Cuban waters at 7:30 P.M. on Saturday last? . . . Later in the night at 10:15, Miss Patterson, the assistant secretary of state, also spoke about the—their desire to enter Cuban waters. Why? Because they were also aware that the incident had taken place here. The U.S . . . has very, very close examination of our military . . . They know very well if something happened, where that happened.

Interview on Cuban television of Juan Pablo Roque, a BTTR member until defecting and returning to Cuba:

Roque: I am in Cuba because I want to denounce to world public opinion the real character of Brothers to the Rescue . . . [BTTR was] born in 1991 in the offices of the Cuban American National Foundation . . . Martín Pérez, with the substantial economic support of the Foundation, advances the idea with ex-CIA agents José Basulto, Billy Shuss, Arnaldo Iglesias, . . . to create an organization with a supposed humanitarian character, to save the lives of men at sea trying to reach the Florida coast.[39]

The four occupants of the two BTTR Cessnas perished (all Cuban born, but three of them U.S. citizens).[40] Washington disregarded the history of violations of Cuban air space and ignored the possibility that the incident could have been a provocation to create a direct confrontation between the United States and Cuba.

The downing of the two BTTR planes could be seen as the product of a miscalculation by Havana and Washington. After having accomplished some bridge-making negotiations and agreements, both sides allowed their mutual misunderstanding to prevail. They forgot the mutually acceptable parameters that had kept their long-standing confrontation within bounds. Clinton's pursuit of the Torricelli Act track two was an attempt to build an anti-Castro force disguised as nongovernmental organizations formed by Cuba's civil society.[41] Washington's failure to stop Brothers to the Rescue violations of Cuban air space was unacceptable to Havana. The effect of these belligerent actions set the stage for Havana's harsh reaction against the BTTR planes.

But Cuba's actions were also unacceptable to Washington. They put Clinton under pressure in a no-win situation. He could not react mildly and still expect that it would not have an effect on his reelection campaign (his major objective at the time). Neither side weighed properly the other's reaction, so that they were provoking each other into actions they should have avoided. Still, it is possible that Havana and Washington acted knowingly and with little regard for the consequences of their own actions.

With his Cuba policy Clinton (a Democrat) has followed a path similar to the one taken earlier by Reagan (a Republican). The obsession with Nicaragua, the support for the Contras, and the negative vision of the Sandinistas led Reagan to the 1987 scandal that almost ruined his presidency. While developments there and in Cuba were not exactly alike, the story repeats itself. First, Clinton supported the Torricelli-Graham bill in what seemed a low-cost political investment that could deliver the votes he needed to win Florida and the election and become president. Second, White House enforcement of track two led to the Cuban reaction, the downing of the BTTR planes, and the signing of the Helms-Burton bill into law.

After having Washington's Cuban obsession forced on them, America's closest allies and trade partners have had to defend their own rights and sovereignty as well as commercial freedom. Whether the easing of economic sanctions by President Clinton following the pope's visit can lead to a better phase in Cuba-U.S. relations is not a guaranteed alternative. According to Cuba, the Cold War is not over; whatever is being done against the revolution has been done many times over, and nobody in Washington seems to know how to end it.[42]

Conclusion

After the demise of European socialism, the Havana-Washington antagonism was defined for what it had been all along: America incapable of accepting a social revolution in a neighboring country. The geographic proximity exacerbated Americans' sensitivities and frustration at having to live close to what they found an unpalatable political phenomenon. American opposition to the Cuban revolution became a pathological obsession: the deeply rooted anti-Castro sentiment in the American psyche would only be satisfied with the end of Castro's leadership.

By the time the Cold War was over, a significant number of Cuban exiles had become American citizens, allowing them to exert a decisive influence in electoral politics, especially in Florida and to a lesser extent in New Jersey. The Cuba policy of the United States became the private domain of the most conservative and wealthiest Cuban Americans, as represented by the late Jorge Más Canosa and the Cuban American National Foundation. Clinton contributed more than most American presidents to this state of affairs—including Republican presidents like Nixon, Reagan, and Bush. Both in 1992 and in 1996, Clinton's electoral needs made him seek Cuban-American political and monetary support in order to win Florida. This marriage of convenience would ultimately carry a high price tag, more than originally expected.

Clinton's support for the 1992 Torricelli-Graham Act, and the implementation of its track two policy, contributed to the events of February 24, 1996, and the downing of two BTTR airplanes, which led to the Helms-Burton bill being signed into law. Next came the internationalization of the American embargo against Cuba and the confrontation between Washington and its closest allies and trade partners, who opposed the Helms-Burton bill for interfering with free trade and their own right to commerce with Cuba.

It took the visit by the pope in January 1998 to move in a more positive direction, provoking some changes in Clinton's Cuba policy. But the easing of sanctions was not aimed at a rapprochement between Havana and Washington. Still, there were other developments in 1998 and early 1999: the Torres-Dodd bill, sponsored by Representative Esteban Torres (D-Calif.) and Senator Christopher Dodd (D-Conn.), which sought to lift the ban on food and medicines, received support in Congress and some sectors of the Cuban-American community. In a letter to President Clinton, fourteen U.S. senators (including eleven Republicans), supported by Henry Kissinger (secretary of state under Nixon and Ford), Lawrence Eagleburger (secretary of state under Bush), and Frank Carlucci (secretary of defense under Reagan), requested the formation of a bipartisan commission on Cuba policy, based on the National Bipartisan Commission on Central America chaired by Kissinger fifteen years earlier. Pressured by Vice President Al Gore, who saw his presidential election in 2000 put at risk, President Clinton nevertheless rejected the initiative while allowing further "people-to-people" contacts (direct mail service, chartered flights, etc.) and the licensing of food and medicine exports to nongovernmental farmers and businesses. Cuba called Clinton's decision a "fraud" and "mere crumbs" but approved the long-awaited exhibition games between the Baltimore Orioles and Cuba's national baseball team.

Ending a forty-year hiatus in official U.S.-Cuba major league contact, the games were held in Havana's Latinoamericano Stadium and Baltimore's Camden Yards on March 28 and May 3, 1999, respectively. Cuba lost the first game 3 to 2 in eleven innings but prevailed the second time by defeating the Orioles 12 to 6.[43] The possible impact of the short-lived exercise in baseball diplomacy and of other developments and problems present in Cuban-American relations under President Clinton are the subject of the next chapter.

Cuban-U.S. Relations under
President Clinton: Part II

Tempestuous Diplomacy at the U.N. and ICAO

Before moving to the diplomatic arena, the Clinton Administration's response to the shooting down of the BTTR planes was to impose punitive measures against Havana. The new White House penalties included the following:

Suspending all charter air travel from the United States to Cuba.

Requesting from Congress legislation providing compensation to the families of the victims using funds from frozen Cuban assets in the United States.

Seeking a compromise with Republican lawmakers on a bill (Helms-Burton) that would expand economic sanctions already imposed on Cuba.

Expanding the reach of Radio Martí (the U.S. propaganda network) throughout the island.

Tightening travel restrictions on Cuban officials living in, or visiting the United States.[1]

By suspending air travel between Miami and Havana, Clinton terminated Cuba's proceeds from those flights. But the suspension meant that Cuban Americans traveling to their native country to visit relatives were also penalized, as were other travelers. The most far-reaching penalty imposed was to end the administration's opposition to the Helms-Burton bill and to agree with its Republican sponsors to have it approved. The decision was made during an international crisis with domestic political ramifications, and the bill's sponsors sought to exact more concessions from the White House. Clinton agreed that henceforth the anti-Castro executive decisions spanning more than three decades could be terminated only with congressional approval.

Washington demanded condemnatory resolutions from the United

Nations Security Council and the International Civil Aviation Organization (ICAO; Washington asked ICAO to conduct an investigation of the incident) but was only partly successful. The Security Council first and ICAO months later sided with the United States, but the resolutions were pale compared to what had been requested, and no sanctions were imposed. Cuba was reprimanded for its actions, but most countries understood that Washington was partly responsible for provoking the incident. Despite Cuban warnings, the United States had allowed Brothers to the Rescue (BTTR) to enter Cuban air space illegally (on one occasion while flying from the U.S. Guantánamo Naval Base in eastern Cuba to Miami), to use southern Florida airports as their base of operations, to falsify flight records to U.S. authorities, and to violate American, international, and Cuban law.

Cuba quoted American specialists on international law and aerial navigation to make its point. In his often cited article, "The Treatment of Aerial Intruders in Recent Practice and International Law," Professor Oliver Lissitzyn stated, "In times of peace, intruding aircraft whose intentions are known to the territorial sovereignty to be harmless must not be attacked even if they disobey orders to land, to turn back or to fly on a certain course . . . In cases where there is reason to believe that the intruder may be hostile or illicit, warning or order to land should normally be first given and the intruder may be attacked if it disobeys." The Cuban government commented:

> By "illicit" intentions, professor Lissitzyn meant "aid to subversive activities, smuggling, or calculated defiance of the territorial sovereign." Brothers to the Rescue violation of Cuban airspace, in addition to being explicitly "hostile," falls precisely within this definition of "illicit." This behavior distinguishes it from the generality of cases upon which the supposed rule of nonuse of weapons asserted by the United Nations is based . . . [The] Cuban air force did not shoot down a commercial passenger airplane. It shot down aircraft belonging to an organization [with] a well-documented record of provocations to the Cuban government and repeated violations of its airspace in spite of reiterated warnings.[2]

Havana launched protests at the Security Council and at the Montreal-based ICAO, denouncing U.S. complicity in BTTR's illegal actions and in using the international bodies for its own purposes. U.S. Secretary of State Madeleine Albright, then U.S. ambassador to the United Nations, presided over the Security Council at the time. She convened the Security Council and put to a vote a resolution condemning Cuba while then

Cuban Foreign Minister Roberto Robaina was still on his way to New York City. By the time he arrived, the Security Council resolution had already been adopted.

As U.S. ambassador to the U.N. Secretary Albright called Castro's downing of the BTTR planes "cowardice, not *cojones*." After promising that the administration would keep its policy on Castro, she stated that "Cuba is an embarrassment for the Western Hemisphere and I think we need to keep making clear that there needs to be a change there." Cuban Americans call her affectionately "the lady of cojones," and applauded her nomination as secretary of state. According to *Newsweek*, "Albright was very much in the mainstream of Democratic thinking on foreign policy. She supported the nuclear freeze, opposed aid to the Nicaraguan contras and urged delay in the use of force against Iraq after it invaded Kuwait in 1990. Over time, though, she became known as a hawk. What accounted for the move? Her friends say she came to trust her latent hawk's instincts. Like fellow refugees Brzezinski and Kissinger, she basically cottoned to the use of U.S. power."[3]

Later, while speaking in San Francisco in 1997, Secretary Albright was interrupted by protesters demanding an end to the U.S. blockade of Cuba. Secretary Albright said: "We would like good and friendly relations with Cuba, but it is up to Cuba to change its behavior, not the United States."[4] Just eight days after Secretary Albright's statement, an old story resurfaced: "The CIA [had] offered $150,000 to assassinate Fidel Castro in the early 1960s, but the mob insisted on taking the job for free, according to a newly declassified document . . . 'We were at (ideological) war,' [said] Robert Mahout, who as a Las Vegas private investigator on the CIA payroll in 1960 hired Chicago crime boss Sam Giancana for the hit . . . [The] murder-for-hire contract was detailed in a summary of a May 1962 CIA briefing for then-Attorney General Robert Kennedy."[5]

Robaina finally spoke to the U.N. General Assembly on March 6.[6] He insisted that the shooting down of the airplanes happened over Cuban territorial waters and also charged that for over thirty years the United States had relentlessly attacked the Cuban revolution. After listing numerous aggressions against Cuba, Robaina asked how the United States could make such unfounded charges.

Still, after Robaina denounced Ambassador Albright's tactics at the Security Council and after discussion of the February 24 events, the Security Council resolution stood as approved. The head of Cuba's National Assembly, Ricardo Alarcón, had problems with the ICAO investigation of the February 24 incident. According to Alarcón's account, at the ICAO deliberations highly improper tactics were used by the American delegation and the final report was "full of falsifications and gaps."[7]

After ICAO had rejected the condemnation of Cuba proposed by the U.S. delegation, and had included a paragraph reaffirming the "obligation of states to adopt appropriate measures to ban the deliberate use of civilian aircraft registered in that state for any purpose not compatible with the Chicago agreement," Castro still called ICAO's report "disgraceful." According to Alarcón, many things were wrong with the report:[8]

> Five days of meetings between ICAO's Investigation Committee and the American delegation resulted in a conspiracy to slant the results to favor the United States.
>
> The United States manipulated data and delayed presenting evidence, leaving the ICAO Council with little time for deliberation before finalizing the report.
>
> ICAO's Investigation Committee did not link BTTR to the U.S. military in spite of having watched a one-hour videotape showing U.S. military officers training BTTR pilots and knowing that the U.S. military frequently uses the same kind of planes.
>
> The chief of ICAO's Investigation Committee, Caj Frostell, admitted that his team never conducted interviews with passengers or the crew of the two ships that witnessed the incident, relying only on the ships' logs.
>
> The single interview conducted by the Investigation Committee in the United States was with the head of BTTR, José Basulto, who after entering Cuba's air space escaped in his aircraft and returned to Opa-Locka, Florida.
>
> The United States provided electronic records of radar tracks from different stations to the Investigation Committee but never the original tapes.
>
> Cuba's proposal to the ICAO Council to correct the report and to consider it later at a proper time was dismissed by the ICAO Council.
>
> A number of ICAO Council members, including Nigeria, Angola, Russia, Indonesia, and India, criticized the Investigation Commission report and were opposed to sending the report as it stood to the Security Council.

The Clinton Administration was operating at two mutually reinforcing levels: the international and the domestic political arenas. First, Washington was determined to have Cuba condemned by the U.N. and ICAO.

Domestically, after some additional punitive measures, President Clinton came out in support of the Helms-Burton bill, and a harsher final version was approved by Congress and signed by the president on March 12.

By signing the Helms-Burton Act, Clinton catered to the anti-Castro domestic political forces. In return, he sought their electoral support in Florida and New Jersey (where the Cuban-American vote could make a difference in the 1996 presidential elections) and also managed to pull the Cuban issue off the electoral agenda. As was noted by a political analyst, "the last few weeks ha[ve] only emphasized how meager a role foreign policy has played during this long campaign, especially when compared with past Presidential contests."[9]

Senator Dole's attempt to bring back the Cuba issue by promising harsher measures against Castro had no political impact. Still, he was quoted as saying: "Here we have Cuba, 90 miles from our shores, and what have we done?" He went on: "We passed a law [the Helms-Burton Act] that gave people a right to sue, and the President postponed it for six months. And it seems to me if you want to send a signal, you have got to send a signal, Mr. President. The sooner, the better off we will be if you put tougher sanctions on Castro, not try to make it easier for him."[10]

The Cuban lobby and its political allies were basically satisfied with Clinton's Cuba policy. What kind of international reasons, if any, Clinton had for signing the Helms-Burton Act were not that obvious. By most accounts, the new twist in the Havana-Washington problem promised to be as harmful to the United States as it was to Cuba.[11]

Track Two and Concilio Cubano

The dissident movement in Cuba planned important political activities the day the two BTTR planes were shot down. Concilio Cubano (CC), made up of small opposition groups, had planned to hold a public meeting on February 24. Almost a hundred dissidents were arrested beforehand, and the meeting never took place.[12] CC received support from external sources (BTTR had pledged thousands of dollars), and BTTR's aerial maneuvers were interpreted as a sign of support for Concilio and of defiance of the Cuban regime. Some analysts saw Havana's response as purposely cracking down on the opposition (financed by Washington, in the Cuban view) and at the same time putting an end to BTTR's violations of Cuba's air space.[13]

The administration's announcement that the New York–based Freedom House was receiving half a million dollars to "promote peaceful change and protect human rights" added to the image "that the American government has taken too much of an activist role in Havana." Also, in October 1995 Washington eased restriction on travel to Cuba by academics and religious and human-rights workers to "encourage its peaceful transition to democracy." In Havana, this was translated as one more attempt to destroy the Cuban revolution.

The United Nations rapporteur on Cuba, Swedish jurist Carl-Johan Gorth, was quoted as saying: "The United States could undermine a growing dissident movement in Cuba with its measures pressuring Havana's government to institute democratic reforms. The [U.S.] measures could drive many dissidents to leave the country." Gorth also stated that Washington's pressure has caused Castro to take more drastic measures rather than heeding any suggestion to democratize Cuba.[14]

Cuba's ultimate reaction, obviously "linked to anger over growing dissent and perceived U.S. meddling in its internal affairs," had been in the making for a while: "The President of Cuba's National Assembly [Alarcón] was visibly angry. He had just emerged from a meeting with a U.S. Congressman [Representative Joseph Moakley (D-Mass.), who was visiting Havana] when he came face-to-face with Cuba's best known dissidents . . . The dissidents had been chauffeured to the hotel in U.S. government vans and were on their way in to see the same Congressman. To Ricardo Alarcón and other top Cuban officials, it was another example of U.S. diplomats aiding and encouraging the dissidents under their very noses."[15]

U.S. officials deny giving Cuban dissidents any money but acknowledge that they have provided them with transportation to "U.S. government–sponsored cocktail parties and that they offer visiting journalists lists of [dissidents'] addresses and telephone numbers." They also provided the dissidents with printed matter: "copies of Miami's El Nuevo Herald and books like *What Is Democracy?* published by the U.S. Information Agency." CC members denied receiving money from Washington but admitted that they were in close contact with Radio Martí and the Cuban American Foundation.[16]

Former foreign minister Robaina had stated that "American officials here 'are walking around freely and putting their noses in where they don't belong'." Another foreign ministry official reacted, saying: "We cannot allow and permit another country to organize dissent to meet and perform in Cuba . . . Are we supposed to stand by and watch the United States drive these people around in their vans?"[17]

Cuba watchers were mostly critical of the shooting down of the BTTR airplanes but were also sympathetic to Cuba's complaints and reasoning:

Philip Brenner (American University): It's hard to know if the Cuban government would have acted as irrationally as it did by shooting down the planes if *Concilio* didn't have these perceived links.

Wayne S. Smith (Johns Hopkins University): Unfortunately, the U.S. government is [highly] involved . . . Castro is authoritarian, but might be able to tolerate a bit of dissidence if there is no evidence of U.S. involvement . . . I don't know if there is a direct link between the shootdown and *Concilio,* but I think that the crackdown on the group [leaders and members of CC were being arrested, mostly temporarily] was the result of the perception that U.S. officials are helping them out.

Nelson P. Valdés (University of New Mexico): *Concilio* would have a better chance for survival if it pulled back from the U.S. government contacts so despised by Cuban officials. The only way you are going to have a viable political movement in Cuba is to declare your complete independence.

In September 1995, President Clinton met in Miami with Más Canosa and other anti-Castro hard-liners as he had before, but this time he also talked to moderate Cuban Americans like Eloy Gutiérrez Menoyo, leader of Cambio Cubano; Alfredo Durán, former chairman of the Cuban Democracy Committee; Ramón Cernuda, representative of a human rights organization operating on the island, and others. The monopoly on U.S. Cuba policy exerted by Más Canosa and the foundation seemed to be eroding, at least partly.

But the trend that had favored moderate Cuban Americans stopped on February 24, 1996, interrupting also their access to the White House. The hard-liners were again in charge. Moderate Cuban Americans reacted angrily to Castro's and Clinton's actions:

Alfredo Durán: Track Two is dead . . .[18] There is no question that there are two sides to Track II. Some people have used it as a Trojan horse, but there are others who are sincere in looking for a solution to a post-Castro Cuba . . . It is unlikely that these [travel] agencies [which operate charter flights Miami-Cuba and contributed $150,000 to Clinton's campaign] will offer any more contributions after [Clinton] closed down their charter flights to Cuba. Clinton took the wind out of the Cuban issue.

Ramón Cernuda: The nonviolent, pro-dialogue approach we propose has been derailed. Helms-Burton is a mistake, repeating the

U.S. mistake of imposing a unilateral policy on the world. It is a triumph for the most aggressive position on Cuba and it will achieve the opposite of what it is pursuing. It will stop any chance of a democratization in Cuba. It has deepened the hard line in Miami. The Treasury Department now has a special telephone number for one to call and tell them who violates the embargo [against Cuba], to tell on your neighbors. It seems that the American government is promoting something similar to Cuba's neighborhood committees to defend the revolution. It is terrible![19]

A segment of the American public responded somewhat critically to President Clinton's response to Cuba's action as not being strong enough, while others were not that interested in his reaction. Two days after Clinton signed the Helms-Burton Act in a White House ceremony with Más Canosa and other foundation leaders, the three anti-Castro Cuban-American congressmen, and Senator Jesse Helms in attendance, a Gallup public opinion survey found that 22 percent of the public had followed the events closely, 47 percent somewhat closely, and 22 percent not closely at all. Also, 7 percent found Clinton's response too strong, 38 percent about right, 43 percent not strong enough, and 12 percent had no opinion. This reaction contrasted with the attention given to such events as Haiti (78 percent), O. J. Simpson charges (77 percent), Jack Kevorkian (77 percent), and the Branch Davidian standoff in Waco, Texas (74 percent). Still, approximately 69 percent of the public had followed the shooting of the two BTTR planes.[20]

Washington had few choices left with which to punish Cuba even before Helms-Burton was approved—short of a military invasion. But after approving such a law, and entrusting the lifting of three decades of executive orders to Congress, Clinton has left no incentives for Cuba to moderate itself while seeking to improve relations with the United States.

A military attack against Cuba had been weighed up in Washington. As requested by the national security adviser, the Pentagon provided a list of possible military actions. It included launching a cruise missile attack on the Cuba MiGs' home base in San Antonio de los Baños or an air attack by U.S. bombers. These possibilities were discarded after the Pentagon failed to recommend either. A government official was quoted as saying an attack was "a bad idea" when the United States had a nuclear power plant at Turkey Point in South Florida, ninety miles from Cuba, and in an air attack, "we were more likely to lose more people in Cuba than in Iraq." Also, a military response would have escalated the shooting of the two airplanes to a very dangerous level.

At the National Security Council meeting, "there were some wild ideas . . . Helms-Burton was the mildest of responses at the table," according to a U.S. official. But the military option was rejected and economic punitive measures were approved. Direct flights from Miami to Havana were suspended and Helms-Burton was supported.[21] However, the law proved almost immediately to be costly and ill-advised.

Signing Helms-Burton into Law

President Clinton signed the Helms-Burton bill coinciding with the Republican primary in Florida, on March 12, 1996. Clinton hardened his nonmilitary response to Castro to safeguard his domestic political objectives. An impression of weakness by Clinton would have been derided by the Cuban lobby and the Republican opposition, which would have denounced it as indecisiveness in a crisis. Clinton's sympathy for the Cuban lobby had been responsible for bringing up the crisis: by allowing BTTR planes' provocative flights over Cuba and by supporting the Torricelli-Graham Act and its track two policy. Still, his behavior had not diminished entirely the negative fallout potential the crisis had for his electoral ambitions.

President Clinton made derogatory remarks about Castro while signing the Helms-Burton bill into law:

> We are here today around a common commitment to bring democracy to Cuba. Two and a half weeks ago . . . in broad daylight and without justification, Cuban military jets shot down two unarmed United States civilian aircraft causing the deaths of three American citizens and one U.S. resident. The planes were unarmed, the pilots unwarned. They posed no threat to Cuba's security. This was clearly a brutal and cruel act . . . Cuba's blatant disregard for international law is not just an issue between Havana and Washington but between Havana and the world."[22]

Besides the unprecedented international condemnation of Helms-Burton, the media examined Clinton's decision somewhat differently. One report concluded that the shooting down of the airplanes determined Clinton's Cuba policy in an irrevocably anti-Castro direction—after the White House had created opposite expectations among hardliners and moderates. "The Congress and the Presidency have turned their pressure on . . . Castro into one of their main objectives, even at the risk of undermining other goals," reported the *Washington Post*. The article recognized both the obsession that Havana had by then become in Washington and the negative impact of Clinton's policy on American world interests.[23]

Two other media reports brought a different light to the president's support for the Helms-Burton bill. *Time* magazine acknowledged that Clinton's southern Florida strategy was increasing his electoral support among Cuban Americans, noting:

> Forty-one percent of Florida's Cuban-Americans plan to vote for Clinton, almost double what he won in 1992, finally giving him a chance to take the state he lost by a squeaker in 1992. It is one of the biggest triumphs of his campaign . . . But the Clinton turnaround has come with costs. The tale of how he brought it off involves excessive influence over foreign policy by a special-interest group, gloves-off bureaucratic in-fighting and a willingness to bash U.S. allies for electoral gain. It also involves peril. Wooing Dade County's 678,000 Cuban-Americans has resulted in the most volatile period of confrontation with Havana since the 1962 missile crisis. The Pentagon fears it is only a matter of time before another event like February's shoot down of two U.S. civilian planes by Cuban MiGs sparks a military confrontation between the two countries.
>
> Four years ago, senior State Department diplomats hoped Clinton would breathe fresh air into U.S.-Cuban relations. Miami's fiercely anti-Castro Cuban-American community has long blocked any thaw, though the Pentagon had concluded that Havana posed no threat to the region, and Washington had made peace with almost all its cold war enemies. *But half a dozen Cuban-American Democrats who raised huge sums for Clinton in 1992 convinced the new President he could win Florida in '96 if he became even more anti-Castro than Ronald Reagan or George Bush had been.* Senior Clinton aides call the cabal the 'core group'. It includes María Victoria Arias, a Miami lawyer married to Hugh Rodham, the First Lady's brother, and wealthy businessman Paul Cejas, who occasionally stays overnight at the White House (emphasis added).[24]

After it was published in the *Miami Herald*, the official Cuban media echoed the report of the Washington-based Center for Public Integrity, linking the Cuban lobby's political contributions to Washington's anti-Castro policies, especially the Helms-Burton Act.[25] (See also table 8.1.) The following are some of the conclusions drawn by the Center for Public Integrity, as cited by *Granma International*:

Directors and officials of the Cuban American National
Foundation have donated almost 3.2 million dollars to the
U.S. political system since 1979. Among beneficiaries receiving the largest amounts is Senator Jesse Helms, one of the
law's co-authors.

The advisors who participated in the drafting of the Helms-
Burton Act were supported by lawyers linked to the interests
of Bacardi, which lost its property in Cuba.

As noted by Charles Lewis, president of the Center for Public
Integrity, Más Canosa and the foundation were able to score
three major political victories: the creation of Radio and TV
Martí, at a cost to American taxpayers of 280 million dollars,
the passage of the Torricelli-Graham Act in 1992, and the
implementation of the Helms-Burton Act in 1996, which
tightened the economic blockade against the island.

The foundation has created a lobbying force that, dollar for
dollar, is the most effective in Washington.[26]

Offended by the report of the Center for Public Integrity, CANF's political allies charged the study's sponsor, the Arca Foundation, with being
a donor for those opposing the Cuban embargo. Mentioned as evidence
were the funding of a Johns Hopkins University study on U.S. trade in a
post-embargo Cuba and the support of Pastors for Peace, the religious
organization that has challenged the U.S. embargo, and of the Cuban
Committee for Democracy. Instead of challenging the report, CANF's
political allies attacked the Arca Foundation for sponsoring opponents of
the Cuban lobby.[27]

Freezing the Bilateral Confrontation

The Helms-Burton Act served to perpetuate the long-held confrontation
in U.S.-Cuban relations. It also undermined the island's economic recovery by discouraging and/or penalizing foreign corporations investing in
properties nationalized by Cuba that belonged to American citizens. The
legal adviser of Havana's Ministry of Foreign Affairs, Olga Miranda,
sheds some light on the dispute:

In the American legislation related to the blockade [of Cuba], not
only [in] Helms-Burton, prevails the notion that there was a confiscation of property in Cuba, because they have not been compensated. But what happened here was a nationalization process

through expropriation—applied because of public interest—and it was in that way that our legislation defined it . . . Confiscation means to apply a punitive measure as a consequence of an unlawful action, as happened with the properties that belonged to the dictator Fulgencio Batista and others guilty of embezzlement of public monies, who had no right to compensation because of the crimes they committed . . . All of our nationalization laws include a compensation [payment] process."[28]

The Helms-Burton Act included a provision codifying into law all executive orders in effect on March 1, 1996, relevant to the trade embargo of the island; some reached back to the early 1960s. The legislation limited the president's power to conduct relations with Cuba and transferred this power to the Congress. Congressional approval would be needed to modify this provision of the law, an impossibility today or in the foreseeable future.

The Helms-Burton Act is organized in four separate titles or sections. Title I solidifies an international network of sanctions against Cuba. It includes:

1. seeking an international embargo sanctioned by the United Nations Security Council;
2. rejecting Cuba's entry to any international lending organization;
3. penalizing former socialist countries aiding Cuba (as in helping to complete the Juraguá nuclear plant in Cienfuegos);
4. supporting independent nongovernmental organizations and individuals;
5. codifying the embargo and transferring any change to congressional authority.[29]

Title II covers U.S. aid to a free and democratic Cuba. It establishes eight major requirements and four additional factors that Cuba would need to address before the United States would lift the embargo, establish diplomatic relations, and begin negotiations to return Guantánamo base to Cuban jurisdiction: (1) releasing all political prisoners, (2) dissolving the State Security Department, (3) holding free elections within eighteen months under international supervision, and (4) guaranteeing the absence of Fidel and Raúl Castro from the transition process. The embargo will continue until a transitional government is established. The president would assess how much progress toward democratization had taken place, subject to congressional review. In sum, the new political and socioeconomic institutions of a post-Castro Cuba would be determined in the United States. Also, all properties nationalized by the revolutionary government since January 1, 1959, would be returned to their original owners.

Title III protects American citizens who lost property. Any corporation currently trafficking in property that belonged to an American citizen (including those who today are American citizens but were not at the time) and was nationalized by Cuba could be sued in American courts. The original owner's property rights would include any investment, improvement, or expansion made in such properties. This revokes the recognition by American courts of the State Action doctrine justifying a government's authority to nationalize property belonging to its nationals or others (recognized in international law). For national security reasons or to promote Cuban democracy, the president has the authority to suspend the application of this title and the legal actions allowed therein for six months at a time. In 1996, 1997, 1998, and 1999 Clinton suspended this provision—and most likely will continue suspending it until the end of his administration. (See table 9.1.)

Title IV empowers the secretary of state and the attorney general to suspend visas of officials from corporations trafficking in American property and of those officials' spouses and children. Two corporations were initially penalized: the Mexican Grupo Domos, which terminated its investment in Cuba's telephone and communications system and in 1997 was notified that its executives were allowed to visit the U.S. again, and the Canadian Sherritt Corporation, which increased its investment in mining and other economic areas. In 1997, a third company that had concentrated on the island's citrus industry was added to the list, the Israeli

Table 9.1. Ten Largest U.S. Certified Claims in Cuba (in 1970 dollars)

Corporation	Claim
Cuban Electric Co.	$268 million
ITT	$131 million
North American Sugar Ind. et al.	$109 million
Moa Bay Mining Co.	$88 million
United Fruit Sugar Co.	$85 million
West Indies Sugar Co.	$85 million
American Sugar Co.	$81 million
Standard Oil Co.	$72 million
Bangor Punta Co. et al.	$53 million
Texaco	$50 million

SOURCE: "Biggest Claims," *Miami Herald*, April 26, 1997.

Grupo BM, which in 1997 announced a new joint venture for $200 million to build a trade and business center in Havana; the executives of both Canada's Sherritt and Israel's Grupo BM were still subject to the U.S. visa ban in 1999.

About half of Americans and most Canadians reject Helms-Burton. Angus Reed, a Canadian pollster, after surveying 1,004 adult Americans and 1,000 adult Canadians in 1997, found that about 48 percent of Americans and 80 percent of Canadians were against the law punishing foreign investors in Cuba.[30]

Cuba's and the World's Reaction

The official Cuban response was unequivocal in its denunciation of the U.S. statute. Explaining the American law on television, Alarcón affirmed that the measures "are going to fail because it is impossible to put them into effect . . . [they are] absurd, stupid and condemned to the most total failure . . . no matter how many times President Clinton signs [them]." He added that the new law was "an insult to the world, [an example of] arrogance, haughtiness and desperation in the face of a failed [Cuba] policy."[31]

In March 1996 the PCC Central Committee held a plenum, the first since October 1992, to discuss the situation facing the country. It was agreed to reinforce the economic planning system based on Marxist-Leninist tenets, and to continue battling the United States in defense of the country's sovereignty and independence. "Socialism does not have an alternative in Cuba . . . Never has revolutionary ideology been as necessary as now," said Castro. The Politburo's report was read by Raúl Castro, Minister of the Armed Forces (FAR). The report attacked track two and those nongovernmental organizations that, as a "Trojan horse," were promoting "division and subversion."[32]

Raúl Castro discussed the challenge posed by the Helms-Burton Act and the nation's situation: the negative effects of self-employment, of youth dissatisfaction, of problems in agriculture, of legalizing the U.S. dollar and tourism, of renting houses to foreigners; and the danger of ideological penetration and the need to defend the national interest from capitalist corruption and bribery (i.e., some foreign investors). He gave credit to those members of the Cuban-American community who constitute "[a] growing minority of brave émigrés [who defend Cuba]." But imprudently, he ended by attacking some of Cuba's main think tanks, the Center for the Study of the Americas, CEA, and the Center for European

Studies, CEE, charging that both were characterized by "arrogance, abandonment of classist principles, the temptation to travel, and the production of articles and books to the liking of those who financed their publications."[33]

The world seemed to agree with Cuba. By having Helms-Burton approved immediately after the shooting of the two BTTR planes, Clinton lost the initial edge he had gained with the international condemnation of Cuba's action. One after another, Canada, England, Mexico, Spain, the European Union, Latin American countries and the Organization of American States, the pope, the Nonaligned Movement, the Rio Group, the Association of East Asian Nations, political parties, political leaders, trade unions, student organizations, religious leaders and groups, and many others voiced their opposition to Helms-Burton, condemning its extraterritoriality. Washington's closest allies claimed that the United States was imposing its Cuba policy on them, infringing on their right to decide their own trade policy. Canada, Mexico, England, and of course Cuba legislated their own antidote (anti–Helms-Burton Act) laws, countering its punitive effect on them.[34]

The issue had grown beyond the U.S.-Cuba problem to become a world problem with bad consequences for international trade practices and agreements. To Latin American and Caribbean nations the latest Washington Cuba policy was a matter of concern due to its destabilizing effect in the region. A military confrontation between the two countries born out of miscalculation and/or a provocation manufactured by militant Miami-based Cuban exile groups was a potential nightmare. As discussed earlier, a military response had been considered by the Clinton White House.

American businessmen felt frustrated because of the Helms-Burton Act. While foreign investors were gaining a foothold in Cuba, Americans were being left out. Dwayne Andreas, chief executive of Archers Daniel Midland, a large processor of oil seed, wheat, and corn, was quoted in the press as stating bluntly: "Helms-Burton is a major mistake." He added: "The only way to improve relations in Cuba is through commerce." Andreas, who met Castro in New York City in 1995 when the Cuban leader attended the United Nations' fiftieth anniversary celebration, called the U.S. embargo a "total and complete failure."[35] Jerry Jasinowski, president of the National Association of Manufacturers (NAM), stated in support of his association's report opposing trade sanctions on Cuba: "Unilateral sanctions are little more than postage stamps we use to send messages to other countries at the cost of thousands of American jobs." In its report, NAM noted that Washington's sixty-one laws and executive actions between 1993 and 1996 authorizing unilateral economic sanctions cost American businessmen their share of business with "2.3 billion potential customers and $790 billion—or nearly 20 percent of the world's export market."[36]

Clinton defended the decision of increasing pressure on Castro. The administration claimed that Helms-Burton did not violate international law (contradicting its earlier position that some sections of the law did) and that it would enforce the measure regardless of worldwide opposition. In July 1996 the law came into effect, but the statute's Title III was suspended.

To calm the international outcry against Helms-Burton, Clinton enlisted Stuart Eizenstat, undersecretary of commerce for international trade. In 1997, with the blessings of Senator Helms, Eizenstat was nominated as the State Department's undersecretary for economics, business and agricultural affairs for his efforts to implement Helms-Burton. Eizenstat's skills were put to a test since his mission was rejected in every country he visited in 1996. Canadian Prime Minister Jean Chrétien was on record saying that Eizenstat would "be told in quite clear terms that we do not accept being told whether or not we can trade with Cuba."[37] Eizenstat's mission became the catalyst for a rejection of Clinton's Cuba policy by the United States' closest allies. It was a triumph for Cuba when true victories were scarce.[38]

Clinton's persistence scored points by the end. Under pressure of the Spanish prime minister, José María Aznar, the European Union established restrictions for aid and investment in Cuba. Aznar's attitude toward Castro created serious friction between Havana and Madrid, damaging what had been cordial relations. The reaction in Spain to Aznar's Cuba policy was characterized by a Spanish political analyst this way:

> Cuba is one of the few hot topics in Spanish foreign policy. That explains the interest of political parties, associations and businessmen to learn the position of the new center-right government, which won the elections on March 3, 1996. Would they toughen policy toward Cuba? . . . Would Aznar continue the policy initiated by General Franco, who, despite being a fierce enemy of communism, never gave in to pressure from North America?
>
> There was the response. Aznar was going to tighten the screws on the Cuban leader to demonstrate that the Popular Party (PP) had its foreign policy straight. What Aznar did not expect was that the apparent tightening united, on one front, the so-called "sociological Spanish left" and the economic right. The first, because foremost in

their minds remained the romantic image of Che Guevara, Coman-
dante Castro, the Sierra Maestra . . . and they could not stand for a
"rightist" government to threaten a new bastion of socialism. The
second, because the policy put their investment in danger . . . In
Cuba there are dozens, perhaps hundreds of Spanish companies,
from Sol Meliá (hotels) to Repsol (petroleum) . . . the Spanish have
discovered that they have taken the lead, ahead of the United States.[39]

Contrary to what Havana expected, American allies in Europe moved
closer to the White House's stance. But in an action supported by Canada
and Mexico, the European Union appealed to the World Trade Organization (WTO), charging that Helms-Burton was extraterritorial and was
contrary to free world commerce. President Clinton's repeated suspension of Helms-Burton's Title III could not solve the dispute with Europe
over Helms-Burton: "The Europeans [were] reluctant to help the United
States in its property disputes with Cuba because all European countries
have already resolved that issue by negotiating compensation agreements with Fidel Castro's government." Moreover, "Why should all the
other countries do something for the United States, which refused to find
the solution that [Europe] did?"[40]

Avoiding a showdown with the European Union (EU) at the WTO in
April 1997, Washington arrived at an informal agreement with its European allies. The Helms-Burton hearing was postponed until October, so
that Clinton could request Congress to waive Title IV of the Helms-Burton Act. But Washington's real objective was that the EU would accept
the Multilateral Agreement on Investment (MAI) regulating confiscated
property, which was being drafted by the Organization for Economic
Development. The new treaty would protect private property worldwide and could be negotiated by the fifteen EU member nations by late
1998.[41]

After missing the October deadline, the United States and the EU accepted a temporary understanding. On May 18, 1998, they ended their
trade dispute over Cuba with an agreement reached "at the eleventh
hour, just before President Clinton was scheduled to meet with EU leaders in London enroute to Geneva to celebrate the founding of the World
Trade Organization." Besides continuing suspending Title III of the
Helms-Burton Act, the White House would refrain from applying Title
IV and the D'Amato Act (which punishes investors in the energy sector
in Iran and Libya). The agreement included the establishment of a global
registry of expropriated properties that would be subject to "binding disciplines," which would ban assistance to European corporations investing in disputed nationalized property.[42]

Castro denounced the U.S.-EU agreement in Geneva during the WTO's fiftieth anniversary celebration. "There are plenty of reasons," he said, "for the world to feel humiliated and concerned . . . the WTO should be capable of preventing economic genocide . . . The dispute between the United States and the European Union about the Helms-Burton Act should not be settled at Cuba's expense."[43]

President Clinton's report to Congress, "Support for a Democratic Transition in Cuba," issued in 1997 in compliance with Title II of the Helms-Burton Act, suggested the creation of an international donor coordination mechanism to which it would contribute between $4 billion and $8 billion for a democratization of Cuba. President Castro retorted that Cuba was not for sale, adding: "Free men can die but no force or money in the world will be capable of turning you into slaves . . . It is unworthy to think that liberty and dignity can be bought."[44]

President Clinton's report, drafted in collaboration with Representative Robert Menéndez (D-N.J.), sought to distance the Cuban military from Castro.[45] It reassured them "that they would not be marginalized or persecuted if they chose to cooperate with a future democratic transition."[46] Rejecting Clinton's offer and proclaiming loyalty to the revolution, "The Declaration of the Twentieth-Century Independent Fighters" was signed by 250,000 officers of the Revolutionary Armed Forces (FAR), the reserves, the Ministry of the Interior (MININT), and Fidel and Raúl Castro. In a ceremony held in 1997, the document was placed inside the José Martí Memorial in Havana's Revolution Square. It stated: "[We] declare that we are the independence fighters of the 20th century and that we shall continue to be those of the 21st century, because in the same way that the Cuban Revolution has been one and the same since 1868, it has also had a single army, called the Liberation Army in the war of independence, then named the Rebel Army at the time of our national liberation; and now, with socialism, we are the Revolutionary Armed Forces, and will continue to defend the same anti-imperialist ideas that we have defended until now."[47]

After the House of Representatives approved seven of ten amendments hardening Helms-Burton, Havana went on an international diplomatic offensive denouncing the congressional action and accusing the White House of not trying to stop it. Alarcón denounced what was happening in Washington in a press conference broadcast worldwide by the CNN office in Havana.[48] Robaina visited Central American and Caribbean nations, Lage carried a similar mission to South America, and other high-ranking officials visited European capitals. They all carried letters from Castro warning the different presidents: the U.S. is doing it to Cuba today, tomorrow could be your turn.[49] As an American Cuba watcher put it: "The [new] bill [in addition to the seven amendments approved by the House], sponsored by Sens. Torricelli and Mack . . . is more outrageously extraterritorial than the Helms-Burton Act itself."[50] Canada actively opposed Clinton's approach to Cuba. In a visit to Havana in 1997, Canadian Foreign Affairs Minister Lloyd Axworthy signed a joint agreement on fourteen areas for further cooperation between his country and Cuba.[51]

Clinton disliked seeing Canada contradicting his Cuba policy in favor of constructive engagement. Others in Washington reacted angrily: "It is a mistake to have a romantic view of Fidel Castro. He is a dictator," declared Secretary Albright. "It is shameful that Canada is participating in this propaganda ploy, " stated Senator Helms's spokesman, Marc Thiessen.[52]

Clinging to a Failed Cuba Policy

Two former Clinton aides were critical of the administration for lacking "a long-range policy on Cuba." The architect of the Torricelli-Graham Act track two and former adviser on Cuba, Richard Nuccio, and the former National Security Council specialist on Latin America, Richard Feinberg, noted that "the U.S. failure to commit to a plan allows Cuban President Fidel Castro to manipulate U.S. policy toward Cuba." Moreover, "Our policy is in the hands of the Cuban government, not because it has to be, but because that's where our administration has left it," stated Nuccio and Feinberg.

Following President Clinton's recognition that his policy has failed, Feinberg stated, "[Clinton's] is a remarkable admission for a president after 35 years [of the U.S. embargo of Cuba]. And even more remarkable that the admission would no way imply in his own mind that we should think about a new policy."[53] Feinberg noted that anti-Castro Cuban Americans' political clout contributed to Clinton's failure to devise an effective Cuba policy.

On the occasion of a visit to Washington by Canadian prime minister Jean Chrétien in 1997, Clinton stated that his policy and Canada's were failing, saying that "since there haven't been appreciable changes in the Cuban regime, neither of our policies can claim success." But the Canadian prime minister defended his policy: "We think that the best way to resolve the problem with Cuba is to open normal relations with them."[54] True to his word, Canada was extending further its relations with Cuba.

The Political Effect of the Pope's Visit

Sponsored by Senator Chris Dodd (D-Conn.) and Representative Esteban Torres (D-Calif.) with the support of Representative Charles Rangel (D-N.Y.) and 135 other legislators, the Dodd-Torres bill proposed lifting the ban on sales of food and medicines to Cuba. It had been presented in Congress with no chance of being widely supported when the correlation of political forces changed somewhat. After gaining twenty-six cosponsors in the Senate and 112 in the House, on March 31, 1998 (the "National Day of Education and Advocacy for Food and Medicine Sales to Cuba"), hundreds of Cuban Americans converged on Capitol Hill to support ending the embargo on food and medicines to Cuba. They were coming from the Miami area energized by the pope's visit to the island and his plea for humanitarian aid to the Cuban people. They visited congressional offices lobbying for their cause and held a press conference supporting, so far unsuccessfully, legislation partially lifting the embargo.[55]

Recognizing the emotional impact of the pope's condemnation of the embargo, and attempting to stop its lifting by Congress or the administration, the Cuban American National Foundation proposed sending up to $100 million in food and medical aid "directly to the Cuban people." The aid would be distributed by the American Red Cross or the Roman Catholic Church, not by the Cuban government. Fearful of the possible abrogation of the embargo, the foundation was endorsing limited humanitarian aid instead of letting Cuba pay for its own purchases of food and medicines.

Suggesting a rift among hard-liners, the three Cuban-American congressmen opposed the foundation's proposal while Senator Jesse Helms supported it.[56] Senator Helms explained that the assistance would be "earmarked for Cubans who cannot afford to buy food and medicine 'because of the brutal, Marxist-Leninist economic policies of the Castro regime'."[57]

The discord in the anti-Castro ranks was felt at the White House, producing mixed results. Secretary of State Albright told an audience at Miami Dade Community College that U.S. Cuba policy needed a "transition." Three days after the National Assembly had reelected Castro for another five-year term, Albright said: "They celebrated Christmas, now they should hold a day of [free] elections." After meeting with anti-Castro groups and delivering a five-minute message to Cuba via Radio Martí, Albright traveled to the Vatican, where she was received by the pope.

Albright told the pontiff that the United States "would like to help the

Cuban people but without supporting the regime" and that she expected Cuba would one day "open itself to the world." A joint communiqué stated that the pope and Albright would watch jointly "Cuba's future following the [pope's] visit." The former U.S. ambassador to the United Nations, Bill Richardson, stated on American television that he found Castro, whom he had met personally, "an interesting, well informed, and intellectually very capable person . . . [but] he is not going to change, and he violates human rights and likes power."[58]

Two months after the pope's visit to Cuba, the White House announced the partial lifting of some of the sanctions for humanitarian reasons. Two of the three curbed penalties had been imposed by President Clinton in 1996. Also, before the 1992 Torricelli Act, Cuba had been able to buy from American subsidiaries in third countries close to $700 million annually, of which 90 percent was food. The 1992 prohibition of these commercial exchanges had been reinforced by the Helms-Burton Act in 1996.

After a formal announcement by the White House, Secretary Albright offered a detailed explanation of the new regulations. The changes affected four areas:

> Allowing the resumption of direct charter flights for humanitarian purposes; regular family visits and tourism are excluded (reversing Clinton's 1996 sanctions).
> Permitting Cuban-American families to send money to their relatives in Cuba: $300 every three months for a maximum of $1,200 per year (reversing Clinton's 1996 sanctions).
> Increasing and facilitating the licensing of nongovernmental organizations that could deliver medical supplies to Cuba for humanitarian reasons (preferably but not limited to the Catholic Church and its charitable organization, Caritas).
> Requesting Congress to work on a bipartisan basis on legislation that would permit the shipment of food to the Cuban people, which is presently prohibited by law.[59]

In less than diplomatic language, Secretary Albright explained Clinton's decision:

> The lifting of sanctions does not represent a change in policy toward the Cuban government.
> The United States will maintain economic pressure through the embargo and the Helms-Burton Act.
> The United States should help the Cuban people without helping the government.

The changes were made in response to the pope's visit to
Cuba, not as a reward to Castro.

When Albright and the pope met at the Vatican in early March,
the pontiff expressed his support for American steps alleviating the suffering and isolation of the Cuban people.

The pope's visit generated "huge amounts of energy and
excitement within Cuba."

Instead of improving relations with Castro, the policy changes
would profit from new possibilities that now exist outside
the government.

Cuba should open its government, release prisoners of conscience, and respect human rights.

As has happened in every other country in the Americas, the
Cuban people should have the right to elect freely their own
government.

The United States will not forget that Cuba shot down two
Brothers to the Rescue airplanes, causing the death of three
American citizens and one legal resident.

The Cuban government is "responsible for murder."

Though the United States would like to see Castro embrace
democracy, it should do as the Cuban people are doing and
start thinking "beyond Castro."[60]

President Clinton expressed similar thoughts. The Cuban people's response to the pope's visit had convinced him "that we should continue to
look for ways to support Cuba's people without supporting its regime,
by providing additional humanitarian relief, increasing human contacts
and helping the Cuban people prepare to be a free, independent and
prosperous nation."[61]

Reacting to the administration's announcement, the former head of
Havana University's Center for the Study of the United States, Esteban
Morales Domínguez, said that the real change would be "simplifying
and accelerating the sale of medicines," adding that "if the decision implies that Cuba could buy medicines [from the U.S.] like any other country, that would be a breakthrough in the embargo."[62]

On the second anniversary of the Helms-Burton Act, Ambassador
James Dobbin, special assistant to President Clinton, confirmed the administration's stance: "there will be no change in American policy as long as
Castro remains in power." He said: "We are 40 years closer to the end of
the Castro regime, [and] it is only prudent to expect a post-Castro era in

which Cubans will choose democracy." While recognizing that American policy has failed to overthrow the Castro regime, he insisted that the U.S. would support a "democratic transition in Cuba."[63]

The archbishop of Boston, Bernard Cardinal Law, expressed an opposing view. "The moment to change U.S. Cuba policy has arrived," he said. Requiring a change in Cuba's leadership for a U.S. policy change was too rigid, and "depending on the means used to provoke such a change [in Cuba], they might also be found morally improper." There had been dramatic changes in religious policy "and they are not going to stop. . . . The toothpaste is out of the tube and it was Fidel Castro who squeezed it," he added.[64]

The New York City–based Catholic Medical Missions Board announced the largest shipment of humanitarian aid it had ever made available for Cuba: $6 million worth of drugs and supplies (antibiotics, insulin, nutritional supplements, vitamins, bandages, gloves, etc.) donated by major U.S. pharmaceutical companies—Johnson and Johnson, Eli Lilly, Merck, and Hoffman-LaRoche. According to the pharmaceutical coordinator of the Catholic Medical Mission Board, they were able to collect $1 million worth of insulin, "enough to take care of every person . . . who has diabetes for the next six months."[65]

Clinton received strong criticism from conservatives in Congress and southern Florida Cuban Americans. While agreeing that "now is the time to pursue the opportunities created by the pope's visit, by supporting the Catholic Church and by decreasing the Cuban people's dependence on the Castro regime," Senator Helms criticized Clinton for having acted alone without consulting Congress. "There is a right way and a wrong way to do it," he said. Senator Robert Torricelli (D-N.J.) stated: "I do not believe that unilateral concessions to Castro without corresponding improvement in his human rights record will bring us any closer to the ultimate goal of freedom for the Cuban people." And Representative Ileana Ros-Lehtinen (R-Fla.) said the measures would send a "terrible" message: "We are forgiving Castro for the death of poor, innocent American citizens. I wish we would be a little tougher with the dictator," she said.[66]

There were other voices in Miami raised against Clinton. The CANF said the moves sent "the wrong signals" to Castro: "Nothing has changed on the part of the Cuban government. Repression has not changed."[67] José Basulto, founder of Brothers to the Rescue, said the sanctions were "being lifted because of private interests who want to do business in Cuba and use its forced labor."[68]

In a CNN interview in Havana, Castro's response was positive: "Those three measures sound to me positive. They would be a positive thing, constructive measures that would be helpful and conducive to a better climate between the United States and Cuba, but . . . we would have to study them fully to express our views on that connection."[69]

Using stronger language, the Cuban foreign minister told the UN Human Rights Commission in Geneva: "We do not need scraps disguised as humanitarian aid. We won't sacrifice our principles in exchange for imperialist pardons." He also denounced the U.S. embargo as "the most flagrant, massive and systematic violation of human rights of [the Cuban] people . . . We are talking of a true war of economic and psychological attrition which has lasted four decades and cost our country $60 billion, not to mention the human victims which are beyond price." But a report prepared for the same organization stated that "the long-standing U.S. embargo against Cuba has provided [the government] with a 'ready pretext' for repressing its people."[70]

The people in Cuba were jubilant "as the word spread that the Clinton administration was loosening economic sanctions." As reported in the *Dallas Morning News,* a housewife in Havana's Miramar neighborhood said: "Now we are waiting for the miracle of miracles, the lifting of the embargo." Referring to the pope's visit as another miracle, a Havana resident said: "This is the second miracle in Cuba this year."

Enrique López, a Havana religious scholar, had similar thoughts: "The easing of travel and other restrictions has recharged the Cuban spirit. People are happy and are celebrating in their homes, calling their relatives in the United States." Pointing to the newly gained role for the Cuban church, López added that this decision would "strengthen the church. It gives the church more credibility with Cubans and the government. The church is proving to Fidel that it can deliver on promises, and Fidel is responding in kind. We are seeing the fruits of a new relationship between government and church and hopefully between the Cuban and American governments."[71]

The scope of Clinton's decision and its objectives for Cuba's future were equally relevant. The changes highlighted the constraints Clinton had in shaping Cuba policy. There is not much a president can do since the Helms-Burton Act has limited the scope of Washington-Havana relations. Also, after courting Cuban American voters, organizations, and leaders, and with circumstances compounded by a Republican-dominated Congress, it was difficult for Clinton to move away from political alliances supporting an antagonistic approach to Castro.

The objectives sought by Clinton were as lasting as his acceding to the pope's plea for a humanitarian approach to Cuba. While his decision lowered the sanctions to almost what they were before the 1994 *balseros* (rafters) crisis and the 1996 shooting down of the BTTR's airplanes, it also resurrected the political objectives sought by track two of the Torricelli-Graham Act. Besides BTTR's repeated violations of Cuban air space in spite of Havana's complaints, what prompted Cuba to react so harshly, precipitating the 1996 confrontation with Washington, was the administration's interference in Cuba's domestic political life, particularly promoting a civil society independent from the government.

It appears that Washington was using a similar approach through the Catholic Church and unnamed nongovernmental organizations: aiming to use the Church to distance the people from the government, making the latter increasingly irrelevant socially and politically. Once the Church has the resources to provide medicines, medical equipment, and eventually food in amounts the government could not afford under the strictures of the embargo, the Church could become a powerful sociopolitical actor rivaling the regime. By then, the people would become materially and psychologically dependent on the Church rather than the government, which would be left retaining a limited scope of authority.

Whether the Church will allow itself to be used in such a fashion, and how and when the Cuban government will react to such challenge to its authority, remain to be seen. However, it seems that this kind of American interference in Cuban social and political life would make a stable, harmonious relationship between the Catholic Church and the government very difficult. They would be seeing each other as political antagonists, ruining the gains made by the liberalization of religious practice and the additional social space accrued by the pontiff. Such an outcome could be a hidden objective built into Clinton's decision to ease sanctions following the pope's visit.

Havana's initial reaction to Clinton's easing of the sanctions was "positive," but it was then rejected as a new version of the old "carrot and stick" trick. "If [the U.S.] want[s] to make a humanitarian gesture, the only really humanitarian [gesture] would be to lift the blockade as the only [decision that is] just and honorable," read a statement from the Ministry of Foreign Relations.

Suddenly, the Vatican became the center of the dispute between Havana and Washington, with American and Cuban representatives visiting in rapid succession. First came Secretary Albright, who told the pope that the United States would be channeling humanitarian aid to Cuba via the Catholic relief organization, Caritas, and after presenting a list of prisoners in Cuban jails, requested their release by Havana. Then came former foreign minister Robaina, who rejected Clinton's offer, expressing reasons similar to the ones included in the foreign ministry's statement.

In a significant political move with nationalistic overtones, Jaime Cardinal Ortega supported Cuba's position. He told the Italian magazine *Christian Family:* "This humanitarian aid is only a palliative, and, to some extent, it is offensive charity." On one hand, he said, "forceful measures are used to drown the economy and suck up our resources and, on the other hand, an aiding hand is extended . . . If this aid is accepted [it is] because one cannot survive without it, but the feeling that none of this respects the dignity of an entire people is very strong. This is the immoral aspect of the embargo that was underlined by the Pope during his visit to Cuba." He blamed the embargo for the shortage of food and medicines, "which must be purchased from far-away countries at very high prices." Cardinal Ortega also accused the United States of forcing Cuba to resort to extremely expensive short-term credits. "Without credits at low interest rates, the island's economy will remain strangled, development projects cannot prosper and the people will suffer the consequences," he said.[72] Cardinal Ortega, the pope, and Cuba were speaking with one voice denouncing Washington's embargo.

Implying a possible mediation role by the Vatican between Cuba and the United States (denied by Havana), the Vatican secretary of state, Angelo Cardinal Sodano, expressed satisfaction with Clinton's easing of sanctions. Partial to a policy of positive but limited steps, Cardinal Sodano said "one moves forward in life with short steps."[73] Still, Cuba rejected Clinton's easing of sanctions as an improper response to the pope's plea for the lifting of the embargo.

Conclusion

For a President limited in international relations initiatives, Clinton's main foreign policy contribution has been the doctrine of democratic enlargement. As former national security advisor Anthony Lake told the Council of Foreign Relations, "[Enlargement] is in the best tradition of American diplomacy, . . . [it] marries our interests and our ideals." Clinton's doctrine was examined as follows: "While campaigning in 1992, Clinton had outlined what he considered to be the three foreign policy priorities that the next commander-in-chief would confront: updating and restructuring American military and security capabilities; elevating the role of economics in international affairs, and promoting democracy abroad . . . America was now the world's only superpower, and that reality demanded that global leadership emanate from the Oval office. *Great foreign policy, Clinton understood, did not only respond to situations, it created them*" (emphasis added).[74]

It was also noted that "free trade remains the heart of enlargement and the core of [Clinton's] foreign policy." But then, "in light of the unilateralism of the Helms-Burton act, which seeks to isolate Cuba economically, and given the administration support for Republican senator Alfonse D'Amato's Iran and Libya Sanctions Act [somewhat changed later], which seeks to reinforce the pariah status of those countries, it should be clear that enlargement means free trade on American terms."[75]

And yet, if the Helms-Burton Act is representative of Clinton's democratic enlargement doctrine, the prospects for its success have not been promising. While foreign policy making based on domestic politics occurred long before the Clinton Administration, it is not an effective way of handling the nation's international priorities. It is implausible to justify persistence in a dated, failed foreign policy. Also, Clinton's democratic enlargement is as intrusive to Cuba as international proletarianism and Cuba's exporting of the revolution were to Washington.

While liberal democracy is the ideology of choice among Western constitutional polities, not every country in the world should be obliged to accept it. And a government should not be punished because it upholds its own political choice and rejects liberal democracy. To use liberal democracy as a justification for destroying such a government is no better than Moscow's interventionism on behalf of communism, which was condemned by Washington.

Interventionism always denies self-determination. Rejecting any interference in Cuban affairs, Castro's defense of national sovereignty and independence is not posturing but real. His stance appeals to his fellow Cubans—the majority who never left the island—motivating them to emulate his nationalistic crusade. After more than four decades of living a revolutionary life, Cubans seem able to endure the hardships brought about by the confrontation with Washington.

During his 1998 tour of Africa, President Clinton received a moral challenge from President Nelson Mandela. "Set an example to all of us and make peace with adversaries in Iran, Libya and Cuba," said Mandela. On the desolate island where Mandela had been in jail in a bleak cell with only a bucket for a toilet for eighteen of his twenty-seven years' imprisonment, he told Clinton: "This was my home." But he said he had forgiven the former South African government that "slaughtered our people, massacred them like flies." The United States, Mandela added, was "the willful leader of the world . . . One of the ways of [being a leader] is to call upon [one's] enemies to say, 'Let's sit down and talk peace'."[76]

Clinton did not respond to Mandela's ethical challenge, but Sandy Berger, national security advisor, told reporters: "On those [issues] we disagree."[77] Berger's remark underscored the difference between Clinton's brand of leadership and Mandela's moral stature in Africa and across the world.[78]

Building New Bridges to the World

To Make New Friends, to Rekindle Old Friendships

The Cuban government's "priorities in foreign policy today are to make friends above anything else, and to multiply business connections with the world."[1] The changes in external relations underscore the island's commitment to a successful adjustment to the world of the 1990s and beyond. New relationships and partnerships are being established, while old ones have been restored under new conditions. The relationship with European socialism that had kept the country economically afloat for three decades had to be replaced with new trade markets, credit and financing, and capital investment. Between 1993 and 1996 Cuba signed Reciprocity Agreements for the Protection and Promotion of Investment with eighteen countries from four different continents, reassuring foreign investors that their investment would be safe.

Cuba followed a twofold approach in the 1990s in international relations. While restoring relations with former European socialist countries and Soviet republics was important (particularly with Russia, which again became Cuba's number one trade partner), establishing relations with countries all over the world remained the new foreign policy centerpiece. Survival was more pressing than ever, and the means to that end had changed.

Cuba's active diplomacy at the United Nations was rewarded in 1999 when for the eighth consecutive year the General Assembly voted to condemn the U.S. economic embargo against Cuba. The European Union members voted against the embargo, expressing their disapproval of the Helms-Burton Act.

The history of the United Nations resolutions condemning the United States embargo against Cuba stands as probably the worst element of

Table 10.1. United Nations' Resolutions Condemning U.S. Embargo Against Cuba (1992–1999)

Year	Votes in Favor	Votes Against	Abstentions	Total
1992	59 (44.36%)	3 (2.25%)	71 (53.38%)	133
1993	88 (59.00%)	4 (2.68%)	57 (38.25%)	149
1994	101 (66.88%)	2 (1.32%)	48 (31.78%)	151
1995	117 (74.05%)	3 (1.89%)	38 (24.05%)	158
1996	137 (83.03%)	3 (1.81%)	25 (15.15%)	165
1997	143 (87.73%)	3 (1.84%)	17 (10.42%)	163
1998	157 (91.81%)	2 (1.16%)	12 (7.01%)	171
1999	155 (92.93%)	2 (1.12%)	8 (4.84%)	165

SOURCE: *Granma International*, November 16, 1997, 5 (online, http://www.granma.cu); *New York Times*, October 15, 1998; "Cuban Officials Claim Moral Victory in Another U.N. Vote Against Embargo," CNN (online, http://www.cnn.com), November 9, 1999.

Washington's diplomatic record at the international body and as Havana's best. From fewer than half the countries (44.36%) voting against the embargo in 1992, the percentage surged to practically universal rejection of U.S. policy by 1998 (91.81%), and even more so in 1999 (92.93%).[2] The vote against the resolution condemning the embargo was never significant; the most votes it received was four (2.68%) in 1993. Also, the declining number of countries abstaining from voting mirrored the increasing international support for Cuba on the issue. Seventy-one nations (53.38%) had abstained in 1992, but by 1999 there were only eight (4.84%). In 1996, when the Helms-Burton Act was signed into law, 137 nations (83.03%) voted against the embargo with only twenty-five (15.15%) abstaining. The opposition to the embargo kept growing in 1999. The director of policy studies at the United Nations Association of the United States commented in 1998 that "as a general principle when a country finds itself totally isolated and has virtually no allies, it should be an occasion for reflection on its foreign policy line."[3] (See table 10.1.)

Havana has approached foreign policy normatively and instrumentally, as an ideological conduit for the revolution and as a resource helping the country's maintenance and development objectives. While past support of revolutionary regimes and movements stemmed from the regime's ideology, it also was a weapon used to neutralize Washington's enmity. The pursuit of such foreign policy motivations and objectives was recognized before 1990:

> The Cuban government has acted according to its own hierarchy of foreign policy goals. In descending order of importance, it has at-

tempted to create and defend a revolutionary regime at home and to establish the relations abroad that will secure and protect that regime; to support Marxist-Leninist regimes in the Third World; to establish relations with other existing governments that do not directly threaten its security; to support revolutionary movements, especially those that oppose the aims of the United States and of governments aligned with it; and, where possible, to promote its own economic relations with other countries, in line with its more important foreign policy goals.[4]

While supporting Marxist-Leninist regimes in the Third World is today a nonissue, defeating Washington's interventionist aims has gained new urgency. Whether a country has close relations with the United States is not a relevant issue as long as it is willing to sustain relations with Havana, but the defense of national sovereignty and of the principles of nonintervention and the right to self-determination remain central to Cuba's values and objectives.

Castro has pursued a personal and almost peripatetic diplomacy in recent years. He has visited every continent and has missed hardly any international forum of significance. His trip to Asia in 1995 included visits to China and Vietnam and a stopover in Japan on his way home. On his first visit to China, Castro visited Beijing, Xian, Shanghai, Shenzhen, and Canton. He studied how the Chinese have adapted "to contemporary global realities without abandoning the basic principles of socialism." Revitalizing trade with China was an important objective. Between 1989 and 1994 commercial exchange had decreased $173.4 million (39.2 percent), from $441.3 million to $267.9 million. Castro stated that "now, as never before, the conditions are ripe for Cuban-Chinese relations to reach their highest levels, to the benefit of both countries." They have improved since, involving some joint ventures. There also was a diminishing trade with Japan to reverse. From $187.9 million in 1989, it had plummeted to $87.5 million in 1994 (53.4 percent). The rescheduling of Cuba's debt with Japan in 1998 could open Tokyo's market again to profitable trade and financial exchange. In Vietnam's Reunification Palace, Castro said: "Ho Chi Minh's dreams have been realized."[5]

At the 1996 United Nations Conference on Human Settlements, Habitat II, in Istanbul, Turkey, Castro spoke on behalf of the world's downtrodden, accusing the rich nations of plundering the planet: "Those who have destroyed the planet and poisoned the air, the seas, the rivers and the earth are the least interested in saving humanity."[6]

In 1998 Castro attended the World Trade Organization's fiftieth anniversary in Geneva, and the Twelfth Nonaligned Movement Summit in Durban, South Africa. He was warmly greeted by President Nelson Mandela, who at a state dinner honoring Castro in Cape Town characterized the sanctions against Cuba as "odious." Castro was among the twenty-three heads of state attending the Eighth Ibero-American Summit in Oporto, Portugal, where thousands of people marched demonstrating support for Cuba and opposition to the U.S. embargo.

A main Cuban objective in foreign policy has been to strengthen relations with Latin American and Caribbean countries. Havana has reestablished relations with nineteen countries in the region, not counting Canada and the United States. While seven Latin American countries reestablished relations in the 1990s, three still remain without diplomatic exchange: Costa Rica, El Salvador, and Honduras (though the latter and Cuba exchanged diplomatic interest sections in 1997). By 1998 the following story reported in the media was no longer unusual: During a visit to Cuba, the president of Panama, Ernesto Pérez Balladares, stated that "relations between Cuba and Panama are excellent on all levels, in the trade, diplomatic and social spheres, and there is a permanent exchange of people and tourism."[7] (See table 10.2.)

Since 1994, Cuba has been a member of the Caribbean States Association, where it has supported the establishment of a free trade area in a region made up of thirty-two islands, even though some still have colonial status under France, England, Holland, and the United States. In 1998 Castro visited Jamaica; Barbados, where he dedicated a monument honoring the seventy-three passengers of a Cubana de Aviación flight who were killed when the airplane exploded off the island as a result of sabotage; Grenada, where he unveiled a monument dedicated to Cuban workers captured or killed in the 1983 U.S. invasion of the island; and the Dominican Republic, where he received a hero's welcome. At the Caribbean Forum (CARIFORUM) Summit held in Santo Domingo during his visit, Castro said: "Unity is the single and true force for the Caribbean . . . only united can we defend ourselves."[8]

After establishing relations with Haiti in 1996, with four more countries a year later, with others including Guatemala in 1998 (a visit by that country's president, Alvaro Arzú, followed in 1999), and Paraguay and Ireland in 1999, Cuba's diplomatic exchanges totaled 168—90.3 percent of U.N. member nations and 87 percent of

Table 10.2. Diplomatic Relations between Cuba and Latin America under the Revolution

Country	Broke Relations	Reestablished Relations
Argentina	1962	1973
Bolivia	1963	1983
Brazil	1964	1986
Colombia	1981	1993
Costa Rica	1961	——
Chile	1973	1995
Dominican Republic	1962	1997
Ecuador	1963	1979
El Salvador	1961	——
Guatemala	1961	1998
Haiti	1961	1996
Honduras	1961	1997 (interest sections)
Mexico	(never broke relations with Cuba)	
Nicaragua	1961	1979
Panama	1961	1974
Paraguay	1961	1999
Peru	1962	1970
Uruguay	1964	1985
Venezuela	1962	1974

SOURCE: "Solo Cuatro Países de Latinoamerica Aun No Restablecieron Relaciones con Cuba," Agence France Presse, January 28, 1998; "Paraguay, Cuba Reestablish Diplomatic Ties," *XINHUA*, November 8, 1999.

all sovereign states. This is more than three times the diplomatic relations Havana had before 1959 (fifty countries, thirty embassies, and half of the sixty consulates in the United States). Of the 185 U.N. member nations, eighty-seven are diplomatically accredited in Havana, while others have consular or other forms of representation. By 1998 Cuba had diplomatic or consular representation in eighty-seven countries and simultaneous accredited representatives in approximately seventy-seven countries.[9]

While Washington has aggravated some of the political and economic issues affecting Cuba in the 1990s, Havana has pursued its own international relations agenda. Breaking the isolation the United States has built around Cuba, the island's international engagement policy has been successful. It has allowed a Cuban presence at almost every international event and has minimized the impact of the U.S. actions against the island.

A Latin American Homecoming

For twenty Latin American, Spanish, and Portuguese heads of state attending the First Ibero-American Summit in Guadalajara, Mexico, in the summer of 1991, Castro was the prodigal son returning to the Latin American family.[10] Cuba's homecoming was greeted by three regional presidents. In Cozumel, Mexico, in 1991, the Group of Three—Presidents César Gaviria of Colombia, Carlos Andrés Pérez of Venezuela, and Carlos Salinas de Gortari of Mexico—unexpectedly invited Castro to join them. At the end of a twenty-four-hour session the Group of Three stated in the Cozumel Declaration: "We aspire to the full inclusion of Cuba in the life of the hemisphere and Latin America."[11]

The Cuban delegation had wondered what kind of reception they would encounter at the First Ibero-American Summit. Ricardo Alarcón, then Cuban ambassador to the United Nations, said after the summit: "We weren't isolated in the least . . . We enjoyed great cordiality and a great connection with the whole world." The *Miami Herald* reported: "By the time Castro had left the Ibero-American summit . . . he had been toasted, queried and cheered repeatedly—but also lectured, scolded and mocked by leaders of lesser fame. Castro's presence so dominated the historic two-day conference of Latin presidents that some dubbed it the 'Fidelo-American' summit."[12]

After the first summit in Mexico came subsequent ones in Spain, Brazil, Colombia, Argentina, Chile, Venezuela, Portugal, Cuba, and the 2000 meeting was scheduled for Panama. Castro has attended all the Ibero-American summits and has been the center of attention at each; his presence has overshadowed that of other heads of state, with the attention of the people and the media centered on him. But he has also been attacked by some Latin American leaders, who seized the opportunity to score some points with Washington and voters at home, and by Cuban exiles exploiting the media attention and launching protests against him (in Venezuela plotting to assassinate him).

Castro was grateful for the opportunity Mexico had bestowed upon him by inviting Cuba to the 1991 Guadalajara summit. As Castro confessed to a journalist there: "The Mexicans were very kind to invite Cuba . . . As you know, Cuba is generally excluded, excommunicated, marginalized . . . But in recent times, there is a different treatment of Cuba. They invite us to the [presidential] inaugurations. It is our elementary duty to accept and take part in what is, to my mind, a historic event. Even if we meet for nothing other than to drink coffee."[13]

The final declaration of the 1996 Ibero-American Summit in Viña del

Mar, Chile, included a rejection of the Helms-Burton Act, but it also included a call for democracy and political pluralism. Castro expressed his support of and agreement with the document and signed it along with the other heads of state. In a veiled criticism of Cuba, the host of the summit, Chile's President Eduardo Frei, expressed support for liberal democratic government and practices: "No one now defends a democracy which has targets but no timetable, which is waiting for a paradise that is always just around the corner but never arrives."[14]

The 1997 Ibero-American summit at Margarita Island, Venezeula, received mixed reviews in the media. It was criticized for being poorly organized and for lacking guidelines to combat poverty and the region's technological and economic underdevelopment.[15] A Venezuelan proposal on "The Right to Truthful Information," promoting the exercise of journalism "with a sense of ethics and social responsibility," was seen as an attack on freedom of the press. After having complained of the Western media distorting the facts about the revolution, Cuba supported the proposal. The original draft was revised to make it more palatable to the nineteen Latin American heads of state and the leaders of Spain and Portugal in attendance.

President Castro was gratified by the "Margarita Declaration" and the subsequent "Porto Declaration" (1998), which again condemned Helms-Burton and rejected any future attempts by Washington to impose sanctions on Cuba. But at Margarita Island the Cuban leader faced harsh criticism from the Argentine and Nicaraguan heads of state; he largely ignored this, instead bantering with Spain's Prime Minister José María Aznar, an ideological adversary. While signing the Margarita Declaration, Castro stated: "I am forced to recall that in Cuba there was, is, and always will be a revolution, the principles of which are not for sale or betrayed."[16] President Ernesto Samper of Colombia invited Castro to join the Friends of Colombia Group (Spain, Mexico, Costa Rica, and Venezuela) to help find a peaceful solution to Colombia's battle with leftist rebels, but the guerrillas rejected Castro's mediation efforts.

The Venezuelan police arrested several Cuban exiles who had traveled to Margarita Island to charge Castro with having failed to honor the promise he made at the Viña del Mar summit to democratize his government.[17] Several Cuban exiles en route to Margarita Island in the boat *La Esperanza* were charged with attempting to assassinate Castro. The boat was seized by the U.S. Coast Guard off Puerto Rico with four Cuban exiles aboard. They were carrying rifles, ammunition, fatigue uniforms, field rations, and communications equipment. The boat was registered to a southern Florida company, and it had been docked at the Miami home of the company's owner, Juan Antonio Llama. A member of the Cuban American National Foundation Executive Committee, Llama is in charge of relations with Madrid's Hispanic-Cuban Foundation, an organization promoted by the CANF.

One of the two .50 caliber sniper rifles found on *La Esperanza* belonged to Francisco Pepe Hernández, another CANF member. While Alberto Hernández headed the CANF after Más Canosa's death, Francisco Pepe Hernández was the organization's number two man. Havana has accused the CANF of organizing the 1997 bombing spree against Cuban tourist hotels and restaurants, but this time it was the FBI who connected the CANF to terrorist actions against the Cuban government.[18] The arrested Cuban exiles were indicted in Puerto Rico on charges of conspiring to assassinate Castro. In Havana four Central Americans were charged with taking part in a bombing campaign that started in 1997 organized by a Cuban exile, Luis Posada Carriles. In 1998 Posada Carriles admitted in a *New York Times* interview to having organized the bombing campaign to hurt the country's tourist industry, its biggest source of foreign exchange.[19]

There were attempts to stop Cuba from participating in important hemispheric affairs. Argentina tried to block Cuba's invitation to the 1996 Chilean summit but was rebuked by the lack of support from other countries. Cuba had become part of the annual event and was readying itself to host the 1999 Ninth Ibero-American Summit. But when Nicaragua's President Arnoldo Alemán said he would not attend the Havana summit, Castro, avoiding antagonizing any head of state so that he would have maximum attendance at the 1999 summit, stated in Portugal that Alemán would always be welcome in Cuba.

The five heads of state who declined to attend the summit had officials from their countries represent them. Chilean president Eduardo Frei refused to go, in protest of Spain's extradition attempt of General Augusto Pinochet, who was receiving medical treatment in a British hospital, to face criminal charges before Spanish judge Baltazar Garzón; Garzón was also indicting eighty-six Argentinian citizens, including seven military officers, on criminal charges.[20] In solidarity with Chile, Argentinian president Carlos Ménem refused to attend the Havana summit. "This is not a boycott," said Ménem. "We have no problems with Cuba or the Cuban president."[21] Nicaraguan president Alemán said he was not attending because of ideological and political differences with Castro, and the presidents of Costa Rica and El Salvador justified their absence by pointing out that their countries did not have diplomatic relations with Cuba. The 1999 summit was a "major diplomatic victory for Fidel Castro over U.S. efforts to isolate him . . . but it also proved to be a historic advance for his domestic foes. An unprecedented string of high-level foreign leaders met with opposition leaders on the island." Nine delegations held talks with political dissidents, and the remarks of some, including Mexico, contained veiled criticisms of Cuba.[22]

Castro, who had finally hosted the Ibero-American Summit in Havana and had replaced his olive-green uniform with an elegant black suit for the occasion, told the officials from twenty-one Latin American countries, Spain, and Portugal with satisfaction that "Cuba had always been left out of every meeting on this continent. Some [people] looked at me with curiosity and even pity. Possibly hardly anyone believed that Cuba could withstand the collapse of the socialist camp." And he added, "We do not need to be summoned or to receive anyone's permission to meet like a family without exclusions."[23] He then listened to King Juan Carlos of Spain, the first reigning Spanish monarch to visit the island (though his father had done so after leaving the throne), wish the Cuban people prosperity and say that "only with an authentic democracy, with full guarantee for liberties and scrupulous respect for human rights by all of us, can our peoples face the challenges of the twenty-first century with success."[24]

The summit's Declaration of Havana condemned the U.S. embargo on Cuba and the Helms-Burton Act; committed the participating nations to the defense of human rights political pluralism, democratic institutions, and the state of law; reaffirmed respect for the principles of sovereignty and nonintervention; and outlined the countries' concern for the effects of economic globalization and of international financial crises on their individual economies.[25]

The Spanish prime minister, José María Aznar, tried to restrict Cuba's participation at the Seventh Ibero-American Summit at Margarita Island in 1997, but the minister in charge of relations with Latin America said later that Cuba should attend the Venezuelan summit. Spain's turnabout could have been intended to avoid an embarrassment similar to that when it reduced Cuba's participation at the Latin American Parliament conference held in Madrid by downgrading Cuba's status from participant to observer. In response, the Latin American Parliament (Parlatino) sent a letter to the Spanish parliament saying that "the invitation diminished to observer status . . . is insulting and inadmissible."[26] (Cuba had rejected the invitation to attend as observer.) Havana was excluded from the Summit Conference on Sustainable Development held in Santa Cruz de la Sierra, Bolivia, in December 1996.

Chile announced that Cuba was not invited either to the second Americas Summit held in Santiago in 1998. The first Americas Summit had been hosted by President Clinton in 1994 in Miami, where it was agreed to establish a hemispheric Free Trade of the Americas by the year 2005. Cuba was the only regional country not invited to attend the Americas Summits and was also excluded from participating in the free trade hemispheric area, which would be the largest in the world. The Chilean summit was held under a cloud caused by Clinton's own political party. In 1997 President Clinton was rebuked by Democrats in the House of Representatives who, unhappy with NAFTA's impact on American labor and environmental issues, voted against his request for fast track legislation that would allow rapid approval of the hemispheric free trade agreement. Clinton told the twenty-one other presidents and twelve prime ministers gathered in Santiago: "Be patient with us. So just stay with us. We'll get there."[27] By the end, they signed the final declaration for free trade in the hemisphere.

The next Americas Summit is being held in Canada in the year 2000, and it is possible that Ottawa may request Cuba's inclusion. Brazilian president Fernando Henrique Cardoso mentioned the embarrassing omission in Santiago: "There is a country that is missing. They have a social commitment. They are very much concerned with education and with health care. Why should we not make steps toward democracy there?" President Cardoso's statement underscored the fact that delegates at the Chilean summit had spent more time discussing social issues (including health care and education) than free trade.[28]

The reception given to Castro during his visit to Uruguay in 1995 demonstrated the sentiment toward the Cuban leader that exists among Latin Americans. Castro could reminisce in Montevideo of the time he had visited the city thirty-six years earlier, only months after the revolutionary warfare in the Sierra Maestra, in eastern Cuba, had come to an end. A public opinion survey indicated that 62 percent of Uruguayans supported President Julio María Sanguinetti's invitation to Castro, and 67 percent opposed the U.S. embargo.

Reviving a request by the Rio Group, the former Colombian president and secretary-general of the Organization of American States (OAS), César Gaviria, joined by Peru and Guatemala, asked in 1997, and again in 1998, that Cuba return to the OAS—it had been expelled in 1962 at Washington's request. But Havana did not see returning to the OAS favorably. Cuba opposes returning to an organization that has been dominated by the United States and in which U.S. influence still counts for much. Cuban scholars have recognized that newly created hemispheric structures have reduced the centrality the OAS used to have in hemispheric matters: "By the end of the Cold War, the prevailing Cuban image among the countries of the hemisphere is that of an obsolete regime, nondemocratic and contrary to the principles ruling the inter-American system. Based on that image, common to those governments whether they said so or not, friends and foes have taken positions in the decision-making mechanisms of the Inter-American system . . . However, among regional organizations formed after the 1960s—SELA, CARICOM, Ibero-American summits, and the Association of Caribbean States—at a time when American hegemony had diminished somewhat, Cuba's membership rights are not questioned, nor are its historic Latin American and Caribbean roots."[29]

In 1997 Havana received support from the Rio Group and the Inter-American Dialogue as well as the OAS. The Rio Group, meeting in Paraguay, discussed taking measures to counter U.S. unilateral actions (and those of the European Union) that affect them, including the U.S. drug certification process and the Helms-Burton Act. The Inter-American Dialogue—a Washington-based organization—"condemned the United States for ignoring the interests of the rest of the hemisphere in its hardline policy toward Cuba." Their report stated that Washington "unilaterally designed and implemented new coercive policies despite the opposition of every other country in the Americas and many beyond." It also noted that U.S. policy has made Castro "less responsive to international pressure to promote change and has increased the prospects for violence when change does occur."[30] The OAS approved the Inter-American Juridical Committee's verdict on the Helms-Burton Act, which resulted in a document strongly condemnatory of the U.S. legislation.

The Canadian-Mexican Connection

Mexico and Canada are the only countries in the Western Hemisphere that have kept uninterrupted diplomatic relations with Cuba since the 1959 revolution. Mexico voted against the OAS decision in 1962 to terminate relations with Cuba; only fourteen nations out of twenty-one agreed, and six countries abstained. The decision was based on Cuba's "adherence . . . to Marxism-Leninism [which] was incompatible with the Inter-American System." Mexico continued its relations with Cuba, arguing that the "measure violate[d] the Principle of Nonintervention in the internal affairs of another state, [which is] part of the OAS charter."[31] Canada was not even confronted with such a dilemma because Ottawa was not a member of the OAS at the time.

Mexico and Canada have different traditions and trade practices, so each has developed its own brand of relationship with Havana. But as Washington's NAFTA and trade partners, they have made public their opposition to Helms-Burton, as they did earlier to the Torricelli-Graham Act. They have also legislated antidote laws, combating the effect of Washington's policy on their relationship with Havana and on free trade practices.

Cuba and Canada

Defying Clinton's Cuba policy, Canada has become the hemisphere's leader in Cuba matters, engaging with the island in diplomatic relations and trade and investment.[32] The relations between these countries have moved into broader areas. Washington has used human rights as a political weapon against Cuba, but Canada has approached the issue by providing a liberal democratic model that could bring the island closer to Western practices, while recognizing that Havana's viewpoint on the subject deserves consideration.[33] Cubans characterize their relations with Canada as "cooperation and business with plenty of [mutual] respect."[34]

Between 1989 and 1996, trade relations between Havana and Ottawa grew from $184.2 million to $491 million ($38.3 million increase per year, or 167 percent in eight years) and moved from a trade exchange favorable to Canada by $79.2 million to one favorable to Cuba by $97 million. In 1996 the volume of trade increased to $491 million (14.6 percent over 1995), and the trade balance remained favorable to Cuba by $97 million (see table 10.3).

In the first ten months of 1996, the trade volume reached $400.1 million for a monthly average of $40.1 million (12.3 percent over 1995's monthly average of $35.7 million). If the last two months of the year had kept the same exchange rate, 1996 would have totaled $480.3 million, $46.3 million over 1995 (10.6 percent), but the actual total was $491 million, $57 million over 1995 (13.3 percent). The trade balance favorable to Cuba grew $63 million (185.2 percent) from 1995 ($34 million) to 1996 ($97 million), and the highest Canadian import remained nickel, which took first place from sugar in 1992.[35]

Diplomacy increased between Canada and Cuba in 1997.[36] Canadian foreign affairs minister Lloyd Axworthy's visit to Cuba with Christine Stewart, secretary for Latin American affairs, was the first at such a high-ranking level since 1976, when then prime minister Pierre Trudeau went to Havana. After meeting with President Castro and senior officials, Axworthy signed a bilateral declaration with Roberto Robaina, foreign affairs minister at the time. The discussions included "the current situation in the two countries, international relations, promotion of invest-

Table 10.3. Cuba and Canada: Import-Export Selected Items and Total Trade, 1989–1996 (in millions of U.S. dollars)

Cuban Exports to Canada	1989	1990	1991	1992	1993	1994	1995	1996
Nickel ores	0.0	0.0	47.4	102.2	84.5	82.2	171.2	232.0
Other nonferrous ore	7.8	0.0	2.7	2.5	1.8	2.8	1.2	3.0
Raw sugar	29.7	95.7	66.9	95.2	31.6	35.6	38.8	43.0
Fish	9.9	9.5	9.2	8.5	9.9	16.9	10.2	9.0
Clothing	1.0	1.0	1.1	1.1	1.6	1.3	1.3	1.0
Tobacco	0.7	1.1	0.8	0.9	0.7	1.2	1.8	3.0
Beverages	0.9	0.5	1.9	0.9	0.5	0.2	0.1	0.0
Total exports*	52.5	111.5	133.0	212.0	132.0	142.3	234.0	294.0
Cuban Imports from Canada	1989	1990	1991	1992	1993	1994	1995	1996
Foodstuffs	100.5	97.1	75.4	54.7	50.1	30.5	70.7	67.0
Raw materials	5.6	2.2	3.3	1.9	0.5	2.2	16.0	14.0
Chemicals	5.4	3.9	2.9	9.7	3.9	5.6	22.2	3.0
Fuels	0.0	0.0	0.0	0.0	4.0	1.0	6.0	1.0
Semifinished goods	10.3	9.6	12.0	7.5	13.0	11.0	24.0	26.0
Machinery	6.6	15.0	16.0	17.0	25.0	15.0	35.0	50.0
Transport	0.9	3.3	2.0	5.0	7.0	9.0	13.0	2.0
Consumer goods	2.0	2.7	3.0	3.0	3.0	6.0	10.0	10.0
Total imports*	131.7	132.5	114.0	98.0	108.0	84.0	200.0	197.0
Total trade	184.2	244.0	247.0	310.0	240.0	226.3	434.0	491.0

*Totals reflect items not listed in this table.

SOURCE: Official Canadian Trade Data, cited in *Cuba: Handbook of Trade Statistics, 1995* (Washington, D.C.: U.S. Directorate of Intelligence, 1995), 31–35; and *Cuba: Handbook of Trade Statistics, 1997* (Washington: U.S. Directorate of Intelligence, 1997), 21–24; Canadian government figures for 1995, cited in *CUBANEWS* 5 (April 1997): 8.

ment, and human rights." After making clear Canada's opposition to the U.S. blockade of Cuba and to the Helms-Burton Act, Axworthy declared that "Canada is willing to help with any changes taking place in Cuba."[37]

Two months later, three separate agreements were signed in Havana by the Canadian fisheries and oceans deputy minister and the Cuban fishing industry deputy minister. The agreements included measures improving "cooperation between their two legislative bodies, extending the right of the Cuban fleet to conduct fishing operations in Canadian waters and extending training in economic planning." The Canadian official stated that "Canada has proven on several occasions that we are not easily influenced. We are friends of Cuba and Cuba is our friend." Also, Canada's House of Commons speaker later signed in Havana an agreement protocol establishing a cooperation program with the Cuban National Assembly.

The National Assembly president stated that "I and my colleagues in the Cuban parliament have learned [from] our Canadian friends and [have much] to thank [them] for." The House speaker stated that the agreement would lead to more visits so that parliamentarians could "exchange mutual experiences and . . . see what advantages can be found in each other's systems, and have a closer relationship, developing the friendship and respect we have built over the past two years."[38]

Furthering Canada's Cuba policy of "constructive engagement," Prime Minister Jean Chrétien visited Havana in 1998, during which visit he stated: "Through good times and bad times, our two countries have always chosen dialogue over confrontation, engagement over isolation, exchange over estrangement. And we have always done this in an atmosphere of mutual respect for each other's independence and sovereignty."[39] While strengthening diplomatic and trade relations and Canadian investments in joint ventures and after discussing human rights issues, Chrétien asked Castro to release several political prisoners, including Vladimiro Roca.

Still, allegedly Canada failed to honor its "informal agreement" with the European Union to battle the United States on two legal fronts against the Helms-Burton Act. Canada should have filed suit under the rules of NAFTA while the European Union was doing likewise under the rules of the World Trade Organization (WTO). Sir Leon Brittan, EU trade commissioner, was reported as saying: "I find it a little curious that we have gone ahead and challenged the United States and taken a very high profile action and got some progress from the United States as a result of that very substantial progress, and Canada has held back on NAFTA."[40]

Stuart Eizenstat's diplomatic efforts on behalf of President Clinton produced a split in the international opposition to the Helms-Burton Act.[41] By neutralizing Canada's legal action in NAFTA, Washington was able to deal with the EU at the WTO alone, producing a failed tentative compromise in 1997. But in 1998 the European Union and the United States negotiated an agreement satisfactory to both parties. (Castro voiced his displeasure with the agreement while attending the WTO fiftieth anniversary celebration in Geneva.) The EU may have come to such an agreement with the United States due to Canada's failure to take action in NAFTA, or the EU blamed Canada to justify its own dealings with Washington.

Just as Canada's close ties with Cuba irked Washington, France's trade agreement with Havana in 1997 (after having delivered an aid package earlier) was criticized by the Clinton Administration. Eizenstat voiced his dissatisfaction with what he said could be a violation of the 1997 negotiations between the White House and the EU on the Helms-Burton Act. EU Trade Commissioner Brittan told Eizenstat that U.S. complaints were baseless. During the official ceremony signing the agreement in Paris, President Jacques Chirac acknowledged "the long-standing ties of friendship between France and Cuba, as well as the mutual feelings of respect." An official of the French foreign ministry denied that France's actions were meant to irritate anyone, though no one from the American Embassy was invited to the signing ceremony. "France needs to protect its investors," he said.

Cuba and Mexico

Mexico and Cuba share a revolutionary tradition that is uniquely Latin American. While Cuba went further in transforming its society than did Mexico, Mexico has defended Cuba's right to self-determination and has opposed Washington's machinations against it. The years Fidel and Raúl Castro and their comrades spent in Mexican exile have reinforced the historic bond between the nations, and their journey in the cabin cruiser *Granma* to their landing in Playas Coloradas in 1956 started the last phase of their revolutionary victory.

Mexico's position on the Helms-Burton Act is that it violates international law, which demands respect for a country's sovereignty, and that it also contradicts the rights of every nation as recognized by the United Nations. The Mexican government stated in 1996 that "the Cuban people have the exclusive right to decide the nature of their economic, social, and political regime." Also, Mexico noted that the OAS Charter and Resolution 2625 of the U.N.'s General Assembly "forbid the imposition of economic or political measures intended to force another state's will."[42]

The Mexican position was supported by the conclusion the Inter-American Juridical Committee of the OAS reached the same year. The Juridical Committee stated that the Helms-Burton Act "is not in conformity with international law"; that the "U.S. Courts are not the appropriate forum for the resolution of State-to-State claims"; and that the United States "does not have the right to take on claims of persons who were not nationals at the time of injury."[43]

The sixth meeting of the Cuban-Mexican Intergovernmental Committee was held in Havana in April 1996, presided over by Mexico's Minister of Foreign Affairs José Gurría and Cuba's Robaina. A political consultation mechanism that would allow Havana and Mexico City to keep each other informed on issues of common interest was established, and a possible visit by President Castro to Mexico was discussed. Approximately 150 programs involving educational, cultural, and scientific exchanges have been endorsed. Mexico's investments in the island are reportedly close to $1 billion, reflecting its rejection of the U.S. economic embargo against Cuba since the early 1960s.[44] Coinciding with intergovernmental meetings on economic cooperation and combating drug trafficking, in 1998 Mexico's Minister of Foreign Affairs Rosario Green paid a three-day visit to Cuba.

Cuban trade with Mexico in 1994 amounted to $185.5 million (down from $192.5 million in 1993). It increased to $363.2 million in 1995 but declined to $343 million in 1996. Throughout the 1990s trade was mostly imports from Mexico (95.5 percent in 1994, 93.8 percent in 1995, and 93.2 percent in 1996), while Cuban exports were consistently small ($12 million in 1994; $6 million in 1995; and $23 million in 1996). Imports in 1996 included semifinished goods ($84 million), chemicals ($62 million), fuels ($46 million), machinery ($38 million), raw material ($31 million), foodstuffs ($24 million), consumer goods ($23 million), and transport ($12 million).[45]

A plan for a Mexico-Cuba ferry service with capacity to carry as many as twelve hundred passengers was announced by the Port Authority of Mexico's Yucatán Peninsula. According to the plan, Sweden's Sanpey shipping company would provide the ferries for the 150-mile trip departing from the port of Morelos, south of Cancún. But there was no immediate reaction from Cuba on the ferry service project.[46]

By 1995, Mexico was second to Canada among Western Hemisphere investors in Cuba, with thirteen joint ventures. However, the Grupo Domos—one of the largest foreign investors in Cuba and with a major stake in the telephone and communication system—announced in 1997 that it was ending its involvement under pressure from the United States. Several Grupo Domos executives and their families had been denied visas to enter the United States under the Helms-Burton Act. Once it ended its Cuban investment, Grupo Domos requested that the visa denials be revoked. After some delay, the State Department notified Grupo Domos that the ban had been lifted.

Relations between Havana and Mexico's ruling PRI have always been close, and the leader of an opposition party has visited Cuba. Santiago Onlate, president of the ruling PRI party, met in Havana with President Castro in 1996 and discussed the possibility that the Cuban Communist Party could join COPPAL, an organization of Latin American political parties, which was meeting in Panama that same year. The head of the Revolutionary Democratic Party, who was also Mexico City's mayor, Cuauhtémoc Cárdenas, has kept close relations with Cuba.

One More Island in the Caribbean

An international scholarly conference held in Caracas, Venezuela, in 1993, discussing relations between Cuba and the Caribbean, arrived at significant conclusions while pursuing common regional grounds. These were some of the points under discussion:

> Cuba [is] tightly bound into the regional network of the Caribbean. In all of the nontraditional security issues, especially those such as drug trafficking, money laundering, migration, disaster response, and navigational cooperation that involved nonstate actors . . . the fate of Cuba is linked to the fate of the other states of the region. While Cuba currently may be less affected by many of these desta-bilizing phenomena than are its neighbors, it cannot escape their effects, and will surely grow more vulnerable as its economy opens further to international influences . . . [However,] the size of [Cuba's] economy and military, its military experience outside of the hemi-sphere, the role Cuba has played in recent years in the Nonaligned Movement, and the unique position that [Cuba] has held on the world stage has made Cuba a world actor of greater significance and weight than any of its island neighbors . . . [These] difference[s] could yet prove a significant obstacle to initiatives for Cuban rein-tegration into the region.[47]

The Cuban pilgrimage of Caribbean leaders that started in December 1996 continued into 1998 and beyond. First came the prime minister of Dominica, Edison James, followed by the prime minister of Grenada, Keith Mitchell.[48] Next was the prime minister of Jamaica, Percival J. Patterson.[49] The ministers of health of Dominica and Jamaica, the minis-ters of education from Haiti and from Trinidad and Tobago, and other Caribbean leaders and officials also paid visits to Cuba. Three agree-ments on economic, technical, and sports cooperation were signed in Havana by Denzil Douglas, prime minister of St. Kitts and Nevis, in 1998. Prime Minister Patterson was the president of the Caribbean Commu-nity (CARICOM), and Prime Minister Mitchell, who headed the Associa-tion of Caribbean States (ACS), replaced Patterson as CARICOM presi-dent in 1998.

During the visit of Jamaica's Prime Minister Patterson to Havana,

Castro stated that "Cuba and Jamaica should not see themselves as rivals, but rather as allies in the common efforts of national and regional economic development . . . the islands of the Cuban archipelago are part of the entire Caribbean's common heritage."[50] Also, rendering his personal respects to an old friend of Cuba, Castro attended the funeral ceremonies in Kingston for former Jamaican prime minister Michael Manley, in 1997.

Bilateral agreements were signed by Cuba and each of the leaders of the island nations during their visits. Cuban teachers will be educating Jamaican students, Cuban technicians will be assisting in the construction of an airport in Dominica, and in Grenada they will be helping in the construction of a national stadium. Cuba's earlier assistance to Grenada to build an airport ended with the 1983 U.S. invasion of the island ordered by President Reagan. While relations were broken at the time, Cuba and Grenada restored them in 1992. Cuban doctors and health workers have been providing their services in Dominica, Belize, Guyana, St. Kitts–Nevis, and St. Vincent and the Grenadines.

In 1996 Cuba hosted the ACS Second Ministerial Meeting, and in 1997 Cuba attended the fifteen-member CARICOM summit held in Jamaica. Havana also hosted the meetings of the Board of Directors of the Caribbean Center for Policy Development and of the Europe-Caribbean Council. (The latter was sponsored by the Caribbean Council for Europe, the organization responsible for promoting cooperation between Europe and the Caribbean.) While Cuba was looking forward to its inclusion in the Caribbean Council, it was preparing itself to host the Fourth Cuba-CARICOM Joint Meeting.

The Jamaica CARICOM summit was a critical meeting for Cuba's integration in the region. CARICOM postponed taking any action on the regional free trade agreement proposed by Cuba until the 1997 meeting in Havana. CARICOM, with a market of some 14 million people, expressed strong support for Cuba's inclusion in any future trade-and-aid agreements. At the Havana meeting, an important report was submitted including the findings of a feasibility study undertaken by the European Union–funded Caribbean Export Development Agency.

Cuba's Minister of Foreign Trade Ricardo Cabrisas held private consultations with the delegations present at the Jamaica summit and attended the meeting with the European Union commissioner on the so-called Lome V discussion on international trade. Prime Minister Mitchell of the Grenadines said CARICOM was fully supportive of Cuba's joining Lome, and the EU commissioner stated that the Cuban "application will be treated like any other." However, a CARICOM official said that "a possible negative reaction from the United States to warmer trade ties between Cuba and its Caribbean neighbors may have been a factor delaying consideration of the free trade accord."

Trade Minister Cabrisas reported that trade between Cuba and CARI-COM had jumped from between $5 and $6 million to $56 million between 1991 and 1996, with representatives of forty Caribbean companies operating in Havana.[51] While Cuban imports from the Caribbean exceeded exports, Havana could also offer skilled labor and technical assistance. With the expansion of the tourist industry more air transportation is now available from Cuba to the region. The 1998 Tourism Convention held in Havana stressed the role the Caribbean should play in the year 2000, in expectation of growth in the number of visitors. The convention offered the fifteen hundred delegates attending the event different commercial options involving Cuba and other Caribbean destinations.[52]

After an earlier visit to Jamaica, Barbados, and Grenada, Castro attended the 1998 summit of Caribbean heads of state and government (CARIFORUM), and in 1999 the second summit of the Association of Caribbean States, both held in the Dominican Republic. The 1998 meeting was the first Cuban participation at a Caribbean summit after Cuba's acceptance into the ACP Group (Africa–the Caribbean–Pacific) with observer status. CARIFORUM coordinates the European Union's assistance to the ACP Group in the framework of the Lome Convention. The current Lome Convention agreement will be replaced in the year 2000. The ACP Group member nations enjoy trade considerations and aid totaling more than $17 billion annually from the European Union. However, according to Edwin Carrington, general secretary of the Caribbean Forum, the group is opposed to Cuba's joining their protocol with the European Union (ACP-EU). The ACP-EU guarantees its members fixed prices and quotas and a protected market for sugar.[53]

Cuba, Spain, and the European Union

Cuban relations with Spain's anti-Communist champion, General Francisco Franco, were always proper and undisturbed but somewhat cool. Franco never allowed Spain to fall in line with Washington's anti-Castro policy. Still, the heyday of Havana-Madrid relations occurred during the administration of socialist prime minister Felipe González. When the new conservative Spanish government of José María Aznar took office in March 1996, relations faltered. The anti-Castro sentiments of the Popular Party's leader had an impact on the European Union's Cuba position as well.

Aznar suspended a development aid loan of 60 million *pesetas* to

Cuba; the ambassador, Eduardo Mirapix, was recalled to Madrid and José Coderch was appointed and "instructed to maintain closer ties with the island dissidents." As the Aznar Administration put it: "If we are changing the message, then it is logical that we should also change the messenger." The new Spanish foreign minister, Abel Matutes, described the bigger picture of Spain's new attitude toward Cuba:

> There are basically four kinds . . . [of] trade with Cuba. Spain is a big exporter to Cuba—let's hope that our exporters get paid—to the order of 40 billion pesetas a year. We hope that we do not have to be paid in toilets and sanitary ware, as happened in the previous ex-propriations when Spanish assets were seized by the Castro regime. [Still] trade between Spain and Cuba remains exactly the same. There are now two forms of cooperation in which the state inter-venes . . . humanitarian aid . . . [and] issues which affect the civilian population. These are going to be maintained in exactly the same way. There is only going to be a change in those government-to-government cooperation projects which in our judgment have been done badly. Cooperation by the European Union, by Spain, when it is government-to-government, is used to help those countries which have needs and at the same time to boost the democratic develop-ment of those societies and regimes which are not democracies, and to promote greater respect for human rights . . . Spain is going to maintain all the humanitarian aid which goes directly to the people . . . [but] those cooperation activities in which money was given, in my view wrongly, to the Cuban government to carry out certain projects are going to be reviewed . . . What we want is to continue promoting reforms in the regime . . . Why should the Cuban people not have the right to freely choose its leaders? Is this not a good aim? This is what we are pursuing with cooperation.[54]

Critics of the Aznar Administration noted that by falling into line with the United States, Spain was losing whatever influence it had on the is-land and that Spanish investments in Cuba were being endangered. Cu-ban-Spanish trade had reached $450 million between 1994 and 1995 and $596 million by 1996 ($131 million in Cuban exports; $465 million in im-ports from Spain). Spanish firms exporting to Cuba received 160 million pesetas per year in credits from Madrid. Matutes responded that Aznar had made clear to U.S. Vice President Al Gore during his visit to Spain in 1996 that Madrid has its own Cuba policy (which might be coordinated with the European Union's) and that it rejected the Helms-Burton Act.

But opponents of Aznar's policy were not satisfied by Matutes's disclaimer and expressed their dissatisfaction.

During trips to the Dominican Republic and Mexico in 1996, Aznar criticized Cuba's one-party system and urged Havana to hold free elections and to democratize the system. The Cuban foreign ministry responded that "Aznar's comments suggest a great lack of knowledge about Cuban reality . . . When someone talks about something he doesn't know about, he runs the risk of making a mistake, and . . . that is the case with Mr. Aznar." In December 1996 Havana announced that it was retracting its approval of the new Spanish ambassador, José Coderch Planas. Coderch's announcement in a press interview that he was planning to give open audience to Cuban dissidents in the Spanish embassy was characterized as interventionist and unacceptable behavior for a diplomat accredited before the government.

The president of the National Assembly told the Cuban media that "the interventionist positions of the government of José María Aznar represent a new capitulation of Spain to Yankee imperialism and adversely affect the political actions of that nation vis-à-vis the Ibero-American community." Matutes responded: "It's typical of certain regimes, when they have internal difficulties, to invent a foreign enemy." Cuba retorted that the Havana-Madrid rift was due to a "sordid conspiracy between Aznar's conservative leadership and the U.S." Making things worse, Más Canosa had inaugurated a Spanish clone of the CANF, the Hispanic-Cuban Foundation, with the purpose of pursuing in Spain activities similar to those of CANF.[55] By then Havana and Madrid realized that a cooling-off period was needed and that the inflammatory rhetoric had to be curtailed.

The 1996 Viña del Mar Ibero-American Summit brought together the heads of Latin American governments, King Juan Carlos and Prime Minister José María Aznar of Spain, and President Jorge Fernando Branco do Sampaio and Prime Minister Antonio Gutiérres of Portugal. As reported in the *Miami Herald*, Aznar took advantage of the opportunity to say: "I have nothing against Cuba, but I have everything against its regime." Castro concentrated his remarks on the United States, attacking its "extraterritorial laws and criminal blockades by that same power that repeatedly has invaded countries of the region and intervened in the internal affairs of our countries."

A direct exchange between Castro and Aznar at the Chilean Summit was chronicled this way: "The Cuban head of state traded neckties with the dapper younger Spanish Prime Minister José María Aznar after the two sat together at lunch Sunday, midway into the Ibero-American summit ending Monday afternoon. The swap took place after Castro complimented Aznar's ties following what Aznar later described as an 'intense' interchange in which he promised to back a European aid package for Cuba if Castro undertook democratic reforms. Not only did Castro refuse, but he walked away with the nicer necktie, Aznar later complained."[56]

It was also reported that Aznar had told Castro, "If you move first, then I move, too" (in a *quid pro quo* exchange), to which Castro responded: "The future of the country is not to be played at a chess table." Soon afterward, after visiting the pope in Italy, Castro added: "We are nearing the 100th anniversary of the end of the war of independence, 'the moment in which [the Spanish] sold us to the United States . . . [our] most powerful enemy."[57]

Under the impact of the pope's plea to "help the world open up to Cuba and Cuba open up to the world," the Aznar Administration announced the appointment of Eduardo Junco as the new ambassador in 1998. He was accepted by Havana. Aznar's change of heart was influenced by King Juan Carlos, who had voiced his intention of visiting the island before the end of 1998, the hundredth anniversary of Cuba's independence from Spain, though he could not carry out the trip until 1999, during Havana's Ibero-American summit which he attended with his wife, Queen Sophia, and Prime Minister Aznar.[58] Cuban-Spanish relations had successfully moved toward normalization by the time the Oporto Ibero-American Summit convened. Castro met privately with Aznar and King Juan Carlos and told the latter "how greatly improved" relations were between the two countries. Confirming the positive trend in relations, Foreign Minister Matutes visited Cuba in November 1998.

Aznar's lobbying efforts with the European Community had paid off in the form of a "Common Position" advocating greater democracy in Cuba—though the document was a watered-down version of Spain's original draft. The EU identified the objective of its relations with Cuba as "encourag[ing] a process of transition to pluralist democracy and respect for human rights." But differentiating itself from Washington's Cuba policy, the EU added: "It is not European Union policy to bring about change by coercive measures with the effect of increasing the economic hardship of the Cuban people."

As Cuba's Ricardo Alarcón noted, the Common Position did not mark a major shift in the EU's policy toward Cuba. But it was now a stance collectively approved by the European Community regarding Cuba, and it had been published as such. Aznar felt he had scored a major victory by turning his Cuba policy into a pan-European one, even if it was more appearance than reality.

In a private meeting with President Clinton in Madrid's Moncloa Palace during NATO's 1997 summit, Aznar assured the U.S. president that his administration "would keep a firm and effective Cuba policy regarding human rights."[59] He had already said Madrid would make its best effort to keep a united European position on Cuba, even though Spain was the only EU country without an ambassador in Havana at the time.[60]

Cooperation talks between Cuba and the EU received mixed reviews. A meeting held in Brussels in 1996 for an economic cooperation agreement ended with the agreement on hold, "due to the Cuban side's inflexibility concerning political and economic reform." However, after holding a meeting in Havana, EU officials stated that negotiations would continue and that "dialogue [was] possible with the Cuban authorities." Cuba was invited to the first European Union–Latin American summit held in the region, and the EU and eleven Latin American countries condemned "any international measure having extraterritorial effect contrary to international law and to established trade rules"—an obvious reference to the Helms-Burton Act.[61]

Reaching Out to Cubans Living Abroad

The 1994 and 1995 Nation and Emigration conferences were dedicated to Cuban migration issues. They were followed by a third meeting in 1997, denouncing the Helms-Burton Act, and other meetings later. While attending to United Nations business, Robaina met with Cuban Americans in New York City, and he met in Madrid with Cuban exiles. Foreign minister Felipe Pérez Roque met with Cuban exiles in New York City while also attending United Nations business. A new publication dedicated to Cubans living abroad and their relationship with their homeland, *Correo de Cuba*, is now published by the Cuban Ministry of Foreign Affairs department in charge of relations with migrants. Havana's policy seeking the normalization of relations with Cubans who have left their homeland is a serious one.

Expatriated Cubans attending these programs are required not to be involved in terrorist actions nor to collude with the United States or any other power to terminate the revolutionary regime. Political and philosophical disagreements, religious affiliation, and past political activism against the revolution do not matter. Most of those attending the conferences fall under one or more of those categories, which in the past would have estranged them from their homeland.[62] Also, the government has issued *vigencias de viaje* (travel permits), on a case by case basis, to Cuban nationals living abroad. Henceforth, they would not need to request permission to visit their homeland.

The rapprochement policy between Havana and Cuban migrants is part of the foreign policy seeking to avoid isolation from the outside world by increasing all kinds of exchange abroad.[63] It also recognizes the "political and ideological diversity within the [Cuban exile] community, which should not be seen as a homogeneous bloc . . . [but as having] different currents of opinion separated from the counterrevolution but still critical of Cuba, including some who from a position of mutual respect oppose the economic embargo and recognize [Cuba's] national sovereignty and the revolution's social justice and independence project."[64]

Of the approximately 1.4 million Cubans living abroad (born in Cuba and/or of Cuban descent), 1.2 million live in the United States (86 percent). Among the latter, 64 percent live in Florida and 16.8 percent in New Jersey and New York. Public opinion surveys conducted in the 1990s (1991, 1993, 1995) revealed a community containing different shades of opinion on issues related to Cuba. However, there were contradictory objectives among and within the different strains of opinion: "Within each population [group] there is a large percentage which supports [applying] pressure strategies in combination with negotiated strategies." Moreover, "71 percent of Dade County [South Florida] and 67 percent of Union City [New Jersey] respondents who support a dialogue also support tightening the embargo."[65]

Track two of the 1992 Torricelli-Graham Act was directed to taking advantage of two related issues: Cuba's policy of welcoming Cuban émigrés and the desire to see the end of the revolution still felt among those who favor a dialogue with Cuba. "A sizable minority of respondents continue to signal that they would support a dialogue with the Cuban government . . . [however,] such a dialogue is seen as important in bringing about a rapid change to the island as well as bringing about the end of the Castro era in Cuba."[66]

According to Havana, by allowing Miami-Havana charter flights in conjunction with increased cultural exchanges (visits by journalists, academics, human rights activists, etc.), the United States pursued a policy of cultural and ideological penetration that sought to erode the Cuban regime from within. The 1994 *balseros* (rafters) crisis brought some of this policy to closure, but it did not really end until the February 24, 1996, shooting down of the two BTTR aircraft.[67] The aftermath of Richard Nuccio's implementation of White House policy until his resignation in 1996 included the emergence of a new generation of supposedly independent groups including journalists, economists, and an array of nongovernmental organizations promoted and supported from abroad. They supposedly represent a civil society independent of governmental control and therefore more legitimate than the government-sponsored mass organizations. International exposure of the existence of *la disidencia política interna* (domestic political dissidents) was a major component of such a policy.

Two Cuban scholars dedicated to studying the Cuban communities overseas have reflected on the political ambitions of Cuban-American organizations: "Admitting that they have some relative autonomy, the actions of most Cuban-American organizations could not be seen as independent as long as they are functional pieces of U.S. Cuba policy . . . Excluding the political left, always respectful of the Cuban process, the common denominator among such organizations is their desire to direct from abroad the course of internal Cuban politics. [They do it] by supporting the extant minuscule internal opposition groups that pose as defenders of 'human rights,' which allows them to pretend a leadership role that has no domestic reality."[68]

A lesser known dimension of the rapprochement policy is the *democracia participativa* (participatory democracy) seminars that started on May 3, 1993, and have continued for several years since. They are held in different Cuban cities (also in Miami), with Cubans living on the island and abroad in attendance. Leaders at the highest and middle levels of government, including Fidel Castro, have met the participants socially or have directly participated in the sessions. The seminars are conducted by Amalio Fiallo, a Roman Catholic Cuban emigré living in Venezuela, with the assistance of Nicolás Ríos, editor of the monthly *Contrapunto* published in Miami until 1997, when it ceased publication due to the boycott it faced in southern Florida.

As different issues of *Contrapunto* chronicling the seminars testify, the discussions are open, with participants offering their own perspectives on political, economic, and social issues. Respectful of the revolution, the proponents of democracia participativa could expose Cubans living on the island to ideas critical of, and in many ways opposed to, official ideology and programs but also critical of United States policy against Cuba.[69] The democracia participativa seminars have been welcomed in Cuba by the government and the numerous participants.

Conclusions

Notwithstanding the obstacles posed by anti-revolutionary forces, Havana continues pursuing a rapprochement with Cuban nationals living abroad. Given that most Cuban exiles reside in the United States, it is surprising that the normalization of relations has been carried out with such consistency. Today, Cuban Americans continue visiting their homeland and providing financial assistance to their relatives (with some restrictions).

The rapprochement between Cuban émigrés and their homeland continues to grow almost with a life of its own. After the pope's visit, Havana's policy of friendly relations with Cubans living abroad and especially with sectors of the Cuban-American community paid off handsomely. Hundreds of Cuban Americans (mostly coming from Miami) converged on Capitol Hill in March 1998 in support of the Torres-Dodd bill proposing ending the embargo on food and medicines for the island.

As in most initiatives undertaken in the 1990s reaching out to the outside world, Cuba's principled pragmatism was paying off, not always but quite often. For a Caribbean island nation that has lived under an American embargo for more than four decades and that is hesitantly lifting itself up from the economic depths of the special period, it was good news. Rather than staying isolated, Cuba has established in the 1990s different kinds of relations with most nations throughout the world; however, the United States persists in its adversarial position.

But the visit to Cuba in late 1999 by George Ryan (R-Ill.), a first by an American governor since 1959, may stand as the harbinger of a political thaw to come. In his five-day visit, Ryan met with Castro for eight hours, lectured students at Havana University on the merits of reconciliation in the "spirit of Abraham Lincoln," donated one million dollars' worth of food and medicine, had lunch with political dissidents, recognized the importance of respecting individual freedoms and other human rights, and emphatically advocated lifting the American embargo on the island. However, upon returning to Illinois carrying a very sick seven-year-old Cuban boy for medical treatment in the United States, Ryan was admonished by the Clinton Administration for talking to Castro. Making clear that Clinton was not lifting the embargo, the State Department spokesperson said: "We wish that there were not high-level contacts with Castro [by American visitors to the island], as long as he is not willing to stop the embargo he has imposed on the Cuban people." At the end of the twentieth century, Ryan's and others' voices asking for the end of the embargo were still ahead of Washington's Cuba policy.[70]

The Pope's Cuban Pilgrimage

The religious and social standing of the Catholic Church had improved since the 1970s from its low point in the early 1960s, but that progress alone probably would not have warranted a papal visit. What made the pope's trip to Cuba possible was the overall betterment of religious life in the 1990s. A visit by the pontiff could reinforce and promote further the Catholic Church's exercise of religious rights. His visit could expand the role in society not only of the Catholic Church but of other churches and religious denominations as well.[1]

Church-state relations under the revolution have been stormy. Given its privileged social class base, the Cuban Catholic Church has been a Latin American anomaly. Its social orientation toward the more affluent social strata disqualified it politically in its initial confrontation with the Cuban revolution:

> Catholic churches existed only in the rich suburbs and old city cen-
> ters. The priesthood was woefully inadequate to its ostensible flock.
> There were only 725 priests in the whole island . . . The overwhelm-
> ing majority—75 percent—of these priests were not Cubans at all
> . . . Thus, when the revolution came, the Church was unable to put
> up any serious resistance. The comparison with, say, Argentina, is
> instructive. The social program of Perón was infinitely less radical
> than that of the Cuban Revolution, yet when the Church joined the
> opposition a successful uprising was almost immediately precipi-
> tated. Faced with a far greater challenge in Cuba, it was helpless.
> The Church was politically a broken reed in Cuba.[2]

The Catholic Church did not hesitate to demonstrate its opposition to the island's communist transformation. The fact that a radical home-grown revolution promoted such a change intensified the averse senti-ment among conservative Christians. The point man for the belligerent church faction was the "popular, extroverted and headstrong" auxiliary bishop of Havana, Monsignor Eduardo Boza Másvidal. He had stated in 1961 that even José Martí, "the revered [nineteenth-century] patriot-revolutionary would [have been] opposed to the fidelista process." Steering Catholics to action, Monsignor Boza Másvidal encouraged them to "vitalize their faith . . . to manifest it publicly and to view it as an ideal for which it [was] worth struggling, making sacrifices and even dying, and to irradiate it around us."

The confrontation came to a head in September 1961, during a procession in Havana on the feast day of the nation's patron saint, Nuestra Señora de la Caridad del Cobre (Our Lady of Charity of El Cobre). The religious gathering of four thousand people outside Monsignor Boza Másvidal's rectory turned into a political demonstration against the regime: "As the afternoon progressed, tension grew, especially when the participants headed toward the presidential palace, shouting slogans against the revolutionary government and the Soviet Union. Some spectators later claimed that a U.S. flag was waved. Apparently, many of the crowd surrounded the demonstrators, and a melee resulted. Shots were fired, and a passing seventeen-year-old was killed."[3]

Monsignor Boza Másvidal claimed that he had tried to calm the angry crowd, but the people had become enraged when they learned that the permit for the procession had been canceled. The government said Boza Másvidal had "stated falsely that the permission had been denied, and [that he] indeed attempted to convert [the celebration] into a counter-revolutionary demonstration." The regime claimed that its intent was not to harass Catholic churches but to curb counterrevolutionary activities disguised as religion. When similar demonstrations were reported in three other cities, the government responded swiftly. One hundred and thirty priests (including Boza Másvidal) were rounded up and deported to Spain.[4] In three years of confronting the regime, the Church paid a heavy toll: it lost its source of income when the affluent faithful left the country, the number of priests declined from eight hundred to two hundred, religious schools were closed, and relations with government leaders became hostile. The Catholic Church had reached its nadir in the twentieth century.[5] After a difficult period of mutual mistrust and antagonism the situation eased and turned into the more positive relationship that exists today.

The Resurgence of the Church and Religion

The religious revival of the 1990s was made possible by the relaxation of the limitations imposed on religious practice, allowing people to express their religious beliefs and to attend mass and other services more freely. The economic hardships of the special period contributed to this phenomenon. According to Jorge Ramírez, a Marxist sociologist, "when a crisis breaks the normal balance of life, there's always a rise in the search for alternative sources of protection, hope, consolation, and the supernatural becomes attractive."[6] But there are other reasons, too, some more obvious than others.

The Fourth Party Congress in 1991 authorized the admission of religious believers to the PCC, and the 1992 constitutional revision declared the Cuban state secular and not atheist. The changes fostered a rapprochement between the revolution and religion, with an increasingly friendly relationship between the government and the Catholic Church. The regime's relationship with the Protestant churches has been harmonious; the Reverend Raúl Suárez, a prominent Baptist minister, is a member of the National Assembly.[7]

Recognizing the magnitude of the ongoing internal changes, Jesuit father Nelson Santana noted: "All the past [religious intolerance] has ceased. Now it doesn't matter if you are a practicing believer. We are seeing an invasion of medallions and crucifixes, of the beads of *santería* . . . People are returning to the Church . . . They now see the Church as humanitarian. Before they saw it as anti-humanitarian, priests as anti-scientific. [The Cuban bishops' 1993 pastoral letter called for] dialogue and reconciliation as a turning point in church-people relations."[8]

Dagoberto Valdés, a lay leader from Pinar del Río Province and editor of the Catholic publication *Vitral*, voiced the new syncretism of religiosity and social concern that seemingly is emerging in Cuba: "We are not in heaven, but we are not in hell. With socialism, we must ask ourselves what kinds of freedom we have been afforded and which dimensions of liberation our people still need."[9]

While critical of the negative aspects of Cuba's political system, Valdés says: "Neoliberalism is not a solution. We must have a just society, not just distributive justice, but something that allows for participation in all of the processes of distribution . . . the market economy should not be without ethical regulation. We must put the human person at the center of economic concerns, not technical production or trade."[10]

Valdés recounts his experience in sessions he had with government officials: "We can now sit down and talk about how we can improve Cuba, how we can all serve the country better from the depths of our Cuban identity, taking Cuba as our common point of encounter."[11]

It is against such an evolving backdrop that Castro's invitation to the pope was issued and accepted. Henceforth they could not envision each other as enemies, not even as adversaries. Castro and Pope John Paul II sensed that a papal visit could be the harbinger of historic developments. The pope could expand the Church's pastoral duty and the believers' practice of their faith, carrying out an evangelizing mission pursuing goodwill and understanding, not enmity or distress. Castro could reassure believers that the regime's religious policy is real—as he confirmed to four Democratic U.S. congressmen in Havana during the pope's visit.[12] He could also affirm that faith in God and in the revolution are not antithetical practices, and that loyalty to both is reconcilable.

As Castro said on national television just before the pope's visit: "Let us think about all those in the world who practice a religion and show them how a socialist and communist revolution can respect all believers and all nonbelievers."[13] His latest stance toward religion could speed up the momentum for Cuban Marxists to find closer kinship with Cuban Catholics who are not adversaries of the revolution. They could build a common identity based on their support for revolutionary social goals and values, while their different epistemological and theological systems would not work as divisive barriers.[14] At such a moment the belief system of the revolution would have expanded its ideological parameters by overcoming a long-held anti-religious bias by the political left: "The Left's difficulty with religion has one of its primary origins in Marx's difficulty with religion. Marx located this difficulty within his doctrine of materialism . . . It is impossible to discuss religion from a socialist perspective without encountering Marx on religion."[15]

While the place of religion in society was being reevaluated with positive effect, the relevancy of Marxism in the wake of the collapse of European socialism was being examined by academics and writers from Havana University and other institutions. The consensus emerging from those discussions reflected a nondogmatic, more flexible understanding of Marxist concepts used in analyzing current social phenomena.

Developments before the Pope's Arrival

When President Castro and Pope John Paul II met at the Vatican in 1996 and the pope accepted the invitation to visit Cuba, a new era of religious life under the revolution had already begun. Significant developments preceded the pope's arrival on the island. Following a ten-hour meeting with leaders of Cuban Protestant churches and of the Jewish community, Castro met for four hours with the Standing Committee of the Conference of Catholic Bishops, headed by Jaime Cardinal Ortega, archbishop of Havana. Reversing a 1969 suspension, Castro first authorized the celebration of Christmas in recognition of the pope's visit and later, in 1998, designated it as a permanent national holiday.[16] Believers attended thirteen open-air celebrations of mass held in Havana's Cathedral Square and in other locations in preparation for the services the pontiff would conduct during his five-day visit. And an exhibition honoring the pope at the José Martí Memorial in Havana's Plaza of the Revolution was inaugurated before his arrival. It included a photographic mural of Pope John Paul II and Castro shaking hands and a video detailing their 1996 meeting at the Vatican and the presents exchanged at the time.

Granma published a Christmas message from the pope addressed to the Cuban people and a detailed account of his itinerary, including the locations where he would be officiating at mass.[17] Reversing past practice, the regime agreed to accept fifty-five new foreign priests to help the overworked Cuban clergy. The Church's request for regular media access and permission to offer religious instruction in schools was not granted, but the issues came up again during the pope's visit.[18] Still, Cardinal Ortega delivered a half-hour address on national television explaining the pope's visit—the first such media exposure ever for a cardinal under the revolution—and catechism groups met regularly in various churches.

Posters with the pope's picture, donated by Latin American churches, appeared everywhere. An eight-story-high mural of Jesus Christ was erected in Havana's Plaza of the Revolution, and a choir from the capital's churches was ready to sing at the pope's Sunday mass, accompanied by the National Symphony Orchestra. The government used its resources to make the pontiff's visit a success. Castro urged Catholics (40 percent of the population are baptized Roman Catholic) and non-Catholics, believers and nonbelievers to welcome the pope and to attend the outdoor masses he would celebrate in four major cities.

Reinforcing the commitment to religious tolerance and rapprochement with the Vatican, and in homage to the pope's visit, Castro addressed the National Assembly about it in December 1997.[19] "We view the Pope's visit as an honor, we see it as a valiant gesture . . . We will do our utmost to make the Pope's visit a success . . . What we want is for the Pope to return to Rome with the impression that this is the best visit he has ever made in any country."[20]

Castro's remarks seemed directed to both internal and external audiences. Rather than allowing the fear of unforeseen consequences from the pope's visit to prevail, he readied himself to test the people's allegiance to the revolution in the worst possible socioeconomic moment under his rule. Castro rejected the notion that the pope's visit could bring about the downfall of Cuban socialism in the same way that the pope's rallying Catholic Poland at the shrine of the Black Madonna had eventually resulted in the fall of Polish socialism. His was a complex, difficult maneuver; but it was in line with the unorthodox decisions Castro was making while adjusting to the post–Cold War world of the 1990s.[21]

When Cardinal Ortega talked about the pope on national television, he was wise enough to minimize the pontiff's anticommunism and heighten his nationalist aspirations: "Cardinal Ortega described [the pope] not as anti-Communist first and foremost but as a nationalist whose patriotic pride was wounded by the Soviet occupation of Poland after World War II. Mr. Castro picked up on that theme in his remarks this weekend [before the pope's arrival], drawing an implicit parallel to his own resistance to the dominance of the United States [in Cuba] before 1959."[22]

However, political analysts, journalists, Catholic priests, and Washington officials decided to politicize the pope's visit, relying on the possible negative outcome awaiting Castro. To them, it was doomsday for Castro once the pontiff started unleashing his liberating message to the Cuban people. An American political analyst wrote: "My . . . long [shot] for 1998 [is] a happier one: Pope John Paul II's visit to Cuba in mid-January will unleash political currents that will lead at last to Fidel Castro's departure from power."[23]

Monsignor Emilio Vallina of Miami's St. John Bosco went on record as saying: "I am sure if the holy father is going to Cuba, Castro will disappear."[24]

Archbishop Ricardo María Carles of Barcelona, who accompanied the pope on his trip to the island, was quoted by the Spanish daily *ABC*: "What happened with the Berlin Wall and what happened in Poland could happen in Cuba."[25]

The White House spokesman, Mike Curry, commented in less ominous terms: "There could in fact be positive results in having the Holy Father in Cuba able to talk about the importance the world attaches to human rights and to the need for relief of the suffering." He added that the "discussion itself might empower those who believe there can be change and might even touch the heart of Fidel Castro."[26]

Those assertions imply that given the magnitude of problems facing Cuba and its proven limitations in overcoming them, Castro had no choice but to reach out to the Vatican in a display of openness that could bring about his downfall. This interpretation disregards any possible positive outcome for the regime stemming from this visit. Besides improving Cuba's image by having the pontiff visit the island while the world watched with interest, Castro expected the pope to address some commonly held concerns, especially condemning the United States' economic embargo of Cuba. The pope's defense of human rights and Christian values (a point of contention with the regime) would be balanced by his opposition to the "vulgar capitalism and materialism" of Western industrialized nations.[27]

In anticipation of the potential impact the pope's rhetoric could have on the populace, Castro went on national television the weekend prior to the pontiff's arrival. Stating that "many people have tried to politicize the visit and use it against the revolution," he added, "many people think the Pope is coming to Cuba to meet with that demon Castro, in the last bastion of communism, and the hope is that this will be the end of the Cuban revolution." Even Clinton, said Castro, was free to visit Cuba "to speak of capitalism, neo-liberalism, globalization . . . We would not raise the least objection . . . Let him try to convince us." Castro went on to say that "some of John Paul's speeches read as if they were written by a journalist from *Granma*, although of course I am not going to accuse him of being a Communist."[28] Later, the pope's critical homilies and remarks proved Castro's assessment wrong.

Castro also noted that the pope is "a big headache for the unipolar hegemonism of the United States [and] of imperialism, because he is not a man who can be manipulated. [He is not the] angel of death for socialism, Communism, and revolution. . . . [The pope] was not the General Secretary of the Communist Party of the Soviet Union." Adding finally, "Instead of a meeting between an angel and the devil, wouldn't it be better to think of a meeting between two angels who are friends of the poor?" (The pope responded, "We are not angels, we are men.")[29]

Noting that Cuba had no expectations that the pontiff's visit could improve relations with Washington, the head of the U.S. Section of Havana's foreign ministry stated that the pope's visit "has nothing to do with the bilateral conflict that Cuba has with the United States." Washington's response to the pope's visit was in effect that this would not change its Cuba policy. But the head of the U.S.-Cuba Trade and Economic Council in New York (which includes a number of major U.S. corporations) said that "there could very well be a new era dawning" in U.S.-Cuba relations.[30]

Havana's archdiocese communications director saw the position of the Church on U.S. punitive policies this way: "We cannot be on either side, not with the government, not with the opposition. The U.S. supports anything that opposes the [Cuban] government. The Clinton Administration has tried to understand the church as an opposition force, but the church is not an opposition party."[31]

Cuban-American sociologist Yolanda Prieto did not expect "anything radical" to come out of the pope's visit. She provided a cautious but far-reaching assessment: "The space for different points of view created by the church and the pope's visit will continue." However, said Prieto, the pope might have an impact on Washington's policy: "Bit by bit, piece by piece, [a] relaxation of some sanctions such as the embargo on humanitarian aid [might come]."[32]

No matter what the outcome of the pope's visit, the formula for the regime's ruin still is for it to become paralyzed by inertia and fear. Besides, the changes implemented in the 1990s have been rated by political analysts as too cautious, as not fast enough and not going far enough.

The Pope's Visit to Cuba

Many questioned why Castro invited the pope to visit Cuba and why the pope accepted. What kinds of risks were they taking, and were the rewards worth the trouble? The pontiff's visit marked a heretofore unlikely convergence of two world personalities. In spite of their differences, the pope and Castro acted upon the realization that they needed common ground to coexist peacefully, so that they would not continue dwelling on past antagonisms. They recognized at their Vatican meeting that the time was ripe for a new direction for both. They could always focus on the social justice issues that brought them closer, like addressing hunger and poverty throughout the world, examining the plight of the Third World, and condemning the lack of concern that industrialized countries show for poor nations.

The risks involved were mentioned in most media reports of the impending papal visit. Could Castro survive the massive demonstration of allegiance to the Church that the pope's visit could provoke? Would the people demonstrate their hunger for something other than food? Also, could Castro afford to bypass the chance of having the pope visit Cuba at this moment? What could the pope gain by legitimizing Castro's rule with his visit? Why should the pope rescue a communist regime on the ropes? Why should he overlook the political sentiments of such devout Roman Catholics as the Cubans who had left their homeland?

The questions were based on dated assumptions about Castro and the pope and about today's Cuba and the Vatican. Jaime Cardinal Ortega, archbishop of Havana, issued a communiqué on behalf of the Church noting "the significance of the meeting between Pope John Paul II and President Fidel Castro in the Vatican." He exhorted "the leaders of those nations whose . . . interests link them to Cuba to also look for the solution to existing conflicts in dialogue."[33] Cardinal Ortega was requesting a breathing space for Cuba, so that it could work out its problems without having to endure the enmity of the United States. He was also asking for the new detente in Church-state relations to flourish without external hindrances.

In a nationalistic sense, it is Cuba that really matters—guaranteeing its national survival as a truly independent and sovereign country—not Catholicism or Marxism or any other religious belief or political ideology. However, Christianity and Marxism should be approached as two value systems that could live side by side. This philosophical and theological syncretism must have pervaded those solemn occasions when the pope and Castro conversed first in the Vatican, and later in Cuba, and when with every word they uttered they were making history.

Evangelizing a Socialist Island

Pope John Paul II's five-day pastoral mission had no precedent in the history of the revolution. His evangelical crusade reached practically the entire Cuban population (the four open-air celebrations of mass were televised nationally), while the rest of the world watched attentively. At the welcoming ceremony at Havana's José Martí Airport, Castro and the members of the PCC's Politburo greeted the pope. The crowd at the airport launched into a cheerful chant, "Juan Pablo Segundo. Te quiere todo el Mundo!" (John Paul II. Everybody loves you!) and "Juan Pablo, hermano! Te quieren los Cubanos!" (John Paul, brother! Cubans love you!). Popular expressions accompanied the pope wherever he went. By the end of his visit, the people's chant had become, "Juan Pablo, hermano, ya eres Cubano!" (John Paul, brother, now you are Cuban!).

The pontiff kisses the earth when he visits a country for the first time, but on this occasion earth was carried in a container by four little children so that he would not have to kneel. The twelve-mile trip from the airport was filled with crowds waving small Vatican and Cuban flags. The pope's welcome seemed to surpass those for Soviet leaders who had visited the island in the past. Government workers were given paid time off to welcome the pope.

At the airport, the pontiff and Castro mentioned some of the religious and nonreligious themes that characterized the pope's visit. To summarize the Cuban president's statements:

> Holy Father, the land you have just kissed is honored by your presence.
>
> Cuba fought alone for its independence with great heroism, and a hundred years ago it suffered a holocaust when a large part of its population perished, mostly old men, women, and children.
>
> Today, genocide is being attempted with hunger, illness, and economic suffocation to subdue people who refuse the dictates of the mightiest economic, political, and military power in history.
>
> As in ancient Rome when Christians were horribly slandered, so we chose a thousand times death rather than abdicate our convictions.
>
> The revolution, like the Church, also has its martyrs.
>
> I was a student at Catholic schools . . . I was taught then that to be a Protestant, a Jew, a Muslim, Hindu, Buddhist, Animist or a participant in other religious beliefs constituted a dreadful sin, worthy of severe and implacable punishment. In some of those schools for the wealthy and privileged, among whom I found myself, it occurred to me to ask why there were no black children there. I have never been able to forget the totally nonpersuasive responses I received.
>
> We feel the same way you do about many important issues of today's world.
>
> No other country could be better disposed to understand your idea that the equitable distribution of wealth and solidarity among men should be globalized.
>
> In matters where our views are different we are most respectful of your strong conviction about the ideas you defend.

In essence, the pope stated:

> I come to share your religious spirit, your endeavors, joys, and sufferings, and to celebrate the mystery of divine love in order to make it more deeply present in the life and history of this noble people who thirst for God.
>
> For five hundred years the Church's presence on this island has not ceased to dispense spiritual values.

I come as a pilgrim of love, of truth, and of hope.

I come with the desire to give a fresh impulse to the work of evangelization, which this local Church continues to sustain with apostolic vitality and dynamism.

My best wishes are that this land may offer to everyone a climate of freedom, mutual trust, social justice, and lasting peace.

May Cuba open itself to the world, and may the world open itself to Cuba.

Castro underlined the destructive impact of the U.S. economic embargo while recognizing how close the revolution's and the pope's stances were on some global issues. Major differences were framed in a context of mutual respect and understanding. The pope emphasized the evangelical nature of his trip but promised to dedicate himself to reinvigorating the work that the Church had accomplished so far. His invitation to the world to open itself to Cuba was understood as a veiled criticism of U.S. Cuba policy.

The following morning in Santa Clara the pope officiated at the first open-air masses. That night Castro and the pope met privately for fifty minutes and exchanged gifts—the pope received a 120-year-old, leather-bound biography of the Reverend Félix Varela, the founder of Cuban national identity in the nineteenth century and currently a candidate for canonization by the Vatican, and Castro received a mosaic of Jesus. As he continued traveling from Havana to the eastern provinces, the Pope said mass on Friday in Camagüey and on Saturday in Santiago—with Raúl Castro in the audience wearing civilian clothing. Finally, on Sunday morning, he said mass in Havana with Castro in attendance, wearing a dark suit, as he did all the time in front of the pope. The pope's homilies and remarks grew stronger, becoming increasingly condemnatory of government policy. Some of the issues raised during the four services were as follows:

> Santa Clara: At the playing fields of the Manuel Fajardo High Institute of Physical Education, the pope emphasized family values to an audience of thirty thousand people. Condemning abortion [high in Cuba, after Vietnam and Russia], he said that in "addition to being an abominable crime, [it is] a senseless impoverishment of the person and of society." He noted the existence of "dissatisfaction for ideological reasons," and "the attraction of the consumer society," which with "measures involving labor and other matters have

helped to intensify a problem that has existed in Cuba for years: people being obliged to be away from the family within the country, and emigration, which has torn apart whole families and caused suffering for a large part of the population."[34]

Camagüey: With fifty thousand people filling the Agramonte Plaza, the pope urged Cuban youth to avoid the emptiness of alcohol, the abuse of sex, drug use, and prostitution. The answer to the country's future, he said, is not "to be sought only in structures, resources, and institutions, in the political system, or the effect of economic embargoes, which are always deplorable because they damage the most needy . . . These are all part of the answer, but they do not touch the heart of the problem." He traced the Church's contributions to Cuba to nineteenth-century priest Félix Varela (who died in 1853 and is revered by believers and nonbelievers, Catholics and socialists alike), calling him the "foundation stone of Cuban national identity" and the precursor of José Martí (the national hero of Cuba's fight for independence from Spain in the nineteenth century, a man referred to by all Cubans as the Apostle).

Santiago: Facing an animated audience of a hundred thousand, after honoring and crowning the icon of the nation's patron saint, Our Lady of Charity of el Cobre, and elevating her to "Queen of Cuba," the Pope called for free expression, free initiative, and free association. He noted the historic links between the Church and Cuban patriotism and stated that Catholics have the duty and the right to participate in public debate. He also urged the Roman Catholic Church to take "courageous and prophetic stands in the face of corruption and of political or economic power." The good of a nation "must be promoted and achieved by its citizens themselves through peaceful and gradual means . . . [so] each person, enjoying freedom of expression, being free to undertake initiatives and make proposals within civil society, and enjoying appropriate freedom of association, will be able to cooperate effectively in the pursuit of the common good," said the pontiff.[35]

Sensing that the pontiff's homily was going to be strongly critical of the regime and feeling protected by his presence,

Santiago's Archbishop Pedro Meurice Estiú greeted the pope, saying that "our people are respectful of authority, and want order, but they need to learn to demystify false messiahs," and that he offered Saturday's mass to the "growing number of Cubans who have confused fatherland with a [political] party, the nation with the historical process [the country has] lived in recent decades, [and] culture with ideology." After the Cuban Church "was decimated at the beginning of the 19th century and spent the better part of this century trying to recover . . . [after having its best days] in the 1950s . . . [and as a] result of the ideological confrontation with state imposed Marxism-Leninism, it returned to being impoverished in pastoral agents and means, but not in spiritual movement." His was the most condemnatory attack on the government yet by a Cuban Catholic clergyman, but no official government response followed his attack.[36]

Havana: This turned out to be the most animated of all four open-air masses (chanting from the audience frequently interrupted the pope), with three hundred thousand people present; accompanying Castro were Nobel Prize winner Gabriel García Márquez, former foreign affairs minister Roberto Robaina, and the head of the National Assembly, Ricardo Alarcón. The pope urged Cubans to seek new paths of reconciliation and to avoid the egoism and inequalities of unrestrained capitalism. "A modern state cannot make atheism or religion one of its political ordinances . . . it should distance itself from all extremes of fanaticism or secularism," said the pope critically. "Various places are witnessing the resurgence of a certain capitalist neo-liberalism, which subordinates the human person to blind market forces and conditions the development of people on those forces . . . At all times, unsustainable economic programs are imposed on nations as a condition for further assistance . . . At stake here is man, the concrete human person . . . For many of the political and economic systems operating today, the greatest challenge is still that of combining freedom and social justice, freedom and solidarity, so that no one is relegated to a position of inferiority," added the pontiff.[37]

Following the Sunday morning mass at Havana's Plaza of the Revolution, the pope met with Jaime Cardinal Ortega and the National Conference of Bishops and urged them to ensure that the Church "occupies her rightful place in the midst of the people and has the possibility of adequately serving the brethren." When the Church demands religious freedom, the pope said, "she is not asking for a gift, a privilege or a permission dependent on contingent situations, political strategies, or the will of the authorities. Rather, she demands the effective recognition of an inalienable human right." Restrictions on the Church's activities must be lifted, concluded the pontiff.[38]

In a meeting with Cuban intellectuals at Havana University the pope stressed the Christian character of democracy. While visiting the San Lázaro shrine in El Rincón, south of Havana, addressing lepers and AIDS patients, he urged the release of prisoners of conscience. After stating that there were not prisoners of conscience in Cuba, the government promised to consider very seriously the request made to free political prisoners.[39] (In response to the pope's request, the government announced that 299 inmates had been released.)[40] The pope also held an ecumenical encounter with leaders of Protestant and Jewish groups, but representatives of Cuban African creeds were not included.

The farewell ceremony at the airport provided the opportunity for some final statements. The pope's historic five-day visit had touched people's inner feelings and concerns deeply. Castro spoke first:

"I think we have given the world a good example: you, by visiting what some choose to call communism's last bulwark; we, by receiving the religious leader who had been imputed [to be responsible] for the destruction of socialism in Europe. There were those who [predicted] apocalyptic events; some even dreamed of them."

"It was ruthlessly unfair to connect your pastoral journey with the mean hope of destroying the noble objectives, and the independence, of a small country subjected to a blockade and a truly economic war for almost 40 years."

"For the honor of your visit, for all the affection you have shown the Cubans, for every word you have said—even those I might disagree with—on behalf of all the Cuban people, Holy Father, I thank you!"[41]

The Pope responded:

"I have experienced intense emotion-filled days with the pilgrim people of God in the beautiful land of Cuba, which have left a profound imprint on me. . . . I am grateful to you for your cordial hospitality, an authentic expression of the Cuban soul, and above all for being able to share with you intense moments of prayer and reflection in the celebration of the Holy Mass in Santa Clara, in Camagüey, in Santiago de Cuba, and here in Havana, as well as the visit completed just a few hours ago to the Metropolitan Cathedral."

"I thank you, Mr. President, and also the other authorities of the nation for your presence here as well as for the cooperation lent in the actual carrying out of this visit . . . either by attending the celebrations or by following them through the media."

"The immediate fruits of [this visit] have already been seen in the warm welcome received; [however] this mission must in some way continue."

"In our day, no nation can live in isolation. The Cuban people therefore cannot be denied the contacts with other peoples necessary for economic, social, and cultural development, especially when the imposed solution strikes the population indiscriminately, making it ever more difficult for the weakest to enjoy the bare essentials of decent living, things such as food, health, and education . . . The roots [of this suffering] may be found . . . in unjust inequalities, in limitations to fundamental freedoms, in depersonalization and the discouragement of individuals and in oppressive economic measures—unjust and ethically unacceptable—imposed from outside the country."

"Dear people of Cuba, as I leave this cherished land, I take with me the indelible memories of these days and a great confidence in the future of your homeland . . . Praised be Jesus Christ!"[42]

Cuba's satisfaction at the pope's condemnation of the U.S. economic embargo was short-lived: the White House initially refused to make changes based on the pontiff's condemnation of the embargo, though it reversed itself partly later. Besides arguing that it was an American law with bipartisan support, the administration claimed that Cuba had to undergo significant changes toward democratization before altering the embargo could be considered.[43] Still, there were expectations that legislation requesting a partial lifting of the embargo (food and medicines) could now have wider support in the U.S. Congress.

In a four-hour appearance on television thanking the people for helping to "make Pope John Paul II's historic visit a success," Castro rejected
the $100 million in aid offered by the Cuban American National Founda-
tion, saying that Cuba "does not ask for handouts," but that "it demands
an end to the economic war against our people . . . The Cuban government, with all the dignity in the world and in the name of the Cuban
people . . . says 'no'." He added, "[This] is a repugnant and immoral
maneuver, a rude reply to the pope's proposals . . . , an insult to the Cuban
religious institutions, and a challenge to the [Cuban] people who resist
and will resist with honor."[44]

Answering the pope's call that "the world should open itself to Cuba,"
Guatemala and the Dominican Republic announced the reestablishment
of full diplomatic ties, and the Venezuelan-American Chamber of Commerce and Industry (Venamcham) demanded in Caracas "the end of the
35-year old U.S. economic embargo against Cuba, which it described as
'a failure'."[45]

After the posters of Pope John Paul II were no longer hanging from
storefronts and after the official media stopped carrying news of the pontiff, the job for the Catholic Church was to move forward in its religious
mission.[46] While the government and the Church had insisted all along
on the pastoral nature of the pope's visit, diminishing its political significance was not appropriate.[47] Its political importance would depend,
however, on several factors, including how strong the position of Jaime
Cardinal Ortega and the Catholic Church would prove as a result of the
pope's visit and whether they would pursue their objectives in a confrontational or conciliatory fashion—that is, whether the Church's objective would be to undo the extant regime or to find a modus operandi
that would broaden Church religious and social space under a socialist
system.

The pope made clear that the Church was not seeking political power,
but he also expressed that the Church should have the place in society it
deserves (as a human and social right and not as a government favor),
without restrictions on its pastoral mission, including on access to the
media and on opening Catholic schools. Even though there are twelve
Church-sponsored publications in circulation, including the politically
critical magazine *Vitral*, published in Pinar del Río Province, television
and radio broadcasting on a regular basis will be limited at best.[48] The
national television coverage provided for the pope's four homilies and
eight speeches was as comprehensive as it was unprecedented. Also, it is
unlikely that the government will grant permission for Catholic educa-

tion to exist again as it did before 1959, but the expansion of catechism instruction already offered by the Church seems promising. It is noteworthy that Castro referred to negative aspects of his own Catholic education during his welcoming remarks to the pope.

By being able to distribute food and medicines to the population, the Church has gained considerable social stature while the state cannot afford to provide many social services, especially imported medicines (this disparity has grown even further following Clinton's 1998 decision partially lifting some sanctions). As we have seen, distribution of food and medicines is conducted through Caritas Cubana, the island's chapter of the charitable Roman Catholic agency, a chapter organized by Cardinal Ortega and which both Washington and Havana allow to receive contributions from the United States. The U.S. economic embargo has played a role in effectively altering social roles favoring the Church and penalizing the regime. The results have been immediate: "Attendance at Catholic mass has doubled since 1992, and baptisms have nearly tripled." These gains were increased further by the Church's evangelization campaign launched prior to the pope's visit with copies of the pamphlet *The Pope Is Coming! But Who Is the Pope?* distributed door to door. In addition, "two million simplified catechisms and nearly one million copies of St. Mark's Gospel" were delivered to the public.[49]

More breathing space for the Church might have political and social consequences. It will mean that a viable alternative to the revolution's ideology will be present and working its way into the population's minds and hearts. This may force the regime to reevaluate its own political strategy and ideological assumptions.[50] A collaborative partnership of the regime and the Church could entail such a radical transformation of political and social values that the partnership is not conceivable. Still, a future modus vivendi defining the nature and extent of government-Church relations may be decided by two very different men—President Castro and Cardinal Ortega—especially if the latter develops a commanding national position that the regime cannot ignore.[51]

The Church's social status is rising at the time when the regime's support base has been eroded by years of economic hardship, but the Catholic Church also has problems of its own. As an actor in a newly gained role in what might become a civil society independent from the government (different from what exists today), the Catholic Church will have to demonstrate that it has "transformed itself from the elite, urban enclave it had been before Castro's revolution" into a church with a convincing social message for a socialist society. It must also prove that it is not in alliance with the "Cuban upper class that had been the church's paro-chial base," which now resides in Miami and elsewhere.[52] Moreover, it will be operating alongside the Protestant churches, which have had a more amicable relationship with the government and have surpassed Catholic churches' attendance.[53]

The imminent presence of the pope in Cuba brought into the open the rivalry between Catholicism and popular Afro-Cuban creeds (Santería, Palo Monte, Abakuá, and others). Leaders of the Afro-Cuban religions complained that the Catholic Church "ha[d] launched an offensive against them on the eve of Pope John Paul II's visit . . . [and that it had] excluded them from meetings with the pope and rejected their offer of a drumming rite of welcome for the pontiff in Havana's cathedral." A Havana Santería *babalawo* (priest) protested that "the church has been more publicly ver-bal in its anti-Santería positions." Cardinal Ortega defensively denied "attacking the [Afro-Cuban] religions," adding that he was merely "criti-cizing efforts by the communist government to promote Afro-Cuban rites as an alternative to Catholicism and [as] a tourism draw." The Church, said Cardinal Ortega, "has always welcomed them [Afro-Cuban religions and their believers] with Christian love."[54]

The pope later compounded the dispute between the Church and Santería by excluding the latter from the ecumenical session held on the last day of his visit, with Protestant ministers and Jewish leaders. He also warned bishops and priests "against putting Santería and other Afro-Cuban religions on par with the Roman Catholic Church." "[Such] tradi-tional beliefs deserve respect but cannot be considered a 'specific reli-gion,'" said the pope.[55]

The Cuban leadership has its own understanding on the validity of different religious persuasions and on the role and space they should have in today's society. When the president of the National Assembly, Alarcón, was asked whether he would permit a bigger role for the Church in Cuban society, he responded: "Yes, in terms of the proper role that the church should have in a lay society. I mean in terms of practicing religion, promoting certain values of spirituality, of human kindness, of human solidarity. I think that would be a positive development. *But we cannot go back to the time when one particular religion had the dominant role, because that is a way to discriminate against others. The obligation of the state is to guarantee freedom of religion, and that implies dealing with all of them on an equal footing"* (emphasis added).[56]

The pope's advocacy of religious freedom as a human right applies to all religious beliefs, but the Catholic Church has claimed that its role in

Cuban history has been central to the formation of the country's national identity. The pope raised this issue during his homily in Camagüey and in the session with Cuban intellectuals at Havana University. The pontiff also expressed this sentiment in his tribute to Father Félix Varela, who played such a decisive role in the formation of the Cuban nation.

Evaluating the Pope's Visit

Who won and who lost by the pope's visit to Cuba? There seem to be gains for most parties. Cuban dissidents were delighted with the pope's remarks. Elizardo Sanchez, president of the Commission of Human Rights and Reconciliation, stated: "The church has spoken for us in a loud voice [but] not with any subversive intent . . . It has issued a call to the conscience of government leaders to take action to guarantee liberty."[57] Francisco Hernández, head of the Cuban American National Foundation after the passing of Más Canosa, said jubilantly: "From now on we will talk about Cuba before the pope's visit and Cuba after the pope's visit." To South Florida Cuban Americans, "their earlier fears that Castro would manipulate the visit to boost his own standing were forgotten as they watched almost incredulously the unprecedented scenes broadcast from Havana of crowds chanting 'liberty' in response to the pope's words."[58]

Some Cuban-American pilgrims joining the pope during his visit returned to the United States resolved to "strengthen the role of the Catholic Church in Cuba." One of the projects in the works is establishing sister parishes between South Florida and Cuban churches, a plan under consideration by the Roman Catholic Archdiocese of Miami. Auxiliary Bishop Thomas Wenski said that it had been discussed with the Cuban bishops in Cuba. And Archbishop J. C. Favalora also discussed the project with a group of Cuban-American priests who had opposed the initial plan (later canceled anyway) for a Miami-Havana cruise ship to take pilgrims to the island during the pope's visit but who changed their minds after the events that took place during the pontiff's visit. He encountered enthusiastic support for the idea, though they realized that "a lot of things have to be put into place before it could happen."[59]

Castro also got what he wanted: "a papal denunciation of the nearly 36-year-old U.S. embargo against [his] country, a critique of consumerism, a vision of a stable yet evolving Cuba and an impression that [he] is open to dialogue even with his harshest critics." Also, Castro was delighted with the pope's denunciation of "growing economic disparities between developed and underdeveloped nations" and of neoliberalism placing "unbearable burdens upon less favored countries."[60]

The Catholic Church came out a winner too: "It emerged from more than three decades of marginalization to center stage as the pope's presence dominated [the] state-run media." Castro told an American congressional delegation that "he expects interest in religion to grow in Cuba."[61] Still, five months after his visit, "frustrated by the [apparent] lack of progress . . . Pope John Paul II . . . called 13 Cuban Roman Catholic Bishops to a week-long meeting at the Vatican." They examined the extent of the Church's gains since the pontiff's visit and the "means to step up pressure for change." As was noted by the Cuban Catholic Church's spokesman, "The church could have a greater presence within a more open society."[62]

The legitimization of religious belief would also benefit Protestantism and Afro-Cuban religions, although, as earlier noted, their relationship with the government has been better than that of the Catholic Church.[63] The Reverend Héctor Méndez, minister of the oldest Protestant church in Havana, welcomed the pope's visit. "I believe," he said, "that when the Christian feeling is awakened, we all benefit . . . The opportunity to have a number of religious symbols displayed in such a public way is already a benefit to society."[64]

Such encouraging and contradictory reactions from so many different or opposing sources (the exception being Washington's response, which was reversed later) underscore the ramifications of the pope's visit to Cuba and the gambit played out by both Havana and the Vatican. That it turned out well took much compromising by Castro and the pope, although the latter seems to have spoken his mind freely, with no limitations or official response other than Castro's welcoming and farewell remarks.

Castro seemed genuinely taken by the pope, never losing perspective that the pontiff's visit had drawn the eyes of the world to his country. The Colombian Nobel Prize winner Gabriel García Márquez, who as a close friend of Castro attended the pope's Havana mass with him, said at a dinner party that Castro was "almost infatuated with the pope." He admitted "never [having] dreamed [that] he would see Mr. Castro going to a Mass."[65]

Describing his Cuba trip, the pope said it reminded him "of his first trip back to Poland a year after being chosen to lead the Roman Catholic Church." Later, at the Vatican, he told a group of Polish visitors: "I wish for our brothers and sisters on that beautiful island that the fruits of this pilgrimage will be similar to the fruits of that pilgrimage [in 1979] to Poland." This was a papal faux pas, perhaps permissible after such a performance in Cuba, but politically counterproductive since that visit to his homeland spawned the Solidarity trade union movement that led to the downfall of communism in Poland.[66]

The pope's statement, coupled with one he made earlier explaining his success in Poland, means trouble for the Cuban Catholic Church during difficult negotiations with the government. The pope explained how, ending the Church's long-standing policy of peaceful coexistence with communist regimes, he "demanded respect for individual human rights and dignity." After the collapse of communism in Europe, he said: "The tree was already rotten; I just gave it a good shake and the rotten apples fell."[67]

It seems that the pope had not heard of Castro's claim on television that Cuba was not Poland and that the revolution had nothing to fear from the pontiff's evangelical mission. Evidently, Castro and the pope had very different perspectives on the objectives of the pontiff's visit to the socialist island. Perhaps the pope did not speak his mind fully while he was in Cuba, preferring to express himself when he was back in the Vatican.[68]

The pope's Vatican statement was condemned by an Italian liberation theologian, Guilio Girardi. In an article published in a supplement of the Roman daily *Il Manifesto*, he characterized the pope's wishes (that what happened in Poland should also happen in Cuba) as "mean spirited." Girardi and other distinguished liberation theologians—Frei Betto and Pedro Ribeiro de Oliveira and Francois Houtart—held a four-hour meeting with Castro after the pope's departure and before his Vatican statement. Also present at the meeting were Cuban leaders, including the party's director of religious affairs. According to Girardi, they talked about such subjects as "Christianity, Marxism, capitalism, liberalism, and the end of communism in Eastern Europe."

Girardi chronicled Castro's account of the pope's visit and his satisfaction with the people's genuine support for the revolution, which to him was unmistakable. Otherwise the conditions for a revolt were there with thousands of people in the streets, controversial speeches about the revolution, the absence of police and soldiers, and international journalists present. Castro mentioned the pope's opposition to neoliberalism and its world effect and disputed that the pope is the "angel of death" of communism. The reasons for the downfall of communism in Poland should be found within that country, he said. "Havana is not Warsaw. Communism in Poland was imposed by Soviet troops, which had committed atrocities that were resented by the Polish people."

The liberation theologians had a more critical view of the pope than did the Cuban leadership and indicated that those leaders should reconsider their positive view. Likening the pontiff's trip to Cuba to his 1983 visit to Nicaragua, they mentioned the internal and external confrontation he had had with the Sandinista revolution. In their opinion, the pope's and the Cuban bishops' prudent behavior during the papal visit were "in reality a new tactic [against the revolution], which is considered today to be more effective." They also viewed the pope's opposition to neoliberalism as being limited to "barbarous capitalism," and that it only amounts to a criticism of the system. Finally, the liberation theologians expressed their appreciation for the importance Castro accorded to meeting with them and to the potential of liberation theology for ethical, cultural, and political contributions to revolution and Christianity.[69]

Castro had religion on his mind. He met with a delegation of U.S. and Latin American Methodist bishops visiting Cuba. The group was headed by the general secretary of the Global Ministries of the United Methodist Church and the president of the Council of Methodist Evangelical Churches of Latin America and the Caribbean. It also included the vice president of the College of Bishops, and others. Social issues discussed at the meeting included "the effects of neoliberalism and the destruction of the environment, as well as the current need to globalize solidarity among nations." Agreeing that their visit to Cuba had been successful, the Methodist delegates stated that it "would help [them to] reinforce their efforts in the fight against the blockade imposed on Cuba."[70] It was the season when religion, social issues, and politics occupied Castro's thoughts and actions and when clergymen from different parts of the world shared those concerns while visiting him.

Conclusion

Having started to rescue the economy from the abyss of the 1990s, the Cuban revolution now faces a serious religious challenge. However, in pursuit of the broader objectives set up by the pope for the Catholic Church, Cuba's Roman Catholic bishops called for "broader discussions with the government" and for "an increased role for the Church in helping the needy." In a document circulated in Cuba (distributed by the Vatican worldwide), the Cuban bishops stated weeks after the pope's visit: "The Church wishes to broaden and increase a frank dialogue with the institutions of the state and the autonomous organs of civilian life . . . [and to] intensify its social service to society, especially those with the greatest need."[71]

Providing a conciliatory bridge between Cuba and Cubans living outside the island, the bishops invited those living abroad "who for various reasons have left the homeland yet still feel they are children of Cuba . . . [to] cooperate with serenity and in a constructive and respectful spirit to the progress of the nation."

Seeking to perpetuate the impact of the pope's visit, and the space gained by the Church, the bishops stated: "The national jubilation and the festival of faith we lived during the papal visit cannot remain as a parenthesis to Cuban history, as a beautiful and indelible though nostalgic moment, but should nurture a permanent reflection that will lead to the renewal of Cuban life."

In order to broaden the Church's appeal in a spirit of coexistence with other beliefs and values, and in recognition of believers and nonbelievers among Cubans, the bishops confirmed: "When the Holy Father says Cuba has a Christian soul, he doesn't mean that the Cuban culture is wholly Christian, which is something different. The values of the Gospel are not exclusive of Christians and do not contradict the nature of the human being. On the contrary, they dignify it . . . The Church does not proselytize when it proclaims, preaches and defends these values."

Also, extending a friendly hand to Protestant churches, the bishops expressed their desire for a "healthy cooperation with the other Christian denominations." The document highlighted the pontiff's condemnation of neoliberalism and his defense of the struggle for social justice. But it also made clear that the pope upholds "justice and freedom, without permitting either to be pushed to the background, which is the greatest challenge facing many political systems today."[72]

Seeking reconciliation within the island and with those Cubans living abroad, and embracing spiritually citizens of all faiths and convictions, the Cuban bishops made their immediate intentions publicly known. Their document did not add new information, but its timing and style were significant. It conveyed the bishops' objective that the country should not return to the single cultural and ideological life that it has had under revolutionary rule. The emerging social and cultural pluralism seems invigorated by a Catholic Church that is making a comeback to a frontline existence.

Satisfying the needs and aspirations of an energized Catholic Church after years of marginalization is going to take creative thinking and compromise by all parties. Religious policy is a public policy area bound to undergo substantive change in the short term. The Church at least would seek that the public and social space gained during the pope's visit not be lost again. However, the harsh rhetoric of the archbishop of Santiago, Meurice Estiú, would be anathema to the regime, even if it drew no official response at the time.

The potential for a collision between the Church and the government has been enhanced by the means and objectives built into President Clinton's 1998 decision easing some of the sanctions against Cuba. Still, the dilemma for the government lies in being able to keep the upper hand in the ideological and social arenas while still acceding to the Church's demands and being able to control the resulting political ramifications. In order to provide sufficient space to the Catholic Church to perform its broadened evangelical mission, the government needs to expand the scope of public life, allowing nongovernmental actors to participate in it with their own discourse. From the regime's perspective, the opening up of the social matrix to new entities and ideas should not endanger the revolution's ideology but should safeguard the socialist system. Castro understands that returning to the long-term status quo that existed before the pope's arrival would destroy whatever was anticipated and accomplished with his visit.

IV

Looking Forward

Reinventing Cuban Socialism

The Dialectics of Adversity

The collapse of European socialism confronted the Cuban regime with a survival crisis. For the Cuban leadership, and especially the Cuban people, these last years have been a time of reckoning, soul searching, and of having to make tough decisions. The revolution's core values and social objectives had to be identified and, in the process, redefined. What Cuba could not do without (the heart of the revolution's gains) had to be prioritized, while many other valued achievements would have to go.

Many social benefits that characterized Cuba's life for three decades are already gone, or nearly so. The burning question has been what should the country strive for as long as it cannot afford to spend its resources to save every social gain? Certainly, the era of total socialism has ended. This is not to say that the country had reached total socialism, but the dream of a socialist society was the ultimate objective that had sustained people's faith and daily efforts in myriad exhausting campaigns and programs since 1959. The policies safeguarding some of what was done before plus the new changes taking place form the contours of what Cuban socialism will look like. The process of reinventing Cuban socialism is already under way, but it will take some time before it is completed.

That people had become accustomed to the revolution's social gains made it more difficult to be without them. Downsizing the social services system was one of the policies chosen to save the revolution. To try to keep the social advantages available during the pre-1991 years would have been fatal for the revolution's survival.

While they stand as the worst years of the revolution's socioeconomic reality, the 1990s still have a potential for growth and improvement. But not everyone was willing to endure the difficult times of the special period years. Numerous defections and the need by many to rely on dollar remittances from relatives living abroad to make ends meet were reminders of how things had run afoul from the early dreams of the 1960s and beyond.

While Marxism has been on the defensive ideologically and politically, Cuba is witnessing a demonstration of the applicability of the dialectical method to social praxis. As dialectics claims, the initial step or event (thesis) should lead to a second one (antithesis), which in turn should lead to a third step or event (synthesis). One by one, every step should be progressing forward and upward, following a spiral developmental growth cycle fed by concerns and aspirations that are both a reflection and the product of extant material reality—Marx's revision or addition to Hegel's notion of an idealistic universal mind arriving at a higher level of self-awareness and freedom.

The collapse of European socialism and its far-reaching sequel ruined the Cuban economy (the dialectical transformation of quality into quantity), leading to Havana's decision to resist and struggle in order to overcome a negative reality, denying adversity the power to determine the nation's fate. The regime did not let the economic crisis stifle the nation's will to resist and fight back (the dialectical interpenetration of opposites or antithesis). The contradiction posed by an ugly socioeconomic reality and the island's resolve to fight adversity created an energy field stemming from the opposite thesis and antithesis poles, which are part of the backlash processes in dialectical analyses. The survival of the Cuban revolution in spite of the ongoing crisis, the fact that it is still battling and alive, is the outcome of the three-step cycle (the dialectical negation of the negation, or synthesis).[1]

How this is being done, and what problems and mistakes are taking place, have been discussed in the preceding chapters. But where is Cuba going from here? What will the socialist system look like at the end of the ongoing complex and, for some, contradictory change process? These questions are answered here through scholarly speculation relying on evidence of what has already happened during the 1990s.

Media Reporting of Cuba's Changing Face

A composite of different media accounts offers a dark image of Cuba's emerging face that slowly turns brighter. Some reports are superficial, but others are insightful. The following story from the beginning of the special period (1991) provides a realistic picture of the abysmal conditions of daily life: "A group of academics visiting Cuba found food shortages, rationing and long lines to buy whatever was available. `People have little to eat,' [says one academic] . . . 'Some of them are surviving on watery soup once a day. Others say Cubans aren't going hungry, but that food is difficult to obtain and that the variety of what can be found is limited. This is producing resentment in a culture that focuses on family meals,' [says another academic]. Even the Cuban elite is being affected. According to a recent visitor, neither coffee nor dessert was available in Havana's most exclusive restaurant, *La Bodeguita del Medio*."[2]

Another report from the same period revealed frustration and anxiety among young people and the need to blame Castro, the revolution, and/ or the government for their predicament and the nation's:

[A friend] I have known for more than a decade, can't wait to tell me how wretched he finds life in Cuba today [1991–92]. "This place is goofier than ever," he says. "I live here," says another of the assembled young people, "even though it is a repressive den of stupidity." Then come complaints, like a torrential rainstorm. There are no light bulbs. Toilet paper hasn't been around for a year. No soap, no cooking oil. The bread ration is insufficient and is made of boniato [sweet potato] flour. "That's because Fidel has roots growing here," a teenager explains to me, "for the boniato up here." He points to his head, and his friends laugh. "Is there no longer any respect for Castro?" I ask. A more serious woman intervenes: "We respect what he's done, what the revolution has accomplished. But we're tired of being told the same old shit about the heroes of 1868 and 1895 and *Granma* and the Sierra and the Bay of Pigs. He is living in the past and he demands that we share that past. Okay . . . [But] this past has no relevance to the world in which we live. The Soviet Union is dead."[3]

Another report from a slightly later period (1993) still rings of scarcity and hardship: "A Western journalist said conditions this month were the worst he has experienced in the four years he has been stationed in Havana. Even the usually well-stocked 'Diplomercado,' the main diplomatic supermarket in Miramar where foreigners pay in U.S. dollars, ran out of meat early this month."[4]

And yet, the following humorous fictional story depicts two things that are real and that were particularly helpful during this period: Cubans' ingenuity and the upbeat attitude they have even when facing adversity: "Making sense of Cuba's economy is not easy. There is a joke I heard in Havana recently: The CIA sends an agent down to live in Cuba and report back on the state of the economy. He returns six months later, babbling, and is carried off to an asylum. 'I don't get it,' he mutters over and over, 'There's no gasoline, but the cars are still running. There is no food in the stores, but everyone cooks dinner every night. They have no money, they have nothing at all—but they drink rum and go dancing'."[5]

What a difference (at least in appearances) a few years can make. The following is an account of the nascent economic recovery by 1997, as reflected in visible imagery of daily life:

> At the level of daily life the economic recovery is dramatic. In 1989 the Malecón, a six-lane seaside highway, had more Chinese Flying Pigeon bicycles on it than cars. The occasional car would be a tourist taxi, or an aging Lada (an inexpensive Fiat manufactured in Russia), or a Chevrolet from the 1950s . . . [In 1996] watching the traffic on the Malecón, I could barely believe I was in Havana. On the street in front of me were a bright-green new Suzuki Sidekick, a new Mercedes-Benz truck, a new Honda sedan, a new Toyota van—and a constant flow of Ladas and '57 Chevies. For those with dollars gasoline was plentiful.[6]

It was for those with dollars to spend that the economic upturn was bright. The grand divide in the 1990s society—fostering the emergence of a small relatively privileged population group—is whether one is limited to the markets operating in the national currency or has access to dollars to purchase goods and services. The economy has become the main factor determining Cuba's new social face.

The reemergence of prostitution, *jineterismo*, is an indicator of how deeply the effects of the plummeting economy were felt. That this prostitution is different from that which existed before the revolution is significant only to a point. Today, there is no need for women to prostitute themselves in order to "buy food for their starving infants"; jineterismo reflects social destitution or official neglect as much as other equally difficult social problems. It shows a "malaise born of boredom and frustration [and the desire for the good things in life] rather than economic desperation (or near starvation)."[7] Mostly unsuccessful police efforts at preventing jineteras from parading in foreign tourist hotels and night clubs can help only momentarily and to a limited extent. A permanent solution might come when the economic recovery lifts the standard of living and ends the dollar/peso social divide as it exists today and when people's confidence is fully restored based on solid economic growth.

Another dimension of Cuba's changing face is the different way younger high-ranking government officials behave and present themselves: "He pedals to work on his purple Phoenix bicycle dressed in jeans and a T-shirt, with an amiable bodyguard tailing behind on another bike. At the office, he changes to his dressed-up look: a suit with a black T shirt. He says he wouldn't be caught dead in a *guayabera*, the traditional tropical shirt favored by older Cubans. With his studied style, Roberto Robaina González [former minister of foreign affairs] looks more like a manager of a rock band than a Marxist model. Yet Robaina [at forty-three] exemplifies *the new face of Cuba"* (emphasis added).[8]

The different outward appearance seems to be more than cosmetics. It signifies that a new generation is climbing today to senior leadership positions and might bring along the key to twenty-first-century Cuba. Signals of continuity in style and substance that characterized the revolution's founding generation prevail today. But this will change with time. While leaders of Robaina's generation (or somewhat younger, like Foreign Minister Felipe Pérez Roque's) are arriving at the top sponsored by Castro and others, they are not in full command yet. Time is on their side, however. When and if they ever become Cuba's rulers (probably along with Raúl Castro), they will carry with them their mentors' imprint, but they will also bring into play their new generation outlook to policy making, so they will be able to deal differently with the world in the next century.

Dogmatic Ideology or Principled Pragmatism

The collapse of European socialism implied a crisis of Marxism as a political ideology that had some impact on the island too. Cubans examined the fall of European socialism searching for its meaning. What went wrong? Are we making similar mistakes? Should we uphold and defend Marxism? Could our commitment to preserve it be taken seriously by others? Answering these questions satisfactorily did not come easily. Still, some tentative answers were given by intellectuals seriously concerned with such issues, providing insightful thoughts.

Examining critically the Marxism of the Cuban revolution, a group of academics from the Philosophy Institute of the Cuban Academy of Science made a comprehensive study of the way communist parties in power have used Marxist theory to explain, direct, and/or justify political decisions to build socialism. These are some of their findings:

> Simply repeating again and again the idea that building
> socialism is a natural evolutionary process—with no contradictions or conflicts, an idealized progression separated from
> reality—does not make it realistic.

Marxism-Leninism is not a straitjacket, nor is it a finished system as a traditional philosophy would be. It leaves an open door to perfect its principles, which gives it strength. Its dialectical nature allows it to be applied to different social conditions.

The collapse of European socialist regimes did not necessarily mean that the ideology they used was wrong. Marxism as a system of ideas, values, and assumptions is not in crisis; what is in crisis is the way it was understood—dogmatically, speculatively, metaphysically. For its own sake, Cuba has distanced itself from that closed-minded interpretation of Marxism.

During the transition period the vision of scientific socialism has been modified. It is a contradictory period in which spontaneity and consciousness are in a dialectical relationship, with the former usually prevailing. Once the image of the transition as a peaceful progression was broken, abstractionist and nonhistorical interpretations were abandoned, and a return to Marx, Engels, and Lenin, plus to Cuba's revolutionary experience, took place. Breaking with idealized conceptions of socialism is not giving up the socialist ideal. Dogmatic idealism has been replaced with genuinely revolutionary Marxist ideals.

It was a mistake to idealize Marxist theory and the Cuban experience. It became necessary to remake the right tools to examine Cuban society. The practice of calling upon Marx or Lenin as a way of justifying certain ideas is wrong. Abstract truth should not be used while concrete situations are ignored. Dogma should never be an instrument of social change.

Socialism has proven itself to be a social system with greater potential for a just society, which makes it superior to capitalism. But its superiority has not been proven in every possible aspect, at least not yet.

We have not come to the end of history, as American political scientist Francis Fukuyama says. Humanity cannot live in a unipolar, neoliberal world surviving under subhuman conditions while a minority reaps all the benefits. Capitalist theoreticians recognize that their system cannot reconcile private property with popular participation, among other contradictions in their system.

> Socialism should not be evaluated according to the Eastern
> European experience, especially after Stalin. Based on the
> experiences of Holland in the sixteenth century, England in
> the seventeenth century, and Europe after Napoleon's defeat
> in 1815, capitalism did not appear to be a viable system.
> Socialism's final fate has not yet been determined. It was
> utopian and naive to assume that we were following a
> predetermined evolutionary system. History is not decided
> by blind alleys but by human actions. In Eastern Europe
> Marx, Engels, and Lenin were wrongly understood.
> Analysis of social reality should be based on empirical re-
> search and content analysis, which are methods not usually
> followed by Marxist philosophers or theoreticians.[9]

The analytical path these scholars followed parallels partly Cuba's policy making in the 1990s: (1) Rejection of Eastern European socialism as a model and a test of socialism's viability (a pragmatic evaluation and an expression of ideological commitment). (2) Marxist thinking should not follow dogma; it should instead facilitate understanding of concrete, real situations (a definition of intentions not followed before). (3) Rejecting capitalism and embracing socialism should lead to a better society (which would allow such a possibility to become real). And (4) dogmatic thinking and reference to Marxist authorities are no substitute for critical revolutionary thinking (nor are they a justification for failed policies).

The study was one of several examining the revolution's philosophical assumptions. *Temas*, a humanities journal, has dedicated some issues to new directions and meaning in Cuban Marxism, including articles by some leading Marxist thinkers on the island. Looking at other dimensions of the same issue (the present and future of Marxism as an ideology and a tool for social analysis), the discussions covered Marxist antecedents in Cuban history; Marxism and the political left; the teaching of Marxism in Cuba; Marxism as a political ideal in pre-1959 politics; and the relevance of Marxism today. Such critical examination of sensitive issues as appeared in the journal, from which the following examples are drawn, would not have been expected before, much less published so prominently:

> Isabel Monal: Stalinism exaggerated the danger of reformist
> and idealistic expressions in order to eliminate any devia-
> tions or disagreements with the closed, fixed system that
> Marxism had become.
> Fernando Martínez Heredia: Rebellion is the closest cultural

activity related to Marxism and Cuban culture. The accumulated radical political culture put into action by the revolutionary vanguard and the people changed antidictatorial politics into a socialist revolution for national liberation. Then everything became political. It would be a mistake to think that everything happened when we became Marxists; the truth is that we became Marxists because of what had happened [during the revolutionary phase, particularly since 1959].

To be a Marxist is not to guess what is expected from you and to follow orders but to be part of the creation of a new path, of a lively project different than capitalism. It includes critical social thought in relation to ideological positions and the formation of socialist culture.

Joaquín Santana Castillo: Searching for and creating a theoretical interpretation of Cuban reality could be the bedrock upon which the credibility of Marxism can be restored, after the damage it has suffered during years of unimaginative teaching.

We cannot seriously assume that Soviet Marxism was always the same throughout history, and in every circumstance, or that everyone involved in academic work in the USSR was imbued with dogma, or even that the Soviet Marxism–Western Marxism polarity is the theoretical-methodological coordinate that can explain the obstacles and progress of Marx's concepts.

Aurelio Alonso Tejada: Any student writing about Marxism and the Cuban revolution should be concerned with how little has been said about the need for rigorous analysis void of doctrinal tensions and with how much it should already have been part of the debate.

The combined effect of the revolution-Marxism sequence, the political and ideological complexity of the socialist context, and the need for survival under a permanent state of siege constitute the framework of Cuban socialism. Equally significant to the island's socialism are the way Marxist thought was incorporated into the ideals of the revolution and what has happened in three and a half decades.

The turnaround in world political thought in the 1970s did not

entail passing from one predominant position to another but
the closing of a long-held debate and the reaffirmation of
theoretical patterns belonging to a position that has existed
all along.

The question of whether Marxism is viable or not cannot be
answered with a doctrinaire, superficial, parochial, or biased
response. Whether Marxism died with its European collapse
must be answered by considering two distinct positions: that
it is extinct and that it is undergoing a revival.

Olivia Miranda: Without the ideas being artificially implanted
from the outside, those leading the struggle assimilated
Marxist and Leninist ideas that already existed in the
revolutionary popular traditions.

Liberal intellectuals were decisive in forming a national anti-
imperialist theoretical consciousness in the country.

Using Martí's politico-historic method to understand politics
socioeconomically did not mean that its anti-imperialist
components contradicted the Marxist-Leninist ideas that
emerged in the 1920s.

Fidel Castro understood that thanks to the Soviet Union, the
correlation of international forces favored a social revolution
that, while not identifying itself as socialist, could not deny
this either, so he trusted that the dynamics of the process
would orient the masses ideologically and would allow
them to assume a leadership role.[10]

That Marxism can be as appealing now as it was in the past if it is
approached imaginatively and creatively (differently than European socialism was) was the verdict arrived at by the Institute of Philosophy
scholars—though they recognized that not all socialist political actors
erred equally during the Soviet era. Looking at lessons learned throughout time, they noted historic occasions when capitalism failed but regimes and societies remained committed to that system nevertheless.

Embracing the subject deeply within a national context, the thinkers
expressed in *Temas* critical views of what the assumptions should be today to reactivate, understand, and apply Marxism. While sharing some
of the thoughts expressed earlier, the *Temas* debate centered on the Cuban
Marxist experience and the role Marxism played during the building of a
national revolutionary identity. Both groups rejected dogma and dogmatic thinking, favoring instead Marxist-based principled pragmatism

as a theoretical framework for critical thinking. This constitutes a positive development, liberating Cuban theoreticians from lingering influences of Soviet Marxist orthodoxy (still shared by hard-liners) and from resorting to it as a normative justification for the regime's policies.

The relevance of Marxism in the post-Soviet world is based not on ideological orthodoxy but on the idea that when rightly used, it is a useful tool to understand social history. A Marxist conceptual framework penetrates the underlying causes of social problems, providing also an instrument for effective decision making. But the caveat is equally important: do not use Marxism as a revolutionary mantra, as if the force of its incantation should stop intelligent examination of the real world. Whenever ideology has been used in a dogmatic way, it has been detrimental to the revolution, and they seem conscious of that. Their reflective, introspective mood underlines a commitment to divest themselves of dogmatism, scholasticism, and orthodoxy, still entrenched among conservative Marxist thinkers.

The revolution's ideology sustains a canvas including more than policy makers and intellectuals. It provided the foundation upon which a new political culture has developed since 1959. Sidney Verba has captured elsewhere the interweaving of subjective perceptions of political reality, values and emotions, and normative social objectives that together may constitute a political culture under this definition: "[Political culture] refers to the system of beliefs about patterns of political interaction and political institutions. It refers not to what is happening in the world of politics, but what people believe about those happenings. And these beliefs can be of several kinds: they can be empirical beliefs about what the actual state of political life is; they can be beliefs as to the goals or values that ought to be pursued in political life; and these beliefs may have an important expressive or emotional dimension."[11]

Political culture is central to a society's understanding of past and present political life, and cultural change permits understanding new social and political objectives and the reasoning behind the policies that pursue them. Marking a departure from past life, the revolution created its own cultural milieu: a revolutionary political culture. As Cubans replaced their old way of thinking with a new cultural *élan vital*, they were able to immerse themselves in action, turning revolutionary thinking and praxis into a single, reinforcing experience.[12]

The teaching/learning (socialization) procedures transforming the pre-revolutionary belief system and the newly created political culture have come into question. The regime's communication control, disseminating biased political messages while performing the political socialization function, has been criticized: "The postulated necessity of developing [a revolutionary] social consciousness, while restructuring the economic system, created a further necessity: the development of appropriate operating methods and techniques. We are in the realm of manipulation—a manipulation may be considered necessary to attain laudable objectives, but is manipulation nonetheless. It can be seen in the uniformity and exclusivity of the revolutionary messages transmitted through the various channels of expression in an attempt to encompass all spheres of existence—and even more clearly in the controlled synergy of the projection of essential changes in revolutionary strategy through those channels."[13]

The characterization of a pervasive governmental communication control system propagating a controlled message is not what the discussion among Cuban intellectuals given earlier in this chapter suggests. One could ask which one is the rule and which the exception, but probably more important today is to know which one is indicative of the country's political direction. The answer should be as candid as the reflections on Marxist ideology already discussed attempt to be. But the scope and substance of cultural life under the revolution have not always been conducive to straightforward analysis of fundamental assumptions and policies. Periods of flexibility and openness for cultural productivity and communication of ideas have been followed by dogmatism and costly errors.

Paradoxically, another analyst questions the effectiveness of the government's communication (socialization) program, noting that the ultimate result is that traditional culture is not replaced but submerged, awaiting an opportunity to reemerge. And in this, according to Julie Marie Bunck, Cuba should be no exception. The initial revolutionary process of building a new political culture is presented as follows:

> The revolutionary government plainly viewed prerevolutionary Cuban culture through the prism of its Marxist-Leninist ideology. Cultural ills such as *machismo* and racism, materialism and laziness, elitism and greed were seen as direct consequences of an exploitative mode of production and of neighboring American imperialism. Fidel Castro and his assistants believed that many of society's most pervasive attitudes . . . could be traced to Cuba's historical experience . . . The revolutionary leaders did not, however, attempt

to destroy every aspect of traditional Cuban culture . . . Castro plainly used Cuba's Hispanic tradition of a strong, highly centralized, authoritarian government to legitimize his communist government.[14]

But, according to Bunck, only failure and disappointment could come next: "Fidel Castro's quest to establish a revolutionary culture in Cuba largely failed. The revolutionary government's attempt to destroy or transform certain aspects of prerevolutionary Cuban culture and to create a culture appropriate for the ideal Marxist society typically met insuperable obstacles. So, too, did the government's efforts to alter behavior often fail . . . Even when confronted with substantial direct and indirect coercion, many citizens failed to change their behavior. If behavior remained unchanged, then the official project to change culture, to change the values, beliefs, and attitudes of citizens, certainly failed as well."[15]

And yet, historic antecedents notwithstanding, the commitment to proletarian internationalism demonstrated by Cubans on numerous occasions—including thousands of volunteers putting their lives on the line in Angola—could be explained by their conviction that such commitment was proper and by their belief that behaving in such a fashion would provoke admiration from their peers. This is an important example of the revolutionary cultural and behavioral paradigm that characterized Cuban society and its emerging political culture after 1959.

However, not everyone shared revolutionary convictions with the same intensity or placed them equally at the center of their lives. Personal commitment to revolutionary values should be measured by a continuum whereby at one pole no cultural connection existed, while the other pole signified total identification. People placed themselves along such a continuum, and probably some individuals changed their standing according to the fortunes or misfortunes the country faced at a given time. As in other societies, there was an instrumental/pragmatic approach to revolutionary society practiced by those who supported the system as long as it delivered what they wanted to satisfy their needs. But once the regime failed to do so, they left the country, even if they occupied leading positions in the system.

The crisis of Marxism following the collapse of European socialism could have contributed to the disillusionment among some defectors, prompting them to emigrate. There is an opportunistic component among those who defected in the 1990s. Besides their past behavior, their departure was spurred by their desire not to be associated with the regime at a time when they expected its imminent downfall.

In a systems analysis approach, the regime faced the adversity of the 1990s with survival measures, while people reacted by providing their input and feedback regarding both the nation's problems and the solutions applied to solve them. While the revolution's survival and the people's support could not be taken for granted, the potential for change was real. In the ensuing cacophony of voices, the need for change was repeated again and again. For some members of the intelligentsia, the revolutionary alternative remained their choice but with major modifications:

> Humberto Solás (film director): "I do not believe in a single-party system. You cannot unify everyone in such an artificial way, because in the heart of the left, you and I think differently."
>
> Guillermo Rodríguez Rivera (university professor): "I believe that today we are advancing toward a new, different society. I don't have a clear idea what it is. I believe, however, that in the long run it should be a true social democracy."
>
> Gerardo González (economist): "The fundamental values we are trying to save are associated with social justice, ethics, morality and national dignity. All of these have to do with two very important things: self-determination and sovereignty. Except for these, everything else is negotiable."
>
> Miguel Barnet (poet, ethnologist, and novelist): "I am for changes. There have to be big changes in the economy. Socialism as it existed in the Soviet Union and the East Bloc no longer exists. We have to create a new type of socialism. But I think that changes have to be introduced very slowly so that people can assimilate them."[16]

Their opinions included opposition to a single political party system and a defense of socialism, the need for major change and a defense of self-determination and sovereignty. While these are not radically opposed ideas, it is likely that more divergent views have been expressed. In discussions across the island, the spectacle of so many people thinking through the different alternatives that could decide their destiny must have been quite a sight. However, as the decade progressed, a national consensus emerged around the policies for the revolution's survival and the defense of national sovereignty and independence.

The regime had to make such decisions in the most difficult of times. Official policies probably helped to shape people's opinions and expectations, but the initial decisions must have been influenced by popular opinion as well. Raúl Castro said publicly in the special period that the nation's number one problem was the shortage of food. He was vocalizing the urgency of the situation and the need to alleviate it, but he was also recognizing that people could not withstand much longer a situation so difficult to endure.[17] The 1994 riots on Havana's waterfront and the ensuing balsero crisis were clear reminders of how explosive the social situation could become if the population's needs at the most basic level remain unsatisfied—anything can happen once the situation goes beyond the threshold of people's fortitude.

The Human Rights Debate

There is no subject that puts Cuba on the defensive more than human rights violations. To allow opposition groups to exist legally, to allow the mass media to function independently from the government, or to have different groups and organizations functioning within their own social space and without governmental interference or control are rights so central to liberal democracy that their absence is difficult to accept. However, besides pressing national security and other issues determining the island's policies, there are fundamental differences between Havana's conception of human rights and that of the West and of liberal democracies in general. For years the White House successfully exploited the issue in the United Nations and elsewhere, until the campaign backfired in 1998. A year later, however, the U.S. strategy was paying off again. By the slimmest of margins—21 votes in favor (39.6 percent) and 20 against (37.7 percent), with 12 abstentions (22.6 percent)—the United Nations Human Rights Commission (HRC) condemned Cuba's human rights record once more by approving a resolution sponsored by Poland and the Czech Republic. It seemed that the sentencing of Vladimiro Roca and his three fellow dissidents, who had received prison sentences a few weeks earlier, tipped the balance against Havana.[18] Although apparently taking a back seat and allowing Poland and the Czech Republic to take the lead on the Cuba debate, the United States lobbied actively to line up the votes against Havana. All in all, the human rights debate has allowed the U.S. anti-Castro campaign to score public relations points as no other issue has.

Sponsored by the United States, the United Nations Social Subcommittee of the Economic and Social Council recommended in 1991 that a special envoy of the secretary general should investigate human rights violations in Cuba. Since then, Washington has annually sponsored successful resolutions at the HRC condemning Cuba: 19 nations voted against it (35.8 percent), 16 in favor (30.1 percent), and 18 abstained (32.1 percent). And then the Polish-Czech resolution was approved in 1999. Support for the American resolution had started to erode by 1995. In 1996, 20 countries favored the resolution (37 percent), while 5 opposed it (9 percent) and 28 abstained (52 percent). In 1997 support for the resolution decreased further with only 19 of the 53 member states voting favorably (35 percent). With barely more than a third of the commission's membership, the resolution prevailed thanks to the support of American allies—10 countries voted against (19 percent) and 24 abstained (45 percent). Having prevailed since 1992, the American resolution was defeated when in 1998, the number of negative votes almost doubled after a third of the 1997 abstentions joined the opposition, and the favorable votes decreased by three. The 1999 vote was so close that it was not certain whether Washington had regained the upper hand or whether Cuba had suffered a temporary setback.[19] (See table 12.1.)

The Cuban representative at the Human Rights Commission called the 1997 resolution "part and parcel of the hostile policy the U.S. has waged for the past 37 years." But in 1998 Robaina, then foreign minister, stated: "All those years when Cuba was condemned, a part of the world believed what the Commission said. Today we call on the whole world to evaluate the result of the voting." In 1999, María de los Angeles Flores,

Table 12.1. U.N. Human Rights Commission Votes on U.S. Resolutions Condemning Cuba, 1992–1999*

Votes	1992	1993	1994	1995	1996	1997	1998	1999
In Favor	23	27	24	22	20	19	16	21
Against	5	10	9	8	5	10	19	20
Abstention	19	15	20	23	28	24	18	12
Total	47	52	53	53	53	53	53	53

*Since 1992 a Human Rights Commission special rapporteur had been appointed yearly to investigate human rights violations. The practice ended in 1998 with the defeat of the American resolution proposing further investigation.

SOURCE: "Historic Defeat by United States in Geneva," *Granma International*, May 3, 1998, 3 (online, http://www.granma.cu); Juan O. Tamayo, "U.N. Panel Puts Cuba on Rights Abusers' List," *Miami Herald*, April 24, 1999.

Cuba's deputy foreign minister, responded to a gesture of support by a fellow diplomat following the HRC's censure of her country by saying laconically, "It happens."

John Kgoana Nkadimeng, South African ambassador to Cuba, had noted in 1998 the role that African nations played in defeating the American resolution at the HRC's fifty-fourth session, and that South Africa was presiding over the commission's proceedings when it happened. In 1999, while most African and Asian nations continued supporting Cuba or abstained, there was a realignment of the Latin American vote: Ecuador, Chile, and Uruguay switched from abstentions in 1998 to votes against Cuba, while Venezuela, Mexico, and Peru changed from abstentions to votes supporting Havana.

El Salvador abstained in 1999 after voting to condemn in 1998, allegedly in exchange for clemency for two Salvadorans sentenced to death early in the year on terrorism charges for sabotaging the Cuban tourist industry in 1997, causing loss of life and considerable damage to several international hotels and a well-known restaurant. The Mexican delegate censured the 1999 resolution saying that it criticized Cuba unfairly and lacked balance because it failed to condemn the U.S. embargo of the island. But Japan, South Korea, Canada, and all European nations voted for the Polish and Czech resolution, which did not include language condemning Cuba as strongly as earlier American resolutions had.

At the time the World Conference on Human Rights was convened, a Forum of Nongovernmental Organizations was also held in Vienna, Austria, in 1993. Making their presence felt on the related issues of human rights and civil society, Cuban delegations attended both gatherings. Joining thirteen hundred NGOs from all over the world, the Cuban organizations with representatives attending the forum were the Cuban Association of Jurists, the Center for the Study of the Americas, the Center for the Study of Europe, the Center for the Study of Youth, the Cuban Pro-Peace Movement, the Cuban Federation of Women, the Félix Varela Center, and Havana's representative of the Tricontinental (OSPAAAL).[20] The need for Cuban NGOs to function autonomously has been recognized: "It is not possible to ignore the need social organizations have for [social] space to function, which corresponds with present requests made while perfecting the political system, as well as [with the] new forms of conducting international relations."[21]

The U.S. denunciation of human rights violations is selective; not all violators are equally denounced. It has become more noticeable with Cuba, given the intensity that has characterized the campaign over a number of years.[22] While not defining the case as such, it is obvious that behind the American stance there is a major and older reason: Washington's anti-Cuba policy. Human rights is one more argument used to justify the policy.[23] Awareness that Washington has politicized the issue, and that it responds to political objectives not related to the defense of human rights, has caused increasing erosion of international support for the American position.

Cuba's human rights practice is based on its socialist system and Marxist ideology and on the commitment to social rights—not just political rights—as an integral component of human rights. It is also a defensive policy, the product of the international context that has surrounded the Cuban revolution. Hostile American actions against Cuba started during the first years of the revolution and have not stopped since. While support from the Soviet Union neutralized American policy in many areas, it did not erase the island-under-siege mentality demanding military readiness to defend itself. Since the collapse of European socialism, the situation has worsened; the combined effects of lacking European socialist support and increased American hostility have taken a toll on the country.

The domestic political opposition is not regarded as a homegrown movement but as the work of Cuban nationals working for the United States. The dissident movement has suffered as a result of its close association with Miami; in the eyes of Cubans, the nexus has rendered it a convenient political tool manipulated by the United States. The human rights campaign has been a collection of internal and external actors working together to denounce Havana's violations of human rights as part of the anti-Castro movement.[24]

The U.N. Commission approved resolution 113, thereby ending the debate on the report issued by the Human Rights Mission after its visit to the island at the invitation of the Cuban government in 1989. But the U.S. did not give up. It continued the denunciation of alleged Cuban violations. After three years of American charges, in 1990 the U.N. Human Rights Commission approved in Geneva the first resolution condemning Cuba. The dissolution of the Soviet bloc allowed the United States to increase its political leverage when members of the commission from former socialist nations turned against Cuba.

The situation repeated itself in 1991 after U.N. Secretary-General Javier Pérez de Cuellar submitted a document reporting positively on a series of contacts with Havana. Unhappy with Pérez de Cuellar's report and confident of increased support among commission members, the United

States put Cuba on the defensive by requesting a special U.N. rapporteur to travel to Cuba, talk to the government and citizens (dissidents), and investigate unanswered questions pending since 1988. The chief of the Cuban delegation at the time, Raúl Roa Kouri, rejected the final resolution approved by the commission: "Cuba will not accept an iota of the resolution amended by the United States."[25] Still, the U.N. Human Rights Commission continued as the political arena of choice for the U.S. human rights campaign against Havana.

In 1995 a Seminar on Definitions of Human Rights was held in Havana with American and Cuban participants.[26] The former head of the U.S. Interest Section in Havana, Wayne S. Smith, reported on Cuban and American viewpoints on human rights discussed at the seminar and on the areas where both delegations agreed:

Areas of agreement between the Cuban and American delegations:

"Human rights . . . do in fact have legal standing under international law."

"Genocide, torture, and arbitrary arrest . . . are universally condemned under international treaty. No government can claim the right to carry on such practices. [Regimes engaging in such practices cannot] maintain that they are acting legally when they do so."

"Human rights do not fall within [either Cuban or U.S.] exclusive, domestic jurisdiction."

"While there are some generally accepted standards governing human rights, they are only partially codified under international law and not always clear. Much remains to be done in this area."

Issues raised by the Cuban delegation:

Cuba proposed and the American delegation accepted that "Under international law it is legitimate for nations to take an interest in the human rights record of other nations. The problem arises [argues Cuba] when such scrutiny is selective and politicized, aimed not at protecting human rights per se, but [at] advancing a political agenda."

Cuba stated that the international community tends to impose not only those precepts generally accepted but also others that are not. There is a difference between international law and "humanitarian law," which signifies how things ought to be. The distinction has been blurred at the meetings of the

U.N. Human Rights Commission in Geneva.

Cuba noted that "there is an unfortunate willingness on the part of some U.N. members to use the organs of that international body improperly . . . The U.N. charter makes clear that the resolution of human rights issues must be brought through cooperation not coercion."

For Cuba, "human rights must be approached as a totality that includes social, economic, and cultural as well as political and civil rights. There should be no priority of some rights over others . . . There should be no priorities for certain groups of people or countries. There is not a single country where improvements are not needed."

"If public order does not contain human rights, then there is no [real] public order."

"[Some] Cubans conceded that there have been abuses and that they should be corrected . . . [All Cubans] stated that Cuba will not be coerced, nor will it cooperate with a campaign against it that is politically motivated."

Issues raised by the American delegation:

"[That] a government provides housing and education in no way lessens its obligation to respect the civil rights of its citizens . . . Without the right to life, no other right has any meaning."

"The right to due process, freedom from torture and from invidious discrimination are priorities. Without them individuals cannot exercise other rights. Economic and social rights . . . are more difficult to specify and implement . . . It is [easier] to protect the right to vote . . .; decent housing and medical care [are] far more difficult."[27]

Reports on violations of human rights in Cuba from such organizations as Human Rights Watch, Amnesty International, the Inter-American Commission on Human Rights of the Organization of American States, and others have been serious and numerous. These bodies have reported and harshly condemned alleged abuses and other human rights violations in Cuba. Most of the evidence for the reports comes from Cuban exiles' organizations and from their informants on the island. Many of those subjected to such abuses have denounced the abuses after leaving their homeland.

Americas Watch has also reported serious human rights violations in

Miami, Florida, among Cuban Americans. Paradoxically, some violations similar to those charged by the Cuban-American community against Cuba have been reported as being committed in Miami. Washington has made no attempt to denounce such violations, but it has sought political support from some of the groups charged with human rights violations by Human Rights Watch, Americas.[28]

The president of the National Assembly told the American delegation attending the human rights seminar in Havana that the government was considering increasing the number of candidates for each seat in the National Assembly contested in national elections to two or more, but that change "would be more likely to happen . . . if U.S. policy were to change." Alarcón added: "We have seen how the CIA and the National Endowment for Democracy come into other countries with money and try to distort the electoral process. We don't intend to let that happen here."[29]

While most problems on the island should not be blamed on Washington, the record shows that U.S. policy against the revolution has been harmful. Politicizing the human rights issue has not helped to improve human rights in Cuba. Political reform could have been more advanced if Havana had not been living under fear of American aggression of one kind or another, knowing that Washington is waiting for any opportunity to harm the Cuban government.

The history of U.S.–Latin American relations includes numerous cases of American-sponsored subversion of governments of which the White House did not approve. The record confirms Cuba's fears. The current Canadian policy of constructive engagement with Havana may yield results in this regard, offsetting entrenched patterns of behavior that have blocked further reform. This could allow Havana to develop fully its democratic promise (which should include respect for social and political rights), without having to fear retaliatory actions by the United States.

Castro's Political Thought and Leadership

Castro's attitude toward creative expression within the revolutionary culture was that no particular school—aesthetically, artistically, or otherwise defined—should prevail or be prohibited. In his "Words to the Intellectuals," delivered at a meeting at Havana's National Library in 1961, he offered to revolutionaries and nonrevolutionaries alike a canvas of cultural creativity framed within the contours of the revolution. He was motivated by political, not aesthetic or cultural reasons: "All artists and intellectuals may find in the revolution [a place] in which to work and create . . . in such a way that their creative spirit, even though they [may] not [be] revolutionary writers or artists, may have the opportunity and freedom to express themselves [and still remain] within the [scope of the] revolution."[30]

Notwithstanding cases of artists and writers facing official intolerance in four decades of revolutionary rule, Cuba never embraced a position similar to the Soviet Union's Socialist Realism, which stood as "the truthful depiction of reality in its revolutionary development."[31] Moscow fostered formal and academic art like Vera Mukhina's sculpture, "A Worker and Collective Farmer" (1936), and Yefim Cheptsov's painting, "A Meeting of a Village Party" (1924), as fine expression of what became officially sanctioned cultural and artistic work.

Revolutionary Cuba's culture was different because it had different roots and direction. In Castro's thinking, his speech to the intellectuals represented a forward leap toward liberated creativity as long as the revolution was the historic event standing for freedom. The same right was given to artists, writers, scientists, agronomists, workers, and peasants. All schools of creative thought should flourish, but within the scope of the revolution. To place oneself outside the revolution was to be against it. Political, artistic, or any cultural work done under such conditions was not acceptable; the revolution could not be destroyed from within. The newly acquired freedom should not be used to destroy its source. Those were the long-held parameters set up by Castro in his famous 1961 speech.

An inherent problem with such a divide (within the revolution everything/without the revolution nothing) is that artistic expression could be seen as political, even critical, when it was not purposely intended thus. Creative artists' social commentary can have unexpected undertones under any kind of government. Also, the interpretation given to an artist's social commentary usually relates not so much to the social event itself as to the political decision maker behind it, either for causing the problem or for failing to prevent it. Having to accept critical commentary on policy making is the price to pay for occupying political office.

Castro's remarks on the film *Guantanamera*—the last (collaborative) work by the late award-winning filmmaker Tomás "Titón" Gutiérrez Alea, an artist of recognized revolutionary credentials—is a case in point. The film depicts humorously life under the special period (satirizing the problems a family undergoes in having to bury a relative) and has been generally acclaimed by critics and audiences. But Castro's concern was political. Why should we focus on the negative, was his train of thought. "To poke morbid fun at tragedies . . . is not a patriotic act," he said. However, for filmmakers like Titón and other artists, it is precisely when difficult social situations are treated humorously (or tragically) that a healthy cathartic effect is achieved, besides this being good art. Was this film conceived within or outside revolutionary creative parameters? For Alfredo Guevara, the director of the Cuban Film Institute (ICAIC), *Guantanamera* is a good film—and he did not change his mind under pressure. For Castro, at the moment he made his remarks, it was not. In a subsequent meeting held at the National Union of Cuban Writers and Artists (UNEAC), attended by Guevara and numerous artists, writers, poets, and others, Castro apologized; he admitted that he had never seen the film in question and "promised to reevaluate the film after a viewing."[32] What might have been clear parameters for artistic creativity in 1961 do not seem so after decades of revolutionary rule, particularly with the compelling need artists have to portray humorously or tragically the kinds of problems confronting the country today.

In 1961 and later, Castro was expressing a radical leftist tradition of political freedom and democracy understood as a single political truth— which in Cuba's case was conceived and implemented by an organically integrated political system.[33] It was not the pluralist liberal democratic notion of divergent political truths struggling to nullify each other (a philosophical difference that fuels the human rights debate discussed earlier). For the revolutionary left, political truth, freedom, and democracy exist to service the people, not to allow sectarian interests to prevail or even to exist as such. So the revolution was the turning point when the people's political truth was finally recognized, and their rights and interests were satisfied. As Cuban national poet Nicolás Guillén put it: "Tengo lo que tenía que tener" (I now have what I was meant to have).[34]

The roots of Castro's political culture can be traced to a tradition of radical Cuban political thought, of which he became a major exponent: "Early Cuban radicals sought to negate privilege, to strike a better balance between the haves and have-nots . . . Radicals do not always choose the safe course. They are often courageous and willing to experiment, and prepared to risk failure. Their actions are not necessarily irrelevant to the mainstream of social and political concerns, but they do not always deal with these concerns in conventional fashion."

Castro's rebelliousness, demonstrated among other actions by his defiance of U.S. might and power, appears to be built into his own charismatic brand of leadership: "[Radicals] respond negatively to the 'obedience syndrome'—respect [fear] for authority or power simply because it exists."[35]

Nelson P. Valdés contends that "for the last two hundred years, Cuban politics [radical and nonradical alike] has followed an identical script" and that "the themes of personal duty, political morality, patriotism, and the historic mission of the nation engaged Cubans from all political perspectives . . . The Cuban revolution did not alter the pattern: Cuban revolutionaries and exiles still conform to the same discourse." These cultural patterns should work themselves out by following four conceptual components: "The four codes are (1) the generational theme, (2) the moralism-idealism syndrome, (3) the theme of betrayal, and (4) the duty-death imperative."[36]

There are distinctions between revolutionaries and exiles in Cuban political history and culture. While studying the roots of Castro's political culture, one should acknowledge his centrality in the development of contemporary radical political thought in Cuba. Also, the way he has practiced Valdés's conceptual codes of political culture is through a political discourse and political actions that have led to a radical social revolution that has sustained itself in power against all odds. Nobody else has done that in Cuban history. Nor has anyone in Latin America led a successful social revolution as radical as the Cuban revolution.

In his seminal work on Castro's political and social thought, Sheldon B. Liss tells us that Castro's political thought and leadership have had a near universal impact—no mean feat for the leader of a small Caribbean island nation.[37] Beyond domestic and national issues, Castro has addressed himself to problems affecting the Americas, international relations, human and social rights, democracy, freedom of expression, social progress, international debt, ecology, and many other spheres. His long-winded oratory is famous. As a close friend, the Nobel laureate Colombian writer Gabriel García Márquez, has said, Castro "rests from talking by talking."[38]

In the 1990s, exercising his charisma on a world stage, Castro became the global spokesman for the poor, the masses of humanity who are usually bypassed by powerful interests and political leaders. In a comeback in the international arena, when so many analysts regarded him as a "has been" leader, Castro has dominated by the strength of his personality every international forum he has attended in recent years. His meeting with the pope in the Vatican in 1996, which he characterized as "very special," and his welcoming the pope to Cuba in 1998 proved him capable of interacting with essentially different interlocutors (especially when compared with former Soviet leaders). But his person and leadership are derisively treated in the United States, where he and his revolution have not been accepted by the government and most likely never will be.[39]

Some political writers and biographers talk about Castro's domineering, authoritarian, uncompromising personality.[40] Cuban exiles and others have accused him of crimes and violations of human rights.[41] Political analysts have said that the Cuban revolution is Castro's revolution and that one could benefit from the social programs instituted since 1959 or could become an important official in his government as long as one accepted his revolution, under his leadership.[42]

Undoubtedly, Castro has a strong personality. As one biographer wrote: "Like his father, Fidel also grew up strong-willed, decisive, and sure of his convictions. [Fidel's father] Angel tolerated little dissent from those around him, and Fidel easily adopted the same style . . . [He] would later become fascinated with discipline for himself and others. It was a vital ingredient in all of his activities . . . Its attraction seemed to be in part based on the importance he attached to it in helping him organize his own unchanneled energies."[43]

Whether Castro is called domineering, authoritarian, or by any other name, even his critics have admitted to being taken in by his charm, magnetism, and the strength he exudes when one is talking to him personally. He is no ordinary man by any standards. Biographers like to point out his questionable activities and associations as a student leader at Havana University while attending law school, when action groups dominated university politics. The important point is that Castro transcended that kind of student politics background to become a political leader of larger-than-life stature.

The demonization of Castro carried out in the United States, especially in Miami, has been evaluated critically by a Cuban-American journalist who left Cuba early in the 1960s and has remained opposed to the revolution, Luis Ortega. Among the many accounts Ortega provided in his articles in *Contrapunto* and other Spanish media in the United States, he offered this one of Miami and Castro: "The monster that has been manufactured by Cuban [exiles] in the United States has become an image for local consumption in Miami. The sizable propaganda made in the United States, during thirty-six years, demonizing Castro could not find an outlet abroad. Castro is one thing in Miami and another outside Miami [or the United States]."[44]

Acknowledging Cuba's new domestic and international relations political objectives, Ortega writes: "It is curious that the Cuban revolution has evolved to the point that references to communism have become a formality. Fidel Castro, on his recent trip to Uruguay, Argentina, Cartagena [Colombia] and New York, did not mention Marxism-Leninism even once. The theme is Cuba's sovereignty."[45]

Castro's political skills are sophisticated; he has a keen sense of what is advantageous for the revolution and goes ahead and does it. He could welcome and embrace with gratitude the aid offered by the Reverend Lucius Walker and the ecumenical U.S.-organized Pastors for Peace "friendshipments" in defiance of U.S. law, specifically the blockade. In 1996, U.S. Customs prevented from crossing the border 350 computers from Pastors for Peace, destined for Cuban hospitals. Only after a hunger strike by Walker and his associates was the friendshipment caravan allowed to cross the Mexican border and from there go to Cuba. In 1997, the Pastors for Peace caravans faced no government obstacles, and new caravans were planned to reach Cuba from the United States, Mexico, and Canada. As former director of Latin American Affairs at the National Security Council Richard Feinberg stated, "[The] Pastors for Peace caravans have no impact on the broad contours of U.S.-Cuba policy but have placed U.S. policy makers 'in something of an embarrassing position' of appearing to block humanitarian aid to Cuba."[46]

Castro also sponsored and provided the setting for the Fourteenth World Festival of Youth and Students held in Cuba from July 28 to August 5, 1997. After a twelve-year hiatus of the annual youth festivals (an earlier one was held in Cuba in 1978), the 1997 celebration brought over twelve thousand people from 136 countries to all Cuban provinces. They engaged in festive celebrations but also, while engaging in an "in-depth analysis of the most acute problems affecting humanity," committed themselves to fight against the U.S. blockade. By the end of the celebrations, the official media reported that "Cuba was the setting for the most significant global youth encounter in 50 years."[47]

In both cases, Castro was acting out his rebellious spirit after effectively tuning it with what is politically correct for the revolution. He interacted first with fellow rebels from the United States, and then with rebel youth from all over the world. The moral indignation that led Castro to the attack on the Moncada Barracks on July 26, 1953, is the same force providing the emotional urging spurring him and fellow rebels into action. Castro was appealing to the traditional generational theme discussed by Valdés and to the radical rebelliousness documented by Liss. At the youth festival he interacted with a young generation, feeding them with his own rebelliousness while he was invigorated by theirs. U.S. Cuba policy provided the raw material awakening the young festival delegates and Pastors for Peace into action, but other social justice causes could have done so as well.

Castro's world vision and ideological universe have been summarized by Liss this way: "When confronted with the anti-intellectuals' position . . . that ideological wars are over, that history is coming to an end, Fidel responded in true Marxist fashion that, on the contrary, history has barely begun. He pointed out that Marxism . . . is a recently implemented method of analysis, not a historical interlude or a failed political system. He has faith in the inexorable historical process that Marx predicted would lead to socialism . . . Most of the capitalist Third World knows only discrimination, misery, and exploitation, and minority social, economic, and political control over majorities. The present might appear to belong to capitalism, but . . . the future does [not], as long as class struggle continues in capitalist societies."[48]

After four revolutionary decades under Castro's leadership, the different themes and codes of Cuba's political culture have been compressed into a new political culture mix that functionally represents a civil (secular) religion. It is not a sacred or divine religion, but a secular religion rooted in the revolutionary values conforming Cubans' political thought. Secular manifestations of the revolutionary civil religion are the defense of national sovereignty and independence, socialism, and anti-imperialism.[49] The nation's civil religion seems to mirror Castro's political thought and objectives even under the special period.

The Making of Cuba's New Socialism

Latin American leftist leaders were conscious before the events of 1989–91 in socialist Europe that they had to distance themselves from political practices abroad. "Even orthodox communists have argued against the mechanical application of policies derived from *perestroika,* considering it an instance of the discredited practice of slavishly defending lines set down by the socialist metropolis."[50] The political left worldwide suffered the disruptive impact of the collapse of European socialism. In the words of Juan Valdés Paz, a Cuban social scientist, "We are in a moment of disorientation for the left . . . What the left has to do is to develop an alternative program . . . [which is] anti-capitalist and anti-imperialist . . . to bring real change . . . not only an economic alternative but a total alternative."[51]

Still, the late Carlos Rafael Rodríguez, the most respected leader among those who belonged to the pre-revolutionary communist party, defended Castro's launching a socialist revolution under conditions that were difficult even before the 1990s: "Fidel Castro has given a primary example of being a revolutionary. He could have waited for socialism to emerge under more propitious circumstances in the continent and not in a country so close to the United States, which is so powerful. But it is not a question of waiting but of accomplishing things. Under extremely difficult conditions, Cuban socialism was [already] ahead of others in the world. That is the way true revolutionaries behave."[52]

The Cuban revolution has been a guiding force for the Latin American left, but during the special period Havana had to concentrate on rebuilding the economy and saving the revolution. It had to reintegrate the island into Latin American life and make clear that Cuba would not interfere in neighboring countries' internal affairs, as it had when exporting its revolution. The São Paulo Forum has been a major initiative attempting to pick up the pieces of the Latin American left and put them back together in a well-articulated political platform. Hence, looking to regain some of the lost influence on the Latin American left, Havana hosted the Fourth São Paulo Forum in 1993.

The Havana São Paulo Forum was an important development for the Latin American left. With the addition of thirty-one new members since the Third Forum held in Managua, 112 member organizations and twenty-five observers from the region attended. Cuauhtémoc Cárdenas, the former mayor of Mexico City and a candidate for the presidency for a second time in the year 2000, was present as a member of the Mexican delegation. The leftist leaders gathered in Havana shared a nationalist, anti-imperialist, socialist, democratic, and progressive identity. The final declaration sought to prove the need for the political left in a continent afflicted by poverty, unemployment, the burden of neoliberal policies, by national economies having to serve the external debt, and by many other ills.

The proceedings of the commission covering relations between the state and political parties and movements included these statements: "Before the false democracy sponsored by neoliberalism it is necessary to oppose it with a profound participatory democracy that will entail not only voting now and then but becoming involved in the task of governing the nation." And "The disregard that some organizations have demonstrated for human and political rights is unjustifiable . . . These rights and freedoms are the product of major social struggles that demanded their implementation and respect by bourgeois governments."[53]

The salient point of the deliberations was to make the Latin American left understand what was happening in Cuba during the special period. It was a call for temperance, making the delegates realize the odds that leftist movements would face if they came to rule a country. As had happened in Cuba, they would be without socialist assistance and would still face the hostility of the United States.

It was in such a political context that the new Cuban socialism was starting to emerge. The government has been accused of not changing fast enough, of pursuing economic but not political reform, and of wanting to safeguard the system but not to democratize it. For Cuba watchers this has been a period of unanswered questions. They have asked if the reforms represent a blueprint detailing Cuba's new socialism or if they are an accumulation of patchwork changes that all together might constitute a reform by the end. In Valdés Paz's view: "It is not even clear when the problems of the [special period] will end or when we will begin to deal with the problems brought about by the solutions to that . . . crisis. All the policies which lead us out of [the special period] will generate a new Cuban society with other social aspirations, with unintended and undesired contradictions. *For this new Cuban society, the economic model will have to be reformulated. The political model, the model of socialism will have to be appropriate to the problems of the times*" (emphasis added).[54]

Some components of the puzzle have become more visible by now. The regime has taken a cautious approach in pursuit of three different but related objectives: to resist and overcome the economic collapse, to safeguard the socialist system, and to integrate the country into the world economy. Every major policy and structural change appears to respond to the pursuit of these three related goals.

The government's firmest decision has been the defense of the revolution, the socialist system, and the nation's sovereignty and independence. These are interrelated elements necessary for Cuba to remain an independent state. Free education and public health care are two social benefits regarded as permanent social equality features of the system. Some of the political, economic, and social changes discussed earlier are among the features forming the silhouette of the emerging socialist system.

The liberalization of religious practice and the visit by the pope in 1998, which reinforced the ongoing religious renaissance and pushed it forward, might have an effect on the ultimate nature of Cuban socialism. Making the revolution's ideology more tolerant of religious beliefs widens the scope of legitimate values and practices in daily life. It would also foster a degree of ideological pluralism, with secular and religious beliefs coexisting in a socialist society. Christian morality could complement the revolution's secular morality in the difficult task of uplifting the nation's ethical standards, especially when creeping materialism seems rampant with the dollarization of the economy, the reemergence of prostitution, the confusion of a young generation deciding what its own present and future objectives should be, and with other negative social traits that emerged under the special period. And yet, while international tourism, dollar remittances from abroad, and the opening of the island to the world have contributed to this state of affairs, they are also necessary pillars of the nation's economic revival.

Conclusions

It is in the details more than at the macro level that the nature of things is defined. How will the reforms be implemented, and what kinds of social relationships will develop between the population and the government and among the citizens themselves? Will the nature of these and other interactions define the emerging system better than grandiose reforms? Sometimes official policy has confirmed what was done at the grassroots level, where informal practices originated. New expectations created by such practices and the official decisions confirming them, even if temporary, should carry some weight in the ultimate character of the emerging system.

Economic liberalization has produced several types of ownership, which might add new modalities in the future. The trend has been to extend the scope of foreign private investment, forming joint ventures in partnership with the government. Self-employment in a growing number of areas is a form of private enterprise accessible to the population. Its scope has been stretched and contracted mostly for political considerations. In the long run, however, even if modestly, it will grow more and then become stabilized. It is hard to imagine a large-scale retrenchment of self-employment given present economic conditions, even if conditions were to improve significantly in the near future.

The system of agricultural cooperatives, UBPCs, is another form of nonstate property. Their productivity has been below expectations, but they allow workers to play labor and management roles—even though they lack land ownership titles. Besides needing to increase productivity as managers, workers should develop a personal stake in the proficiency of agricultural enterprises.

The mix of public and private enterprise under a socially interventionist state that keeps a firm hand in many economic areas appears to be a
lasting feature of the emerging economic system. While still retaining a
socialist character, the new economy will be a far cry from the pre-1991
era of nearly total socialism. Also, future economic planning should have
a broad participatory input, different from the narrow bureaucratic control that has dominated it.

Keeping the single-party system and turning that party into the political party of the Cuban nation would safeguard the political system while
broadening its mobilization and participatory political base. In the long
run, however, the Cuban Communist Party would have to change its
name and identity, so that it could be the political party of the entire
Cuban nation. To be truly inclusive, even if most of the membership ad-
heres to a Marxist orientation (probably with a definition of Marxism
different from what it was before), the party should include revolutionary Christian believers.

As religious believers effectively become party members, providing a
non-Marxist but revolutionary presence, change in the party's name and
identity would constitute recognition of what has taken place at the
grassroots level. Also, the change would institutionalize a broader ideological matrix (blending Marxist and Christian ideologies) for a national
political party rooted in the revolution and committed to its defense. As
improbable as it looked not long ago, this could happen in the not too
distant future. The idea of a single political party representing the nation
as a whole in order to foster the revolution and democracy was initially
suggested as far back as January 1959 by Faure Chomón, head of Havana
University students' Revolutionary Directorate during the anti-Batista
struggle.[55]

The electoral system is a compromise between limited political reform
and the need for defensive measures. While it allows a direct secret vote
and the possibility of relatively unknown elected representatives becoming legislators in the National Assembly and even being elected to the
Council of State, the lack of candidates competing at the national and
provincial levels detracts from its potential as a democratic representative system. There should be a new electoral system providing the electorate with a choice among competing candidates at all jurisdictional
levels.

Alarcón has stated that American punitive policies are holding back
the implementation of further political reform, including changing the
electoral system. The situation places the country physically and psycho-

logically in a state of readiness to withstand any external aggression. This is not Cuba overreacting; history has demonstrated that economic, political, and cultural aggression can be as harmful as military aggression.

Cuba needs to continue on the path of reform while adjusting to international realities and domestic expectations. While the changes already made have recognized such exigencies, future change should respond to Cuba's interests and objectives. The reform process must continue uninterrupted regardless of hostile U.S. policies. This is not to say that national security should be disregarded but that the ongoing transformation of the political and economic system should not be hostage to the Cuban-U.S. relations problematic. Although 1998 and 1999 were not the years for a rapprochement, perhaps President Clinton's decision easing some of the sanctions may pave the way for a future normalization of relations with a new administration in Washington.

As regards continuing the political and economic reform process, the suggestion Morales Domínguez made close to forty years ago still applies: "If it were possible, it would be convenient for Cuba to forget that the United States [exists]."[56] That way the newly emerging socialism could develop according to the expectations of the Cuban people and the revolutionary leadership about what it should be like. But regardless of these considerations and obstacles, or perhaps because of them, Cuba will continue reinventing its own brand of socialism today and tomorrow.

APPENDIX A

Composition of the Council of Ministers and Other High Government Posts, October 1997

Council of Ministers

President[1]	Fidel Castro Ruz
First Vice President	Gen. Raúl Castro Ruz
Vice Presidents of the Council of Ministers	José Ramón Fernández Álvarez
	Carlos Rafael Rodríguez Rodríguez[2]
	Osmany Cienfuegos Gorriarán
	Jaime Crombet Hernández Baquero[3]
	Adolfo Díaz Suárez
	Pedro Miret Prieto
Secretary of the Council of Ministers	Carlos Lage Dávila
Minister of Agriculture	Alfredo Jordan Morales
Minister of Basic Industry	Marcos Portal León
Minister of Communications	Brig. Gen. Silvano Colás Sánchez
Minister of Construction	Juan Mario Junco del Pino
Minister of Construction Materials Industry	José Canete Álvarez
Minister of Culture	Abel Prieto Jiménez
Minister of Domestic Trade	Barbara Castillo Cuesta
Minister of Economy and Planning	José Luis Rodríguez García[3]
Minister of Education	Luis I. Gómez Gutiérrez
Minister of Finance and Prices	Manuel Milláres Rodríguez
Minister of the Fishing Industry	Orlando Felipe Rodríguez Romay
Minister of the Food Industry	Alejandro Roca Iglesias
Minister of Foreign Investment and Economic Cooperation	Ibrahim Ferradáz[4]
Minister of Foreign Relations	Roberto Robaina González[5]
Minister of Foreign Trade	Ricardo Cabrisas Ruiz
Minister of Higher Education	Fernando Vecino Alegret
Minister of the Interior	Corps. Gen. Abelardo Colomé Ibarra
Minister of Justice	Roberto Díaz Sotolongo

Minister of Labor and Social Security	Salvador Valdés Mesa[6]
Minister of Light Industry	Jesús Pérez Othón
Minister of Metallurgic and Electronics Industry	Ignacio González Planas
Minister of Public Health	Carlos Dotres Martínez
Minister of the Revolutionary Armed Forces	Gen. Raúl Castro Ruz
Minister of Science, Technology, and the Environment	Rosa Elena Simeón Negrín
Minister of the Sugar Industry	Gen. Ulises Rosales del Toro
Minister of Tourism	Osmany Cienfuegos Gorriarán[4]
Minister of Transportation	Alvaro Pérez Morales
Minister Without Portfolio	Wilfredo López Rodríguez
Minister-President, Central Bank of Cuba	Francisco Soberón Valdés

Other High Posts

Attorney General	Juan Escalona Reguera
Principal Officer, Cuban Interests Section (Washington, D.C.)	Fernando Remírez de Estenoz Barciela
Permanent Representative to the United Nations (New York)	Bruno Rodríguez Parrilla

---

[1]The president of the Council of Ministers and of the Council of State becomes the country's president. Fidel Castro has occupied the office since its creation in 1976. He was reelected as president of the Council of Ministers and of the Council of State for a fifth time in 1998, and will be seventy-six years old by the end of his term in 2003.

[2]Deceased (December 8, 1997).

[3]Jaime Crombet Hernández was replaced by José Luis Rodríguez Garcia as vice president of the Council of Ministers.

[4]In 1999 Osmany Cienfuegos Gorriarán was replaced as minister of tourism by Ibrahim Ferradáz, minister of foreign investment and economic cooperation. Ferradáz's deputy, María Lomas Morales, became foreign investment minister.

[5]Felipe Pérez Roque became minister of foreign relations in mid-1999.

[6]Salvador Valdés Mesa was replaced as minister of labor and social security by Alfredo Morales Cartagena—it was the third ministerial change in a five-month period in 1999.

Source: Central Intelligence Agency (online) http://www.odci.gov/cia/publications/chiefs/fea2.html (Washington, D.C.: U.S. Government, 1997, 1999); *CubaINFO* 9 (November 13, 1997): 5–7; *CubaINFO* 11 (September 14, 1999): 7; "Nuevo Ministro de Trabajo en Cuba," Reuters, October 23, 1999.

APPENDIX B

Election of the Council of State
by the National Assembly
(February 24, 1998)[1]

President and Vice Presidents[2]	Votes Received[3]
Fidel Castro Ruz (PB),[4] President	595 (100%)
Gen. Raúl Castro Ruz (PB), First Vice President	595 (100%)
Other Vice Presidents	
Juan Almeida Bosque (PB), Commander of the Revolution	595 (100%)
Gen. Abelardo Colomé Ibarra (PB), Minister of the Interior	595 (100%)
Carlos Lage Dávila (PB), Vice President of the Council of Ministers	595 (100%)
Esteban Lazo Hernández (PB), First Secretary of the PCC in Havana	595 (100%)
José Ramón Machado Ventura (PB), Head of the Organization Department of the Central Committee of the PCC	591 (99.3%)
José M. Millar Barruecos, Minister Secretary	594 (99.8%)

Other Members of the Council of State
Reelected Members

José Ramón Balaguer Cabrera (PB), Head, Department of International Relations and Ideology of the PCC	594 (99.8%)
Vilma Espín Quillot, President, Cuban Women's Federation (FMC)	593 (99.6%)
Armando Hart Dávalos, Director, José Martí Program Office	589 (98.9%)
Orlando Lugo Fonte, President, National Association of Small Farmers	592 (99.4%)
Pedro Miret Prieto (PB), Vice President, Council of Ministers	591 (99.3%)
Felipe R. Pérez Roque, Foreign Relations Minister	594 (99.8%)
Marcos Javier Portal León (PB), Minister of Basic Industry	595 (100%)
Pedro Ross Leal (PB), Secretary General of Cuban Workers' Union	587 (98.6%)
Rosa Elena Simeón Negrín, Minister of Science, Technology, and the Environment	592 (99.4%)

New Members   **Votes Received[3]**

Maria Caridad Abreu Ruiz, President, Municipal Assembly, La Palmira, Cienfuegos province	590 (99.1%)
Marcos Raúl Aguilera, Director, Central Oil Company	594 (99.8%)
Gen. Julio Casas Regueiro (PB), First Substitute, Revolutionary Armed Forces Minister	593 (99.6%)
Juan Contino Aslan, National Coordinator, Committees for the Defense of the Revolution (CDRs)	595 (100%)
Sergio Corrieri Hernández, President, Cuban Friendship Institute (ICAP)	594 (99.8%)
Roberto T. Díaz Sotolongo, Minister of Justice	594 (99.8%)
Caridad del Rosario Diego, Head, Office of Religious Affairs of the PCC	590 (99.1%)
Regla Martínez Herrera, President, Popular Council, Los Sitios, Havana	587 (98.6%)
Conrado C. Martínez Corona, President, Municipal Assembly, Havana	595 (100%)
Roberto Fernández Retamar, President, Casa de las Américas	590 (99.1%)
Otto Rivero Torres, First Secretary, Union of Young Communists	595 (100%)
José Luis Rodríguez, Minister of Economy and Planning	592 (99.4%)
Salvador Antonio Valdés Mesa, Minister of Labor and Social Security	592 (99.4%)
Carlos M. Valenciaga Díaz, President, University Students Federation (FEU)	592 (99.4%)

Replaced Members

Luis Abreu Mejías
Hipólito Abril Santos
Enith Alermo Prieto, Head, Cuban Young Pioneers Union
General Sixto Batista Santana
Concepción Campa Huergo (PB), President, Finlay Institute
Senén Casas Regueiro (deceased)
Osmany Cienfuegos Gorriarán, former Tourism Minister
Carlos Dotres Martínez, Minister of Public Health
Juan Escalona Reguera, Attorney General
Eslinda Orosco Moreno
Abel Prieto Jiménez (PB), Minister of Culture
Roberto Robaina González (PB), Former Foreign Relations Minister
Carlos Rafael Rodríguez (deceased)
Division General Ulises Rosales del Toro (PB), Minister of the Sugar Industry

1. In the 1998 National Assembly there were 166 women (27.6%) and 435 men (72.3%), for a total membership of 601. Their social composition included: workers in production and service sector (workers, peasants, education and health workers, and others) 145 (24.1%); researchers and scientists 26 (4.3%); athletes 7 (1.1%); intellectuals and artists 30 (4.9%); military personnel 35 (5.8%); political leaders 64 (10.6%); religious representatives 3 (0.4%); representatives of mass organizations 36 (5.9%); state officials 41 (6.8%); representatives of the Organs of People's Power 83 (13.8%); Popular Councils delegates 90 (14%); and other leaders 21 (3.5%).

2. The president of the Council of State (and the Council of Ministers) becomes the country's president. Fidel Castro has occupied the office since its creation in 1976. Reelected as president of the Council of State for a fifth time on February 24, 1998, he will be seventy-six years old by the end of his term in 2003.

3. On February 24, 1998, the National Assembly reelected its president, vice president, and secretary: Ricardo Alarcón, Jaime Crombet, and Ernesto Suárez, respectively. Of the 601 newly elected National Assembly deputies, 595 were present at the opening session and voted to elect the new Council of State. After all ballots were declared valid, the 31-member Council of State had 14 newly elected members (45.1%) and 17 reelected members (54.8%), including the president, first vice president, and five other vice presidents.

4. PB indicates a member of the Politburo of the Cuban Communist Party (PCC).

SOURCE: "Elección del Consejo de Estado," RV/RHC [Radio Habana Cuba], February 24, 1998; Pablo Alfonso, "Castro Is Again Picked Leader of the Council of State," Miami Herald, February 25, 1998; Rodolfo Casals, "Cuba Ratifies Its Socialist Option: There Will Be No Transition to Capitalism," Granma International, March 8, 1998, 3; CUBANEWS 6 (March 1998): 12.

APPENDIX C

Membership of the Political Bureau of the Communist Party of Cuba after the Fifth Party Congress, October 8–10, 1997

Fidel Castro Ruz	First Secretary of the Central Committee of the Communist Party of Cuba, and President of the Councils of State and Ministers
Gen. Raúl Castro Ruz	Second Secretary of the Central Committee of the Communist Party of Cuba, First Vice President of the Councils of State and Ministers, and Minister of the Armed Forces
Ricardo Alarcón de Quesada	President of the National Assembly of People's Power
Juan Almeida Bosque	Major of the Revolution, Vice President of the Council of State
José Ramón Balaguer Cabrera	Member of the Council of State
Concepción Campa Huergo	Member of the Council of State
Julio Casas Regueiro, Division General	First Substitute for the Minister of the Revolutionary Armed Forces
Leopoldo Cintra Frías, Division General	Head of the Western Army
Abelardo Colomé Ibarra, Army General	Vice President of the Council of State and Minister of the Interior
Misael Enamorado Dager*	First Secretary of the Party's Provincial Committee in Las Tunas
Ramón Espinosa Martín,* Division General	Head of the Eastern Army
Yadira García Vera	First Secretary of the Party's Provincial Committee in Matanzas
Alfredo Jordan Morales	Minister of Agriculture
Carlos Lage Dávila	Vice President of the Council of State, Secretary of the Executive Committee of the Council of Ministers

Esteban Lazo Hernández	Vice President of the Council of State, First Secretary of the Party's Provincial Committee in the City of Havana
José Ramón Machado Ventura	Vice President of the Council of State, Head of the Organization Department of the Party's Central Committee
Marcos Javier Portal León*	Member of the Council of State, and Minister of Basic Industry
Abel Prieto Jiménez	Member of the Council of State, Minister of Culture
Roberto Robaina González	Member of the Council of State
Juan Carlos Robinson Agramonte*	First Secretary of the Party's Provincial Committee in Santiago de Cuba
Ulises Rosales del Toro	Member of the Council of State, Minister of the Sugar Industry
Pedro Ross Leal	Member of the Council of State, General Secretary of the Central Organization of Cuban Trade Unions
Pedro Saez Montelo*	First Secretary of the Party's Provincial Committee in Sancti Spiritus
Jorge Luis Sierra Cruz*	First Secretary of the Party's Provincial Committee in Holguín

Note: The Fifth Party Congress agreed to downsize the party's leadership by reducing the Politburo from 26 members to 24 (7.6 percent) and the Central Committee from 225 members to 150 (33.3 percent) and to add younger political leaders to the highest political ranks. The decision sought to increase the party's effectiveness by concentrating its function on political leadership rather than on administration and legislation. Six new members were added to the Politburo and eight old leaders were demoted to the Central Committee. Nelson Torres, sugar minister; Alfredo Hondal, the first party secretary in Ciego de Avila Province; and Cándido Palmero, first party secretary in Havana Province also lost the government and party offices they had held before the party congress. Osmany Cienfuegos, former minister of tourism; Jorge Lezcano, head of the National Assembly Foreign Affairs Commission; Julián Rizo, National Assembly deputy; and María de los Angeles García were also removed from the Politburo. Because of his advanced age (eighty-four years) and infirmity, Carlos Rafael Rodríguez lost his Politburo post but, having had an illustrious party and government career, retained his seat on the Central Committee. Confirming his commitment to the revolution in spite of his precarious health, Rodríguez attended the Fifth Party Congress only two months before he passed away on December 8, 1997. With Fidel and Raúl Castro in attendance, Ricardo Alarcón, president of the

National Assembly, delivered the funeral oration evoking the outstanding life of Carlos Rafael, as he was popularly known, and his contributions to the regime.
* New Politburo member.

SOURCE: *Granma International*, October 26, 1997: 8–9; *CUBANews* 5 (November 1997): 8–9; *CubaINFO* 9 (October 23, 1997): 7–8; and "Fallece Comunista Cubano Carlos Rafael Rodríguez," *El Nuevo Herald*, December 10, 1997.

APPENDIX D

Provincial Secretaries of the Cuban Communist Party (PCC) and Number of Central Committee Members per Province and the Isle of Youth Municipality after the Fifth Party Congress, October 8–10, 1997

Province	Provincial Secretary	Number of Central Committee Members*
Pinar del Rio	María del Carmen Concepción	3
Havana	Pedro Saez	3
City of Havana	Esteban Lazo	93
Matanzas	Yadira García	4
Villa Clara	Miguel Díaz-Canel	9
Sancti Spiritus	Juan A. Díaz	1
Ciego de Ávila	Edildo L. Companioni	3
Holguín	Jorge L. Sierra	3
Guantánamo	Rider Díaz	3
Santiago de Cuba	Juan C. Robinson	8
Granma	Armando Hamut	5
Las Tunas	Misael Enamorado	4
Camagüey	Carlos Díaz	3
Cienfuegos	Manuel Menéndez	3

Municipality	Municipal Secretary	Number of Central Committee Members*
Isle of Youth	Roberto F. García	1

*There are four additional Central Committee members not included in the provincial membership listed here.

SOURCE: *CUBANEWS* 5 (December 1997): 12.

APPENDIX E

Membership of the Cuban Communist Party (PCC) during the Fifth Party Congress, October 8–10, 1997

Total membership   780,000*
New members
    1986–1991   168,432 (28,072 per year)
    1992–1996   232,456 (46,492 per year)
New members who belong to the Union   52.9%
    *of Communist Youth (UJC)***
Membership by age group
    28 to 35 years   22.5%
    36 to 45 years   29.3%
    46 to 55 years   26.6%
    over 55 years   19.7%
Membership by educational level
    Less than sixth grade   1.7%
    Up to sixth grade   9.5%
    Elementary   30.7%
    High school   34.9%
    College   23.2%
Membership by ethnic group
    White   66%
    Black   12%
    Mixed   22%
Members retired from the labor force
    110,461 (14.35%)
Number of party base organizations
    56,656 nucleuses

---

*Membership includes 9.4% of the population over 28 years of age; 29.4% of PCC members are women, 4.4% more than in 1990.

**16.8% of the population between 16 and 30 years of age belong to the UJC. The combined membership of the UJC and the PCC represents 13.1% of the population 16 years of age and older.

SOURCE: "El Partido en Cifras," *Correo de Cuba* 3, no. 4: 8.

APPENDIX F

Cuban Roman Catholic Personnel Divided by Dioceses, 1998

Diocese/ archdiocese	Bishops	Auxiliary bishops	Diocesan priests	Religious order priests	Permanent deacons	Nuns/ sisters	Secular institutes	Friars/ brothers	Totals
Santiago de Cuba	1		10	18		32	1	4	66
Havana	1*	1	41	71	13	258	6	18	409
Pinar del Río	1		15	4		36			56
Cienfuegos	1		11	12	2	20			46
Camagüey	1		14	9	5	35	5	3	72
Matanzas	1	1	9	11	1	60	7		90
Holguín	1		21	6	2	42	4	1	77
Santa Clara	1		12	9	6	32			60
Bayamo/Manzanillo	1		6	2	10	1			20
Ciego de Ávila	1		4	2	4	9			10
Guantánamo/Baracoa	1		1	4		4			10
Totals	11	2	144	148	43	529	23	26	927

Note: Catechists are not included. There are 21 male religious communities in Cuba, with 148 priests and 26 friars/brothers, and 52 female communities with 562 members. The Cuban Roman Catholic Church's personnel's nationality with the highest number is Cuban (381), followed by Spanish (178), Mexican (84), Colombian (59), Dominican (31), Canadian (22), Argentinian (21), Indian (19), United States (16), Italian (14), Brazilian (13), and others, for a total of 34 nationalities.

*Jaime Cardinal Ortega.

Source: *La Iglesia Católica en Cuba, 1998* (online, http://www.nacub.org)

NOTES

Chapter 1. Introduction

1. Examining the reasons behind the Cuban government's staying power despite the collapse of the Soviet Union and Eastern European socialist regimes, Jorge I. Domínguez states: "Besides the fact that communism in Cuba was not guaranteed by Soviet tanks, Cuba is clearly different from the regimes of Eastern Europe. As early as the spring of 1990 the Cuban people understood that communism was reversible. Cubans had already witnessed its collapse elsewhere, and they were feeling the negative economic effects. A public opinion poll taken at the time showed that only one-fifth of respondents said that the food supply was good and only one-tenth could say the same of the quality of transportation. Such results made the poll credible, and therefore we ought also to believe that three-quarters of respondents thought health services were good and that four-fifths believed the same about their schools. *Cubans supported their regime because they made differentiated judgments about its performance. They understood its many failings but they could also identify its successes*" (emphasis added). Jorge I. Domínguez, "The Secrets of Castro's Staying Power," *Foreign Affairs* (spring 1993): 97.

2. "Citizens perceive that a government is legitimate to the degree that they believe it has the rightful power to compel obedience. When citizens believe that they ought to obey the laws, the legitimacy is high. If they see no reason to obey, if they comply only from fear, then legitimacy is low . . . A government with high legitimacy will be more effective in making and implementing policies and more likely to overcome hardships and reversals." G. A. Almond and G. B. Powell, Jr., eds. *Comparative Politics Today: A World View* (New York: Harper Collins, 1996), 37.

3. On the occasion of his visit to Cuba, Santiago Onlate Laborde, a leader of the Mexican political party in power, the PRI, and of the Permanent Conference of Latin American Political Parties (COPPAL), stated that both organizations were studying the decisions taken by Havana "in the construction of a new economy without sacrificing the social structures." He added that he would like to see Mexico applying the Cuban social protection policies. Onlate had an interview with Fidel Castro and extended an official invitation to the Cuban Communist Party to join COPPAL. See Antonio Garza Morales, "Invitarán al Partido Comunista Cubano a Ingresar a la COPPAL: Onlate Laborde se Entrevistará con Fidel Castro para Deliberar el Tema," *Excelsior* (Mexico City), February 10, 1996.

4. Joaquín Oramas, "The People Say 'Yes' at the Polls," *Granma International*, January 18, 1998: 1, 3–6.

5. Patrick Oppman, "'Che' Is Put to Rest in Santa Clara," *CubaINFO* 9 (October 1997): 8; John Rice, "Che Guevara's Bones to Be Buried in Cuba," Associated Press, October 12, 1997.

6. "Elecciones: ¿Se Retirará Fidel Castro?" *Contrapunto* 8 (August 1997): 5–6.

7. Castro was "very happy" after the January 11, 1998, elections, according to the president of the National Assembly, Ricardo Alarcón. Still, days before the pope's visit, Castro's state of mind was characterized this way: "A friend who has known Castro since their university days, film-institute president Alfredo Guevara, describes Fidel as obsessed. His friend was always a volcano 'that sometimes does harm but sometimes fertilizes the soil'. For 40 years he has obsessed—Guevara keeps using the word—over the consummation of the revolution that we know has not been fully achieved'. Yet Fidel is intensely proud that he has again defied world predictions of his imminent demise, as satisfying a triumph to him as any that went before." Johanna McGeary, "Clash of Faiths," *Time*, January 26, 1998: 26–32, quotes at 30.

8. A Cuban physician exiled in Costa Rica, Elizabeth Trujillo Izquierdo, claimed that President Castro was treated for a life-threatening brain disease, hypertensive encephalopathy, on October 22–26, 1997. According to Trujillo, Castro was hospitalized at the same hospital where she worked as a member of an elite medical team, the Center for Medical and Surgical Research. Castro denied the report, calling it a "lie from beginning to end." Foreign journalists who looked at Havana University's academic records said that "Trujillo was not listed as graduating from a school of medicine on March 30, 1987," as she claimed. The Vatican spokesman, Joaquín Navarro Valdés, stated that he had a six-hour conversation with Castro on October 25, during the time Trujillo claimed he was in the hospital. Navarro Valdés described his talks with Castro as "cordial and relaxed." See *Miami Herald*: "Defector: Castro Had Brain Disease," July 19, 1998; "Castro in Excellent Health, Cuban Foreign Ministry Says," July 21, 1998; "Report of Brain Disease a Lie, Cuban Leader Says," July 24, 1998; "Validity of Cuban Defector's Diploma Questioned," July 29, 1998.

9. As was reported at the time, "three months after his older brother Fidel formally selected him as his eventual successor, Raúl Castro appears to be assuming a wider range of official duties and playing a more prominent role in the running of the Cuban Government and the Communist Party, Cuban officials and foreign diplomats say. . . . [R]ecent developments suggest, a diplomat here said, 'that Fidel has finally begun to prepare for the day when he will no longer be on stage'.

"Another diplomat said: 'Above all, *Fidel wants continuity and an orderly transition. He is certainly not ready to abandon power any time soon, but he wants to be sure the house is in order when that day comes, and he thinks the best way to do that is to gradually expand Raúl's responsibilities*" (emphasis added). Larry Rohter, "As the Heir to Fidel, Raúl Castro Takes a Bigger Role in Cuba," *New York Times*, February 2, 1998, A6. At the time of his two-week visit to China in late 1997, Raúl Castro gave some intimations of what would he do upon succeeding his brother: "Raúl Castro has made it clear that no full-scale Tienanmen [sic] re-enactment will take place in

Cuba under his authority." He reportedly said in a private meeting: "I am not going to be responsible for bringing out the tanks . . . We have to find solutions to avoid this at all costs." Domingo Amuchástegui, "Chinese Model Poses Dilemma for Fidel's Cuba," *CUBANEWS* 6 (January 1998): 10.

10. In a long speech following his reelection on February 24, 1998, as president of the Council of State (and therefore of the country) for another five-year term, Castro denied having chosen his brother Raúl Castro as his successor (which had been reported during the Fifth Party Congress in October 1997): "I have no authority to do it," he said, "this is not a monarchy." Regarding the news published abroad reporting that his brother had been chosen as his successor, Castro said that "no one should 'play games' with the destiny of other countries." "Castro Fija Línea Dura en Discurso de 8 Horas," *El Nuevo Herald*, February 26, 1998.

11. "Free Zones and Industrial Parks: New Options for Foreign Investment," *Business Tips on Cuba* 4 (July 1997): 1–54.

12. Marta Bares Gómez, "Banco Popular de Ahorro: Acercándonos Más al Cliente," *Correo de Cuba* 3 (1997): 34.

13. The death of Jorge Más Canosa on November 23, 1997, after a prolonged illness marked a turning point for hard-line politics among Cuban-Americans, the influence they have exerted on Washington's Cuba policy, and future United States–Cuban relations. His death was mourned by thousands of grief-struck Cuban Americans in Miami. He was honored as if he had been a head of state, especially in the United States. President Clinton, Secretary of State Madeleine Albright, and other high dignitaries sent messages of condolence to his family. At the University of Southern California in Los Angeles, during the opening ceremony of an exhibit celebrating the contributions made by Cuban Americans to the state of California, a minute of silence was kept in his memory.

Más Canosa's death received wide media coverage. These are some examples:

(1) Senator Robert Torricelli (D-NJ), representing President Clinton at Más Canosa's funeral, stated: "Unjust is the death of a liberator while the tyrant lives." Still, "left unsaid was that Más had done everything he could as the most effective advocate of a hard line against Cuba, and that policy, tried and tested for more than 37 years, had simply failed to reach the exiled leader's objective." Ana Radelat, "A Death in Exile," *CubaINFO* 9 (December 1997): 9–10.

(2) The *New York Times* editorialized: "No individual had more influence over United States policies toward Cuba over the past two decades than Jorge Más Canosa, who died Sunday. Mr. Más, who fled to Miami in 1960, the year after Fidel Castro seized power, founded the Cuban-American Foundation and turned it into the most powerful lobbying organization on Cuban issues in Washington. The passing years never eroded his belief that Cuba's Communist dictatorship was ripe for overthrow. That dubious assumption drove his campaigns for successive tightenings of Washington's economic embargo on Cuba, culminating in the regrettable Helms-Burton law of 1996." "Turning a Page on Cuba," *New York Times*, November 25, 1997.

(3) Not long after Más Canosa's death, the foundation started to show signs that its former political clout was slipping away: "Three months after [Más Canosa's] death, the Cuban American National Foundation that [he had] built into a lobbying powerhouse [was] moving down an uncertain path, alienating some of its longtime supporters and antagonizing its Washington allies . . . The turmoil comes as the custodians of the hard-line U.S. policy towards Cuba face mounting criticism in the wake of Pope Paul John II's visit to the island [January 21–25, 1998], as pressure grows from American religious, humanitarian and business groups to relax U.S. sanctions in hopes of easing the suffering of the Cuban people." Christopher Marquis, "Without Más Canosa's Lead, Foundation May Be Losing Its Way," *Miami Herald*, February 24, 1998.

(4) *Religious Socialism* published a rather critical commentary on Más Canosa and his legacy: "Jorge Más Canosa is dead! Long live the Cuban Revolution! . . . Mr. Más was a multimillionaire who profited supremely from the largess of government . . . He had quite the deal going, but then divine retribution, or just luck (not from his point of view of course), caught up with him. Más died at age 57, never having his dream come true—his dream of returning to Cuba as its supreme ruler . . . Más came to see himself as dictator timbre; he was the one who could return to Cuba and fill the shoes of Batista—the man the Cuban Revolution overthrew . . . Más was not hugely successful because he deserved success, or worked hard. He was successful because he served those with power and money, so they kept him around . . . Our policy towards Cuba will change, not because Más is no longer here to advocate for it, but because Más is no longer here to provide the pretense of government responding to the will of the people. Contrary to the picture painted by his fans, Más was not an engine of U.S. foreign policy, but its front man. He was not the man behind the curtain; he was the man in front of it." Richard Curtis, "A Specter Is Haunting America," *Religious Socialism* (spring 1998): 18.

14. Lisandro Pérez, "El Fin del Exilio: Una Nueva Era en la Política Migratoria Hacia Cuba," *Correo de Cuba* 3 (1997): 10–16. See also Félix Masud-Piloto, *With Open Arms: Cuban Migration to the United States* (Totowa, N.J.: Rowman and Littlefield, 1988); David Rieff, "From Exiles to Immigrants," *Foreign Affairs* 74 (July–August 1995).

15. "Clinton Prepared to Develop Bilateral Relations," Itar-Tass, January 10, 1998.

16. Cuban-American Representatives Ileana Ros-Lehtinen (R-Fla.) and Lincoln Díaz-Balart (R-Fla.) have been rather vocal combating any possible easing of sanctions against Castro, no matter how limited the lifting of penalties could be. According to Díaz-Balart, "The Clinton administration can dialogue all it wants with the Havana regime, *but the embargo against Cuba cannot be changed without the approval of Congress*" (emphasis added). *Miami Herald*, December 19, 1997, as cited in *CUBANEWS* 6 (January 1998): 3.

Recognizing that U.S. Cuba policy has been taken away from the president by

Congress under the Helms-Burton Act, Canadian Minister of Foreign Affairs Lloyd Axworthy told the 28th Leadership Conference of the Center for the Study of the Presidency, convened in Ottawa in October 1997: "May I share with you a concern—that is, the increasingly isolationist trend taking place in the U.S. Congress. The Congress does not recognize this increasing need to work in partnership, work according to a broad-based international set of rules, but in fact, tends more and more to want to go it alone . . . We saw that most dramatically in the case of the Helms-Burton Bill, which we have strongly opposed, not simply because we believe we have a right to relate to Cuba the way we want to relate, not the way some other assembly tells us to relate, but also—and this is the critical point—[because] once we get into a position where any parliament or assembly or congress, particularly one that is in a very powerful nation, begins to assert a right unilaterally to change international rules, we begin to then really put almost a virus into the system, which I think could then really begin to erode away at the superstructure that has been built up." "Excerpts from the Major Policy Address 'Canadian-American Relations in the New Millennium,' by Hon. Lloyd Axworthy, Canadian Minister of Foreign Affairs," *Center House Bulletin* 8 (winter 1998): 6–7.

17. "CIA Official Discusses Policy with Cuba," *CubaINFO* 10 (January 1998): 1.

18. Ana Radelat, "U.S. Lawmaker Proposes Sanctions against CARICOM Nations," *CubaINFO* 9 (August 1997): 1.

19. "Fidel at the World Food Summit: 'What Will We Do to Prevent One Million People in the World from Dying of Starvation Every Month?" *Granma International*, November 27, 1996: 16.

20. Alessandra Galloni, "Fidel Castro Is Acclaimed, Praised in Rome," Associated Press, November 18, 1996.

21. Javier Rodríguez, "Encuentro del Papa y Fidel: Cuba y el Vaticano Apuestan por Relaciones Fructíferas," *Correo de Cuba* no. 3 (n.d.): 24–26.

22. "The Pope Will Visit Cuba in 1998," Associated Press, January 4, 1997.

23. Ann Louis Bardach and Larry Rohter, "Authorities Knew of Bombing Campaign, Says Cuban Exile," and "Life in the Shadows, Trying to Bring Down Castro," *New York Times*, July 12, 13, 1998; Juan Tamayo and Gerardo Reyes, "Posada Carriles Sigue Conspirando Contra Castro," *El Nuevo Herald*, June 7, 1998.

24. "The Revolution at 30," *Newsweek*, January 9, 1989: 36–37.

Chapter 2. The Impact of the Demise of European Socialism

1. Max Azicri, "The Institutionalization of the Cuban Revolution: A Review of the Literature," *Cuban Studies/Estudios Cubanos* 9 (July 1979): 63–78.

2. Cole Blasier, "The End of the Soviet-Cuban Partnership," in *Cuba after the Cold War*, ed. Carmelo Mesa-Lago (Pittsburgh: Pittsburgh University Press, 1993), 59–98.

3. International Institute of Strategic Studies, *The Military Balance 1990–1991* (London: IISS, 1990), 192–93, as cited in Blasier, "End of Soviet-Cuban Partnership," 72.

4. Jorge G. Castañeda, *Utopia Unarmed: The Latin American Left after the Cold War* (New York: Vintage, 1993); Wayne S. Smith, "The End of World Revolutions in Latin America," 37–43, and Georgi Mirsky, "World Revolution and Class Struggle: Outdated Concepts?" 29–36, both in *The Russians Aren't Coming—New Soviet Policy in Latin America*, ed. Wayne S. Smith (Boulder, Colo.: Lynne Rienner, 1992).

5. On the activity in Guerrero, see "Mexican Rebels Demand Aid for Poor," Associated Press, January 5, 1997.

6. Francis Fukuyama, "The End of History," *National Interest* (summer 1989): 3ff.

7. For insightful speculation about what the Soviet foreign policy alternatives were by the end of 1990, following the resignation of Foreign Minister Eduard Shevardnadze in December of that year, see the work of two political analysts from the Soviet Academy of Sciences, Alexei Izyumov and Andrei Kortunov, "The End of 'New Thinking,'" *Newsweek*, December 31, 1990: 54.

8. Mikhail Gorbachev, *Perestroika: New Thinking for Our Community and the World* (New York: Harper and Row, 1987), 9, 17, passim.

9. Ibid., 135–60, quote on 141. Also see his *Gorbachev: Mandate for Peace* (New York: Paperjacks, 1987).

10. Blasier, "End of Soviet-Cuban Partnership," 71.

11. For a critical discussion of the events leading to the breakdown of the Central Eastern European socialist regimes, see Daniel Chirot, ed., *The Crisis of Leninism and the Decline of the Left: The Revolutions of 1989* (Seattle: University of Washington Press, 1991). For a discussion of Gorbachev's policies and the Kremlin's political dynamics during his tenure, from the perspective of a Kremlin insider in the early years of perestroika, see Yegor Ligachev, *Inside Gorbachev's Kremlin* (New York: Pantheon Books, 1993).

12. Besides the effect that the events in Eastern Europe had on the Soviet Union, the changes in the latter under Gorbachev had a more direct and larger bearing on its final destruction. A structural-functional comparison of the distribution of systemic political functions among the different political structures from 1987 (two years into the Gorbachev era) to 1994 (three years after the breakdown of the Soviet Union) is revealing. The two dominant structures in the former Soviet political system, the Communist Party and the bureaucracy, ended with the party (by then under a different name) void of any policy and interest aggregation function and with the bureaucracy lacking its former socialization input and having a significantly reduced role in any other systemic function. Prior to Gorbachev's reforms, both the party and the bureaucracy had concentrated tremendous power unto themselves while performing such central functions as socialization, recruitment, policy making, policy implementation, policy adjudication, and others. See Almond and Powell, *Comparative Politics Today*, 30–31.

13. The rectification process (RP) was "pointed in a direction contrary to perestroika and the ideological gap between the two countries has expanded since 1985. Actually Soviet-Cuban relations cooled after Brezhnev died, and in 1984–1985 Castro attended neither the CMEA [Council for Mutual Economic Assistance]

meeting in Moscow nor Chernenko's funeral." Carmelo Mesa-Lago, "Cuba's Economic Counter-Reform (Rectification): Causes, Policies and Effects," in *Cuba after Thirty Years: Rectification and the Revolution*, ed. Richard Gillespie (London: Cass, 1990), 126.

14. *Granma Weekly Review*, December 17, 1989: 2.

15. Fidel Castro, "Press Conference Held by President Fidel Castro Ruz at the International Center of Higher Journalism Studies for Latin America (CIESPAL) in Quito, Ecuador, August 13, 1988," *Granma Weekly Review*, August 28, 1988: 2.

16. Estervino Montesino Seguí, "The Cuban Perspective on Cuban-Soviet Relations," in Smith, *The Russians Aren't Coming*, 136–49.

17. Castro, as expected, has repeatedly stood against the destruction of the Soviet Union, but, surprisingly, his comments on Gorbachev have not been very critical. In his conversational interview with Sandinista leader Tomás Borge, Castro said: "We [initially] approved of the Soviet efforts to perfect socialism in the Soviet Union, but we could not agree with—nor could we ever agree with—the destruction of the Soviet Union, or with not only the destruction of socialism in the Soviet Union but the destruction of the Soviet Union itself, because of the terrible danger that this entails for the peoples of the world and the position in which this places the Third World, in particular . . . But he [Gorbachev] did not want the destruction of the Soviet Union. *Gorbachev even spoke of defending socialism and [of] more socialism, not of less socialism.* He said it and repeated it many times, and I have no doubts that he meant it; but a process unfolded there, in which Gorbachev, of course, has a responsibility, as well as the Soviet leaders, the leadership of the Soviet party, and the leadership of the Soviet government altogether; there is a form of collective responsibility. *Terrible mistakes were then made that led to self-destructive processes for socialism and the Soviet Union, because when a process starts destroying a country's values, that kind of process is very negative*" (my translation; emphasis added). Fidel Castro, *Un Grano de Maíz: Conversación con Tomás Borge* (Havana: Oficina de Publicaciones del Consejo de Estado, 1992), 47–48.

18. Jorge I. Domínguez, "The Political Impact on Cuba of the Reform and Collapse of Communist Regimes," in Mesa-Lago, *Cuba after the Cold War*, 99–132; Castro, *Un Grano de Maíz*, 47–48.

19. The internal struggle within the Soviet Union under Gorbachev between conservatives (supporting Cuba) and liberals (opposing Cuba) was mirrored in the Soviet press: "The advantage . . . was progressively gained by the liberals who, protected by their position in the mass media, starting in 1989 launched a violent campaign against [Soviet] relations with Cuba." Santiago Pérez, "El Fin de la URSS y Cuba," in *Cuba en Crisis: Perspectivas Económicas y Políticas*, ed. Jorge Rodríguez Beruff (San Juan, Puerto Rico: Editorial de la Universidad de Puerto Rico, 1995), 6.

20. Mesa-Lago, "Cuba's Economic Counter-Reform," 127–30. Also, the special nature of Cuban-Soviet relations had created cleavages and alignments within opposing camps of the Soviet political establishment: "The high level of such a close relationship implied the formation of groups and interests that had their own

autonomous interests and sphere of action in the USSR. It was vox populi until August 1991 that the military and political circles in the Communist Party of the Soviet Union (CPSU), and leaders of the centralized economy favored decisively no concessions [internally and externally] on the Cuba issue. That was the so-called Cuban lobby in Moscow . . . *The position on Cuba became an internal political issue at the republic and [federal] Soviet level. More than [arguing over] an international political issue, what was taking place was an ongoing political and ideological struggle between contending political forces. The 'conservatives' defended Cuba as their own ideological agenda, while the 'liberals' in parliament and in the government saw it as a totalitarian state, a remnant of the Soviet past, and a political and economic expenditure [the Soviet Union] could not afford"* (emphasis added). Pérez, "El Fin de la URSS y Cuba," 5–6.

21. Blasier, "End of Soviet-Cuban Partnership," 76–81.

22. Smith, *The Russians Aren't Coming*, "New Policy from New Thinking," 55–86, and "The Soviet Union in Central America," 87–116. See also Gorbachev, *Perestroika*, "The Third World in the International Community," 171–89.

23. "Soviet Delegation Explains Aspects of Its Visit to Cuba," *Granma Weekly Review*, December 16, 1990: 5.

24. "U.S. Wins Vote to Press Cuba on [Human] Rights," *Miami Herald*, March 7, 1990.

25. Applications for the 5,000 U.S. visas approved in the 1995 U.S.-Cuba migration agreement went up 43.17% between 1995 and 1996, from 189,000 to 437,725. In a new visa lottery round, the number could go as high as 700,000. Andres Oppenheimer, "Latin America: '97's Potential Trouble Spots," *Miami Herald*, December 31, 1996.

26. José Luis Rodríguez, "Economic Relations between Cuba and Eastern Europe: Present Situation and Possible Developments," in *Cuban Foreign Policy Confronts a New International Order*, ed. H. Michael Erisman and John M. Kirk (Boulder, Colo.: Lynne Rienner, 1991), 53–62, quote at 53.

27. Carmelo Mesa-Lago, "The Economic Effects on Cuba of the Downfall of Socialism in the USSR and Eastern Europe," in his *Cuba after the Cold War*, 139.

28. Rodríguez, "Economic Relations between Cuba and Eastern Europe," 53–57. Also, see Manuel Pastor, Jr., and Andrew Zimbalist, "Cuba's Economic Conundrum," *NACLA Report on the Americas* 29 (September–October 1995): 7–12.

29. Rodríguez, "Economic Relations between Cuba and Eastern Europe," 53–55.

30. A. Zimbalist and C. Brundenius, *The Cuban Economy* (Baltimore: Johns Hopkins University, 1989), 152; J. I. Domínguez, *To Make a World Safe for Revolution: Cuba's Foreign Policy* (Cambridge, Mass.: Harvard University, 1989), as cited in Rodríguez, "Economic Relations Between Cuba and Eastern Europe," 61.

31. Mesa-Lago, "Economic Effects on Cuba of the Downfall of Socialism," 138–47.

32. Richard A. Dello Buono, "Cuban Socialism and the Reconstruction of Viability: A Profile of the 'Survival' Economy," *Proceedings*, 17th International Latin American Studies Association Congress, Los Angeles, 1992, 3.

33. Mesa-Lago, "Economic Effects on Cuba of the Downfall of Socialism," 145.

34. Rodríguez, "Economic Relations between Cuba and Eastern Europe," 56.

35. Amuchástegui, "Chinese Model Poses Dilemma for Fidel's Cuba," 10.

36. United Nations Development Program (UNDP), *Human Development Report, 1994,* cited in Pastor and Zimbalist, "Cuba's Economic Conundrum," 9.

37. "FAO Reports Scarcity of Food," *CubaINFO* 6 (April 1994): 11.

38. Max Azicri, "Notes about the Normalization of Relations between Cuba and the Emigration," *NOTICIERO* (September–October 1994): 4, 10–11, 15.

39. Ambrosio Fornet, "Rethinking the Revolution—Nine Testimonies from Cuba," *NACLA Report on the Americas* 29 (September–October 1995): 27–28.

40. Juan Antonio Blanco, "Rethinking the Revolution—Nine Testimonies from Cuba," *NACLA Report on the Americas* 29 (September–October 1995): 29–30.

Chapter 3. Rectifying the Revolution's Mistakes

1. It has been argued that the RP had started before it was announced by Castro at the Third Party Congress in 1986. So it could have started when criticism of the free farmers' market and of self-employment was first voiced in 1982, or when some of the functions of the Central Planning Board (JUCEPLAN) were transferred to the Council of Ministers' "Central [Economic] Group" in 1984, or, as stated by Cuban Vice President Carlos Rafael Rodríguez, before perestroika in 1984. See Mesa-Lago, "Cuba's Economic Counter-Reform," 99. Additional antecedents to the RP in the 1980s include the Fourth Congress of the Cuban Union of Communist Youth (UJC) and the Sixth Congress of the National Association of (Small) Private Farmers (ANAP) held in 1982, at which existent economic and mercantilist tendencies were denounced as contrary to the revolution's nature and objectives. At the closing session of the National Assembly of People's Power (the country's national legislative body) in 1984, a special call was issued to rectify economic working conditions to guarantee effectively people's participation. However, the ceremony commemorating the twenty-fifth anniversary of *Playa Girón* (the 1961 Bay of Pigs invasion of Cuban exiles trained, organized, and financed by the CIA), a ceremony held on April 19, 1986, when Castro denounced serious economic problems and irregularities, has been identified as the beginning of the RP policy. José Luis Rodríguez, "Aspectos Económicos del Proceso de Rectificación," *Cuba Socialista* 44 (April–June 1990): 88–89.

2. According to a leading official in the PCC's Department of Revolutionary Orientation (DOR) and frequent contributor to *Contrapunto* (a liberal magazine formerly published in Miami, Florida), "The process of 'Rectification of Errors and Negative Tendencies' that purposely sought solutions to . . . [difficult] situations, *would have definitely distanced the Cuban revolution from the USSR's and Eastern Europe's erroneous conception of socialism,* but it lost momentum due to the collapse of socialism, which *imprisoned Cuba under the double grip of the imperialist blockade*

and the loss of all supplementary economic, financial, and technical-scientific mechanisms, as well as the sudden dissolution of political alliances, which brought the country to its most difficult moment in its revolutionary history" (emphasis added). Jorge Gómez Barata, "Cuba: La Revolución Diferida," *Contrapunto* 8 (February 1987): 28–29.

3. The bibliographical collections recording the works of Fidel Castro, Ernesto Che Guevara, Carlos Rafael Rodríguez, Raúl Roa, Osvaldo Dorticós Torrado, and other Cuban leaders, writers, poets, and intellectuals are so numerous that it is impossible to give a proper listing here. As a sample of the numerous articles, books, anthologies, bibliographies, interpretative studies, interviews, and reference materials available, and besides many editions in different languages of Castro's *History Will Absolve Me* and Guevara's *Reminiscences of the Revolutionary War,* see Francisco Fernández-Santos and José Martínez, eds., *Cuba: Una Revolución en Marcha* (Paris: Cuadernos de Ruedo Ibérico, 1967); Fidel Castro, *La Revolución Cubana: 1953–1962* (Mexico City: Ediciones Era, 1973); and his *El Pensamiento de Fidel Castro, Enero 1959–Abril 1961,* 2 vols. (Havana: Ediciones Políticas, 1983); *La Primera Revolución Socialista en América* (Mexico: Siglo XXI, 1977); *Un Grano de Maíz,* already cited; *Fidel and Religion: Talks with Frei Betto* (Havana: Publications Office of the Council of State, 1987); *Un Encuentro con Fidel: Entrevista Realizada por Gianni Mina* (Havana: Oficinas de Publicaciones del Consejo de Estado, 1987); Fidel Castro, Osvaldo Dorticós, and Raúl Roa, *Asi se Derrotó al Imperialismo: Preparando la Defensa* (Mexico: Siglo XXI, 1978); Fidel Castro and Alvaro Prendes, *Asi se Derrotó al Imperialismo: El Combate y la Victoria* (Mexico: Siglo XXI, 1978); Martin Kenner and James Petras, eds., *Fidel Castro Speaks* (New York: Grove Press, 1969); Sheldon B. Liss, *Fidel! Castro's Political and Social Thought* (Boulder, Colo.: Westview Press, 1994); Ernesto Che Guevara, *Guerrilla Warfare* (New York: Vintage Books, 1961); his *El Socialismo y el Hombre Nuevo* (Mexico: Siglo XXI, 1979), and his *Escritos y Discursos,* 9 vols. (Havana: Editora Política, 1977); Fernando Martínez Heredia, *Che, El Socialismo y el Comunismo* (Havana: Casa de las Américas, 1989); Carlos Tablada, *Che Guevara: Economics and Politics in the Transition to Socialism* (Sydney, Australia: Pathfinder, 1989); R. E. Bonachea and Nelson Valdés, *Che: Selected Works of Ernesto Guevara* (Cambridge, Mass.: MIT Press, 1969); Carlos Rafael Rodríguez, *Letra con Filo,* 3 vols. (Havana: Editorial de Ciencias Sociales, 1983, 1987), and his *Palabras en los Setenta* (Havana: Editorial de Ciencias Sociales, 1984); and Raúl Roa, *Retorno a la Alborada,* 2 vols. (Havana: Editorial de Ciencias Sociales, 1977).

4. From 1962 to 1965 a policy debate took place that was central to the meaning of the revolution itself, inquiring into subjects like the role of money and market under socialism and the importance of material incentives in a socialist society. Although the controversy dealt with fundamental economic issues, in reality the core principles sustaining a revolutionary society's ethical values were the underlying theme. See Bertram Silverman, *Man and Socialism in Cuba: The Great Debate* (New York: Atheneum, 1971).

5. Max Azicri and José A. Moreno, "Cultura, Política, Movilización Indirecta y Modernización: Un Análisis Contextual del Cambio Revolucionario en Cuba:

1959–1968," *Revista Mexicana de Sociología* 43, 3 (July–September 1981): 1245–70.

6. The economist C. Mesa-Lago, recognizing frequent policy changes under the revolution, provides a critical account of successive stages of economic organization from 1959 to the rectification process in the late 1980s. "In the economic realm, an important feature of the Cuban revolution has been numerous, frequent shifts in policy. Over 30 years there have been six stages of economic organization, with varying degrees of change: (1) 1959–60, the liquidation of capitalism; (2) 1961–63, the failed attempt to introduce the pre-1965 Soviet centralized-planning, command economy model; (3) 1964–66, debate over and test of alternative socialist economic models (Guevara's idealistic, mobilizational, moral economy model versus the 1965 Soviet timid economic reform model); (4) 1966–70, the failed application of the Guevarist model with radicalized features and other Castroite adaptations; (5) 1971 until the mid-1980s, the shift to, and gradual application of, a moderate version of the pre-Gorbachev Soviet economic reform model—the System of Direction and Planning of the Economy (SDPE); and (6) since the mid-1980s, the Proceso de Rectificación (Rectification Process: RP), a reversal of the previous direction, away from decentralization and the use of market mechanisms." Mesa-Lago, "Cuba's Economic Counter-Reform," 98.

7. Susan Eva Eckstein, *Back from the Future: Cuba under Castro* (Princeton, N.J.: Princeton University Press, 1994), 60.

8. *Granma Weekly Review*, July 5, 1987: 5.

9. For two different views on the state of workers and grassroots participation, and the need for improvement, see for a negative view Carollee Bengelsdorf, *The Problem of Democracy in Cuba: Between Visions and Reality* (New York: Oxford University Press, 1994), and for a positive view Linda Fuller, *Work and Democracy in Socialist Cuba* (Philadelphia: Temple University Press, 1992).

10. Mesa-Lago, "Cuba's Economic Counter-Reform," 98–139; George Black, "Toward Victory Always, but When?" *Nation*, October 24, 1988: 374.

11. Ibid.

12. Bengelsdorf, *Problem of Democracy in Cuba*, 141.

13. Fernando Martínez Heredia, *Desafíos del Socialismo Cubano* (Havana: Centro de Estudios Sobre América, 1988),104–5.

14. Rodríguez, "Aspectos Económicos del Proceso de Rectificación," 86.

15. Ibid., 87.

16. James F. Petras and Morris H. Morley, "Cuban Socialism: Rectification and the New Model of Accumulation," in *Cuba in Transition: Crisis and Transformation*, ed. Sandor Halebsky and John M. Kirk (Boulder, Colo.: Westview Press, 1990), 15–36.

17. Ibid., 15, 34.

18. Andrew Zimbalist, "Incentives and Planning in Cuba," *Latin American Research Review* 24 (1989): 88.

19. *Granma Weekly Review*, February 11, 1990: 2–3.

20. For a discussion of the positive potential role the United States could have played during the 1980s if the Washington-Havana problem could have been

worked out satisfactorily (something that has not happened), see Alfonso Casanova Montero and Pedro Monreal González, "Cuba's External Economic Constraints in the 1980s: An Assessment of the Potential Role of the United States," in Gillespie, *Cuba after Thirty Years*, 84–97.

21. "Now, when Cuba is starting to breathe, *when it depends on no one but itself and there are no longer dogmatic deformations of revolutionary thought, the Cuban revolution can provide its best contribution:* showing its ideology and offering a viable alternative" (emphasis added). Gómez Barata, "Cuba: La Revolución Diferida," 29.

22. Max Azicri, *Cuba: Politics, Economics and Society* (London: Pinter, 1988), 86–88, 125–26.

23. Fidel Castro, "Diálogo Sostenido con los Participantes en el III Congreso de la Asociación de Economistas de América Latina y el Caribe, La Habana, 23–26 de Noviembre de 1987," *Por el Camino Correcto* (Havana: Editora Política, 1988), 264, cited in Rodríguez, "Aspectos Económicos del Proceso de Rectificación," 89–90.

24. Reportedly, the budget deficit had increased in 1987 by 279 percent. Thomas C. Dalton, *Everything within the Revolution: Cuban Strategies for Social Development since 1969* (Boulder, Colo.: Westview Press, 1993), 49.

25. This section draws largely from Rodríguez, "Aspectos Económicos del Proceso de Rectificación," 88–94.

26. Informe Central, I Congreso del Partido Comunista de Cuba (Havana: Departamento de Orientación Revolucionaria, 1976), 113; Fidel Castro, "Versión de las Partes Fundamentales de Sus Intervenciones y Conclusiones en el II Pleno del Comité Central del Partido Comunista de Cuba, La Habana, 17, 18 y 19 de Julio de 1986," *Cuba Socialista* 23 (1986): 168.

27. Castro, "II Pleno del Comité Central del Partido Comunista de Cuba, 1986," 144.

28. Banks summarized Castro's mid-1980s predicament: "Faced with a manifestly worsening economic situation, President Castro launched a major campaign against bureaucratic corruption and inefficiency . . . [He] later announced a major austerity program to compensate for a severe decline in foreign exchange earnings and Soviet subsidies, which had earlier been estimated at $6 billion a year." A. S. Banks, ed., *Political Handbook of the World: 1987* (Binghamton, N.Y.: CSA Publications, 1987), 139–40.

29. Carlos Cabrera, "Rectification: Renewal in Cuba Socialism?" *Granma Weekly Review,* September 18, 1988: 3.

30. Rodríguez, "Aspectos Económicos del Proceso de Rectificación," 94–97.

31. Bengelsdorf, *Problem of Democracy in Cuba*, 145.

32. *Granma Weekly Review,* November 8, 1987: 9.

33. Rodríguez, "Aspectos Económicos del Proceso de Rectificación," 94–101.

34. Mesa-Lago, "Cuba's Economic Counter-Reform," 118–26.

35. Eckstein, *Back from the Future*, 79–87.

36. Bengelsdorf, *Problem of Democracy in Cuba*, 152.

Chapter 4. The Quality of Life under Severe Austerity and Scarcity

1. Beatriz Díaz, "El Modelo de Desarrollo Equitativo en Cuba," *Proceedings,* 17th International Latin American Studies Association Congress, Los Angeles, California, 1992.

2. "Chile, after a decade of applying a neoliberal model with a monetarist policy of balance of payments or open economy, has not been able to achieve 'stable development'—its policy objective—but stability without development. The inflationary rate was reduced with high unemployment, salary contraction, investment coefficient stagnation, rising external debt, industrial infrastructure erosion, and national banks lost to foreign entities." Rene Villareal, *La Contrar-revolución Monetarista: Teoría Económica e Ideología del Neoliberalismo* (Mexico: Ediciones Océano, 1983), 18.

3. Following the 1994 midterm elections (when the Democratic Party lost both houses of Congress to the Republican Party), former Democratic Party National Chairman Fred Harris said: "While it's true . . . that the average per capita income has risen . . . that has been caused by increases for the highest wage earners . . . The upper fifth of our population is getting 48.2 percent of the income while the lowest fifth is getting 3.5 percent. That's the worst inequality of any industrialized democracy." "Chautauqua at Gannon: Former National Party Chiefs Take a Look at GOP's Success," *(Erie, Pa.) Morning News,* November 10, 1994, 1B. Twenty years earlier, according to a World Bank publication, the distribution of income throughout the United States population in 1975 before taxes totaled 26.7 percent to the top decile while the bottom decile received 0.8 percent. The top fifth's share was 44.7 percent (somewhat lower than in 1994), and that of the bottom fifth was 3.8 percent (somewhat higher than in 1994). The maldistribution of wealth ratio grew somewhat worse between 1975 and 1994. Also, the Gini Index (measuring income maldistribution) was 0.38 in 1970, but it got slightly worse in 1976 when it increased to 0.391. See S. Jain, *Size Distribution of Income* (Baltimore: Johns Hopkins University Press, 1976).

4. David Briscoe, "U.S. Blacks, Hispanics Worse Off than Some Third World Citizens," Associated Press, May 18, 1993. For a well documented report on hunger in the United States affecting most racial and ethnic groups in spite of the current economic recovery, see Second Harvest National Report, *Hunger 1997: The Faces and Facts* (Chicago: Second Harvest, 1997).

5. This section draws from Joan M. Caivano, "Cuba's Deal with the Dollar," in "Dollars, Darkness and Diplomacy: Three Perspectives on Cuba." *Cuba Briefing Paper Series* no. 6 (Georgetown University, July 1994), 1–3.

6. Frank T. Fitzgerald, *The Cuban Revolution in Crisis: From Managing Socialism to Managing Survival* (New York: Monthly Review Press, 1994), 172.

7. Luis Sexto, "Psicología: Oiga, ¿Es Su Problema el Estrés?" *Bohemia,* June 18, 1993, B9–11.

8. Eckstein, *Back from the Future,* 96–99, 113–26; Dello Buono, "Cuban Socialism

and the Reconstruction of Viability," 8–10; Max Azicri, "The Rectification Process Revisited: Cuba's Defense of Traditional Marxism-Leninism," in *Cuba in Transition: Crisis and Transformation,* ed. Sandor Halebsky and John M. Kirk (Boulder, Colo.: Westview Press, 1992), 37–54.

9. Eckstein, *Back from the Future,* 99.

10. "Inusual Debate Sobre Prostitución Abre Órgano de Prensa," International Press Service, April 22, 1996.

11. "Castro to Clean-Up Tourism Image," *CubaINFO* 6 (June 1994): 9.

12. "Inusual Debate Sobre Prostitución Abre Órgano de Prensa."

13. "Ofensiva Oficial Contra 'Corruptos y Prostitutas,'" International Press Service, April 30, 1996.

14. Rosa Miriam Elizalde, "Prostitution in Cuba: The Truth about the Women Called Jineteras," *Granma International,* September 4, 1996, 8–9.

15. Ibid., 9.

16. Elizalde, "Prostitution in Cuba," 9.

17. Teresa Meade, "Cuba: Twenty-Seven Years Later," *Radical Historians Newsletter* 77 (December 1997): 1–4, 16, quote at 2.

18. "Public Health: Prostitution, Medical Breakdown Promote Spread of Sexual Disease," *CUBANEWS* 4 (August 1996): 10.

19. "American Association for World Health Report," *CubaINFO* 9 (March 1997): 2–3.

20. Molly Moore, "The Hemorrhaging of Cuba's Health Care; Doctors without Data, Patients without Drugs: U.S. Embargo, Economic Crisis Cripple a Showcase System," *Washington Post,* February 23, 1998, A12.

21. José de la Osa, "Infant Mortality Rate at 7.2 in 1997!" *Granma International,* January 11, 1998, 11.

22. "Health in Cuba: An Example of Equity, Solidarity and Respect," *Granma International,* December 7, 1997, 4.

23. "Neuropathy Epidemic May Have Ended," *CubaINFO* 5 (October 1993): 11.

24. "Cuba Announces Altered AIDS Policy," and "Government to Relax Policies toward HIV Carriers," *CubaINFO* 5 (September 1993): 8, and 6 (January 28, 1994): 8.

25. Carolina Aguilar and Rita Maria Pereira, "The Challenges of Daily Life," *CUBA Update* (April–June 1995): 9–10.

26. Margaret Randall, *Cuban Women Now* (Toronto: Women's Press, 1974).

27. Ann Froines, "Women's Changing Consciousness," *CUBA Update* (April–June 1995): 11–12; Lois M. Smith and Alfred Padula, *Sex and Revolution: Women in Socialist Cuba* (New York: Oxford University Press, 1996); Max Azicri, "Cuba," in *Women's Studies Encyclopedia,* ed. Helen Tierney (n.p.: New York Press, 1999).

28. Vilma Espín, *Cuban Women Confront the Future* (Melbourne, Australia: Ocean Press, 1991); see also Elizabeth Stone, *Women and the Cuban Revolution* (New York: Pathfinder Press, 1981), and Heidi Steffens, "FMC: Feminine, Not Feminist," *Cuban Review* 4, no. 2 (n.d.): 22–33.

29. See Smith and Padula, *Sex and Revolution*, passim.

30. Max Azicri, "The Women's Revolution within a Revolution," in *Integrating the Neglected Majority: Government Responses to Demands for New Sex-Roles*, ed. Patricia A. Kyle (Brunswick, Ohio: King's Court Communications, 1976), 62–81, quote at 78.

31. Ibid. "The FMC magazine, *Mujeres* (Women), a publication discussing women's issues, still dedicates a significant number of pages to 'fashion . . . recipes, embroidery, hair styles, child and household care . . . [without exploring] the changing sexual mores,'" 78 n. 32.

32. Smith and Padula, *Sex and Revolution*, 52.

33. Ibid., 56.

34. Mirta Ojito, "Divided Loyalties Tugging at Cuba's Children," *New York Times*, February 18, 1998, A1, A4.

35. Meade, "Cuba: Twenty-Seven Years Later," 2.

36. Marelys Valencia, "Young People: Interrupted Dreams," *Granma International*, January 29, 1997, 8–9.

37. "Education Minister Announces Greater Link between College and Ideology," *CubaINFO* 6 (September 1994): 10.

38. "Comenzó la Dura Lucha Anual por las Plazas Universitarias," Agence France Presse, April 1, 1997.

39. Valencia, "Young People: Interrupted Dreams," 9.

40. Ibid.

41. Ibid.

42. Lucien O. Chauvin, "The Many Struggles of Cuban Academics," *Chronicle of Higher Education*, May 31, 1996, A33.

43. Ibid., A35.

44. "Más de 14,000 Niños de Chernobil Fueron Atendidos en Cuba," EFE [online, http://www.efe.es], March 30, 1997.

45. Chauvin, "The Many Struggles," A33, A35.

46. *Bohemia*, January 8, 1995, B4–7, quote at B5.

47. "Partido Comunista Hace Llamamiento contra la Corrupción," EFE, March 25, 1997.

48. Ibid.

49. "Gobierno Descarta por Ahora Autorización Empresas Privadas," EFE, April 1, 1997.

50. "Rehabilitación en Centro Turístico Provocó Desalojo de Vendedores," EFE, April 2, 1997.

51. "The government announced in late May (1997) that the National Bank of Cuba, founded in 1948, would be replaced by a new Central Bank that will supervise monetary and credit policy and promote the modernization of the banking institutions . . . Francisco Soberón Valdéz, principal architect of the reforms in banking, will remain as head of the banking system with the rank of cabinet minister." "New Central Bank," *CUBANEWS* 5 (June 1997): 3.

52. "Cuba Toma Medidas contra el Blanqueo de Dinero," Agence France Presse, March 30, 1997.

53. The foreign banks include Internationale Nederlanden Bank, of the Netherlands; Netherlands Caribbean Bank, Dutch Antilles; four banks based in Spain—Banco Exterior de España, Banco Bilbao Vizcaya, Banco Central Hispanoamericano, and Banco de Sabadel; Fransabank SAL, Lebanon; Havana International Bank, a United Kingdom–registered subsidiary of Banco Nacional de Cuba; National Bank of Canada; Société Générale, France; and Banco Nacional de Comercio, Mexico. Besides the new Central Bank, the Cuban banking entities include the Banco Nacional (National Bank); Banco de Crédito y Comercio (Bank of Credit and Commerce); Banco Popular de Ahorro (People's Savings Bank); Banco Internacional de Comercio (International Bank of Commerce); Financiera Internacional (International Finance Bank); Cadenas de Casas de Cambio (Currency Exchange Houses); Banco Metropolitano (Metropolitan Bank); Banco de Inversiones (Investment Bank); Banco Financiero Internacional (International Financial Bank), and Havana International Bank (a subsidiary of the National Bank of Cuba located in London). "Foreign Banks in Cuba," *CUBANEWS* 5 (August 1997): 12.

54. Susana Lee, "Code of Ethics for Cuban State Cadres Approved," *Granma International*, August 7, 1996: 4.

55. Harry Anderson, Stryker McGuire, and David González, "I Have No Reason to Live," *Time*, July 10, 1989, 25.

56. Andres Oppenheimer, *Castro's Final Hour* (New York: Simon and Schuster, 1992), 104, 115, 127; *Case/1989: End of the Cuban Connection* (Havana: José Martí Publishing House, 1989); and Eckstein, *Back from the Future*, 84–86.

Chapter 5. Political Reform under the Special Period

1. After visiting Spain, France (where he received the Human Rights Award of the French Republic from President Jacques Chirac), Latin American countries, and the United States, Elizardo Sánchez Santa Cruz, the head of the Cuban Commission for Human Rights and National Reconciliation and a well-known dissident, stated: "I have no doubt that transition in Cuba is inevitable." But he added: "I do not think that President Fidel Castro wishes to carry out any real reform." *CubaINFO* 9 (February 1997): 1. For critical political and economic evaluations of the regime's reforms in the early 1990s and assessments of future ones, see *Transition in Cuba: New Challenges for US Policy* (Miami: Florida International University, U.S. Department of State, and U.S. Agency for International Development, n.d.), passim. Also, see *CUBANEWS*, a monthly publication emphasizing economic trends, formerly published by the Miami Herald Publishing Company, Miami, Florida. For an official Cuban government source reporting on the extent of the economic changes and business opportunities, see *Business Tips on Cuba*, a monthly publication that is also available online at the Cuban government web site, http://www.Cubaweb.cu. *Granma International*, Prensa Latina, Havana's Tropicana nightclub, and others are also available via the Internet.

2. Carmelo Mesa-Lago, *Are Economic Reforms Propelling Cuba to the Market?* (Miami: University of Miami, 1994).

3. Among the Cuban leaders some have "been uneasy about the political effects of increased self employment [and other reforms]. As one government official reflected in late 1993: 'Once some (economic) freedom from the state is offered, there is always the risk that some people will demand still greater freedom from the state.' . . . As it became evident that the food program was not resolving shortages, the most reformist wing of the [PCC] advocated re-establishing some form of the 'free farmers' markets' . . . The cautious sector of the party dissented, claiming that expanding private farming would lead to price gouging and unequal distribution of food products." Gillian Gunn, "Balancing Economic Efficiency, Social Concerns, and Political Control," *Cuba Briefing Paper Series* no. 5 (Georgetown University, 1994), 3.

4. "Editorial: Saquemos Las Lecciones y Sigamos Adelante," *Granma: Resumen Semanal,* September 10, 1989, 1, 11.

5. Jorge I. Domínguez, "Cuba en un Nuevo Mundo," in Rodríguez Beruff, *Cuba en Crisis,* 23–42.

6. Ibid., 39–40.

7. Gillian Gunn, "Prospects for Change in Cuba: The Perspectives of Cuba's Political Leadership," in *Transition in Cuba,* 67–96.

8. The subject of a political transition has received special attention in Miami. A Cuban-American group rated as politically moderate, the Cuban Committee for Democracy (CDC), held a seminar in early 1997 discussing the Helms-Burton Act and the political transition in Cuba. The discussion on Cuba's transition sought answers to such questions as: Is the transition desirable or not? How should it be? And in what direction should it go? "La Transición en Debate," *Contrapunto* 8 (April 1997): 14–15.

9. "Fidel's Address at the Closing Ceremony of the 4th São Paulo Forum— 'Neoliberalism Is the Doctrine of Stripping Our Nations Bare,'" *Granma International,* August 18, 1993, 8–10.

10. A similar sentiment was echoed by the editor of a monthly published in Miami, Florida: "The Cuban Revolution belongs to all Cubans. It should be open to all; all should be part of it and make it their own. This should be noticed by those who control its leadership, and by all Cubans, including those living overseas, independently of their past." Nicolás Rios, "La Revolución Pertenece a la Nación Cubana," *Contrapunto* 8 (May 1997): 15–16.

11. "Castro Continues Hard-Line on Economic Changes," *CubaINFO* 9 (May 1997): 6–7.

12. Max Azicri, "Comparing Two Social Revolutions: The Dynamics of Change in Cuba and Nicaragua," in Gillespie, *Cuba after Thirty Years,* 36.

13. Arnold August, *Democracy in Cuba and the 1997–98 Elections* (Montreal: Editorial José Martí, 1999), 94–95; and José Martí, *El Partido Revolucionario Cubano* (Havana: Editorial de Ciencias Sociales, 1975).

14. Juan Marinello, "El Partido Revolucionario Cubano, Creación Ejemplar de

José Martí," *Siete Enfoques Marxistas Sobre José Martí* (Havana: Editora Política, 1985), 145.

15. T. M. Magstadt and M. Schotten, *Understanding Politics: Ideas, Institutions, and Issues* (New York: St. Martin's Press, 1996), 310. Also, see Jules Lobel, "The Meaning of Democracy: Representative and Participatory Democracy in the New Nicaraguan Constitution," in *The Nicaraguan Constitution of 1987*, ed. K. J. Mijeski (Athens: Ohio University, 1991), 253–345.

16. When asked what he thought of the first debate in the 1996 U.S. presidential elections, Castro responded that he "was bored. It was a lot of theater and very little substance." His distaste for America's brand of electoral politics echoes Martí's. According to Martí's biographer John M. Kirk, "when describing the practice of democracy in North America at times [Martí] accepted with reservations but more often he roundly condemned the fraudulent practices surrounding the polling booth . . . He criticized severely the phenomenon of 'bossism,' the controlling of politics by influential party leaders." In Martí's own words: "The despicable 'boss' was described earlier; the ringleader of the party; the one who prepares the elections, twisting them, taking advantage of them, handing them on a plate to his friends but denying them to his foes—and selling them to his opponents; the person who holds sway over the electoral commissions; the same one who demands financial contributions of employees, enabling him to bring about the elections, which will keep them in their jobs." John M. Kirk, *José Martí: Mentor of the Cuban Nation* (Gainesville: University Press of Florida, 1982), 70. See also "President Castro's Reaction," *CubaINFO* 8 (October 1996): 2, and Sheldon B. Liss, *Roots of Revolution: Radical Thought in Cuba* (Lincoln: University of Nebraska Press, 1987).

17. On April 16, 1961, in a multitudinous ceremony held at the intersection of 23rd and 12th Streets in the Vedado section of Havana, Castro proclaimed the socialist nature of the Cuban revolution. It was a day before the Bay of Pigs invasion would start and a day after Cuban airplanes and airports had been attacked by airplanes departing from South Florida. Even though the PCC was inaugurated on October 3, 1965, the April 1961 date has been chosen as the anniversary of the Cuban Communist Party. Alberto Alavariño Atienzar, "The Cuban Nation's Single Party," *Granma International*, May 3, 1997, 2.

18. The congress is the PCC's highest decision-making body. The election and composition of the delegation were as follows: one-third had been directly elected by local party branches, while provincial party officials elected the remaining two-thirds on recommendation from local offices; almost two-thirds were under forty-five years of age (forty-four was the average age); half were directly involved in production, services, or education; over one-third had served in internationalist missions in developing nations; more than half had university degrees, and 16 percent were women. Ninety-three percent of the delegates attended all sessions; but absent from some or most sessions were Minister of Armed Forces Raúl Castro and Minister of Interior Abelardo Colomé Ibarra, who were attending to defense-related matters. The party membership had reached 611,627 by 1991, representing

11 percent of the population over thirty. Approximately 15 percent of the population sixteen years or older belonged to the party or the Union of Communist Youth. Gail Reed, *Island in the Storm: The Cuban Communist Party's Fourth Congress* (Melbourne, Australia: Ocean Press and Center for Cuban Studies, 1992), 20.

19. Ibid., 21.

20. This section draws from Gail Reed, "Summary of Resolutions Adopted at Party Congress," *CUBA Update* (March–April 1992): 16.

21. Reed, *Island in the Storm*, 81.

22. Rhoda Rabkin, "The Communist Party of Cuba: Fighting for Survival," in *Transition in Cuba*, 199–236.

23. "A process was unleashed destroying the party's authority, and destroying the party's authority meant to destroy one of the pillars of socialism's existence and of the Soviet Union's existence, because the party founded by Lenin was the fundamental pillar, the cement that created the Soviet Union, which was a historic feat, one without precedent." Castro, *Un Grano de Maíz*, 44–53, quote at 48.

24. "Viceministro Chino se Reune con Presidente Cubano," Agence France Presse, May 17, 1997.

25. See Linda Fuller, *Work and Democracy in Socialist Cuba*, especially chapter 4.

26. "Partido Comunista Asegura que Sus Filas Crecieron en los Años de la Crisis," Agence France Presse, May 1, 1997.

27. "Convocatoria al V Congreso del Partido Comunista de Cuba," Cuban Government web site [http://www.Cubaweb.cu], April 16, 1997.

28. "The Party of Unity, Democracy, and the Human Rights We Defend, 5th Congress of the Communist Party of Cuba," *Granma International* [online, http://www.granma.cu], May 1997; "Documento del PCC Mantiene 'Modelo Estalinista,'" *El Nuevo Herald*, May 25, 1997; and Juan O. Tamayo, "Cuba Chills Talk of Change," *Miami Herald*, May 26, 1997.

29. "Congress Vows Commitment to Socialism, One Party-Rule," *CubaINFO* 9 (October 1997): 6–7; Domingo Amuchástegui, "'More of Same' or 'Move to Reform'?" *CUBANEWS* 5 (November 1997): 5–9.

30. "Efficiency Must Become Our Way of Behaving, Monitoring and Demanding," *Granma International*, October 19, 1997, 10–11.

31. Amuchástegui, "'More of Same' or 'Move to Reform'?" 5.

32. Domingo Amuchástegui, "Future of Cuba Riding on New Politburo," *CUBANEWS* 5 (July 1997): 6.

33. Some speculative comments by political scientists (the first two) and economists (the last two) are given in Mimi Whitefield, "Cuba Ratifies New Constitution," *Miami Herald*, July 13, 1992, as follows.

Damian Fernández (Florida International University): "I don't think these changes mean much to people's daily lives in Cuba, but I look at them as an elitist maneuver to try to make the system more flexible so it will survive in the short and medium term . . . The emphasis is still on a one-party system, but they are trying to define that one party as a political option to everyone."

Wayne Smith (Johns Hopkins University and Center for International Policy): "The Cubans have studied the PRI [Mexico's ruling party] extensively and some argue they could have a more open system that's still dominated by one party . . . The question is will they allow the formation of other parties?"

Sergio Roca (Adelphi University): "It opens the potential for ownership of small businesses and even medium-size businesses by foreigners and maybe even Cuban-Americans some day. Of course I don't see this happening in the near future."

Andrew Zimbalist (Smith College): They need to move in the new world, and they are trying to accommodate themselves to this new reality . . . This is the type of legislation that Hungary was introducing when it began to move toward a market-oriented economy."

34. "Se Realizaron 296 Intervenciones Sobre Proyecto de Ley," *Granma*, July 13, 1992, 1–5.

35. This section draws from Hugo Azcuy, "Aspectos de la Ley de Reforma Constitucional de Julio de 1992" in Hugo Azcuy, Rafael Hernández, and Nelson Valdés, eds., *Reforma Constitucional Cubana* (Albuquerque: Centro de Estudios Sobre América and New Mexico University, 1992), 1–11; and Susana Lee, "Constitución de la República de Cuba: Nuestras Reformas Ratifican el Rumbo de Nuestra Revolución Democrática y Socialista," *Granma*, September 22, 1992, 3–10.

36. "Cuban Communist Party Emphasizes 'Democratic Centralism,'" *CubaINFO* 8 (August 1996): 7.

37. Lee, "Constitución de la República de Cuba," 4–7.

38. Whitefield, "Cuba Ratifies New Constitution."

39. Pedro Prada, "XII Periodo Ordinario: Ley Electoral a Debate," *Granma*, October 20, 1992, 1.

40. Juan O. Tamayo, "Dissidents Ask Cubans to Boycott Elections," *Miami Herald*, May 6, 1997, 7.

41. According to a UPI report, "Mexican media reported an annulment rate of approximately twenty percent . . . Some foreign reporters observing ballot counting reported a 10 to 20 percent rate of ballot annulment. Fidel Castro estimated the rate of ballot annulment would be about ten percent, and official Electoral Commission announcements placed the amount at just over 7 percent." Ibid., 7.

42. According to Cuban telecommunications analyst Leonard Cano, between February 8 and February 23 Radio Martí broadcast 452 "calls" imploring the Cuban population to spoil their ballots in order to symbolize rejection of the regime. Cano reported that eleven short-wave and four medium-wave radio stations were broadcasting to Cuba during the month of February and were "orchestrated and designed to harm the election process by calling for nullification of one's ballot or abstaining from participation in the elections, or [were] attempts to discredit this election process by trying to make it appear undemocratic." Cuba commentator Roberto Morejón reported on "a propaganda bombardment of 1,112 hours of broadcast time per week by 15 medium and short-wave radio stations." "National

Election Results," *CubaINFO* 5 (March 1993): 7–9.

43. *Granma International*, March 14, 1993, 8.

44. Mimi Whitefield, "Draft of Cuban Election Law Aired," *Miami Herald*, October 8, 1992.

45. "National Election Results," 7–9.

46. A national campaign characterized voting as an expression of national unity in support of the revolution and as an act of patriotism. Youngsters were wearing fashionable T-shirts with a legend reading: "Electoral Ballot, February 24, Candidates: 1. Fatherland, 2. revolution, and 3. socialism." Castro campaigned for several days in his own district, Santiago de Cuba, and a public letter inviting people to vote for the entire slate, in his own handwriting, was published in *Juventud Rebelde*, a national newspaper. "National Elections as Front-Line Battle," *CubaINFO* 5 (February 1993): 5–7.

47. "97.59 Percent of Electorate Votes," *Granma International*, November 2, 1997, 3; "Cubans Vote for Local Officials," *CubaINFO* 9 (October 1997): 9.

48. "Cuba to Remain Communist, Castro Vows at Latin Summit," Associated Press, November 9, 1997; Jim Thompson, "Cuba's Broken Promises Elicit Rebukes at Summit," *Miami Herald*, November 8, 1997.

49. "U.S., Castro 'At an Impasse,'" *Miami Herald*, November 10, 1997.

50. Rodolfo Casals, "Massive Voter Turnout: Cuba's Democratic Electoral System Is Second to None, Declares President Castro," *Granma International*, October 26, 1997, 15.

51. "Cubanos Acuden a Votar en Comicios de un Solo Partido," *Miami Herald*, October 20, 1997. Besides claiming that Cuba's electoral system, while not perfect, reflects Cuba's definition of democracy that is not for others to emulate, Castro has reasons for looking at America's multiparty electoral system as an exercise of power based on money and interest peddling by the wealthy and powerful and with little regard for the general good. As a major contributor to President Clinton's 1996 reelection victory asked: "Why did Clinton win so easily in 1996? Why did his lead hardly vary? What was his strength with the voters that Dole could never shake? . . . In my opinion, the key to Clinton's victory was his early television advertising. There has never been anything remotely like it in the history of presidential elections. In 1992, Clinton and Bush each spent about forty million dollars on TV advertising during the primary and general elections. In 1996, the Clinton campaign and, at the president's behest, the DNC [Democratic National Committee] spent upwards of eighty-five million dollars on ads—more than twice as much!" Dick Morris, *Behind the Oval Office: Winning the Presidency in the Nineties* (New York: Random House, 1997),138, passim. Even before the 1997 U.S. Senate hearings on election financing scandals, it was reported that "raising tons of campaign cash from special interests is a bipartisan sin—and it's only getting worse." Jonathan Alter and Michael Isikoff, "The Real Scandal Is What's Legal," *Newsweek*, October 28, 1996, 30–32.

Miami's Cuban-American politics and elections mirror past Cuban political practices:

"Questions of Vote Fraud: A flood of absentee ballots decisive in the November [1997] race for Miami mayor. Former Mayor José Carollo would have won outright on Nov. 4 were it not for Mayor Xavier Suarez's lopsided advantages of absentees . . . Now, the Florida Department of Law Enforcement is investigating allegations of widespread absentee fraud . . . The *Herald* has reported that the produce peddler witnessed a ballot cast in the name of a dead man—Manuel Yip, who died four years ago and is buried in a pauper's grave. At least 40 possibly fraudulent absentee votes came from homes linked to supporters of Miami Chairman Humberto Hernandez in Little Havana and the Roads." Joseph Tanfani and Karen Branch, "Dozens Cast Votes in Miami Mayoral Race—for $10 each," *Miami Herald*, January 11, 1998.

"The city without a mayor has a new one: Joe Carollo. In a stunning decision that provided a definitive resolution to Miami's leadership crisis, a state appeals court late Wednesday declared the businessman-politician to be the city's mayor. They said the absentee ballots that deprived Carollo of a victory over Xavier L. Suarez in November are null and void because they were infected with fraud. And the panel called off a new election ordered by a trial court judge." "Joe Carollo Is Back," *Miami Herald*, March 13, 1998.

"As Joe Carollo was installed as Miami mayor, prosecutors and state agents were finishing their criminal probe into voter fraud in Miami and preparing charging documents." "Carollo Is Installed as Mayor," *Miami Herald*, March 13, 1998.

52. Electronic mail electoral report from Havana to author, January 15, 1998.

53. "A Vote for the Nation," *Granma International*, January 18, 1998, 3–6, quote at 6.

54. "Fidel Castro: Candidate, Voter, Winner," *Miami Herald*, January 12, 1998.

55. For a detailed discussion of the PCC, the OPP, and other governmental institutions, see Azicri, *Cuba: Politics, Economics and Society*, chapters 4 and 5.

56. "The most serious problem concerning the authenticity of participatory democracy in Cuba arises from the dominant role played by the Party in the OPP. The Party is empowered by the Constitution to play a pervasive guidance function in Cuban society generally, and the OPP and mass organizations specifically . . . It would be an exaggeration to view the OPP at all levels, as only a front or a facade, to be used to legitimize the actions of the Party, and to improve the efficiency with which Party decision can be implemented." Archibald R. M. Ritter, "The Organs of People's Power and the Communist Party: The Nature of Cuban Democracy," in *Cuba: Twenty-Five Years of Revolution, 1959–1984*, ed. Sandor Halebsky and John M. Kirk (New York: Praeger, 1985), 270–90, quote at 288.

57. Haroldo Dilla, Gerardo González, and Ana Teresa Vicentelli, "Participación y Desarrollo en los Municipios Cubanos," in Rodríguez Beruff, *Cuba en Crisis*,59–100; Susana Castañeda Donate, ed. *Proceso Electoral Cubano*, dossier no. 1 (Albuquerque: Centro de Estudios Sobre América and New Mexico University, 1993), 1–206, *passim*.

58. "At the local level, where citizens directly elect neighbourhood leaders, and at the municipal level where citizens elect candidates and directly elect their representatives, democracy defined in terms of control over leadership selection exists to some degree. Accountability and recall reinforce the influence of the electors, although recall conceivably could be employed to keep elected delegates in line with Party policy. Direct elections, the importance of neighbourhood circumscription electoral meetings, and the practice of accountability sessions appear to operate so as to ensure some responsiveness on the part of elected delegates to their electors' wishes." Ritter, "People's Power and the Communist Party," 288.

59. "Opinión Pública: ¿Que Piensa el Pueblo de Su Poder?" and "La Democracia Cubana Frente al Espejo," *Bohemia*, July 6, 1990: 4–9, and 10–11, respectively.

60. "Resolución Sobre el Perfeccionamiento de la Organización y Funcionamiento de los Órganos del Poder Popular" (El Cuarto Congreso del Partido), in Castañeda Donate, *Proceso Electoral Cubano*, 7–19.

61. Gunn, "Prospects for Change in Cuba," 73.

62. Santiago Feliú, "Procedencia de los Diputados a la Asamblea Nacional del Poder Popular," in Castañeda Donate, *Proceso Electoral Cubano*, 205.

63. Información Mínima Sobre los Procesos Electorales, "Nominación de Candidatos y Elecciones a Delegados (Balance Nacional)," in Castañeda Donate, *Proceso Electoral Cubano*, 206.

64. Mayda Álvarez Suárez et al., *Mujer y Poder: Las Cubanas en el Gobierno Popular* (Havana: Federación de Mujeres Cubanas, 1994), 1–44.

65. Haroldo Dilla, Gerardo González, and Ana Teresa Vincentelli, "Los Municipios en Cuba: Una Experiencia Más Allá de los Paradigmas," in "Cuba," *Síntesis* 15 (1992): 205–22, quote at 206.

66. "'We have to guarantee the revolution,' Castro said in a four-hour speech at the close of the Fifth Party Congress . . . [He] said that the party was fortunate that his 66-year-old brother was the No. 2 man. 'Raúl is younger than I,' said the 71-year-old Cuban leader. 'He can count on much more time.' . . . Castro made it clear that his brother was his choice in an unusually explicit discussion of Cuban succession, one that seemed aimed at rumors Castro suffers from ill health, though he made no direct reference to that and Cuban officials have denied it." John Rice, "Castro: Brother Is His Successor," Associated Press, October 13, 1997.

67. "High profile trips to China and Italy [following the Fifth Party Congress] by Cuban Armed forces Chief Raúl Castro have stocked speculation that he has slowly begun to assume some of the powers of his brother, President Fidel Castro. . . . 'This is raising Raúl's profile, giving him a new image—the image of the man who will follow Fidel,' said Nicolás Rios, a Cuban American magazine publisher with good contacts in Havana . . . [Still, no] one in Cuba believes that Castro will surrender power anytime soon, although the inner workings of Havana's leadership is a highly guarded secret in the island." Juan O. Tamayo, "Raúl Castro Appears to Assume Some Powers," *Miami Herald*, December 17, 1997.

68. Cathy Booth, "Here Come the Yummies," *Newsweek*, June 21, 1993, 42–43.

69. It was officially announced several months after his replacement by Felipe Pérez Roque that "former Cuban foreign minister, Roberto Robaina, was about to enroll at the School of National Defense, a higher level educational institution for 'important leaders of the government and the Communist Party'. The foreign ministry spokesman, Alejandro González, said that the former foreign affairs minister is 'doing fine' and that he took a vacation before starting his studies at this 'higher center of political strategy'. Former minister of sugar, Nelson Torres, and former first secretary of the Union of Young Communists (UJC), Victoria Velázquez, attended this school after they were 'freed' from their posts, as it happened to Robaina." "Estudiará Ex Canciller Cubano en Centro de Estudios Estratégicos," *NTX*, October 8, 1999.

70. "Robaina on Collective Leadership in Cuba," *CubaINFO* 5 (December 1993): 8.

71. Booth, "Here Come the Yummies," 42.

72. Marelys Valencia Almeida, "This Is a Young People's Revolution," *Granma International*, December 20, 1995, 7.

73. "Cuba: Año 39," *Contrapunto* 8 (February 1997): 5–8, quote at 5. For an opposite viewpoint, see Marifeli Pérez-Stable, "La Cuba que Aún Puede Ser," in Rodríguez Beruff, *Cuba en Crisis*, 157–73.

74. Susana Lee, "Interview with Carlos Lage," *Granma International*, November 6, 1996, 6.

75. Raúl Castro, "Speech Marking the 36th Anniversary of the Proclamation of the Socialist Nature of the Revolution and Day of the Militia," *Granma International*, April 30, 1997, 7.

Chapter 6. Economic Reform under the Special Period: Part I

1. There are three distinct stages in the development of the Cuban revolution and several phases within the second stage: (1) the democratic-popular stage (1959–60); (2) the socialist stage (1961–90), which in turn can be subdivided into several phases—first (1961–63), second (1964–75), third (1976–86), fourth (1986–90), and since then; and (3) the current special period stage (1990–). In the first stage, the revolution had not yet been characterized as socialist. The second stage began with Castro's socialist proclamation on April 16, 1961. During this period important policy shifts, sometimes implying radical and contradictory changes, took place. Among others, the issues under discussion included the emphasis on moral or material incentives, the implementation of the system of planning and direction of the economy, and the rectification process. The last stage is the special period. The socialist character of the revolution and the political system has been confirmed. At the same time a profound process of change is taking place, leaving the final features of Cuba's socialism as an open-ended question. For a discussion of the first and second stages see José Luis Rodríguez, *Estrategia del Desarrollo Económico en Cuba* (Havana: Editorial de Ciencias Sociales, 1990).

2. This section draws from Gerardo González Nuñez, "Cuba y el Mercado

Mundial," in Rodríguez Beruff, *Cuba en Crisis*, 43–58; José Luis Rodríguez and George Carriazo Moreno, *Erradicación de la Pobreza en Cuba* (Havana: Editorial de Ciencias Sociales, 1987), 35–54; and Rodríguez, *Estrategia del Desarrollo Económico en Cuba*.

3. González Nuñez, "Cuba y el Mercado Mundial," 43–50.

4. Ibid., 48–49.

5. Rodríguez and Carriazo Moreno, *Erradicación de la Pobreza*, 51–52.

6. Carmelo Mesa-Lago, *The Economy of Socialist Cuba: A Two-Decade Appraisal* (Albuquerque: University of New Mexico Press, 1981), 35, *passim*.

7. Ibid., 175.

8. Claes Brundenius, "Cuba: Redistribution and Growth with Equity," in Halebsky and Kirk, *Cuba: Twenty-Five Years of Revolution*, 209.

9. The special relationship that Cuba had with the Soviet Union came under severe criticism under Gorbachev by the late 1980s. Its opponents wanted to replace it with one more advantageous to Moscow. The main points covering trade and economic issues were as follows: "Five-year based agreements; the central state organs of both countries were in charge of its enforcement; the price of sugar, nickel, and cereals were based on a floating ruble; trade imbalances were covered with development credits for specific economic sectors . . . Relations were more advantageous to Cuba than what it could have had with any capitalist country; however, this should not be understood as a large Soviet 'aid' or 'subsidy' package . . . First of all, no one can afford to buy 4 million tons of sugar at international market prices. Second, the quality of the highly priced Soviet merchandise Cuba bought with rubles was not comparable to the quality of regular merchandise bought in the world market. Third, it is not the same to speak of rubles as it is of U.S. dollars." Pérez, "El Fin de la URSS y Cuba," 6.

10. Jorge Rodríguez Beruff, "Introducción: ¿Hacia Dónde Cuba?" in his *Cuba en Crisis*, ix–xxvi.

11. *La Economía Cubana: 1994* (Havana: Oficina Nacional de Estadísticas, 1995), 7–9, 1–12; José Luis Rodríguez, "Economía: ¿Hacia Dónde Va Cuba?" *Contrapunto* 7 (February 1996): 53–56, 58–59; Elsa Barrera, ed., *Reajustes y Reformas en la Economía Cubana: 1994*, Dossier no. 8 (Albuquerque: Centro de Estudios Sobre América and New Mexico University, 1995), 1–209, see especially 19.

12. González Nuñez, "Cuba y el Mercado Mundial," 50–58.

13. Julio Carranza Valdés, "Report on Cuba," *NACLA Report on the Americas* 29 (September–October 1995): 31–32.

14. Julio Carranza Valdés, Luis Gutiérrez Urdaneta, and Pedro Monreal González, *Cuba: La Restructuración de la Economía* (Havana: Editorial de Ciencias Sociales, 1995).

15. Fidel Castro, "Speech to the Central Committee of the Communist Party of Cuba, October 10, 1991," *Granma International*, November 3, 1991, and his "Speech at the National Meeting of Presidents of the Provincial Organs of People's Power," *Granma International* [online, http://www.granma.cu], January 13, 1997, and

"Castro States That Transition Would Be a 'Transit to Hell,'" *El Nuevo Herald*, March 15, 1997; Carlos Lage, "Primer Semestre: La Economía al Trote," *Contrapunto* 7 (September 1996): 48–50; Susana Lee, "Carlos Lage's Statement at the Second Meeting of Entities Operating in Freely Convertible Currency," *Granma International* [online, http://www.granma.cu], January 27, 1997; Rodríguez, "¿Hacia Dónde Va Cuba?": 53–56, 58–59, and his "Rodríguez: The Economy," *CUBANEWS* 5 (February 1997): 12 (originally published in *El País*, January 1997).

16. Mesa-Lago, *Are Economic Reforms Propelling Cuba?* i–iv, 1–84, see quote at ii.

17. Jorge Pérez-López, "Learning from Others: Economic Reform Experiences in Eastern Europe, Latin America, and China," in *Transition in Cuba*, 367–417, quote at 368.

18. A. R. M. Ritter, "Financial Aspects of Normalizing Cuba's International Relations: The Debt and Compensation Issues," in *Transition in Cuba*, 501–66, quote at 501.

19. Pablo Alfonso, "Panorama de las Reformas Económicas en Cuba: 1993–1994," (Miami: Association for the Study of the Cuban Economy, 1994) [online, http://www.lanic.utexas.edu/la/cb/cuba/asce].

20. "Council of State Issues Formal Decree Legalizing Dollars," *CubaINFO* 5 (September 1993): 7–8.

21. Haroldo Dilla Alfonso, "Cuba: Crisis, Socialismo y Dólares," in *La Despenalización del Dólar, Trabajo por Cuenta Propia y Cooperativización en Cuba: Documentos y Comentarios*, ed. Caridad Rodríguez and Nelson Valdés, Dossier no. 3 (Albuquerque: Centro de Estudios Sobre América and New Mexico University, n.d.), 83–85.

22. Gerardo González Nuñez, "La Economía Cubana: Entre la Urgencia y la Meditación," in Rodríguez and Valdés, ed., *La Despenalización del Dólar*, 78–80.

23. "Castro Says Small Business on Horizon," *CubaINFO* 7 (March 1995): 11.

24. "Hard Currency Payments to Cuban Workers," *CubaINFO* 7 (April 1995): 7.

25. Pablo Alfonso, "Aumentan las Divisas en Manos de la Población," *El Nuevo Herald*, January 19, 1997.

26. Joy Gordon, "Cuba's Enterpreneurial Socialism," *Atlantic Monthly* (January 1997): 12, 18, 20–22, 30, quote at 20.

27. "Reforms: Market Results," *CUBANEWS* 3 (March 1995): 6.

28. Pedro Morales, *El Programa Alimentario: Una Visión Realista* (Havana: Agencia de Datos y Referencias, Grupo Empresarial UFO, n.d.), 1–13.

29. Luis Báez, "Entrevista a Raúl Castro: Si Hay Comida para el Pueblo No Importan los Riesgos," *Bohemia*, September 30, 1994, B16–23.

30. "Acuerdo del Buró Político para Llevar a Cabo Importantes Innovaciones en la Agricultura Estatal," in Rodríguez and Valdés, ed., *La Despenalización del Dólar*, 71–72.

31. "Government Eases Hold on Agricultural Sector," *CubaINFO* 5 (September 1993): 6.

32. Armando H. Portela, "Reforms/Agriculture: UBPC Reforms Called Timid, Insufficient," *CUBANEWS* 4 (November 1996): 11.

33. Gregorio Trueba González, "Potencialidades del Desarrollo Agroindustrial Cubano," 19th Latin American Studies Association Congress, Washington, D.C., 1995, 13–14.

34. Carranza Valdés, et al., *La Restructuración de la Economía*, 45.

35. "UBPC Reforms Designed to Stop Collapse," *CUBANEWS* 5 (May 1997): 8.

36. "El Sector Privado en Cuba: El Más Dinamico en Términos de Empleo," Agence France Presse, February 20, 1998.

37. "Reforms: New Rules, Taxes Hit Self-Employed Workers," *CUBANEWS* 4 (June 1996): 2.

38. Enrique Rangel, "Cuban Capital Renovating to Attract Tourists," *Dallas Morning News*, June 11, 1997.

39. "In Full-Employment Cuba, Layoffs Are Major Issue," *CUBANEWS* 3 (June 1995): 2.

40. Carlos Batista, "Ley de Arrendamiento de Viviendas Afectará a Numerosos Cuentapropistas," Agence France Presse, May 24, 1997.

41. "New Decree on Housing Rentals," *Granma International*, May 27, 1997: 6.

42. "Ley Vivienda: Las Autoridades Denuncian las Carencias de la Administración," Agence France Presse, May 31, 1997.

43. "Demographics: 'Illegals' in Havana," *CubaINFO* 5 (July 1997): 11.

44. "Confiscation, Evictions Reported in Housing Fight," *CubaINFO* 5 (July 1997): 11.

45. Armando H. Portela, "Where Do Residents Come From?" and "House-by-House Screening Enforced by CDRs," *CUBANEWS* 5 (November 1997): 10.

46. Still, the black market remains an attractive alternative under unusual circumstances. "With a marriage license a couple could buy four cases of beer, three of soft drinks, three large family-size pastries and a wedding cake that is sold by the government at regular [subsidized] prices. If the strict rationing in place is considered, it is not bad. However, no one will eat or drink at the reception . . . As a matter of fact, there will be no reception, because the newlyweds are not united by love, but interest. After paying the divorce expenses, and selling the supplies for the party on the black market, they would still be left with a profit equal to a weekly salary, about 4 [U.S. dollars]." William Santiago, "Mercado Negro, Robo y Estafas Permiten Vivir a los Cubanos," *El Nuevo Herald*, February 19, 1997.

47. "Industrial Markets: Consumers Unimpressed," *CUBANEWS* 3 (April 1995): 4.

48. *Cuba: Informe Económico, 1996* (Havana: Ministerio de Economía y Planificación, 1996), 1–8.

49. "Impuestos: Molestos, Pero Efectivos," *Correo de Cuba* 1 (n.d.): 29.

50. Ibid.

51. "Special Report: Cuba's New Contributors," *CubaINFO* 8 (August 1996): 8–10.

52. Octavio Lavastida, "Renewed Taxpayers' Awareness," *Granma International*,

May 7, 1997, 8–9; "Taxes: Thousands Miss First Income Tax Deadline," *CUBANEWS* 5 (April 1997): 6

53. "CEPAL Report on Economy Contains Good, Bad News," *CUBANEWS* 5 (August 1997): 7.

Chapter 7. Economic Reform under the Special Period: Part II

1. The law on foreign investment in force in Cuba defines two types of investment that can be agreed upon between national and foreign capital. One of the modalities is that in which the stock is divided into shares or other securities, public or private. This supposes the future possibility of foreign investments being made by acquisition of shares, although this is not possible at present, nor does the country have stock markets or exchanges. The other variant is direct investment, characterized by the effective participation of the foreign investor in the management of a joint venture or an enterprise with totally foreign capital or through contracts of international economic association. "Investments in Cuba: Flexibility in Forms and Types," *Business Tips on Cuba* (July 1996): 45.

2. Elsa Barrera López, ed. *Las Inversiones Extranjeras en Cuba* (Havana: Centro de Estudios Sobre América and New Mexico University, 1995). Also, see the different issues of *Business Tips on Cuba,* a Cuban government publication promoting foreign investment. For business opportunities today and tomorrow, see T. A. Babun, Jr., *Business Guide to Cuba* (Miami: Miami Herald Publishing Company, n.d.).

3. *Cuba: Inversiones y Negocios, 1995–1996* (Havana: Consultores Asociados, CONAS, 1995), 16–23.

4. Charles Thurston, "Cuba Invites Foreign Investment in Its Biotechnology Industry," *Journal of Commerce,* June 15, 1992.

5. At a meeting of the Association for the Study of the Cuban Economy, a U.S.-based organization made up of academics disaffected with the Cuban regime, a Chilean economist challenged those figures. The actual figure could be as low as $500 million, which placed Bulgaria as the only country behind Cuba in foreign investment in the last few years, according to Maria Werlau. While Havana's estimate could be too high (for obvious reasons), Werlau's estimate could be too low (also for obvious reasons). Juan O. Tamayo, "Economist: Foreign Investment in Cuba Lower than Nation Claims," *Miami Herald,* August 11, 1996.

6. *Cuba: Informe Economico, 1996* (Havana: Ministerio de Economía y Planificación, 1996) 2.

7. "Taladrid on U.S. Law," *CubaINFO* 8 (August 1996): 6.

8. "El Sector Privado en Cuba: El Más Dinámico en Términos de Empleo," INS, 1996.

9. "News from Cuba," February 20, 1998, Washington, D.C.: Cuban Interests Section.

10. "Sherritt Plans Cuban Expansion," *CUBANEWS* 3 (December 1995): 7; "Grupo Domos Sells 25% Cuba Phone Venture to Italian Firm," *CubaINFO* 7 (April 1995): 8.

11. "Power Project Expands Sherritt Holdings in Cuba" and Barry Brown, "Sherritt Buys Cuban Cell Phone Network," both in *CUBANEWS* 6 (March 1998): 2.

12. "Cubanacán at Center of Tourism Boom," *CUBANEWS* 5 (December 1997): 9.

13. "Tourism: The Heart of the Economy," *Granma International*, March 15, 1998, 8–9.

14. "Economic Report for 1997 Finds GDP Grew 2.5 Percent; Forecast Is Gloomy," *CUBANEWS* 6 (January 1998): 6–9, quote at 8.

15. "Tourism: The Heart of the Economy," 8.

16. *Cuba: Inversiones y Negocios, 1995–1996*, 44.

17. "Tourism: Officials Predict 1.2 Million Tourists in 1997," *CUBANEWS* 5 (April 1997): 4.

18. "48 Airlines Fly to Cuba from 27 Countries," *CUBANEWS* 6 (April 1998): 9.

19. Juan O. Tamayo, "Bomb Kills Italian in Havana: Explosions, Minutes Apart, Jolt 3 Neighboring Hotels" and "Havana Restaurant Is the Latest Target of Bombing Spree," *Miami Herald*, September 5, 6, 1997.

20. Juan O. Tamayo, "South Florida Link to Cuban Bombs Probed," *Miami Herald*, June 5, 1997, and his "Bomb Shook Havana Hotel; Blast First Since '60s; 4 Detained; Government Silent," *Miami Herald*, May 31, 1997.

21. Carlos Batista, "Nuevos Sabotajes Hoteleros dejan Saldo Negativo para Ambas Partes," Agence France Presse, September 4, 1997.

22. Orlando Oramas León, "Terrorism in Cuba Is Financed and Organized in the United States," *Granma International*, September 26, 1997, 8–9; Larry Rohter, "Cuban Bombings Stop but the Tensions Persist," *New York Times*, October 13, 1997, A6.

23. Juan O. Tamayo, "Exiles Directed Blasts That Rocked Island's Tourism, Investigation Reveals," *Miami Herald*, November 16, 1997. Not surprisingly, the Cuban media reported the *Miami Herald*'s findings: Nicanor León Cotayo, "Cuba Never Lies: *Miami Herald* Investigates Explosions in Havana Hotels," *Granma International*, November 30, 1997, 15. In spite of the arrest of Raúl Cruz León, it was reported that "'two more bombs targeted at Cuban tourism, and alleged by police to be part of a bombing spree financed by Miami exiles, were placed in Havana in October but failed to explode,' knowledgeable Cuban sources say." Juan O. Tamayo, "Cuba Finds 2 Bombs after Arrest, *Miami Herald*, December 22, 1997. The bombing spree continued into late December. This time it was aimed at disrupting the forthcoming visit by Pope John Paul II to Cuba on January 21–25, 1998. A small bomb exploded outside La Merced church in the Old Havana district. "Iglesia Católica 'Lamenta' Explosión en Templo de La Habana," Agence France Presse, December 27, 1997.

24. "Update on Armed Forces Financing," *CubaINFO* 8 (January 1996): 4

25. Phyllis Greene Walker, "Challenges Facing the Cuban Military," *Cuba Briefing Paper Series* no. 12 (Georgetown University, 1996), 1–8, quote at 6.

26. Andres Oppenheimer, "Cuban Forces Cut in Half, General Says," *Miami Herald*, February 21, 1998.

27. Ibid.

28. Christopher Marquis, "Report Downplaying Cuba Threat Back for Review," *Miami Herald*, April 8, 1998. "A new assessment from the Pentagon concludes that Cuba poses no military threat to the U.S., has no chemical or biological weapons capability beyond those of any nation with a pharmaceutical industry, and has no ability to project armed forces beyond its borders . . . Reaction to the report in Washington was . . . unsurprising. The report's release was delayed so its conclusions could be "reviewed—the *Washington Post* suggested so it could be made more consistent with current policy. Nevertheless, Marine Gen. Charles Wilhelm, South Com[mand]'s Commander, defended the report against tough questioning before a congressional panel." Mark Seibel, "Editor's Note," *CUBANEWS 6* (April 1998): 1.

29. Domingo Amuchástegui, "The Economy: FAR's Growing Role," *CUBA-NEWS* 5 (January 1997): 8.

30. "Update on Armed Forces Financing," 4. For data on Cuba's military budget and other information see the annual series, *World Military Expenditures and Arms Transfers* (Washington, D.C.: U.S. Arms Control and Disarmament Agency).

31. Domingo Amuchástegui, "Newsmakers: Raúl Castro's Rising Star," *CUBA-NEWS* 3 (April 1995): 10.

32. "Economic Report: First Semester, 1996, Ministry of Economy and Planning" in "News from Cuba," July 29, 1996, Washington, D.C.: Cuban Interests Section.

33. *CUBA: Informe Economico, 1996,* 1.

34. Carlos Lage, "The Effects of the Results of the First Half of the Year Are Directed Mainly Toward the Solution of the Economy's Fundamental Problems," *Granma International,* August 7, 1996, 5–7.

35. Ibid.

36. As reported in "Sugar Industry Is Economy's Loss-Leader," *CUBANEWS* 5 (August 1997): 7.

37. Charles Hoots, "Higher Interest, Better Terms Demanded by Investors," *CUBANEWS* 5 (September 1997): 6.

38. "The Economy: Debt Placed at $11 Billion," *CUBANEWS* 4 (August 1996): 2.

39. "Cuba Scores Debt Breakthrough in Deal with Japanese Private Creditors," *CUBANEWS* 6 (April 1998): 6.

40. "Debts to Over 180 Japanese Companies Rescheduled," *Granma International,* March 29, 1998, 1, 6.

41. Elaine Lies, "Top Japan Firms to Sign Accord on Cuba Debt," Reuters, March 18, 1998; "Japón Inicia Colaboración en Programas de Salud en Cuba," Agence France Presse, March 22, 1998.

42. *Cuba: Handbook of Trade Statistics, 1997* (Washington, D.C.: U.S. Directorate of Intelligence, APLA 97-1006, 1997), 1.

43. José Luis Rodríguez, "¿Hacia Donde Va Cuba?" 53–56, 58–59, quote at 54.

44. *Cuba: Handbook of Trade Statistics, 1997,* 1.

45. Eloy Rodríguez, "Duty-Free Zones Begin Operating," *Granma International,* May 20, 1997, 9; "Trade and Commerce: Two Trade Zones Open: Two More Are Planned," *CUBANEWS* 5 (May 1997): 5.

46. Juan O. Tamayo, "Cuban Officials Fear an Economic Slowdown in {ap}97," *Miami Herald,* December 19, 1996.

47. *La Economía Cubana: Reformas Estructurales y Desempeño en los Noventa,* booklet (Washington, D.C.: Comisión Económica para América Latina y el Caribe, 1997), 15–16.

48. "Among the measures Cuba has taken to boost employment and economic output, 'self-employment' stands out because it relies on the initiative of individual Cuban citizens. Cuba's cuentapropistas (trabajadores por cuenta propia, or workers on one's own account) have made a difference: they have brought small enterprise to the streets, increased and diversified the supply of goods and services, improved their standard of living, and learned the habits of independent actors in competitive markets. Since 1993 their growth has been dramatic, peaking at over 209,000 licensed cuentapropistas in 1996." Philip Peters, "Cuba's Small Business Experiment: Two Steps Forward, One Step Back," *Cuba Briefing Paper Series* no. 17 (Georgetown University, 1998), 1.

49. Ken Cole, *Cuba: The Options* (Norwich, England: University of East Anglia, 1996), 29. Also see his *Cuba: From Revolution to Development* (London: Pinter Publishers, 1998).

Chapter 8. Cuban-U.S. Relations under President Clinton: Part I

1. The invitation issued to Russia to join the Paris Club was characterized by a high-ranking U.S. official as "the financial end of the Cold War." "As Summit Opens, Russia Invited to Join Elite Economic Group," *Washington Post,* June 21, 1997. Still, in what sounded like Cold War rhetoric regarding Cuba, U.S. Treasury undersecretary Lawrence Summers said that "Russia arrived at an agreement . . . with the Paris Club over the principles of its 'full participation' in the group." He added that "Cuba would not receive any relief" and that "no action will be taken as long as Cuba does not 'regularize' its relations with the international community." "Entry of Russia in Paris Club Won't Ease Cuban Debt," *EFE,* June 20, 1997.

2. Terence Hunt, "Clinton Limits New NATO Members to 3," Associated Press, June 13, 1997. The three countries joining NATO were Poland, Hungary, and the Czech Republic.

3. "John Quincy Adams believed that the island was one of the most vital elements in the economic and strategic future of the United States. He wrote: 'Such indeed are, between the interests of the island and of this country, the geographical, commercial, moral, and political relations, formed by nature, gathering in the process of time that in looking forward to the probable course of events for the short period of half a century, it is scarcely possible to resist the conviction that the annexation of Cuba to our federal republic will be indispensable to the continu-

ance and integrity of the Union itself.' Thomas Jefferson wrote in 1807: 'I remember candidly that I have always looked at Cuba as the most interesting addition we could make to our state system'." Robert Freeman Smith, *Background to Revolution: The Development of Modern Cuba* (New York: Alfred A. Knopf, 1966), 5. John Quincy Adams also applied the "ripe fruit" doctrine to Cuba: "Just like a fruit separated from the tree by the force of wind cannot help but fall on the ground, likewise Cuba with the artificial connection with Spain ended, incapable of sustaining itself alone would necessarily have to gravitate toward the North American Union and only to it, and because of its own obligations, the Union could not refuse to take Cuba in." Lázaro Barredo Medina, "El Litigio Más Extenso de la Época Contemporánea," *Contrapunto* 8 (April 1997): 19–22.

4. Esteban Morales Domínguez, "Cuba en la Política Norteamericana: Una Reflexión Desde la Perspectiva Actual," in *Política de Estados Unidos Hacia Centroamérica y el Caribe* (Mexico: Cuadernos del CISEVA, FLACSO-CISAU, 1962), 193–95.

5. Pérez, "El Fin de la URSS y Cuba," 19.

6. *Cuba: Handbook of Trade Statistics, 1997,* 56–57.

7. "Intercambio Comercial entre Rusia y Cuba a los Niveles de 1991," Agence France Presse, June 7, 1997. After a difficult period in their relations following the collapse of the Soviet Union in December 1991, six months later President Boris Yeltsin reported during a visit to the United States that "after having corrected the well-known imbalances in [their] relations," Russia and Cuba would continue commercial exchanges (with no subsidies involved). "[Cuba] is one of our Latin American partners. Our commerce with Cuba is based on universally accepted principles and is conducted to mutual benefit using world prices." Yeltsin, quoted in the *Miami Herald,* June 18, 1992. Also, see Jean-Michel Caroit, "Food Campaign Helps Castro to Defy 'Second Blockade,'" *Manchester Guardian/Le Monde,* August 16, 1992. Under the 1997 agreement, Cuba should deliver 3.25 million tons of sugar for 9.75 million tons of Russian oil—a deal favorable to Havana with one ton of sugar for three tons of oil. Economic analysts were skeptical that Cuba could make such sugar deliveries when it still owes China 500,000 tons of sugar from an earlier agreement, and the 1997 sugar harvest was not expected to exceed 4.2 million tons—of which 600,000 tons are for the domestic market. "Reports of Oil/Sugar Exchange Raise Questions," *CUBANEWS* 5 (June 1997): 2.

8. Dennis Rousseau, "Rusia Relanza Proyecto de Central Nuclear," Agence France Presse, June 6, 1997. The U.S. Congress was also considering legislation prohibiting American aid to the U.N. International Atomic Energy Agency if it provides assistance to Cuba for any nuclear energy project. As happened before when Havana's close relationship with Moscow was a major reason for Washington's hostility, the U.S. did not welcome a full rapprochement in Russian-Cuban relations in the late 1990s either. "Energy: Doubts Raised over Nuclear Plant . . . Again," *CUBANEWS* 5 (June 1997): 4.

9. Wayne Smith, "La Política Sobre Cuba de la Administración Clinton Ahora se

Dicta desde Miami," *Contrapunto* (April 1996): 45, and *The U.S. Cuba Imbroglio: Anatomy of a Crisis* (Washington, D.C.: Center for International Policy, 1996).

10. Carla Anne Robbins, "Dateline Washington: Cuban-American Clout," *Foreign Policy* (fall 1992): 162–82, quotes at 166–67.

11. Tom Fiedler, "How Candidates Were Squeezed on Castro Policy," *Miami Herald*, April 26, 1992.

12. Jane Franklin, *Cuba and the United States: A Chronological History* (New York: Ocean Press, 1997), 161.

13. Christopher Marquis, "Bush Gives Support to Cuba Bill," *Miami Herald*, May 6, 1992.

14. Fiedler, "How Candidates Were Squeezed."

15. Ibid.

16. Pat Jordan, "After Fidel, Mr. Más? From Exile, the Most Influential Cuban in America Plots His Archenemy's Fall," *Los Angeles Times*, May 3, 1992.

17. Ibid.

18. "Más Scorns U.S. in *El País* Interview," *CubaINFO* 6 (August 1994): 12.

19. "Florida Election Results," *CubaINFO* 4 (November 1992): 10.

20. "102nd Congress Faces U.S.-Cuba Legislation," *Cuban-American Committee Report from Washington* 1 (spring 1991): 1–2.

21. Christopher Marquis, "House Committee Backs Torricelli's Bill on Cuba," *Miami Herald*, June 5, 1992. For a clarification of what is and is not permitted under the Cuban Democracy Act, see "Commentary," *CubaINFO* 4 (December 1992): 11.

22. "Cuban Humanitarian Trade Act of 1997 (HR 1951 IH), 105th Congress, 1st Session." (New Mexico University: Cuba-L [email: Cuba-L@unm.edu], 1997).

23. "Proyecto Para Suavizar el Embargo contra Cuba Divide al Congreso de EE.UU.," Agence France Presse, June 18, 1997. Lincoln Díaz-Balart and Ileana Ros-Lehtinen resigned from the House Hispanic caucus following the selection of Xavier Becerra (D-Calif.) as caucus president. Becerra had met President Castro during a four-day trip to the island with Congressman Esteban Torres (D-Calif.) in December 1996. The trip had been organized by the Southwest Voter Research Institute. "The caucus has long been divided between those such as Ros-Lehtinen and Díaz-Balart who want to tighten sanctions on Cuba to bring about Castro's downfall, and others, including Becerra, who have argued that the U.S. embargo has hurt the Cuban people." After their defections (Menéndez decided to stay in the caucus), seventeen of twenty-one Hispanic congressional representatives belong to the caucus. "Two Dade Lawmakers Quit House Hispanic Caucus, Protest Comes over Chairman's Cuba Visit," *Miami Herald*, January 9, 1997. Also in December 1996, two Republican congressmen, Toby Roth of Wisconsin and Jon Christensen of Nebraska, visited Cuba. Their trip was sponsored by an association of former U.S. congressmen, in an attempt to learn what changes the Helms-Burton law had brought to Cuba.

24. Isabel Sánchez, "Incertidumbre en Cuba por Futuro del Embargo," Agence France Presse, June 20, 1997.

25. "Al Menos Diez Muertos por Epidemia de Dengue en Cuba, Segun CARI-TAS," Agence France Presse, June 17, 1997.

26. William Raspberry, "Cuba: A Threat Only to Politicians' Egos," *Morning News,* February 26, 1997.

27. Robbins, "Dateline Washington," 167.

28. Ibid.

29. Wayne S. Smith, "Cuba's Long Reform," *Foreign Affairs* (March–April 1996): 99–112, quote at 99.

30. Robbins, "Dateline Washington," 168.

31. Wayne S. Smith, "Presidential Hypocrisy on Cuba," *CubaINFO* 9 (May 1997): 9–11.

32. Armando Hart Dávalos, "Civil Society and Non-Governmental Organizations," *Granma International,* September 18, 1996, 3

33. Jorge I. Domínguez, "U.S. Policy toward Cuba: Implementing Helms-Burton," *Cuban Affairs/Asuntos Cubanos* III (summer–fall 1996): 1, 10.

34. "South Florida's Cuban-Americans Turn Out for Clinton," *CubaINFO* 8 (November 1996): 10.

35. "Cronología de las Violaciones del Espacio Aéreo Cubano, 1994–1996," Cuban Government web site [online, http://www.cubaweb.cu], February 25, 1996, 1–2.

36. "Cuba Defends Shooting Down of 'Pirate' Planes," Reuters, February 2, 1996.

37. This section draws from "The Incident," *CubaINFO* Supplement (February 1996): 1–14, quotes at 2–3.

38. See Peter Dale Scott, "José Basulto León: Background," Real History Archives: *Cuban History,* February 28, 1996 [online, http://www.webcom/~lpease].

39. Ibid., 3, 9–10.

40. The names of the four pilots and passengers who perished in the incident of February 24, 1996, were Armando Alexander, Jr., Carlos Costa, Mario de la Peña, and Pablo Morales. José Basulto and the three passengers (two men and one woman) in the third aircraft returned to Florida safely. "The Incident," 3.

41. Hart Dávalos, "Civil Society and Non-Governmental Organizations," 3.

42. The economic warfare against the Cuban government is becoming more serious, with several bomb explosions in Havana's major foreign tourist hotels and Cuban charges at the United Nations of U.S. biological warfare against the island. On July 12, 1997, two bombs exploded in the Nacional Hotel and the Capri Hotel in Havana, which resulted in four people injured and material damage. There were similar terrorist actions earlier and later in the year in an attempt to sabotage international tourism, the fastest-growing economic sector in the country (see chapter 7). According to reports published in the United States, National Assembly President Ricardo Alarcón confirmed that Cuba has "proof that the people responsible and materials for the July 12 blasts at the Nacional and Capri

Hotels came from the United States." Juan O. Tamayo and Christopher Marquis, "Few Facts Point to Who is Responsible," *Miami Herald*, July 21, 1997. Also, Cuba officially refuted the U.S. State Department justification for the activities of the American S2R plane that on October 21, 1996, was flying over Cuban national territory. According to the Cuban government, the U.S. aircraft "sprayed crops with a blight of the insect known as *Thrips palmi*." While the United States admitted that the flight took place, it stated that "the aircraft in question was merely trying to specify its position to a nearby Cuban aircraft, via smoke signals." Cuba's counterclaim stated that the "U.S. aircraft was flying under instrument flight rules, where responsibility for keeping airplanes apart during flights is assumed by the air traffic controller directing them, and not by pilots, as the U.S. version alleges." Moreover, in a statement given by an eyewitness, the Cubana Airlines pilot Erlan Romero Llush, "It was liquid and not smoke [that] the [U.S.] aircraft sprayed" while flying over the Giron air corridor in western Cuba. Cuba's report, "Technical Consideration[s] Related to the Activities of the U.S. S2R Aircraft during Its Flight over National Territory on October 21, 1996," was presented to the United Nations. The report followed the charges filed on May 12, 1997, with the Russian Federation, which acts as trustee for the nations that form part of the Convention on the Prohibition [of] the Development, Production and Storage of Bacteriological Weapons. As stated in the report, "Small, medium and large-capacity commercial transport aircraft, those used in general aviation, and fumigation planes manufactured and operated throughout the world are not equipped with smoke generators, nor are these a requirement established by the ICAO [International Civil Aviation Organization]. Smoke generators are usually only installed in aircraft used for acrobatic displays and similar activities." *Granma International* [online, http://www.granma.cu], July 23, 1997.

Havana has also identified previous cases of U.S. biological warfare against Cuba:

In 1961 and 1962 the CIA organized Operation Mongoose, which included a plan to incapacitate sugar industry workers during the harvest through the use of chemical means that would make them ill.

On May 29, 1964, balloons of various sizes were dropped from a high altitude and dissolved on contact with the earth, leaving a gelatinous substance similar to that used in bacterial cultures.

In 1971, the Long Island daily *Newsday* reported that a virus had been transported on a fishing boat from Fort Gulik, in the Panama Canal Zone, to agents operating inside Cuba.

The book *The Fish Is Red* confirmed that CIA agents introduced swine fever into Cuba for the first time in 1972. As a consequence, more than half a million pigs were sacrificed to combat the epidemic.

Between 1979 and 1981, four diseases were introduced that seriously affected the population and crops vital to the Cuban economy: hemorrhagic conjunctivitis, hemorrhagic dengue, sugarcane smut and tobacco blue mold. Hemorrhagic dengue alone killed 158 Cubans, 101 of whom were children. In the first seven weeks of the epidemic, 273,404 people were infected.

In 1979, the *Washington Post* reported that there was a CIA program aimed against Cuban agriculture and that Pentagon specialists had been manufacturing biological agents for it since 1962.

In 1984, before a U.S. jury, Eduardo Arocena, leader of the Omega-7 terrorist group, admitted that he had participated in an operation to introduce germs into Cuba as part of the biological war against the island. *Granma International*, July 23, 1997.

43. "The Baltimore Orioles knew the Cuban players could hit hard. What they didn't know was that the Cuban second-base umpire could hit, too. The umpire, César Valdéz, body-slammed and punched an anti-Castro demonstrator in shallow center field Monday night as the Cuban all-star team embarrassed Baltimore 12–6. Omar Linares and Daniel Castro each had four hits, and Andy Morales spread his arms wide as he steamed around the bases after a three-run homer in the ninth inning." "'O's Are No Shows in Loss to Cubans," Associated Press, May 4, 1999.

While political controversy surrounded the exhibition games, reactions were different in Cuba and the United States: "Cubans rushed home early from work and crowded television sets to cheer their hometown baseball heroes during Monday's rematch with the Baltimore Orioles at Camden Yards. The childhood home of one of Cuba's biggest baseball stars, Javier Méndez, was packed with relatives and neighbors watching the game. 'I am so proud of my son because he fought hard to be on the Cuban team . . . [I hope] the game [will] bring the American and Cuban people closer together,' said his father." "Orioles vs. Cuba: Streets of Cuba Deserted for Game," *Miami Herald*, May 4, 1999. Though the Cuban team enjoyed the support of approving fans during the Baltimore game, outside Camden Yards Park "several hundred anti-Castro demonstrators denounced the event . . . The demonstrators, many from South Florida, were joined by two Cuban-American congressmen, Republican Lincoln Díaz-Balart of Miami and Democrat Bob Menéndez of Union City, N.J." Politicizing the sport event, Díaz-Balart told the crowd: "This game is an insult." Frank Davies, "Cubans Win on U.S. Soil: 12-6 Rout Follows Controversy," *Miami Herald*, May 4, 1999. Upon the Cuban teams' arrival at José Martí Airport the day after the game, Fidel Castro greeted the team and the three-hundred-member Cuban delegation, which included journalists, ballplayers, ordinary citizens, members of youth groups, and outstanding students. Six members of the delegation, who overslept after the all-night victory celebration and missed the charter plane, returned a day later. But one assistant pitching coach, Rigoberto Herrera Betancourt, refused to return and requested political asylum in the United States. Michael Janofsky, "As Cubans Take Home a Victory, One Coach Is Said to Seek Asylum," *New York Times*, May 5, 1999.

Chapter 9. Cuban-U.S. Relations under President Clinton: Part II

1. "Sanctions at a Glance," *New York Times*, February 27, 1996.

2. *Granma International* [online, http://www.granma.cu], February 14, 1997.

3. Matthew Cooper and Belinda Liu, "Bright Light," *Newsweek*, February 10, 1997, 23–31, quote at 27; Carol Giacomo, "Albright Takes Firm Position on China, Cuba," Reuters, January 24, 1997. See also Matthew Cooper, "The Lady Is a Hawk," *Newsweek*, December 16, 1996, 25–28.

In her Senate confirmation hearings for secretary of state, Albright answered Senator Helms's question "Are you committed to the full implementation of the Libertad [Helms-Burton] Act?" by stating: "Senator, I believe that the Libertad Act has had a very important effect. The points that you cite about the action of the European Union and of Latin American states at the Ibero-American Summit as well as actions by labor unions and the non-governmental organizations have created an entirely new situation. And that is, rather than the U.S. being isolated in its policy, Castro is being increasingly isolated by the democracies of the world." "Albright Responds to Questions on Cuba," *CubaINFO* 9 (January 1997): 2–4, quote at 3. Congressman Bill Richardson (D-N.M.) was President Clinton's replacement for Ambassador Albright at the U.N. Richardson had reportedly told *Palm Beach Post* in January 1996: "If we're going to open up the island, maybe some consideration should be given to lifting the embargo." However, at his Senate confirmation hearing for the U.N. post, Richardson answered a question on the Helms-Burton Act (after having voted against it) saying: "Let me state that as . . . the U.S. representative to the United Nations I will vigorously support the administration policy on Cuba. The Helms-Burton law is the law of the land." "Richardson Comments on Cuba in Senate Confirmation Hearing," *CubaINFO* 9 (February 1997): 4. The extreme politics and bitter personality of Senator Helms are having a negative impact on the U.S. Senate. On the occasion of Helms's refusal to hold hearings for the confirmation of his fellow Republican William Weld, governor of Massachusetts, nominated as ambassador to Mexico, Richard Cohen wrote in his syndicated column: "Jesse Helms is an odd chairman of the Senate Foreign Relations Committee. Since taking over the committee [1995] he has never made a major pronouncement on foreign policy and has been out of the country just once—a quick trip to the funeral of Israeli Prime Minister Yitzhak Rabin. If travel does indeed broaden, we can understand why Helms is so narrow . . . Chairman Helms has vowed never—but never, never, never—to hold a hearing on [Weld's] nomination . . . [Helms] is an ornery man, it is true, but he's one of the few people in Washington who is untroubled by his national image. He cares only for the voters back home—the white, conservative voters, that is—and not how he appears on the 'Today' show. It matters little to him if he is liked or respected. He'll settle for feared—and that, as the record shows, he is . . . Weld has . . . illuminated Jesse Helms as a man possessed of shabby, antique thoughts. Lacking the ability to persuade, he can only obstruct. In the end his strength amounts to that of your standard off-the-shelf bully—the weakness of his opponents." Richard Cohen, "Chairman Helms Relies on Senate's Cowardice," *Erie* (Pa.): *Morning News,* August 7, 1997, 3B.

4. "Protestantes por Embargo contra Cuba Interrumpen Tres Veces a Albright," Agence France Presse, June 24, 1997.

5. Laura Myers, "Mob Would Have 'Hit' Castro for Free," Associated Press, July 2, 1997. Scholarly studies noting that the almost four-decade-old U.S. policy toward the Castro regime has been characterized by hostility and transgressions of legality include Michael Krinsky and David Golove, *United States Economic Measures Against Cuba: Proceedings in the United Nations and International Law Issues* (Northhampton, Mass.: Aletheia Press, 1993); Franklin, *Cuba and the United States;* Fabian Escalante, *The Secret War: CIA Covert Operations against Cuba, 1959–1962* (Melbourne, Australia: Ocean Press, 1995); and Claudia Furiati, *ZR Rifle: The Plot to Kill Kennedy and Castro* (Melbourne, Australia: Ocean Press, 1994).

6. "Statement by H. E. Mr. Roberto Robaina González, Minister of Foreign Affairs of the Republic of Cuba, to the Resumed 50th Session of the U.N. General Assembly, New York, March 6, 1996." (New Mexico University: Cuba-L [email: Cuba-L@unm.edu]), March 16, 1996).

7. See "Deberá Decidir OACI Esta Semana Entre Dignidad o Vasallaje"; "Denuncian que Estados Unidos Intenta Manipular a la OACI"; "Conferencia de Prensa de Alarcón sobre OACI," all in "Síntesis sobre Cuba," Prensa Latina, June 24, 1996.

8. "ICAO Finds Exile Planes Shot Down in International Airspace," *CubaINFO* 8 (July 1996): 4–9; "Conferencia de Prensa de Alarcón sobre OACI," Prensa Latina, June 27, 1996.

9. R. W. Apple, Jr., "Foreign Policy: Voters Pay a Price for a Campaign of Domestic Issues," *New York Times,* September 24, 1996, A14.

10. "U.S. Presidential Debates Touch on Cuba," *CubaINFO* 8 (October 1996): 1–2.

11. Rex Nutting, "U.S. Isolated in Struggle against Cuba," United Press International, March 5, 1996.

12. However, the leaders of Concilio Cubano vowed to try again: "*Miami Herald* quoted Concilio's vice-president, Hector Palacio Ruis, as saying that 'Concilio is indestructible . . . More than anything, it represents a determination and a patriotic design of a peaceful transition' of power in the island." "Cuban Concilio to Try Again," *CubaINFO* 8 (March 1996): 12.

13. This section draws from Anita Snow, "American Diplomats in Cuba Walk Fine Line," Associated Press, March 15, 1996.

14. Robert Evans, "EU Criticado en Ginebra por Sus Tacticas con Cuba," Reuters, March 16, 1997.

15. Ibid.

16. "Robin Meyer, the former human rights officer at the U.S. mission in Havana, was expelled by the Cuban government in August [1996] for 'activities incompatible with her status,' which Havana officials said included aiding and organizing Castro opponents. Last month, Undersecretary of State Peter Tarnoff

bestowed upon Meyer one of the department's highest honors for her 'dedication, bravery and consistently sound policy recommendations.' In a rare interview, Meyer recently reflected on life in the cross hairs of the Cuban government, on her role as ally and friend of the island's untouchables . . . 'I am an exile,' said the Chicago-born diplomat. 'Who knows when I'll get back? When am I going to see my friends again?'" Christopher Marquis, "Expelled U.S. Envoy to Cuba: 'I am an Exile,'" *Miami Herald*, November 24, 1996.

17. The quotations in this paragraph and the ones that immediately follow were cited in Jim Cason and David Brooks, "Miami—Imperio de Terror," *La Jornada*, March 17, 1996.

18. Cason and Brooks, "Documentos: Funerales Para el Carril Dos," *Contrapunto* 7 (May 1996): 34–45.

19. Cason and Brooks, "Miami—Imperio de Terror."

20. Lydia Saad, "Gallup Poll on Cuba," *Los Angeles Times*, March 14, 1996.

21. Andrés Oppenheimer and Christopher Marquis, "Missile Attack Weighed after Shootdown," *Miami Herald*, October 1, 1996.

22. "Helms-Burton Legislation Becomes Law; Global Community Protests and Cuba Threatens Retaliation," *CubaINFO* 8 (March 1996): 1–10, quote at 4.

23. *Washington Post*, quoted by Thomas W. Lippman in "Derribo Definió la Política de Clinton," *El Nuevo Herald*, February 25, 1997.

24. Douglas Wallar, "Clinton's Cuban Road to Florida: How Policy Was Turned by a Few Cuban-Americans, Including His Own Sister-in-Law," *Time*, October 24, 1996.

25. Christopher Marquis and Josh Goldstein, "Study: Cuban Exile-Lobby Is Most Cost-Effective," *Miami Herald*, January 24, 1997, 1A.

26. "U.S. Report Links Helms-Burton Act to Political Donations," *Granma International* [online, http://www.granma.cu], February 14, 1997.

27. Christopher Marquis, "Group Gave $1 Million to Promote Dialogue With Cuba," *Miami Herald*, January 24, 1997.

28. Ernesto Montero Acuña, "Entrevista con la Doctora Olga Miranda, Nacionalizaciones y Bloqueo, La Ley Helms-Burton No Es Aplicable en Cuba," *Correo de Cuba* 1 (n.d.): 6–8.

29. "The final version of the Helms-Burton legislation approved by the U.S. Congress codifies the long-standing U.S. embargo against Cuba in an effort to make it impossible for President Bill Clinton—or any future U.S. president—to modify the sanctions without approval from Capitol Hill." Ana Radelat, "New Embargo Legislation Makes Reversal Harder," *CUBANEWS* 4 (special report) (March 8, 1996): 2.

30. "Helms-Burton Down in Poll," *CubaINFO* 9 (April 1997): 4.

31. On January 18–19, 1997, 130 Cubans living abroad in eight different countries attended a conference held in Havana to discuss the negative implications for Cuba of the Helms-Burton Act. Among the speakers were José Ramón Balaguer, member of the Communist Party's Politburo; Roberto Robaina, foreign affairs

minister; José Luis Rodríguez, minister of economy and planning; and Ricardo Alarcón, president of the National Assembly. Experts on international law from Cuba and other countries also addressed the audience. "Cubanos Contra la Ley Helms-Burton," *Correo de Cuba* no. 3: 7–10.

32. "PCC Central Committee Meets; Castro Calls for 'Ideological Battle' with U.S." *CubaINFO* 8 (April 1996): 7–11; "Socio Political News: Politburo Declaration," *CUBANEWS* 4 (April 1996): 4–5.

33. Ibid. As a student of Cuban affairs, I have had the opportunity of interacting for years in Mexico, the United States, Canada, and Cuba with scholars who worked at the Center for the Study of the Americas. I always thought that in their papers and lectures they did their best to present the Cuban perspective in an honest, intelligent, and convincing way. If there was any adjustment to the outside world it was mainly for Cuba's benefit, in the sense that they understood how to articulate better an argument to an outside audience. The fact that most of them are presently occupying other government-related positions of responsibility is testimony that they never purposely meant to hurt the revolutionary cause.

34. See "Summary of European Union Legislation in Retaliation to the Helms-Burton Act," "Summary of Mexico's Position Regarding the Helms-Burton Act and Cuba," "Summary of Canadian Legislation in Retaliation to the Helms-Burton Act," and "Summary of the OAS' Response to the Helms-Burton Act," all in Washington, D.C.: Center for International Policy [online, http://www.ciponline.org], 1997; and "Reaffirmation of Cuban Dignity and Sovereignty Law," *Granma International*, January 22, 1997, 4.

35. Quoted in Kristin S. Krause, "American Shippers, Carriers Miss Out as Foreign Investment Floods Cuba," Knight Rider/Tribune Business News, July 29, 1996.

36. "Helms-Burton: NAM Study Criticizes Unilateral Embargo," *CUBANEWS* 5 (April 1997): 6.

37. Christopher Marquis, "Clinton to Name Diplomat on Cuba: Commerce Department Official Will Urge Allies to Pressure Havana," *Miami Herald*, August 14, 1996.

38. "Defeat is the best term used to describe what happened to Stuart Eizenstat, former ambassador to the European Union, and Madeleine Albright, the U.S. representative in the United Nations, when just a few days ago they tried to secure the support of their European allies and Latin American governments regarding the Helms-Burton Act." "Unsuccessful Hunting: U.S. Support-seeking Missions in the European Union and Latin America Fail," *Granma International*, September 18, 1996, 14.

39. Carlos Salas, "Commentary: A Strange Game of Chess," *CubaINFO* 9 (February 1997): 12–14.

40. Ana Radelat, "U.S., E.U. Still Far Apart in Talks," *CUBANEWS* 5 (July 1997): 5.

41. "U.S. Presses Europeans to Deal with Confiscated Property in New Investment Treaty," *CubaINFO* 9 (May 1997): 1–2; "Helms-Burton: Wider Proposal May Resolve WTO Dilemma," *CUBANEWS* 5 (May 1997): 7.

42. Ana Radelat, "Understanding May Prevail in Helms-Burton Deal," *CUBANEWS* 5 (December 1997): 5.

43. "Fidel Denounces U.S. Attempts to Internationalize Blockade," *Granma International*, May 24, 1998, 4–5.

44. Fidel Castro, "It Is Infuriating that Some People Could Imagine that the Freedom and Dignity of a People Could Be Bought," *Granma International*, February 12, 1997, 3.

45. Armando Correa, "Menéndez Logra Alto Cargo en el Congreso," *El Nuevo Herald*, March 15, 1997.

46. "White House Releases Report on Cuba in Compliance with Title II," *CubaINFO* 9 (February 1997): 3–4.

47. "Declaration of the 20th Century Independent Fighters: A Salute to the Memory of José Martí," and Octavio Lavastida, "We Won't Surrender Our Weapons without a Fight," both in *Granma International*, March 26, 1997, 6.

48. After a protracted period of waiting for Washington's approval, the White House agreed on February 12, 1997, to grant licenses to ten U.S. media organizations to open news bureaus in Cuba. These included CNN, ABC, CBS, the *Miami Herald*, Univision (U.S. Spanish TV network), the *Chicago Tribune*, the *Sun Sentinel* (South Florida), and *CubaINFO*. So far, out of the ten, Havana has approved only CNN to open a news bureau.

49. (Costa Rica/Cuba): "Relaciones con Cuba Siguen Igual Tras Visita de Canciller Robaina," Agence France Presse, June 10, 1997; (Nicaragua/Cuba): "Alemán Se Entrevistará con Canciller Cubano," Agence France Presse, June 10, 1997; (Uruguay/Cuba): "Vicepresidente Cubano Expone en Uruguay Sus Diferencias con EE.UU.," Agence France Presse, June 17, 1997.

50. Wayne S. Smith, "Congress Throws Cold Water on Eizenstat-EU Agreement," *CubaINFO* 9 (June 1997): 12–13.

51. Rodolfo Casals, "Fourteen Areas of Further Cooperation with Canada," *Granma International*, February 5, 1997, 6; "Canada-Cuba Pact Irks Washington," *CubaINFO* 9 (February 1997): 5–6.

52. "Ever since her gooey confirmation hearings, Secretary of State Madeleine Albright has made it her business to charm the courtly porcupine who chairs the Senate Foreign Relations Committee, eschewing the diplomatic handshake in favor of kissing his Moon Pie face (both cheeks) and interrupting her global travels to tour his home state, where she gave the Jesse Helms Lecture at Wingate University . . . As Helms and Albright toured a bit of North Carolina together, they looked like an old couple trying to find a nice place to retire . . . She gave him a T shirt inscribed SOMEONE AT THE STATE DEPARTMENT LOVES ME . . . When he showed up at a Washington softball game between her staff and his, he was wearing it." Margaret Carlson, "The Love Connection," *Time*, August 4, 1997, 28.

53. "U.S. Policy on Cuba Criticized: Two Former Aides Blame Clinton," *Miami Herald,* April 21, 1997.

54. "Clinton: U.S. Cuba Policy a Failure," *CubaINFO* 9 (April 1997): 4.

55. George Gedda, "Cuban Americans Lobby on Capitol Hill for Ending of Embargo," Associated Press, April 1, 1998.

56. "Congress' three Cuban American members, Reps. Ileana Ros-Lehtinen, R.-Fla., Lincoln Díaz Balart, R-Fla., and Robert Menéndez, D-N.J., who usually fall in step with the CANF and Helms on Cuba policy, opposed the measure saying it sends mixed signals." Ana Radelat, "Humanitarian Aid Issue Splits Anti-Castro Lawmakers," *CubaINFO* 10 (February 1998): 1.

57. "Helms Backs Cuban Aid Proposal," Associated Press, January 30, 1998. In a document drafted by Senator Helms's advisors Roger Noriega and Marc Thiesen in collaboration with Caleb McCarry, an aide to Representative Benjamin Gelman, chairman of the International Relations Committee of the House, it was recommended that while political and economic sanctions should be maintained, a relaxation of the supply of food and medicines should be initiated. Their recommendation was based on conversations with Cuban dissidents and workers, talks they had had with the help of independent organizations and the Church while visiting Cuba at the time of the pope's pilgrimage. The document stated: "The Pope planted the seeds of Cuba's liberation . . . The challenge for the Cuban people and for the North Americans who want to help them is to find ways to make those seeds grow." U.S. Representative Ileana Ros-Lehtinen rejected their recommendation, arguing that "those advisors that traveled to Cuba do not vote [in Congress] and do not reflect our opinion." Olance Nogueras, "Sugieren Ayudar a Cubanos y Mantener el Embargo," *El Nuevo Herald,* March 10, 1998.

58. "Madeleine Albright Hablará el Sábado al Pueblo Cubano," Agence France Presse, February 27, 1998; "Albright Quiere Ayudar a Cuba, No a Su Gobierno," and "Richardson Elogia y Critica a Castro," *El Nuevo Herald,* March 8, 1998.

59. "U.S. Announces Steps to Increase Humanitarian Aid to Cuba," CNN [online, http://www.cnn.com], March 20, 1998; "Anuncia Estados Unidos Suspensión de Algunas Medidas contra Cuba," *Granma* [online, http://www.granma.cu], March 20, 1998.

60. Richard Whittle, "Albright: Cuba Will Remain under Tight Economic Embargo," *Dallas Morning News,* March 21, 1998.

61. Carol Giacomo, "Clinton Looks 'Beyond Castro' with Cuba Moves," Reuters, March 21, 1998.

62. Ibid.

63. Quoted in "Arzobispo de Boston Llama a EE.UU. a Cambiar Política Hacia Cuba," Agence France Presse, March 22, 1998.

64. Ibid.

65. Ana Radelat, "U.S. Pharmaceuticals Donate $6 Million Medical Gift to Cuba," *CubaINFO* 10 (March 1998): 3.

66. Whittle, "Albright: Cuba Will Remain under Tight Economic Embargo."

67. Angus MacSwan, "U.S. Cuba Moves Slammed, Welcomed in Miami," Reuters, March 20, 1998.

68. "Clinton's Shift on Cuba Brings Mixed Reactions," UPI, March 20, 1998.

69. "Castro Wants to Hear Details on Expected Easing of U.S. Sanctions," CNN, March 20, 1998.

70. Clare Nullis, "U.N. Report Criticizes Cuba Embargo," Associated Press, March 20, 1998.

71. Alfredo Corchado and Tracey Eaton, "Cubans Call Easing of Restrictions a Miracle," *Dallas Morning News,* March 21, 1998.

72. Carlos Batista, "Cuba Rechaza la Zanahoria Norteamericana," Agence France Presse, March 28, 1998; Mauricio Vincent, "Cuba Desconfia de la Apertura de Clinton," Reuters, March 29, 1998.

73. Kelly Velázquez, "Canciller Cubano Rechaza la Ayuda Humanitaria a Través de la Iglesia," Agence France Presse, March 29, 1998.

74. Douglas Brinkley, "Democratic Enlargement: The Clinton Doctrine," *Foreign Policy* 106 (spring 1997): 111–14.

75. Ibid., 126–27.

76. "Mandela said that just as he received Clinton, he has welcomed Fidel Castro, Moammar Gadhafi and former Iranian President Hashemi Rafsanjani, and will remain loyal to them. They supported Mandela in the battle against apartheid." Terence Hunt, "Mandela to Clinton: 'Set Example'—Make Peace with Enemies," Associated Press, March 28, 1998.

77. Ibid.

78. "What's new is that the enduring example of Nelson Mandela has heartened all Africans with a fresh vision of leadership, how men of their own kind can be admired, respected, and even emulated." "Africa Rising," *Time,* March 30, 1998: 34–37, 40–46, quote at 36.

Chapter 10. Building New Bridges to the World

1. "Relaciones Diplomáticas y Consulares," in *Todo de Cuba, All about Cuba,* multimedia encyclopedia (Madrid: CEDISAC and Prensa Latina, 1997).

2. "Cuba is beginning a new legal campaign to fight the U.S. economic embargo, starting with a lawsuit against the U.S. government seeking more than $100 billion to compensate the Cuban people for their suffering. Ricardo Alarcón, president of Cuba's National Assembly, announced the campaign shortly before the U.N. General Assembly voted overwhelmingly for the eight straight year to demand that the U.S. embargo be lifted immediately." Edith M. Lederer, "Cuba Suing U.S. for Over $100B," Associated Press, November 10, 1999.

3. Youssef M. Ibrahim, "U.N. Votes, 157–2, in Nonbinding Referendum against U.S. Embargo of Cuba," *New York Times,* October 15, 1998.

4. Jorge I. Domínguez, *To Make a World Safe for Revolution: Cuba's Foreign Policy* (Cambridge, Mass.: Harvard University Press, 1989), 6.

5. "Speech Given by President Fidel Castro at the Reception Held in the Reunification Palace, Ho Chi Minh City, Viet Nam, on December 10, 1995," *Granma International*, December 20, 1995: 3.

6. *Granma International*, June 26, 1996, 14–15, quote at 15.

7. "Panamanian President Describes Ties with Cuba as Excellent," *Granma International* [online, http://www.granma.cu], February 27, 1998.

8. "Second Summit of the Association of Caribbean States: Fidel Calls for Third World Unity," *Granma International*, April 25, 1999, 5; Fidel Castro, "We Form Part of that Globalized World and Our Destiny Is the Same as the Destiny of All Those Countries," *Granma International*, May 2, 1999, 10–11, quote at 11.

9. José R. Bauza, "Diplomacia: ¿Cuba una Isla . . . Aislada?" *Correo de Cuba* 3, no. 3 (n.d.): 39–40.

10. The Ibero-American summits have been in Guadalajara, Mexico, July 1991; Madrid, Spain, July 1992; Bahia, Brazil, July 1993; Cartagena, Colombia, July 1994; San Carlos de Bariloche, Argentina, October 1995; Viña del Mar, Chile, November 1996; Margarita Island, Venezuela, November 1997; Oporto, Portugal, October 1998; Havana, Cuba, November 1999; and Panama City, Panama, 2000. At the 1994 Colombia summit the locations of those from 1995 to 2000 were designated.

11. Gustavo Robreño, "24 Hours That Have Become History," *Granma International*, November 3, 1991, 8–9.

12. Christopher Marquis, "Castro's Summit Reviews Mixed," *Miami Herald*, July 21, 1991.

13. Christopher Marquis, "Castro 'Worried' about Cuba's Economic Fate," *Miami Herald*, July 19, 1991.

14. Imogen Mark, "US Curb on Cuban Trade Rejected," *Financial Times*, November 12, 1996.

15. Pablo Alfonso, "VII Cumbre Se Va Sin Penas Ni Glorias," *El Nuevo Herald*, November 10, 1997.

16. Tim Johnson, "Latin Leaders, Castro Spar at Summit," *Miami Herald*, November 9, 1997; "Castro Brushes Aside Criticism, Wins Leadership Role at Ibero-American Summit," *CubaINFO* 9 (November 1997): 5–6.

17. Pablo Alfonso, "Arrests in Venezuela Block Exiles' Anti-Castro Protest," *Miami Herald*, November 4, 1997.

18. Javier Valenzuela, "El FBI Vincula a un Líder del Exilio Cubano con un Presunto Atentado a Castro," *El País*, December 22, 1997; Gerardo Reyes, "Before Assassination Plot, Boat Was at Gables Dock," *Miami Herald*, November 7, 1997; and "U.S. Arrests Four Suspected of Plotting to Kill Castro," *CubaINFO* 9 (November 1997): 1–2.

19. "Cuba Charges 4 Suspects in Bomb Attacks," *New York Times*, October 30, 1998, A3.

20. "Caso Pinochet Marcó la Cita de Oporto y Daña la de Habana," EFE, November 8, 1999.

21. "Ménem Dice que Su Ausencia en la Cumbre no Es Boicot contra Cuba," Reuters, November 9, 1999.

22. "Summit Is Victory for Castro but Also Advance for Critics," CNN [online], November 15, 1999. In addition, David Gonzalez of the *New York Times* reported: "Cuban participants said issues included multiparty democracy, open markets, freedom of expression, and—they pointedly added—an end to the United States embargo against Cuba. They said the meetings were held at the request of the delegation and passed without comment" ("A Higher Profile for the Dissidents in Cuba," November 17, 1999, A12).

23. "Ibero-American Summit Opens in Havana," CNN [online], November 16, 1999.

24. Ibid.

25. "Main Points of the [Havana] Declaration," Agence France Press, November 17, 1999.

26. "Latins Protest Spanish Action," *CubaINFO* 9 (June 1997): 5–6.

27. John M. Broder, "Clinton Urges Latin America to 'Be Patient' on Free Trade," *New York Times*, April 17, 1998, A3.

28. Tom Raum, "Western Leaders Set Trade Talks: 34 Nations Move Forward on Plan for Duty-Free Trade by 2005," Associated Press, April 20, 1998; Calvin Sims, "Free-Trade Zone of the Americas Given a Go-Ahead," *New York Times*, April 20, 1998, A1, A10.

As Florida International University's Eduardo Gamarra has noted, "The No. 1 crisis in the entire region is the crisis of personal security . . . [but it was not] "the subject of a single formal discussion at the summit." Moreover, "the crisis in security is warping the region's social and economic development. And it consistently ranks as the top public concern in opinion polls throughout Latin America. It's easy to see why: Latin America now averages 30 homicides per 100,000 inhabitants, six times the world average, three times the rate in the United States and twice that of Africa and the Middle East. The fear of common crime—theft, assault, kidnapping—affects nearly everyone . . . And the situation is only getting worse. Fueled by a widening gap between rich and poor, an ineffectual legal system and a surplus of weapons left over from cold-war conflicts, crime is rising in nearly every country in Latin America. In Mexico crime has multiplied faster in the past four years than in the previous six decades. Colombia, aside from its drug violence, has become the world leader in kidnappings, with more than 2,000 reported last year—one abduction every four hours. El Salvador has surpassed Colombia as the world's most murderous country, with more homicides per year than during the height of its bloody civil war. And a recent United Nations survey reports that 78 percent of Chileans expect to be robbed—while 47 percent of Chilean women expect to be sexually attacked . . . The Inter-American Development Bank called violent crime 'the principal barrier to regional development.' Its annual cost: $168 billion, or 14 percent of the region's GDP." Martha Brant, "A Special Breed of Bandit," *Newsweek*, April 27, 1998, 44.

29. Ana Julia Faya, "Cuba ante el Sistema Interamericano y los Mecanismos de Concertación Política Regionales," in *Cuba en las Américas: Una Perspectiva Sobre Cuba y los Problemas Hemisféricos*, ed. Rafael Hernández, dossier no. 6 (Havana: Centro de Estudios Sobre América, 1994), 38–42, quote at 38.

30. "Panel Slams U.S. Cuba Policy," *CubaINFO* 9 (May 1997): 4.

31. Franklin, *Cuba and the United States*, 48.

32. See John M. Kirk, *Back in Business: Canada-Cuba Relations after 50 Years* (Ottawa: Canadian Foundation for the Americas, 1995).

33. "During a two-day session of talks in Havana, the governments of Canada and Cuba shared their opinions on the issue of human rights, of interest to these two countries and the rest of the international community. [During his visit to Cuba in January 1997, Canada's Foreign Affairs Minister Lloyd Axworthy] pointed out that Canada's way of dealing with the subject of human rights is different from the United States and the European Union. Further bilateral cooperation in this area will include organizing seminars, establishing academic links and exchanging opinions on the work carried out by the specialized agencies in the United Nations. The first meeting in Havana took place just before the initiation in Geneva of the latest session of the U.N. Human Rights Commission." Rodolfo Casals, "Talks with Canada on Human Rights, *Granma International* [online, http://www.granma.cu], April 1, 1997.

34. Luis Melián, "Cuba-Canada: Cooperación y Negocios con Mucho Respecto," *Correo de Cuba* 3, no. 2 (n.d.): 11–12.

35. "Canadian Exports to Cuba; Canadian Imports from Cuba," *CUBANEWS* 5 (April 1997): 8. "The improving output of nickel refineries located on the eastern side is offering Cuba a dynamic growth sector in an otherwise fragile economy, attracting more hard currency at a time when the government desperately needs it . . . It has been Cuba's good fortune that the recovery of the nickel industry coincides with an upswing in the price of the metal in the worldwide market." "Mining: Nickel Output Gives Cuban Economy Hope," *CUBANEWS* 5 (June 1997): 11. Moreover, "KWG Resources, Inc. of Montreal has announced plans to invest $300 million in Cuba to build a nickel refinery that will process ore from a mining complex on the eastern tip of the island." "New Nickel Deal," *CUBANEWS* 5 (July 1997): 3. See also Gillian McGillivray, "Trading with the 'Enemy': Canadian-Cuban Relations in the 1990s," *Cuba Briefing Papers Series* no. 15 (Georgetown University, 1997), 1–16, and John M. Kirk and Peter McKenna, *Canada-Cuba Relations: The Other Good Neighbor Policy* (Gainesville: University of Florida Press, 1997).

36. "'Viva el Embargo!' or 'Turn the Page on Cuba'? These two titles from recent articles in the Canadian press reflected Canada's somewhat ambiguous position vis-à-vis the U.S. embargo of Cuba. Economically, Canada should benefit from the embargo; Cuba is an increasingly open market in which Canadian companies do not have to compete with Americans. Politically, Canada's Cuba policy has provided, at least until recently, a relatively painless way for Canada to assert its

independence from the United States in the realm of foreign policy." McGillivray, "Trading with the 'Enemy'," 1.

37. Casals, "Fourteen Areas of Further Cooperation with Canada," 6.

38. "Canada Report: Cuba, Canada Sign Cooperation Pacts," *CUBANEWS* 5 (April 1997): 8.

39. "Cuba-Canada: Constructive Engagement," *Granma International*, May 3, 1998, 6–7.

40. "Trade and Commerce—Canada: EU: Canada 'Scared'," *CUBANEWS* 5 (May 1997): 4.

41. "Since his selection as the Clinton Administration's point man on Helms-Burton in mid-August [1996], veteran U.S. official Stuart Eizenstat has traveled nearly 35,000 miles, visited 12 countries and met with 18 heads of government in a vigorous but frustrating attempt to win support for U.S. policy toward Cuba." "Helms-Burton Change Called Unrealistic," *CUBANEWS* 4 (November 1996): 9.

42. "Summary of Mexico's Position Regarding the Helms-Burton Act and Cuba," Washington, D.C.: Center for International Policy [online, http://www.ciponline.org], 1996.

43. "Summary of the OAS's Response to the Helms-Burton Act," Washington, D.C.: Center for International Policy [online], 1996.

44. "Gobiernos se Reunen para Alentar Cooperación," International Press Service, April 2, 1996.

45. *Cuba Handbook of Trade Statistics, 1997*, 3–7.

46. "Mexico-Cuba Ferry Service Eyed," *Miami Herald*, March 13, 1998.

47. Joseph S. Tulchin, "Introduction," in *Cuba and the Caribbean: Regional Issues and Trends in the Post–Cold War Era*, ed. Joseph S. Tulchin, Andrés Serbon, and Rafael Hernández (Wilmington, Del.: SR Books, 1997), xiv–xv.

48. "Shortly before his departure, Keith Mitchell, the prime minister of Grenada, affirmed that his country's relations with Cuba would be totally different as a result of his visit. At the conclusion of his official trip to the island, Mitchell was honored by the Revolutionary Armed Forces' ceremonial unit, and was seen off by President Fidel Castro." Orlando Oramas León, *Granma International*, May 7, 1997, 15.

49. Upon the visit to Havana by Jamaican prime minister Percival Patterson, Castro said: "It is concrete actions like these that truly help to achieve integration . . . It is an honor to be a comrade in arms of men like him . . . I feel my affinity and affection for him grow." Castro recalled that "when no country in the hemisphere, except Mexico and Canada, dared to establish relations with Cuba, it was the Caribbean nations which broke the isolation." The Cuban media reported that "[Percival] Patterson had announced publicly to President Clinton [Jamaica's support for Cuba's integration in CARICOM] during the recent summit in Barbados" and that Jamaica had "traditionally voted for the Cuban resolutions against the U.S. in the U.N. General Assembly." "Real Results Evident in the Signing of Four Accords between Jamaica and Cuba" and Orlando Oramas León, "From Jamaica, A Friend," *Granma International*, June 8, 1997, 3.

50. "Real Results Evident in the Signing of Four Accords," 3.

51. Orlando Oramas, "Cuban-Caribbean Relations Closing the Distance," *Granma* [online, http://www.granma.cu], July 18, 1997; "CARICOM Delays Decision on Free Trade With Cuba," *CubaINFO* 9 (July 1997): 4–5; "International: CARICOM Improves Ties," *CUBANEWS* 5 (July 1997): 5; and Luis Melián, "New Stage of Relations with Jamaica," *Granma International*, June 1, 1997, 1.

52. Rodolfo Casals, "1998 Convention to Accentuate Commercial and Caribbean Character," *Granma International* [online, http://www.granma.cu], February 27, 1998; "Caribbean: A Single Destination," *Granma International*, May 16, 1999, 8–9.

53. "Caribbean-Regional Group Backs EU Benefits for Cuba," *Miami Herald*, March 19, 1998.

54. "Spain's New Cuba Policy Beginning to Unfold," *CubaINFO* 8 (June 1996): 6–7.

55. "Cuba Reneges Approval of New Spanish Ambassador," *CubaINFO* 8 (December 1996): 5–6.

56. Katherine Ellison, "Castro Rebuffs Latin Summit Reforms Pleas," *Miami Herald*, November 12, 1996.

57. "John Paul II Accepts Invitation to Visit Cuba," *Granma International*, November 27, 1996, 1.

58. "Spain's Naming of Envoy to Cuba May Ease Tension," Agence France Presse, April 2, 1998.

59. "When Ralph Waldo Emerson famously observed that 'consistency is a stranger to great minds,' he must have had forewarning of the Clinton Administration's human rights policy. Certainly, its decisions over the past week display a charmingly haphazard pattern. Over China, Southeast Asia, Bosnia and the Caspian Sea [and Cuba], the administration has reached openly inconsistent positions. A great mind, it seems, must be at work." Jonathan Clarke, "If U.S. Seeks to Stand Up for Human Rights, We Can't Play Favorites," *Erie (Pa.) Morning News*, August 9, 1997, 2B.

60. "Aznar Reafirma que se Mantendrá Firme con Cuba," Agence France Presse, July 9, 1997.

61. "Castro Invited to EU Summit," *CubaINFO* 9 (April 1997): 6.

62. In reality, the first conference of this kind was held in 1978 in Havana. The so-called Dialogue Conference was followed up by two more soon afterward in order to negotiate the release of most of those in political prison at the time. But it was not until 1994 that another conference like this would be held.

63. For an insightful analysis from an economic perspective of Cuba's opening to external exchange policy, see Elena C. Álvarez González, "Características de la Apertura Externa Cubana," 19th Latin American Studies Association Congress, Washington, D.C., 1995.

64. Milagros Martínez Reinosa and Jorge Hernández Martínez, "Algunas Facetas de la Emigración Cubana," New York: NY Transfer News Collective [online, http://www.blythe.org], 1996, 1–7.

65. Guillermo Grenier, Hugh Gladwin, and Douglas MacLaughen, "The 1995 FIU Cuba Poll: Views on Policy Options Held by Cuban-American Residents of Dade County, Florida, and Union City, New Jersey," (Miami: Florida International University, 1995), 1–18.

66. Ibid., 1–2.

67. See Ernesto Rodríguez, "La Crisis Migratoria Estados Unidos-Cuba en el Verano de 1994," in *Migración Cubana: Crisis de los Balseros en el Verano de 1994* (Albuquerque: Centro de Estudios Sobre América and New Mexico University, n.d.), 1–22.

68. Martínez Reinosa and Hernández Martínez, "Algunas Facetas de la Emigración Cubana," 2–4.

69. "Si se Puede: Democracia Participativa," *Contrapunto* 8 (May 1997): 3–6; Amalio Fiallo, *Hacia una Democracia Participativa* (Caracas, Venezuela: PH Editorial, 1996).

70. "Mejor no Reunirse con Castro," EFE, October 28, 1999; "EE.UU. Advierte que no Suspenderá Embargo a Cuba," Associated Press, October 28, 1999. The State Department announced in 1999 that "in a bid to help Americans understand the maze of rules and regulations governing travel to Cuba, the U.S. embargo against the island and related issues, [it had] unveiled a new web site focus[ing] exclusively on Cuba." George Gedda, "New Web Site Explains Rules on Cuba," Associated Press, November 7, 1999. The web site address is: http://www.state.gov/www/regions/wha/cuba/index.html.

Chapter 11. The Pope's Cuban Pilgrimage

1. "Church people from abroad visiting Cuba in the late 1960s and early 1970s regarded the churches as being in a transition period in which there were some tentative attempts to reconcile religious beliefs with an increasingly institutionalized revolution. One U.S. Protestant felt that the government's attitude toward the churches was positive and that active Christians did not run afoul of the government unless they were counterrevolutionaries. Rabbi Everett Gendler, who visited Cuba in 1969, felt that those Christians and Jews who were recognized as making positive contributions to Cuban society did not suffer discrimination except by 'sectarian' Communists, who he felt were outnumbered by 'liberal' Communists." In response to allegations of discrimination against practicing Catholics, Castro told a delegation of three U.S. Catholic bishops in 1985 that "pressure against Catholics was not part of Cuban government policy . . . however, [he admitted] that historical circumstances could result in discrimination." Still, the bishops concluded that "improved communication between the Catholic church and the Castro government was a 'real cause of hope'." A Protestant leader stated at the time that "relations with the government have never been better." Margaret E. Graham, "Freedom of Worship in Revolutionary Cuba," in *The Cuba Reader: The Making of a Revolutionary Society,* ed. P. Brenner, W. M. LeoGrande, D. Rich, and D. Siegel (New York: Grove Press, 1989), 211–19.

2. Robin Blackburn, "Themes of the Cuban Revolution," in Brenner et al., *The Cuba Reader*, 42–58, quote at 46.

3. John M. Kirk, *Between God and the Party: Religion and Politics in Revolutionary Cuba* (Tampa: University of South Florida Press, 1989), 102–5, passim.

4. Monsignor Eduardo Boza Másvidal was able to return later to Cuba for short visits, including the pope's five-day pilgrimage.

5. Kirk, *Between God and the Party*, 103.

6. Juan O. Tamayo, "Cubans Flock to Religion's Comforting Arms," *Miami Herald*, November 11, 1997.

7. Before the 1959 revolution Cubans were overwhelmingly Catholic but perhaps more in appearance than in practical reality. Today, Professor Enrique López Oliva, a Havana University religion expert, estimates that there are 650 Catholic churches and 900 Protestant churches in Cuba, with attendance higher at the latter. "Cuba: Other Christians," Associated Press, January 8, 1998. Havana's Martin Luther King Memorial Center promotes religious social activism and reflection and publishes *Caminos*, a journal dedicated to sociotheological thought. Some issues include articles by American social scientist Noam Chomsky, Brazilian theologian Leonardo Boff, and former Cuban foreign minister Roberto Robaina.

8. Leslie Wirpsa, "Catholic Cubans Nurture New Freedoms," *National Catholic Reporter*, July 4, 1997, 16–17.

9. Ibid.

10. Ibid.

11. Ibid.

12. "A group of [four] U.S. Democratic Congressmen in Cuba for Pope John Paul II's visit said they had found a 'mellower' President Fidel Castro and reiterated their opposition to Washington's 35-year-old economic embargo . . . 'He was much more laid-back than last time we met two years ago, though no less committed to the revolution,' Massachusetts Democrat Jim McGovern told Reuters . . . [The four U.S. congressmen] held a rare meeting for U.S. politicians with Castro for about two hours [on January 23] . . . McGovern, speaking on behalf of the group, quoted Castro as saying that the Roman Catholic Church was gaining space on the communist island . . . 'One of the questions we asked him [Castro] was whether religion was growing on the island and his response was that this was correct,' McGovern said . . . He added that their conversation ranged from theology to U.S. politics. 'With a man like that, you talk about everything,' he said . . . Also present at the meeting were Osvaldo Paya, leader of the Christian Movement, and Manuel Cuesta, of the Democratic Socialist Group, two of Cuba's small and illegal dissident organizations . . . McGovern said the dissidents were 'very much committed to internal reform and an end to the U.S. embargo on Cuba'." Andrew Cawthorne, "U.S. Congressmen Meet 'Mellower' Castro," Reuters, January 25, 1998. Obviously, an important aspect of the two-hour meeting of Castro and the four U.S. congressmen was the presence of two representatives of domestic dissident groups. Paya and Cuesta must have been with the four American legislators

when they met President Castro, and under such circumstances they could not have been asked to leave. The encounter seems more a signal of how relaxed the mood was during the pope's visit than of the possibility of a political opening for dissident groups in the near future.

13. "We Must Receive the Pope as a Man Who Is Concerned about Many Major Problems in the World Today," *Granma International*, January 25, 1998, 1, 4–6.

14. As Castro told a Brazilian Dominican friar, "As a political principle, respect for believers is right, because we live in a world with many believers, and confrontations between revolutions and religious believers aren't advisable. When they take place, the reaction and imperialism may use religious beliefs as a weapon against the revolutions . . . I feel that every citizen's right to his own beliefs should be respected, along with his rights to health, life and freedom and all other rights. That is, I believe that the individual has the inalienable right to have or not to have his own philosophical ideas or religious beliefs . . . [This is] not just a question of political tactics." Frei Betto, *Fidel and Religion: Talks with Frei Betto* (Havana: Publications Office of the Council of State, 1987), 232.

15. James R. Willems, "The Practice of Consciousness," *Religious Socialism* 17 (summer 1993): 1, 8–10.

16. "The Israeli government has broken years of silence about a secret operation that brought four hundred Cuban Jews to Israel over the past five years. . . . Cubans have been trickling into Tel Aviv's Ben Gurion Airport since 1995, the resettling in Israeli immigration centers . . . with other Jews from Ethiopia, Chechnya and Yemen. . . . Secrecy was a major component of the deal between Fidel Castro's government and the Jewish Agency for Israel, an organization that resettles Jews in Israel." "Quiet Exodus of Cuban Jews to Israel," *CubaINFO* 11 (October 27, 1999): 5–6. However, according to Dr. José Miller Freedman, president of the Cuban Jewish Community, "There is no sentiment against the Jewish people [in Cuba], either among the population or in the government. Neither is there any secret pact to 'rescue' Jews by sending them to Israel; that's a total lie. Those who wish to leave the island can do so, just like any [other] Cuban citizens who fulfill the immigration and exit requirements of the nations concerned." *Granma International*, October 31, 1999, 4.

17. Cuba's Jaime Cardinal Ortega referred to the impact that the pope's itinerary could have on his health: "His years weigh on him more than on others . . . a trip like this is a great effort, to change time zones, to move from one place to another . . . [after having] suffered from illness." "Cuban Cardinal Cites Pope's Health," Associated Press, January 10, 1998.

The pope's visit to Cuba was indeed demanding. It included traveling long distances to say mass in four cities: Santa Clara, Camagüey, Santiago de Cuba (mass and coronation of Cuba's patron saint, the Virgin of Charity of el Cobre), and the Plaza of the Revolution in Havana (facing a mural of Che Guevara that is permanently on display across from José Martí's monument; behind the altar was an eight-floor mural of Jesus Christ especially built for the occasion). In addition, the pope paid a courtesy visit to President Castro at the Palace of the Revolution; visited both the monument housing the remains of Father Félix Varela at Havana University and the Sanctuary of San Lázaro in El Rincón, province of Havana; met with the Conference of Catholic Bishops of Cuba at the archbishopric; and conducted a liturgical celebration at Havana's cathedral. "Itinerary for Visit by Pope John Paul II," *Granma International*, December 21, 1997, 7.

18. Larry Rohter, "Cuba and Church Keep Maneuvering over Pope's Visit," *New York Times*, January 19, 1998, A1, A6.

19. Reportedly, in late 1997 the pope's visit was almost called off by Rome: "A Madrid newspaper reported that angry Vatican officials had briefly threatened to cancel the trip after a bugging device was found in a house where the pope was scheduled to rest." Havana explained that this was not its doing, that the bugging device dated from the pre-revolutionary Batista period. "The Battle for Cuba's Soul," *Newsweek*, January 19, 1998, 36–37.

20. *Granma International*, December 21, 1997, 21; and December 28, 1997, 1, 3–6. It was reported that "when Pope John Paul II steps onto this communist-ruled island . . . he will find that the church and the government have set aside mutual suspicions and occasional enmity for the sake of their institutional interests . . . Catholic leaders hope the Pope's presence will galvanize believers in Cuba and help broaden the church's influence among the country's 11 million people . . . Fidel Castro's government, meanwhile, hopes a successful papal visit will enhance its image abroad and demonstrate its tolerance for religion. A windfall from the visit would be a papal denunciation of the longtime U.S. economic embargo of Cuba." Associated Press, December 13, 1997. Cuba also profited financially from the pope's visit: "'From commemorative cigars to jacked-up prices for hotels and services, Cuba is preparing to reap a huge financial windfall from Pope John Paul II's upcoming visit' . . . 'This will be more than pennies from heaven. It'll be millions from heaven,' said [a] Montreal travel agent . . . who books Canadians on vacations to the island' . . . 'A rock-bottom estimate by the New York–based U.S.-Cuba Trade and Economic Council put Havana's potential income from the papal visit at $20 million, and acknowledged it had not covered all incidentals'." Juan O. Tamayo, "Cuba's Papal Windfall," *Miami Herald*, January 11, 1998. The pope's visit to Cuba caused division and controversy among Cuban Americans. A cruise ship sponsored by the Archdiocese of Miami and capable of carrying up to a thousand passengers was canceled by Archbishop John C. Favalora in response to objections from Cuban-American Catholics (more than four hundred people had bought tickets on the cruise ship by then). In its place, a more modest pilgrimage was organized using a charter jet with capacity for 180 people. "'We have been overwhelmed with calls,' said the Rev. Patrick O'Neill, who [was] organizing the Miami trip. 'I've been here since the crack of dawn.'" Christopher Marquis and April Witt, "Flight to Cuba for Pope's Visit Filling Up Fast," *Miami Herald*, January 8, 1998. In the end six Catholic pilgrimages went to Cuba from Miami, Tampa, La Place (Louisiana), Boston, and Puerto Rico, carrying eleven hundred people, many of them Cuban Americans. Eddie Domínguez, "Cuban Exiles Become Pilgrims during Papal Visit," Associated Press, January 17, 1998.

21. Castro made clear to the National Assembly the risks the government was taking, given the country's international exposure during the pope's visit: "A great many journalists have asked to come. Suffice it to say that one of the U.S. networks has requested accommodation for 200 television workers; another also asked for that much, for positions all over the place, here, there, on the route, in Santiago, everywhere. I think five of the important U.S. networks are coming. As far as we know over 1000 journalists have been accredited [reportedly 3000 international journalists]. A great amount of attention is going to be focused on the country during the time of the visit and, naturally, we are interested in all that is said internationally on this subject." *Granma International*, December 28, 1997, 3–6.

22. Rohter, "Cuba and Church Keep Maneuvering over Pope's Visit," A6.

23. Jim Hoagland, "On the Foreign Policy Horizon," *Washington Post Weekly Edition*, January 22, 1998, 5.

24. David Briggs, "Papal Trip: Defining Moment for Exiles," Associated Press, January 18, 1998.

25. Ibid.

26. "Pope's Visit Stirs Emotions, Provokes Conflicting Views," *CubaINFO* 10 (January 1998): 2–3, "Pope's Visit to Cuba," *CUBANEWS* 6 (January 1998): 1–2. For a critical evaluation of how the U.S. media reported the pope's visit, see "Pope's Visit through the U.S. Media Lens," *Cuba Update* (April 1998): 9–19; for various anti-Castro views of the historic event, see "The Pope in Cuba, The Response to Date," *Cuba Brief* (Spring 1998): 5–22.

27. "'It is a marriage of convenience, not conviction,' says a religious scholar in Havana. 'The pope and Fidel need each other, but for their own agendas'." Brook Larmer, "The Battle for Cuba's Soul," *Newsweek*, January 19, 1998, 36–44, quote at 40.

28. John Rice, "Cuban Officials Skeptical that Pope Can Improve U.S.-Cuba Relations," Associated Press, January 19, 1998.

29. Rohter, "Cuba and Church Keep Maneuvering over Pope's Visit," A6.

30. Rice, "Cuban Officials Skeptical that Pope Can Improve U.S.-Cuba Relations."

31. Leslie Wirpsa, "Catholic Cubans Nurture New Freedoms," 16–17. See also "Fidel Describes Meeting with the Pope as Special," *Granma International*, December 4, 1996, 15.

32. David Briggs, "Papal Visit Expected to Have Lasting Impact on Religious Freedom in Cuba," Associated Press, January 17, 1998.

33. "Cuban Catholic Church Praises Fidel's Meeting with the Pope," *Granma International*, December 4, 1996, 15.

34. "Pope's Words: Family and Responsibility," *New York Times*, January 22, 1998, A9.

35. Ibid.

36. "Excerpts from the Greeting of the Rev. Pedro Meurice Estiú, the Archbishop of Santiago," *Miami Herald*, January 25, 1998. "It was the sharpest and most direct criticism ever heard in revolutionary Cuba. People in the audience looked at each other in disbelief. 'What did he say?' asked a woman who admitted being a

member of the Communist Party. Some people in the audience, especially Catholic activists, applauded. Others discreetly left the plaza. An earthy mulatto woman left rapidly saying, 'I am leaving, just in case.' At times, the tension could be felt as strongly as the terrible heat of the hot sunny day, which seemed to be melting the Polish Pope." Mauricio Vicent, "Misa en la Cuna de la Revolución," *El País*, January 25, 1998.

A few days later, the National Assembly President Ricardo Alarcón deplored Archbishop Estiú's remarks, saying that they were "reminiscent of a regrettable period when many clerics held an antipatriotic attitude . . . [However] during that period [the 1950s] there were Catholic voices that denounced the crimes committed by the dictatorship of Fulgencio Batista in Santiago de Cuba." Spokesmen for the archbishops of Havana and of Santiago stated that there was no official or unofficial response from the government regarding Archbishop Estiú's statement at the pope's mass in Santiago. "Alarcón: Las Críticas de Monseñor Meurice 'Recuerdan Una Época Lamentable,'" Agence France Presse, January 27, 1998. Archbishop Pedro Meurice Estiú's adversarial dichotomy of Catholics vs. Marxists resembles a request for help for Cuban Catholics made in April 1936 by an American Catholic publication: "We cannot overemphasize the need of assisting our Cuban brothers. Unless American Catholics show interest, Cuban Catholics will turn to those only too willing to help them, namely the Marxists." As cited in Jeremy Scahill, "Advent of the Cuban Church," *Catholic Worker*, January–February 1998, 1, 7.

37. Larry Rohter, "Pope Asks Cubans to Seek New Path Toward Freedom," *New York Times*, January 26, 1998, A1, A8.

38. Ibid.

39. "A 43-year old physician and long-time human rights advocate, Dr. [Dessi] Mendoza was arrested last summer after publicizing an outbreak of dengue fever, a painful tropical disease. The indictment against him contends he did so with 'the intention of creating uncertainty, confusion and panic in the Cuban population,' an accusation his wife dismissed as absurd. 'He was acting according to his conscience in his dual capacity as doctor and defender of human rights,' Dr. Piñon Rodríguez, 34, who is also a physician, said in an interview." Larry Rohter, "Jailed Cuban's Wife Pins Hopes on Pope's Words," *New York Times*, January 30, 1998, A7.

40. A spokesman for the foreign ministry announced that the government intended to "free 'more than 200 inmates' held on political and other charges." Cuba would "pardon 'several dozen' prisoners whose names were on a list that the Vatican's Secretary of State, Angelo Cardinal Solano, gave to Cuban authorities during the Pope's visit [in January] . . . [and] scores of other prisoners [would also be released] on humanitarian grounds," said the spokesman. Larry Rohter, "Cuba Announces That It Will Free 200 in Bow to the Pope," *New York Times*, February 13, 1998, A1, A9. "Cuba said yesterday it had freed 299 prisoners, including more than 70 political detainees, in response to a clemency appeal from Pope John Paul II last month, but a Foreign Ministry spokesman would not confirm whether the par-

dons included well-known political dissidents whose release had been sought by several foreign governments and international human rights organizations. Spokesman Alejandro González denied media reports that the Cuban government had not freed all of the nearly 300 prisoners it announced a week ago would be pardoned. He said the 299 freed were all those included in an official pardon approved February 12." "Cuba Frees 299 in Response to Pope's Appeal," *Washington Post*, February 20, 1998, A20.

41. "Pope John Paul II, Castro Texts," Associated Press, January 25, 1998.

42. Ibid.

43. Nonetheless, President Clinton received unexpected support from President Castro on the sex scandal that rocked the White House starting the same day that the pope arrived in Cuba, January 21, 1998. "Fidel Castro wished President Clinton luck today in overcoming problems linked to allegations he had an affair with a White House intern, blaming Senator Jesse Helms for fomenting the scandal." Castro was reported as saying: "I think the actions are really dirty . . . It's a real example of the things that occur in that country, of the lack of ethics." (It was reported that Senator Helms had been instrumental in having Kenneth W. Starr appointed as independent counsel handling the case.) "Castro-Clinton," Associated Press, February 3, 1998; and Francis X. Clines, "First Lady Attributes Inquiry to 'Right-Wing Conspiracy,'" *New York Times*, January 28, 1998, A1, A22.

44. Frances Kerry, "Castro Says Furious 'No' to U.S. Aid Plan," Reuters, February 3, 1998; Anita Snow, "Castro Thanks Cuba for Pope's Visit," Associated Press, February 3, 1998.

45. "Politics—Cuba. Guatemala Answers the Pope's Call," International Press Service, January 30, 1998; "Venezuelan Businessmen Demand End of Cuban Embargo," *XINHUA* (China), January 29, 1998.

46. "Now comes the hard part. With Pope John Paul II back in Rome after a five-day visit, responsibility for carrying out his call for Catholics to play a larger role in Cuban society falls to a local church whose mission has been severely circumscribed under Communism for nearly 40 years." Larry Rohter, "After the Visit: Mission Lies Now with Cuban Church," *New York Times*, January 27, 1998, A3. "'What happened here in Cuba was a true miracle of God,' said Roberto González, 42, a lifelong Catholic . . . 'The religious culture in Cuba always has been very poor and we must change that'." "Pope Strengthens Cuban Church," Associated Press, February 2, 1998.

47. "[Former] Cuban Foreign Minister Roberto Robaina said on Wednesday people abroad were trying to 'politicize' Pope John Paul's visit to the island this month but it was first and foremost a religious event." Frances Kerry, "Don't Read Politics into Pope's Visit—Cuban Minister," Reuters, January 8, 1998.

48. "'The church is the ultimate sanctuary, the last redoubt of freedom,' says Dagoberto Valdés, the editor of *Vitral*, a magazine of independent—and occasionally critical—ideas . . . [Of all Church sponsored publications, it is] the most troublesome to the Castro government . . . Valdés, a lay Catholic, delivers most of

the 2,000 copies of the bimonthly on bicycle. But its articles talk about the need for a civil society not so different from the ones nurtured by dissidents in Eastern Europe. More prickly yet: Valdés has established the Center for Civic and Religious Formation, a series of workshops on ethics and politics which he says 'plants the seeds of democracy'." Larmer, "The Battle for Cuba's Soul," 43.

49. Ibid., 42.

50. "In a recent pastoral letter, the Cuban Conference of Bishops declared, 'The action of the church in society is not limited to the free exercise of worship'." According to Cardinal Ortega, the Church's main challenge after the pope's visit would be "a dialogue with the state that has yet to start seriously, and which did not advance during the year of preparation for the papal visit." Rohter, "Cuba and Church Keep Maneuvering over Pope's Visit," A6.

51. Mark Fineman, "Cardinal Ortega Emerges as a Political Leader in Havana," *Los Angeles Times*, January 18, 1998.

52. Ibid.

53. "About 4.7 million of all 11 million Cubans are baptized, but only about 150,000 attend Sunday mass. (There are about 1 million active Protestants, and a much greater number—roughly 6 to 7 million—who practice Afro-Cuban religions.)" Larmer, "The Battle for Cuba's Soul," 42.

54. Juan O. Tamayo, "In Cuba, A Clash between Religions—Afro-Cuban Creeds, Catholics at Odds," *Miami Herald*, January 12, 1998.

55. "Pope: Afro-Cuban Cults Not Religion," Associated Press, January 25, 1998.

56. "You Should Not Expect a Miracle," *Time*, January 26, 1998: 34.

57. "Dissidents: 'Church Has Spoken for Us,'" *Miami Herald*, January 25, 1998.

58. Angus MacSwan, "Cuban Exiles Cheer, Weep at Pope's Words," Reuters, January 25, 1998.

59. Fabiola Santiago, "Sister Parishes in South Florida and Cuba? Archdiocese Discussed It with Island's Bishops," *Miami Herald*, March 15, 1998.

60. Serge F. Kovaleski, "Castro, Catholic Church Both Appear to Gain from John Paul's Visit," *Washington Post*, January 26, 1998, A18.

61. Ibid.

62. "Pope Calls Cuban Clerics to Vatican," *CubaINFO* 10 (June 1998): 6–7.

63. Rachel L. Swarns, "Cuba's Protestant Churches: A Growing Flock," *New York Times*, January 29, 1998, A1, A8.

64. David Briggs, "Papal Visit to Cuba Was Ecumenical Awakening," Associated Press, February 14, 1998.

65. Celestine Bohlen, "Pope Captivates His Marxist Host," *New York Times*, January 26, 1998, A9.

66. William Drozdiak, "John Paul Voices Hope for Repeat of History: Pontiff Evokes Cuba-Poland Parallel," *Washington Post*, January 29, 1998, A21.

67. Larmer, "The Battle for Cuba's Soul," 37.

68. The pope's remarks to a group of his countrymen visiting the Vatican likening Cuba to Poland could have been given a different meaning than what was

intended, especially once they were quoted out of context. The media had been looking for signals of conflict between Cuba and the Vatican, or more directly between Castro and the pope, during the latter's visit to the island. The three anchormen of America's major television networks returned to the United States immediately after the pope's arrival to cover the then breaking White House sex scandal story involving President Clinton. Their sudden departure from Cuba could be seen as an admission that the pope's visit was not turning into the kind of (conflict) news that so many had expected. For a Cuban perspective on this issue see, Gabriel Molina, "The Pope's Voyage to Cuba: The Charges against Clinton Were a Pretext to Detract from the Visit's Importance," *Granma International,* February 15, 1998, 4.

69. Kelly Velásquez, "Derrota del Régimen Cubano 'Mezquina Esperanza' del Papa: Teólogos de la Liberación," Agence France Presse, February 17, 1998.

70. "Fidel Meets with Bishops and Other Representatives of United Methodist Church," *Granma International,* February 22, 1998, 4.

71. "Cuban Bishops Call for 'Positive Dialogue,'" *Miami Herald,* February 21, 1998.

72. Ibid.

Chapter 12. Reinventing Cuban Socialism

1. "[Dialectics] is possibly the most contentious topic in Marxist thought . . . The most common emphases of the concept in the Marxist tradition are as (a) a method, most usually scientific method, instancing epistemological dialectics; (b) a set of values or principles, governing some sectors of the whole of reality, ontological dialectics; and (c) the movement of history, relational dialectics [the main concern for us here]. All three are to be found in Marx." T. Bottomore, L. Harris, V. G. Kiernan, and R. Miliband, eds. *A Dictionary of Marxist Thought* (Cambridge: Harvard University Press, 1983), 122, 126.

2. Robert S. Greenberger, "Cuba's Troubles Look Worse than Ever," *The Wall Street Journal,* June 26, 1991: A4.

3. Saul Landau, "Is Fidel Washed Up?" *Progressive,* August 1992, 17–23, quote at 18.

4. William E. Deibler, "Cuba's Dark Days Growing Darker," *Pittsburgh Post-Gazette,* August 12, 1993, A1, A8.

5. Gordon, "Cuba's Entrepreneurial Socialism," 18.

6. Ibid., 20.

7. Booth, "Here Come the Yummies," 42.

8. Ibid.

9. Ariel Terreiro, "¿Crisis del Marxismo?" *Bohemia,* September 9, 1991, 26–29.

10. Isabel Monal, "La Huella y la Fragua: El Marxismo, Cuba y el Fin de Siglo"; Fernando Martínez Heredia, "Izquierda y Marxismo en Cuba"; Joaquín Santana Carrillo, "Algunos Problemas de la Filosofía Marxista y Su Enseñanza en Cuba";

Aurelio Alonso Tejada, "Marxismo y Espacio de Debate en la Revolución Cubana"; Olivia Miranda, "El Marxismo en el Ideal Emancipador Cubano durante la República Neocolonial," in the special issue titled "La Cultura Marxista en Cuba," *Temas* 3 (July–September 1995): 4–57. See also articles by Marta Pérez-Rolo, Juan Antonio Blanco, Miguel Lima, Delia Luisa López, and Jonathan Quirós in a 1998 series of features under the overall title "Controversia—El Socialismo y el Hombre en Cuba: Una Mirada en los 90," *Temas* 11 (1998): 104–19.

11. Sidney Verba, "Comparative Political Culture," in *Political Culture and Political Development*, ed. Lucian W. Pye and Sidney Verba (Princeton: Princeton University Press, 1965), 516. "Political culture, conceptualized roughly, is the pattern of distribution of orientations members of a political community have towards politics. This patterned collectivity of orientations influences the structure, operation, and stability of political life." Richard E. Dawson and Kenneth Prewitt, *Political Socialization* (Boston: Little, Brown, 1969), 27.

12. Regarding the socialization (normative teaching/learning process communicating political value messages) and the transformation of cultural orientations toward the old and the new political systems: "Political socialization shapes and transmits a nation's political culture. More specifically, political socialization maintains a nation's political culture insofar as it transmits that culture from old to new constituencies. It [could also] transform the political culture insofar as it leads the population or part of it, to view and experience politics differently from the way they did previously." Dawson and Prewitt, *Political Socialization*, 27.

13. Tzvi Medin, *Cuba: The Shaping of Revolutionary Consciousness* (Boulder, Colo.: Lynne Rienner, 1990), 167.

14. Julie Marie Bunck, *Fidel Castro and the Quest for a Revolutionary Culture in Cuba* (University Park: Pennsylvania State University Press, 1994), 3–4.

15. Ibid., 215.

16. "Rethinking the Revolution," *NACLA Report on the Americas* 29 (September–October 1995): Humberto Solás, 24–25; Guillermo Rodríguez Rivera, 26–27; Gerardo González, 32; Miguel Barnet, 33.

17. Baéz, "Entrevista a Raúl Castro: Si Hay Comida Para el Pueblo," B16–23.

18. Juan O. Tamayo, "U.N. Panel Puts Cuba on Rights Abusers' List," *Miami Herald*, April 24, 1999.

19. See "Historic Defeat by United States in Geneva," *Granma International*, May 3, 1998, 3 (online, http://www.granma.cu), and Tamayo, "U.N. Panel Puts Cuba on Rights Abusers' List."

20. Mirta Rodríguez Calderón, "Derechos Humanos: ONG Cubanas en Viena," *Bohemia*, July 9, 1993: B32–35.

21. Graciela Chailloux Laffita, "Cuba: Organizaciones Sociales, ONGs y Política Exterior," 19th International Latin American Studies Association Congress, Washington, D.C., 1995, 15. For a different viewpoint, see Gillian Gunn, "Cuban NGOs: Government Puppets or Seeds of Civil Society?" *Cuba Briefing Paper Series* no. 7 (Georgetown University, 1995).

22. Clarke, "If the U.S. Seeks to Stand Up for Human Rights, We Can't Play Favorites."

23. For a discussion of the U.S.-Cuba problematic and the changing charges justifying it, see Max Azicri, "Cuba and the United States: What Happened to Rapprochement?" in *The New Cuban Presence in the Caribbean*, ed. Barry B. Levine (Boulder, Colo.: Westview Press, 1983), 183, 189–90.

24. Ernesto Rodríguez Chavez and Jorge Hernández Martínez, "De la Campaña Acerca de las Supuestas Violaciones de los Derechos Humanos Hacia una Alternativa de Poder Político para la Revolución," in Ernesto Rodríguez Chavez, ed. *Cuba: Derechos Humanos* (Havana: Editorial José Martí, 1991), 234–35.

25. Ibid., 262.

26. The American delegation included William J. Butler, president of the American Association for the International Commission of Jurists; Norman Dorsen, professor of law at New York University; Thomas Farer, professor of law and international relations at American University; Christian Herter, Jr., professor of law at Johns Hopkins University; Ralph G. Steinhardt, professor of law at George Washington University; and Nita R. Manitzas and Wayne S. Smith of the Center for International Policy. The Cuban delegation included Miguel Alfonso, Higher Institute of International Relations; Hugo Azcuy, Center for the Study of the Americas (CEA); Lázaro Barredo, vice president of the International Relations Committee of the National Assembly; Jorge Bodés, justice of the Supreme Court; Ramón de la Cruz, former attorney general; Julio Fernández Bulté, professor of law at Havana University; Rafael Hernández, CEA; Arnel Medina, president of the National Union of Jurists; Luis Suárez, then director of CEA; and Luis Toledo, dean of the Havana University School of Law. Wayne S. Smith, "Human Rights in Cuba: Initiating the Dialogue," *International Policy Report*, September 1995, 1, 2.

27. Ibid., 1–7.

28. See, among other reports, Americas Watch, *Tightening the Grip, Human Rights Abuses in Cuba*, 1992, 1, 4; Human Rights Watch, Americas, *Cuba: Repression, the Exodus of August 1994 and the U.S. Response*, 1994, 6, 12, and *Cuba: Improvements without Reform*, 1995, 7, 10; Amnesty International, *Cuba: Dissidents Imprisoned or Forced into Exile*, 1996; Inter-American Commission on Human Rights, Organization of American States, *Annual Report of the Inter-American Commission on Human Rights, 1996* (Washington, D.C.: OAS General Secretariat, 1997). For violations of human rights in Miami, Florida, see Human Rights Watch, Americas, *Dangerous Dialogue: Attacks on Freedom of Expression in Miami's Cuban Exile Community*, August 1992, 6, 7.

29. Smith, "Human Rights in Cuba," 6.

30. José Portuondo, "Literature and Society," in *Latin America in Literature*, ed. Cesar Fernández Moreno et al. (New York: Holmes and Meier, 1980), 287–88.

31. E. Lucie-Smith, *Art of the 1930s: The Age of Anxiety* (New York: Rizzoli International Publications, 1985), 44–65, quote at 53. For a discussion of cultural and artistic disagreements between artists and writers and the government in the early

years of the Cuban revolution, see Lourdes Casal, *El Caso Padilla: Literatura y Revolución en Cuba* (Miami: Ediciones Universal, n.d.). For a discussion of the revolutionary government's cultural policy, see Armando Hart, *Del Trabajo Cultural: Selección de Discursos* (Havana: Editorial de Ciencias Sociales, 1978), and *Política Cultural de la Revolución Cubana: Documentos* (Havana: Editorial de Ciencias Sociales, 1977).

32. "Castro Meets with Cuban Artists after Criticizing Popular Film," *CubaINFO* 10 (March 1998): 8.

33. J. L. Talmon, *The Origins of Totalitarian Democracy* (New York: Praeger, 1961).

34. Nicolás Guillén, "Tengo," in his *Antología Mayor* (Mexico City: Editorial Diógenes, 1972): 251–2, quote at 252.

35. Liss, *Roots of Revolution: Radical Thought in Cuba*, xvii–xviii.

36. Nelson Valdés, "Cuban Political Culture: Between Betrayal and Death," in Halebsky and Kirk, *Cuba in Transition*, 207–8.

37. Liss, *Fidel! Castro's Political and Social Thought*.

38. Ibid., 1.

39. For a contrary view claiming that the American media is responsible for presenting a benign image of Castro to the American public, see William E. Ratliff, ed. *The Selling of Fidel Castro: The Media and the Cuban Revolution* (New Brunswick, N.J.: Transaction Books, 1987).

40. Among others, see Peter G. Bourne, *Fidel: A Biography of Fidel Castro* (New York: Dodd, Mead, 1986); Tad Szulc, *Fidel: A Critical Portrait* (New York: William Morrow, 1986); Georgie Anne Geyer, *Guerrilla Prince: The Untold Story of Fidel Castro* (Boston: Little, Brown, 1991).

41. Organizations such as Freedom House, the Cuban American National Foundation (CANF), and others are constantly pouring out and distributing anti-Castro materials, which are usually mailed free to a wide audience. A sample of Cuban exiles' publications denouncing Castro and the Cuban government includes Reinol González, *Y Fidel Creo el Punto X: Un Testimonio Revelador sobre el Régimen de Castro* (Miami and Caracas: Saeta Ediciones, 1987); Angel Cuadra, *The Poet in Socialist Cuba* (Gainesville: University Press of Florida, 1994); *El Presidio Político en Cuba Comunista: Testimonio* (Caracas, Venezuela: ICOSOVOC, 1982); José Sainz de la Peña, . . . *Y Castro Quedo Atras: Memorias de un Desterrado* (Buenos Aires, Argentina: Editorial Lectorum, 1970); Mario Lazo, *American Policy Failures in Cuba: Dagger in the Heart* (New York: Funk and Wagnalls, 1968); Jaime Carbonell Vice, *La Verdad de la Revolución de Castro* (Barcelona, Spain: Talleres Gráficos A. Estrada, n.d.); Manuel Urrutia, *Fidel Castro y Compañia, S.A.* (Barcelona, Spain: Editorial Herder, 1963); José Luis Massó, *Cuba R.S.S.* (Miami: Casablanca Printing, 1964); Agustín Tamargo, *Furias e Improperios* (San Juan, Puerto Rico: Editorial San Juan, 1972); Bernardo Viera Trejo, *Militantes del Odio: Y Otros Relatos de la Revolución Cubana* (Miami: Editorial AIP, 1964).

42. Lee Lockwood, *Castro's Cuba, Cuba's Fidel* (Boulder, Colo.: Westview Press, 1990); Frank Mankiewicz and Kirby Jones, *With Fidel: A Portrait of Castro and Cuba* (New York: Ballantine Books, 1975).

43. Bourne, *Fidel: A Biography*, 18.

44. Luis Ortega, "Las Dos Imágenes de Fidel Castro," *Contrapunto* 6 (December 1995): 19–21.

45. Ibid., 20.

46. "Pastors Roll On," *CubaINFO* 9 (May 1997): 4; *Granma International*, August 10, 1997, 2.

47. "A Multinational Force Resounds in Havana," and "World Youth Movement Strengthened and Extended in Havana," *Granma International*, August 3, 1997, 1, and August 10, 1997, 6.

48. Liss, *Fidel! Castro's Political and Social Thought*, 183–84.

49. "Liberty, nationalism, and faith are fused in the American civil religion. As Norman Mailer put it, 'In America, the country was the religion. And all the religions of the land were fed from that first religion'." Connor Cruise O'Brien, "Thomas Jefferson: Radical and Racist," *Atlantic Monthly*, October 1996, 53–54.

50. Steve Ellner, "Introduction: The Changing Status of the Latin American Left in the Recent Past," in *The Latin American Left: From the Fall of Allende to Perestroika*, ed. Barry Carr and Steve Ellner (Boulder, Colo.: Westview Press, 1993), 1.

51. "Voices on the Left: Cuba, Juan Valdés Paz," *NACLA Report on the Americas* 31 (July–August 1997): 26–27.

52. Luis Baéz, "Mundo Contemporáneo: Diez Preguntas a Carlos Rafael Rodríguez," *Bohemia*, May 14, 1994, B16–23.

53. "Acuerdos y Resoluciones del IV Encuentro del Foro de Sao Paulo, La Habana, del 21 al 24 de Abril de 1993," *IV Encuentro del Foro de Sao Paulo*, July 1993, 1–27, quotes at 9–10.

54. "Voices on the Left: Cuba, Juan Valdés Paz," 27.

55. Emma Pérez, "De Usted También Diremos Algo . . .," *Bohemia*, January 18–25, 1959, 15.

56. Esteban Morales Domínguez, "Cuba en la Política Norteamericana," 195.

INDEX

Abakuá, 268
abortion issue, 261
Abrantes, José, 67, 98
accounting systems, 66
Adams, John Quincy, 351–52n. 3
Africa, 84–85
Afro-Cuban creeds, 268, 270
agricultural cooperatives: Basic Units of
    Cooperative Production (UBPCs), 144–46;
    deficits, 111; emergence, 9; free farmers'
    markets, 63; future trends, 305; irregulari-
    ties, 56
agriculture: economic recovery, 166; special
    period, 76; women's participation, 85
AIDS, 84–85
air conditioning, 76
airlines, 158
airspace, violations of, 191
air travel, 197, 243
Alamar Associates, 154
Alarcón de Quesada, Ricardo, 123–24; on
    archbishop's remarks, 374n36; Brothers to
    the Rescue planes downed, 193; Church
    role, 268; Clinton policy, 214; dissident
    reaction, 202; election to National
    Assembly, 124; elections and U.S.
    interference, 296; First Ibero-American
    Summit, 230; Helms-Burton Act, 210;
    humanitarian aid, 220; ICAO investiga-
    tion, 199–200; influence, 126; pope's visit,
    263; reappointment, 111, 314; Spanish
    interference, 247; U.S. policies and reform,
    306–07
Albright, Madeleine: anti-Castro discord,
    216; anti-Castro rhetoric, 12; Brothers to
    the Rescue incident, 198–99; Canada's
    approach, 215; confirmation hearings,
    357–58n3; embargo, 199; embargo
    softened, 217; Helms-Burton Act, 360n38;
    Helms relationship, 361n52; humanitarian

aid, 221–22; pope receives, 216–17;
    protests against, 199
Alemán, Arnaldo, 118–19, 232
Almeida Bosque, Juan, 97, 314
Alonso Tejada, Aurelio, 109, 284
American Association for World Health, 187
Americas Summit, 233–34
Americas Watch, 295–96, 379n26
Andreas, Dwayne, 211
anti-corruption campaigns, 97–99
antigovernment leaflets, 191
anti-market reforms, 66
Arca Foundation, 207
Archers Daniel Midland, 211
Argentina: blocking Cuba, 232; Catholic
    Church, 251; democratization criticism,
    118–19; health care, 81; infant mortality,
    82; life expectancy, 82; tourism, 158
armed forces: budget, 162; size of, 162;
    transition scheme, 214
arts and letters, 295–98
Association of Caribbean States (ACS), 241,
    242–43
austerity measures, 54, 66, 75–77, 332n28
autonomous enterprises, 115
Axworthy, Lloyd, 215, 236–37, 325n. 16, 366n.
    33
Aznar, José María: aid suspended, 243–44;
    Castro with, 231; Clinton meeting, 247;
    criticizing Cuba, 245; critics of, 244, 245;
    EU stance on Cuba, 14, 212–13; in Havana,
    246; relations, 243; Venezuelan Summit,
    233

Bacardi Corporation, 207
balseros (rafters) issue, 11, 248, 290
banking system: currency crimes, 97; foreign
    banks, 10, 336n. 53; money laundering, 97;
    reorganized, 335n. 51; savings accounts
    frozen, 143

Barbados, 228
Barnet, Miguel, 289
baseball diplomacy, 196, 356n. 43
Basic Units of Cooperative Production
    (UBPCs), 144–46
Basulto, Jorge, 192–93, 194, 219, 354n. 40
Batista, Fulgencio, 208
Berger, Sandy, 224
bilateral agreements, Caribbean nations, 241
bilateral relationship, between former USSR
    and Cuba, 27–30
biological warfare, 354–56n. 42
biology, 93
biotechnology, 93, 153
black market: after dollarization, 140; early
    1990s, 133; flea markets, 97; fraud, 347n.
    46; industrial markets versus, 149
Blanco, Juan Antonio, 44
Blas Roca Calderío contingent, 64
Boza Másvidal, Eduardo, 262
Brazil, 234
Brenner, Philip, 203
Brezhnev doctrine, 23
bribes, 98
Brittan, Leon, 238
Brothers to the Rescue (BTTR) planes
    downed, 10–11; Clinton's remarks, 205;
    consequences, 22; described, 191–95;
    fatalities, 354n. 40; public opinion, 204; U.S.
    penalties for, 197; U.S. responsibility, 198,
    200
budget: education, 66; housing, 66; medical
    care, 66
budget deficits: 56, 56t3.1; early 1990s, 133;
    growth, 66
Bulgaria, 29
Bunck, Julie Marie, 287–88
bureaucracy, rectification process, 54, 67–68
Bush administration, embargo, 183, 184

Cabello, Mario, 148
Cabrisas Ruiz, Ricardo, 180, 242–43, 309
Campa, Concepción Huergo, 126, 314
Canada: Americas Summit, 234; approach,
    215; Clinton approach, 215; close relations,
    14; constructive engagement, 238, 296;
    criticized, 215; diplomatic relations, 235–
    36; embargo, 366–67 n.36; health care, 81;
    Helms-Burton Act, 209, 211, 212; human
    rights issue, 237, 292, 366n33; infant
    mortality, 82, 83; joint ventures, 237;

leader in Cuban matters, 236; life
    expectancy, 82; tourism, 158; trade, 236,
    237t10.3; on U.S. isolationism, 325n16
Candidacy Commissions, 117
capital accumulation, sugar economy, 129
capital goods, 130
capitalism: Castro on, 110; creeping, 147;
    pope on, 263; self-employment, 147
capitalist modalities, 109, 110. See also
    foreign investment; free farmers'
    markets; joint ventures; self-employment
Cárdenas, Cuauhtémoc, 241, 303
Cardoso, Fernando Henrique, 234
Caribbean: Cuba as part of, 241–43;
    diplomatic activism, 14, 228
Caribbean Center for Policy Development,
    242
Caribbean Community (CARICOM), 241,
    242, 243
Caribbean Export Development Agency, 242
Caribbean Forum (CARIFORUM) Summit,
    228, 242
Caribbean States Association, 228
Caridad del Cobre, Nuestra Señora de la,
    252, 262
Caritas, 172, 187, 188, 222, 267
Carollo, José, 342n. 51
Carranza Valdés, Julio, 134
Casas Regueiro, Julio, 162, 314
Castro Ruz, Fidel: assassination attempts,
    199, 232–33; ballots, marking, 118; on
    capitalism, 110; centralized power, 124–25;
    charisma, 54, 298–99; Clinton approach,
    12; on Clinton's sex scandal, 375n. 43; on
    conciencia and moral incentives, 51–52;
    consummation of revolution, 322n7; on
    creative expression, 296–98; demonization
    of, 300; downfall predicted, 256–57; early
    inexperience, 49–50; on economic reform,
    141; election in 1998, 8–9, 310n. 1, 322n. 7;
    on elections, 119; end predicted, 188–89;
    on Gorbachev, 327n. 17; on Guevara, 8;
    health issues, 322n. 8; on Helms-Burton
    Act, 214; on humanitarian aid, 220; ICAO
    report, 200; ideological significance, 17;
    international reputation, 299–300;
    obsession of U.S. with, 188–90, 194–95; on
    perestroika, 25; personal diplomacy, 227–
    30; on Poland, 271–72; on political change,
    100; political culture, 298; political skills,
    301; political thought and leadership, 17;

Castro Ruz, Fidel—*continued*
  pope's arrival, 259, 260–61; on pope's
  visit, 254, 256–57, 264, 269–70, 373n. 21; on
  private property, 111; on prostitution, 78;
  rebelliousness, 298–99, 301–02; rectification process, 6; on religion, 254, 255–56,
  272, 370n. 12; strong personality, 300;
  succession, 9, 110, 125, 322–23nn. 9, 10,
  343nn. 66, 67; on U.S. elections, 338n. 16,
  341n. 51; world vision and ideological
  universe, 302
Castro Ruz, Raúl: on defending socialism,
  128; ethics code, 97; Fidel's succession, 9,
  125, 322–23nn. 9, 10, 343nn. 66, 67; on food
  shortages, 290; on food supplies, 144;
  Helms-Burton Act, 210–11; on military
  preparedness, 127; military's economic
  resources, 164; new generations, 127;
  pope's visit, 261; prostitution dilemma, 78
Catholic Church: Afro-Cuban creeds, 268;
  after pope's visit, 266, 269; believers,
  numbers, 376n. 53; detente with state, 259;
  dialogue with state, 376n. 50; early
  transition, 369n. 1; easing embargo, 220;
  food and medical aid, 216; personnel by
  diocese, 319; pope's visit, 251, 270;
  problems, 267–68; religious revival of
  1990s, 252–54, 370n. 7; religious and social
  standing, 251; U.S. humanitarian aid
  policy, 221–22
Catholic Medical Missions Board, 219
censorship, critical Soviet publications, 27
Center for European Studies (CEE), 210–11
Center for Public Integrity, 206–07
Center for the Study of the Americas (CEA),
  210–11, 360n33
Central American conflict, 29
Central Intelligence Agency (CIA), 199
centralization of power, 124–25
Cernuda, Ramón, 203–04
charter flights, 203, 217, 248
Chernobyl nuclear disaster, 27, 93
child-care centers, 58
child mortality rates, 39, 40, 42t2.8
children: education, 89; special period, 88–92
Chile, 81, 231, 333n. 2, 365n. 28
China: Castro's diplomacy, 227; Chinese
  model, 108; joint ventures, 36, 108, 227;
  military corruption, 164; quasi-Chinese
  model, 101; trade, 35, 38–39, 38t2.1, 227
Chirac, Jacques, 239

Chomón, Faure, 306
Chrétien, Jean, 238
Christmas, celebration of, 255
church-state relations: broadening space, 274;
  detente, 259; human rights issue, 18; papal
  faux pas, 270–71; pope's conditions, 16;
  pope's visit, 3; under the revolution, 251
Cienfuegos, Osmany, 78
CIMEX agency (Department of Convertible
  Currency), 99, 142
civil society: Torricelli-Graham bill track two,
  189; U.S. interference, 221, 248–49
Clinton, William J.: anti-Castro stance
  analyzed, 205–07; Canada's approach, 215;
  Cuban-American vote, 186, 206;
  defending Helms-Burton Act, 212;
  doctrine of democratic enlargement, 222;
  easing sanctions, 12; Más Canosa's
  political game, 184–85; pope's visit, 218;
  sex scandal, 375n. 43; southern Florida
  strategy, 206; transition scheme, 214
Coderch Planas, José, 244, 245
Cohen, William, 161
Cold War, 195; Cold War, end of, U.S. versus
  Moscow meanings, 29. *See also* European
  socialism, collapse of
Cole, Ken, 176
College of Bishops, 272
Colombia: crime, 365n. 28; revolutionary
  activity, 22, 231
Committees for the Defense of the Revolu-
  tion (CDRs), 122, 149
Common Position on Cuba, 246
communication control system, 287
Communist Party, Cuban: in 1990s, 104–07;
  Central Committee, 107; centrality, 107–08;
  congress, 338n. 18; constitution, 114;
  debate, 105; economic policy, 106;
  elections, 106; electoral opposition, 101;
  Fifth Party Congress, 7, 110–12, 314–16,
  318; foreign policy, 106–07; Fourth Party
  Congress, 105–07; future trends, 306;
  Helms-Burton Act, 210; internal rule, 105;
  leadership, 314–16; membership, 108–09,
  314–16, 318, 338–39n. 18; OPP relationship,
  121–22; Organs of People's Power, 106;
  origins, 50; Political Bureau membership,
  314–16; political reform, 7; program, 105–
  06; provincial Central Committee
  members, 317; provincial secretaries, 317;
  rectification process, 55, 105; religious

believers, 104; religious practice, 253; structure, 338n. 18; tourist sector, 156
compensation to U.S. nationals, 137–38, 207–08; Helms-Burton Act, 209, 209t9.1; registry of expropriated properties, 213
conciencia, revolutionary, 5, 51–52, 61
Concilio Cubano (CC), 201, 203, 358n. 12
Confederation of Cuban Workers (CTC), 108
Conference of Catholic Bishops, 254–55, 264, 272–73, 376n. 50
Constitution (Cuban): amendments to, 112; political reforms, 113; reforming, 112–13; speculative comments, 339–40n. 33
construction contingents, 61; Blas Roca Calderío contingent, 64; output, 65f3.3
construction sector, 58
consumerism, 25
Consumer Price Index (IPC), 150
Contrapunto magazine, 249, 300
convertible peso mechanism: adopted, 36; rectification process, 66
Coordination and Inspection Board (JUCEI), 122
COPPAL (Permanent Conference of Latin American Political Parties), 240, 321n. 3
Correo de Cuba, 247
corruption, 54; anti-corruption campaigns, 97–99; bribes, 98; Chinese military, 161; drug trafficking scandal, 67, 98–99; military leaders, 67; special period, 96–99
Council of methodist Evangelical Churches of Latin America and the Caribbean, 272
Council of Ministers, composition, 309–10
Council of Mutual Economic Assistance (CMEA), 31, 130, 180
Council of State, 113, 121, 311–13
counterrevolutionary activism, 18
creative expression, 296–98
credit, 10
crime and delinquency, 55, 365n. 28
crisis management, 102–3
Cruz León, Raúl Ernesto, 159
Cubana de Aviación, 158
Cuban Academy of Science, 281–85
Cubanacán: finances, 115; joint ventures, 155; leading hotels, 156t7.3; occupancy rate, 156
Cuban-American lobby in congress, 13, 182t8.1, 206, 324n. 16, 353n. 223
Cuban American National Foundation: aid

rejected, 266; anti-Castro materials, 380n. 41; anti-Clinton, 219; assassination attempts, 232; Brothers to the Rescue origins, 193–94; Bush administration, 183; campaign contributions, 207; food and medical aid, 216; funding lobbies, 182t8.1; illegal operations, 18; pope's visit, 269
Cuban Americans: anti-Castro organizations, 18; CANF influence, 195; Castro demonized, 300; Catholic Church, 269; Clinton reelection, 190–91, 206; Clinton's Cuba policy, 1, 201, 206; core group, 206; Cuban bishops, 273; democratization pressures, 127; Dialogue Conference, 368n. 62; election practices, 341–42n. 51; Más Canosa's death, 323, 324n. 13; military threat, 161–62; moderate, 203–4, 210, 337n. 8; numbers in U.S., 248; organizations critiqued, 248–49; pope's visit, 216, 219, 256, 269; reassessing relations, 139; rift among hard-liners, 215; terrorism by, 159, 232
Cuban Committee for Democracy, 207, 337n. 8
Cuban Conference of Bishops. *See* Conference of Catholic Bishops
Cuban Democracy Act of 1992 (CDA), 81, 181, *See also* Torricelli-Graham bill
Cuban Humanitarian Trade of 1997, 107
Cuban Interests Section, 29–30
Cuban Liberty and Democratic Solidarity Act of 1996. *See* Helms-Burton Act
Cuban-Mexican Intergovernmental Committee, 239
Cuban revolution: core values, redefining, 277; creativity, 297; early Catholic Church opposition, 251–52; early debates, 330n. 4; gains and deficiencies, 53; institutionalization of, 20; for Latin American left, 303; liberal democracy versus, 298; Marxism examined, 281–86; nonnegotiable features, 19, 304; political culture, 286–87; rectification process, 52; reformulating the project, 43–44, 45; riddle of its survival, 4; risking socialist system, 102; as secular religion, 302; space for Church, 267; stages and phases, 344n. 1; survival under RP, 68; young people, 279
Cuba-socialist exchange analyzed, 33–35
cultural exchanges, 248
Czechoslovakia, 29–30, 137, 290, 291

D'Amato Act, 213, 223
debt burden of poor nations, 16
decentralization reforms, 52, 54
decision making, 52
defections, 4, 277; collapse of European
    socialism, 30; opportunism, 288–89;
    special period, 69
defense expenditures, 162, 163t7.4
De la Guardia, Antonio, 98
De la Guardia, Patricio, 98
Del Pino, Rafael, 99
democracy: concept of, 102; liberal
    democracy, 223, 231, 236, 298; neoliberal,
    303; participatory, 303; pope on, 264
democratic centralism, 114
democratization issue: Ibero-American
    summits, 118–19; pressures on Cuba,
    127–28
dengue fever, 188, 374n. 39
dependency on Soviet bloc: benefits of, 31;
    complacency, 132; criticisms, 345n. 9;
    economic integration and, 30–31;
    economic policy, 130; trade imbalance,
    132; unpreparedness for collapse, 5
dependency on USSR, historical alignment, 20
dialectical analysis, 278, 282, 377n. 1
Dialogue Conference, 368n. 62
Díaz Balart, Lincoln, 187
dictatorship of the proletariat, 122
diplomatic activism, 13–14; baseball
    diplomacy, 196, 356n. 43; embargo, 225;
    United Nations, 225
diplomatic relations: Canada, 235–36, 236–39;
    Mexico, 235–36, 239–41; pope's call for,
    266
Diplomercado, 279
dissent issue: religious rights, 17; summa-
    rized, 17–18; U.S. policy, 248
dissidents: association with Miami, 293;
    BTTR planes downed, 201, 202; Castro on,
    370n. 12; Concilio Cubano (CC), 201, 203;
    Domestic Dissidence Working Group, 116;
    elections, 116, 117; as loyal opposition, 17;
    major problem, 127, 128; on reform, 336n1;
    Spanish ties, 243, 244–45; special period,
    69
Doctors of the World, 172
doctrine of democratic enlargement, 222, 223
Dodd, Christopher, 196, 216
Dole, Robert, 191, 201
dollarization: consequences, 74–75;

inequality, 45, 71; legalization process,
    140–42; population participating, 142;
    prostitution, 79–80; social cleavage effect,
    140–41; social implications, 141
dollar/peso social divide, 7, 71, 140–41, 280
dollars-only stores/sites, 7, 139, 142, 279
Domestic Dissidence Working Group, 116
Domínguez, Jorge, 101
Dominica, 241
Dominican Republic, 228, 243, 266
drug certification process, 235
drug smuggling, 152, 240
drug trafficking scandal, 67, 98–99
Durán, Alfredo, 203

economic development: aid from USSR, 32–
    33; armed forces role, 160–64; social equity
    principle, 70
economic downfall, social impact, 7
economic growth rates, 56, 131–32; per-
    formance 1995–1996, 165t7.5; recovery,
    164–68
economic indicators, 39–41, 56
economic planning system, 115
economic policy: Communist Party, 106; early
    shifts, 331n6; future trends, 305; main
    objectives, 129; rectification process, 132
economic problems: current, 19; dialectical
    analysis, 278; of early 1990s, 132; Fifth
    Communist Party Congress, 111; impact of
    Helms-Burton Act, 168–69; performance
    of 1960s, 131; public confidence, 120,
    121t.5.3; recovery period, 39; social
    impact, 19; Soviet collapse effects, 26
economic recovery: nascent, 280; sugar
    economy, 10; trade, 38–39
economic reform, 9–10; comparative
    analysis, 137; dollarization effect, 141;
    economists on, 133–34; government
    leaders on, 135–36; ideological beliefs, 136;
    scholars abroad on, 136–38; special period,
    138–40; views of, 133–38
economists' views of economic reform, 133–34
ecumenical approach, 270, 273
education: budget, 66; Catholic schools, 266–
    67; children in primary school, 70f4.1;
    children in special period, 89; public
    opinion polls, 120; rectification process
    reforms, 61; religious instruction in
    schools, 255; schooling, years of, 39, 40,
    41t2.5; shortages in special period, 76;

universal, free, 96; women's participation, 87, 87f4.3

Eizenstat, Stuart, 212, 238–39, 360n. 38

elections: annulment of ballots, 340–41nn. 41, 42; candidacy commissions, 117; Castro on, 119, 341n. 51; as compromise, 306; electoral law of 1992, 115; first, 7–8; human rights issue, 296; local, 343n. 58; nominating systems, 117; opposition opening, 101; system reformed, 7; television advertising, 341n. 51; under new law, 115–19; "unity" vote, 116; voter turnout, 119; voting campaign, 341n. 46

elites, 279

El Salvador, 159, 292

embargo: Albright on, 199; Bush administration, 183, 184; Canada, 237, 366–67n. 36; Catholic Church favored, 267; challenges to, 207; CIMEX agency, 99; Clinton administration, 31; Communist Party, 107; Cuban American lobby, 353n. 23; food and medicine, 81, 82, 222; health and nutrition effects, 187, 188; Helms-Burton Act provisions, 208; history of, 180; informer hotline, 204; legal fight against, 353n. 2; pope on, 265; pope's visit, 261; public opinion, 234; U.S. nationals' compensation, 138; Venezuela on, 266

emigration: bishops on, 273; pope on, 262

employment: college graduates, 91; higher education, 91; leading generator, 146; rectification process, 62

energy sector, 173

England, 211

English-only movement, 191

enterprise managers, 58, 305

enterprise-to-enterprise agreements, 35

entertainment industry, 76

equality, special period, 139

equity issues: distribution of goods and services, 5; revolution's record, 5; social equity principle, 70; special period, 69, 77, 139

Escalante, Aníbal, 50

Escalona, Juan, 117

Espín, Vilma, 78, 85–86

ethics code, 97–98

Europe: Europe-Caribbean Council, 242; human rights issue, 292; tourism, 158

European socialism, as influence, 51; Castro predicting, 5; collapse of: 6; Cuban government's staying power, 321n. 1; dialectical analysis, 278; disruption of left, 302; domestic effects, 21–22; impact on Cuba, 30; living under two blockades, 180; political structures, impact, 326n. 12; rectification process, 55; survival crisis, 277

European Union, 212, 213; Aznar's lobbying, 246; Caribbean trade, 242; Common Position on Cuba, 246; cooperation talks, 247; embargo, 225; Helms-Burton Act, 238

Europe-Caribbean Council, 242

exchange rates, 133, 143

exchange system, Cuba-socialist, 33–35

exiles: on Castro, 300; communities abroad, 247–49; human rights issue, 295; Ibero-American summits, 230; rapprochement between émigrés and Cuba, 250; Venezuela, 231–32

expatriated Cubans, 247–49. See also Cuban Americans; exiles

exports: collapse of European socialism, 32; economic policy, 129; future trends, 136; rectification process, 65

family: constitution, 115; jineterismo, 80

fast track legislation, 234

Federation of Cuban Women (FMC), 78, 85–86, 122

Feinberg, Richard, 215, 301

feminist approaches, 85–86

Fernández, Damian, 339n33

Fernández de Cossio, Carlos, 13

ferry service, Mexico-Cuba, 240

Festival of Youth and Students, 301–2

Fiallo, Amalio, 249

financial assistance, USSR, 33

First Clinton Administration, fund-raising, 182t8.1, 183–84

fisheries agreements, 237

fish farming, 160

fishing, economic recovery, 166

flea markets, 97

Flores, María de los Angeles, 291

Food and Agriculture Organization (FAO), 15

food issues: Castro on, 15; emergency measures, 145–46; food shortages, 111, 278–79, 290; reforms in system, 144–46 food and medical supplies: Catholic Church role, 267; Cuban Americans supporting, 216; largest medical shipment, 219; sales by U.S. subsidiaries, 186, 187; sanctions lifted, 217; Torres-Dodd bill, 196

food production, 143–44

food self-sufficiency program (Programa Alimentario), 76–77; described, 143–44; productivity, 166

food supply: calorie consumption, 40, 42t2.7; free farmers' markets, 63

foreign debt: calculations, 137; categories, 170; convertible currency, 171n 7.8; country creditors, 170; early 1990s, 33; failure to service, 169–70; hard currency, 67; Japan, 10, 172; origins of problem, 170; rectification process, 54, 60; rescheduling, 169–72

foreign investment: banking, 336n53; bribes, 98; Canada, 154–55; Communist Party, 106; as economic reform, 9; enterprises by nation, 154t7.1; Fifth Communist Party Congress, 110; financing sugar harvests, 169; free-trade zones, 173–74; Mexico, 154–55, 240; modalities allowed, 348n. 1; Reciprocity Agreements for the Protection and Promotion of Investment, 225; rectification process, 67; from socialist bloc, 32, 33; special period, 153–55; top investors, 153

Foreign Investment Act of 1995 (Law 77), 153

foreign policy, Cuba, 13–14; Castro's diplomacy, 227–30; Communist Party, 106–07; goals, 226–27, 228

foreign policy, U.S., domestic politics as base, 223

foreign trade, new economic model, 136. See also trade

Forum of Nongovernmental Organizations, 292

France, 238–39

Franco, Francisco, 243

freedom of expression: 120, 121t5.2; criticism of revolution, 127–28

Freedom House, 201–02, 380n41

free peasant/farmer markets: Communist Party, 106, 337n. 3; elimination, 62–63; industrial markets compared, 149; irregularities, 56; National Association of Small (Private) Farmers (ANAP), 143;

problems caused, 60; rectification process, 25; reopened, 142–43

free trade, 223; Caribbean, 228, 243

Free Trade Area of the Americas, 234

free zones, 9

Friends of Colombia Group, 231

fuels, 173

Fukuyama, Francis, 22

García Márquez, Gabriel, 263, 270, 299

gasoline supplies, 280

Gaviria Trujillo, César, 230, 234

generational theme, 299, 301–02; new leadership, 125–27, 281–82

geological prospecting program, 33

Germany, 158; GDP share, 73

Girardi, Guilio, 271

glasnost: Cuban reaction, 24–26; Cuban resistance, 26; Soviet publications on Cuba, 27

GNP. See gross national product

gonorrhea, 81

González, Felipe, 243

González, Gerardo, 289

González Nuñez, Gerardo, 133–34

Gorbachev, Mikhail, 22–25, 26, 27, 44; Castro on, 327n. 17; reforms' outcome, 49, 108

Gorth, Carl-Johan, 202

Graham, Bob, 161, 183

Green, Rosario, 240

Grenada, 228, 241, 367n. 48

Grenadines, 242

gross national product (GNP): early 1990s, 132–33; growth rates, 164–68; purchasing power parity (PPP) to measure, 39, 39t2.3

Group of Three, 230

Grupo BM, 210

Grupo Domos, 209, 240

Guáimaro Constitution, 103; by sectors, 130, 130t6.1

Guantanamera (film), 297–98

Guatemala, 228, 266

guerrilla warfare, 22

Guevara, Alfredo, 298, 322n7

Guevara, Ernesto Che, 8; early inexperience, 49–50

Guillén, Nicolás, 298

Gurría, José, 239

Gutiérrez, Tomás (Titón), 297–98

Gutiérrez Menoyo, Eloy, 203

Gutiérrez Urdaneta, Luis, 134

Haiti, 228
Hart, Armando, 189
health care, special period, 81. *See also* medical care; food and medical aid
Hegel, F.R.W., 278
Helms, Jesse, 207, 216, 219, 361n. 52, 362n. 57, 375n. 43
Helms-Burton Act: anti-Castro electoral support, 201; Brothers to the Rescue (BTTR) planes downed, 197; Canada, 238–39; Clinton's anti-Castro stance, 205; compensation to U.S. nationals, 209, 209t9.1; condemnation by U.S. allies, 181, 184; criticized, 203–4, 359–60n. 31; Cuban reaction, 210–11; economic impact, 168–69; effects on Cuba-U.S. relations, 204; executive powers circumscribed, 208, 359n. 29; foreign investment, 153; freezing the bilateral confrontation, 207–10; impact on economy, 174; Inter-American Juridical Committee, 234, 239; international reaction, 211, 238; joint ventures, 154; Mexico on, 239; North American opposition, 14; pope condemning, 15; presidential authority reduced, 12; rejected by Ibero-American summits, 231; second anniversary, 218–19; Title I, 208; Title II, 208–9, 214; Title III, 12, 209, 212, 213; Title IV, 209–10, 213; titles or sections described, 208–10; toughening embargo, 188; U.S. business, 211–12
Hernández, Francisco Pepe, 232, 269
higher education: access to, 91; career opportunities, 91; competition for slots, 91; employment, 91; history, 93–96, 94f4.6; tourist sector employment, 74; youth, 92–96
high wages, low productivity, 57–58, 59
historical symbols, 114
history, Cuban, studying, 93–96
housing: distribution manual, 66; minibrigade construction, 65; regulations, 147–49; rentals, 147–49; shortages in special period, 90–91; special period, 77
Housing Law (1984), 56
housing shortage, growth, 58
human capital, Moscow aid, 32
humanitarian aid, 218–19, 222; Castro on, 220; Cuban Catholic Church, 221; Cuban reaction, 221, 222; Pastors for Peace, 301
humanitarian reasons, for lifting sanctions, 217

human rights issue: Canada, 237, 366n. 88; Cuban practice, 293; Cuban-U.S. seminar, 294–95; debate, international, 17; internal opposition, 249; opposition issues, 290; pope's visit, 257; reports on violations, 295–96; social-economic versus political, 110, 293, 295; social vs. political rights, 17; U.S. mission officer expelled, 358–59n. 16; U.S. policy criticized, 368n. 59
Hungary, 29, 137
hunger: Castro on, 15; pope on, 16

Ibero-American summits, 230–34; Castro's diplomacy, 230–32; democratization pledge, 118–19; Guadalajara, Mexico, 230; listed, 14, 364n. 10; Margarita Declaration, 231; Porto Declaration, 231; Porto, Portugal, 228; Viña del Mar, Chile, 231, 245
Iglesias, Arnaldo, 194
immigration regulations, 11, 148–49
imports: collapse of European socialism, 32; medicine, 153; rectification process, 65; from Russia, 36
import substitution, 129
individualism, 58
industrialization: early policy, 9, 129; healthy growth, 56; obstacles, 133–34; rectification process, 65
industrial markets, 149–50
industrial parks, 9
inequality, special period, 139
infant mortality rates: comparative, 82, 83, 83t4.2; U.S., 73, 83t4.2
informal economy, 150
informal sector, 137
Integral Tax System, 150–52
Integrated Revolutionary Organization (ORI), 50
Inter-American Dialogue, 235
Inter-American Juridical Committee, 235, 239
International Civil Aviation Organization (ICAO), 198, 199–200
internationalism, proletarian, 288
international law, 294
international reserves, 67
interventionism, 223
inventory control, 59–60
investment, government, 130–31
Ireland, 228
Israel, 185–86, 209–10, 371n. 16

Italy, 15, 154, 158
ITT (International Telephone & Telegraph), 13

Jamaica, 228, 241, 367n. 49
Japan: average earnings, 73; foreign debt,
172; GDP share, 73; health care, 81; human
rights issue, 292; infant mortality, 82;
rescheduling debt, 10; trade, 227
Jasinowski, Jerry, 211–12
jineteras. See prostitution (*jineterismo*)
John Paul II (Pope): Albright received,
216–17; bishops to Vatican, 270; Castro
meeting at Vatican, 15–16, 255, 256; health
issues, 371n. 17; political effects of visit,
216–22; Spanish government response,
245–46; visit as harbinger, 254
joint ventures, 9; Canada, 238; China, 36, 108,
227; foreign investment, 153–54; growth
rates, 166; Israel, 210; Mexico, 240; Soviet,
36; Spain, 153; tourism, 155
Juan Carlos (King), 233, 246
Junco, Eduardo, 246
Juraguá nuclear power plant, 35, 76, 181,
352n. 8

Kennedy, John F., 21
Kozak, Michael, 13
Kruschev, Nikita, 21

labor force: hard currency incentives, 142;
marital status, 87–88; tourism, 156;
women, 85, 87–88
labor norms, 57, 58
labor productivity, 57–58, 59; construction
contingents, 64; growth, 130
labor surplus, 147
Lage Dávila, Carlos, 126, 314; Clinton policy,
214; on economic problems, 111, 167;
economic recovery, 128, 164; on economic
reform, 135–36; health care, 84; Helms-
Burton Act, 168; on *paladares* restaurants,
97; special period, 41–43
land distribution, 145
land use, 62
language issues, English at university level, 93
Latin America: diplomatic activism, 14;
diplomatic relations, 228, 229t10.2;
exporting revolution, 21–22; human rights
issue, 292; left wing, 303–04; left wing in
1990s, 22; living standards, 73–74; public
health, 82; trade, 136

Latin American Methodist bishops, 272
Latin American Parliament (Parlatino), 233
Law, Bernard Cardinal, 219
Lazo Hernández, Esteban, 96, 315
leadership: Castro, 124–25; early inexperi-
ence, 49–50; new generations, 125–27,
281–82
legitimacy, 4, 30, 321n. 2
Lenin, Vladimir I., 103
liberal democracy, 223, 231, 236, 298
liberation theologians, 271–72
life expectancy, 39, 40, 41t2.6, 81–82, 83t4.3
Lissitzyn, Oliver, 198
Liss, Sheldon B., 299, 302
literacy rates, 39, 41t2.4
living conditions, special period, 75
Llama, Juan Antonio, 232
Local Powers, 122
Lome V discussion, on international trade,
242, 243
López, Enrique, 220
Lourdes electronic intelligence-gathering
station, 27
Lugo Fonte, Orlando, 143

male attitudes, 85
management, 58–59
Mandela, Nelson, 223–24, 228, 363nn. 76, 77
manufacturing, 130, 166
Mariel boat lift, 184
Marinello, José, 103
market economies: GDP share, 72–73, 73t4.1;
trade with, 31–32, 32f2.2
market reforms: Gorbachev's, 24–25;
"negative tendencies," 51
market socialism, 175
Martí, José, 103, 104, 113–14, 338n. 16
Martínez, Jesús, 126
Martínez Heredia, Fernando, 52, 53, 283–84
Martínez Valdés, Jorge, 98
Marxism: Castro on, 302; crisis after
European collapse, 281; debates over
role, 16; future trends, 306; reexamined,
281–86; relevance in post-Soviet world,
286; socialist crisis, 22; viability, 278;
youth, 96
Marxism-Leninism, 282, 301; political
culture, 287–88
Más Canosa, Jorge: Clinton meeting, 11, 203;
critical commentary, 324n. 13; death and
eulogies, 323–24n. 13; donor to lobbies,

182t8.1; political one-upmanship, 184–86, 188; Torricelli-Graham bill, 183

Más Canosa, Ricardo, 185

material incentives, 25; labor discipline, 59; SDPE system, 57

materialist doctrine, 254

maternal mortality ratio, 82, 83t4.2, 84

Matutes, Abel, 244, 245

media: accounts of special period, 278–79; coverage problems during rectification process, 61; Soviet, 27, 327n19; U.S., in Cuba, 361n. 48

medical care: access to services, 70f4.1; after rectification process, 60–61; AIDS, 84–85; babies delivered by medical personnel, 70f4.1; budget, 66; Chernobyl nuclear disaster, 27; contraceptives, 82, 83t4.2; deficits, 56; dengue fever, 188, 374n. 39; eye disease, 84; facilities shortage, 58; family doctors, 60–61; health care in special period, 81; infant immunization,70f4.1; population per physician, 40, 42t2.9; public opinion polls, 120; special period, 77, 81; women and public health, 81–84

medical supplies, embargo, 82

medicine imports, 153

Méndez, Hector, 270

Menéndez, Robert, 187, 214

mercantilism, 58

Mesa-Lago, Carmelo, 137, 138

Meurice Estiú, Pedro, 263, 274, 373–74n. 36

Mexican model, 101

Mexico: close relations, 14; crime, 365n28; diplomatic relations, 235; foreign debt, 171; foreign investment, 154–55; Group of Three, 230; health care, 81; Helms-Burton Act, 209, 211; human rights issue, 292; Ibero-American Summit in Guadalajara, 230; joint ventures, 240; Mexico-Cuba trade agreement, 171; revolutionary activity, 22; revolutionary tradition, 239; tourism, 158; trade, 240

migration to Havana, 148–49

migration issues, 247–49, 328n. 25

migration law, internal, 148

military: defense expenditures, 162, 163t7.4; economic involvement, 160–64; special period, 77

military assistance: Moscow's commitment, 20; Sovietization, 20; Soviet personnel, 21

military intervention, Soviet-Yugoslav Statement of Principles, 24

military leaders, 67

military option, against Cuba, 204–05

military threat, by Cuba, 161, 360n28

Millares Rodríguez, Manuel, 145, 309

minibrigade movement, 60, 61; housing, 65; output, 64f3.2; revival, 64

Miranda, Olga, 207–08

Miranda, Olivia, 285

missile crisis, 21

Monal, Isabel, 283

Monreal González, Pedro, 134

Morales Domínguez, Esteban, 179, 218, 307

most favored nation (MFN) status, 29

Mujeres magazine, 86

Multilateral Agreement on Investment (MAI), 213

NAFTA, 234, 238

National Assembly (Poder Popular): constitutional reforms, 113; deputies analyzed, 124; nominating assemblies, 124; opening elections, 296; social composition, 312–13n. 1; women leaders, 85

National Association of Manufacturers (NAM, U.S.), 211–12

National Association of Small (Private) Farmers (ANAP), 143

National Commission for [Crime] Prevention and Social Assistance, 66

National Commission for the Direction of the Economic System (CNSDE), 62

National Defense Council, 113

National Electoral Commission, 117

National Housing Institute, 148

nationalism, younger generation, 127

nationalization process, 207–08

National Office of Tax Administration (ONAT), 150–51

National Union of Cuban Writers and Artists (UNEAC), 298

neoliberalism: Chile, effects, 333n. 2; church on, 253; contradictions, 282; disagreement, 136; Fukuyama, 22, 282; pope on, 263; social downside, 71–74; social impact, 72–74

neo-Stalinist model, 108

neuropathy, 84

newspapers, 76

Nicaragua: democratization criticism, 118–19; Nicaraguan model, 101, 102–03; pope's visit, 272; Reagan policy, 194
nickel plants, 76, 366n35
Nkadimeng, John Kgoana, 292
nominating assemblies, 124
nonaligned movement summit, 228
nongovernmental organizations: anti-Castro movement, 189, 221, 249; Cuban, listed, 292
Nuccio, Richard, 190, 215, 249

OAS. See Organization of American States
objective conditions, 51
Ochoa, Arnaldo, 67, 98–99
Office of Foreign Assets Control (OFAC), 187
officials, younger government, 281–82
oil, Soviet imports, 34, 75, 352n7
Onlate Laborde, Santiago, 240, 321n3
optic neuritis, 84
Organization of American States (OAS), 234–35, 239
Organs of People's Power (OPP): Communist Party relationship, 106, 121–22; Communist Party role, 342n. 56; described, 121–22; direct election, 113; economic strategies, 176; elections, 115–16, 117–18; improving its performance, 122–24; objectives, 122–23; origins, 122; political reform, 7; public opinion, 123
Ortega, Jaime Cardinal, 222, 254–55, 256; Afro-Cuban religions, 268; Caritas, 267; pope meeting, 263–64; significance of pope's visit, 259
Ortega, Luis, 300–301

Padrón, Amado, 98
paladares restaurants, 97, 146, 147
"Palestinians," 149
Palo Monte, 268
Panama, 228
paper factories, 76
Paraguay, 228
Paris Club, 60, 179, 351n. 1
participatory democracy seminars, 249
Pastors for Peace, 207, 301
patriotism, 95
Penal Code, 66
pensions, 66
Pentagon, 204

perestroika, 23–24; Castro questioning, 25; Cuban resistance, 26, 326–27n. 13; exchange problems, 35; glasnost, Cuban reaction, 24–26
Pérez Balladares, Ernesto, 228
Pérez, Lisandro, 11
Pérez, Martín, 194
Pérez de Cuellar, Javier, 293
Pérez-López, J., 137, 138
Pérez Roque, Felipe, 126, 310n. 5
performing artists, 76
Peru, 22
peso: improvement, 143; taxable transactions, 150
pharmaceuticals, 153
pimping, 78
pluralism, dangers of, 103
Poland: Castro on, 271–72; economic reform, 137; human rights issue, 29, 290, 291; pope in, 256, 270–71, 376–77n. 68
police repression, 4
political attitudes: measuring, 120–21; opinion polls, 121tt5.2, 5.3
political change: Castro on, 100; need for, 128; reasons for, 101; unintended effects, 101
political culture, 286–87; Castro's, 298; conceptual codes, 299; Marxism-Leninism, 287–88
political prisoners, 222, 264, 374n40
political reform, 7–9; Castro on Gorbachev's, 44, 49, 108; Constitution, 113; slow change, 9; special period, 100
political system: Canadian agreement, 238; centralization of power, 124–25; changes of special period, 304; Latin American criticisms, 231; Mexico's PRI, 240; political change, 101; religious policy, 273–74; three objectives, 303; transition, 337n8
Ponce Solazábal, José Ramón, 75
pope's visit: background to, 254–58 ; Clinton on, 12; critical remarks, 261–65; crowds greeting, 259–60; developments before arrival, 254–58; evaluating, 269–72; expectations prior to, 372–73n. 20; incident before, 372n. 19; open-air masses, 261; political effect, 216–22; pope's health, 371–72n. 17; risks involved, 258–59; significance, 3, 251; speeches at airport, 260–61; summarized, 14–16
Popular Councils, 113

Popular Savings Bank (BPA), 10
Popular Socialist Party (PSP), 50
Posada Carriles, Luis, 160, 232
power, centralization of, 124–25
prices, 111
priests: in Cuba, 255; deportation of, 252
Prieto, Yolanda, 258
Prieto Jiménez, Abel Enrique, 111, 126, 315
principled pragmatism: Marxist-based, 286;
    as policy axis, 50; rectification process, 53;
    special period, 102
private enterprise, emergence of, 9
private property: Castro on, 111; constitution,
    115; socialist property and, 115, 134
privatization, 111, 136
productivity: agricultural cooperatives, 305;
    complacency, 132; economic policy, 130
Programa Alimentario, 76–77
proletarian internationalism, 288
property crimes, 59, 60
property and ownership, 115, 134, 136, 305
prostitution (jineterismo): economic problems
    and, 19; public health problem, 81; reasons
    for, 101, 280; return of, 7, 77–81; women in
    special period, 85
Protestant churches, 253, 254, 270, 273,
    370n. 7
Provincial Organs of People's Power, 119
public health, Japanese aid, 172. See also
    medical care
public opinion polls: 121tt5.2,, 5.3; Brothers
    to the Rescue (BTTR) planes downed, 204;
    Canada, 210; Latin America, 365n28; OPP
    changes, 123; Uruguay, 234; U.S., 210
public transportation, 75–76
publishing: Church-sponsored, 266, 375–
    76n48; special period, 76; women's
    magazines, 86, 335n. 31
purchasing power, 133, 143
purchasing power parity (PPP), 39

quality of life. See standard of living

radicals, 298
Radio Martí, 116, 202, 207
Ramírez, Jorge, 253
Rangel, Charles, 216
rapprochement between émigrés and Cuba,
    250
rationing system, 76, 278–79
Reagan administration, 194

rebellion, 283–84; Castro's, 298–99, 301–02
Reciprocity Agreements for the Protection
    and Promotion of Investment, 225
rectification (of errors and negative
    tendencies) process (RP), 6–7, 51–52;
    announced, 55; antecedents, 329n. 1;
    assessment overall, 58; balance sheet, 66–
    68; collapse of European socialism, 329–
    30n. 2; Communist Party, 105; concrete
    changes, 53–55; contrary to perestroika,
    326–27n. 13; criticisms of, 66–68;
    decentralization reforms, 52; economic
    strategies, 176; evaluating, 52–53;
    exchange problems, 35; foreign debt, 54;
    initiated, 25; justifying changes, 53;
    measures instituted, 62; origins, 49–50;
    scope and content, 55–59; timing, 54–55;
    two years after, 59–62
Red Cross (American), 216
regional (Caribbean) issues, 241–43
regional organizations, 230–35
religion: civil religion (U.S.), 381n. 49;
    Communist Party, 104
religious life: analyzing, 9; believers as party
    members, 306; Communist Party
    supervision, 122; future trends, 273–74,
    304–5; human rights issue, 18; official
    policy, 17
religious rights, regime control vs., 45
religious tolerance, 3; Castro on, 255, 371n.
    14; constitution, 114, 115; other religions,
    270
remittances from relatives abroad, 10, 277–
    78; Más Canosa on, 11; as revenue source,
    139
rentals, housing, 147–49
resist, will to, 43
restaurants, 97
revolt, as possible scenario, 101–02
revolution, conditions for, 303
revolutionary activity, 22
Revolutionary Armed Forces (FAR):
    commercial structure, 162, 164; economy,
    160–64
Revolutionary Directorate (DR), 50, 306
revolutionary voluntarism, 49
Richardson, Bill, 217
Rio Group, 234, 235
Ríos, Nicolás, 249
riots on waterfront in Havana, 290
Ritter, A.R.M., 137–38

Roa Kouri, Raúl., 294
Robaina González, Roberto, 315; BTTR
    planes downed, 199; Clinton policy, 214;
    exile community, 247; humanitarian aid
    rejected, 222; human rights issue, 291;
    Mexican meetings, 239; new face of Cuba,
    281; new generation, 127, 128; pope's visit,
    263, 375n. 47; School of National Defense
    training, 344n. 69
Roca, Sergio, 340n33
Roca, Vladimiro, 116, 237, 290
Rodríguez, Carlos Rafael, 49–50, 303, 315–16
Rodríguez, José Luis, 309, 310; capitalist
    modalities, 110; on economic reform, 135–
    36; Helms-Burton Act impact, 168–69; new
    generation, 126; regime's dilemma, 53; on
    tourism, 157; trade deficits, 173
Rodríguez Llerena, Otto René, 159
Rodríguez Rivera, Guillermo, 289
Roque, Juan Pablo, 193–94
Rosales del Toro, Ulises, 162, 310, 315
Ros-Lehtinen, Ileana, 187, 219, 324n. 16
Ross Leal, Pedro, 147, 315
RP. See rectification process
Ruiz Poó, Miguel, 98
Russia: end of Cold War, 179; post-Cold War
    trade, 35–36, 352n. 7; trade, 6, 38
Ryan, George, 250

St. Kitts and Nevis, 241
salaries, 65
Sánchez Santa Cruz, Elizardo, 110, 336n. 1
Santana, Nelson, 253
Santana Castillo, Joaquín, 284
Santería, 268
São Paulo Forum, 303
Sawyer, Diane, 8
scarcities, 279–80
schooling, years of, 39, 40, 41t2.5
scientific studies, 93
Second Clinton Administration: Cuba policy
    characterized, 180; plan lacking, 215;
    policy litmus test, 190; scope of action
    analyzed, 220–21
self-determination, 223
self-employment: authorized, 146–47;
    Communist Party on effects, 337n. 3;
    controls over income, 56; emergence, 9;
    future trends, 136; growth, 351n. 48;
    industrial markets, 149, 150; rectification
    process, 62; regulated, 147; taxes, 150

Seminar on Definitions of Human Rights
    (1995), 294
Sherritt Corporation, 154–55, 209
Shining Path, 22
Shuss, Billy, 194
Siata company (Italy), 155
single-party politics: Communist Party, 107,
    108; Communist Party and OPP, 122;
    democratizing the Communist Party, 128;
    early experience, 50; future trends, 306;
    Lenin and Martí, 103–4; opposition to, 289
Smith, Wayne S., 203, 294, 340n33
Soberón Valdés, Francisco, 97, 310, 335n. 51
social benefits, 277, 304
social class: Catholic Church, 251; notion of,
    122
social cleavage effect, of dollarization, 140–41
social equity principle, main objectives, 70
social indicators, 39–41, 70–71, 72f4.2
socialism: economic modalities, 175–76; fate
    of, and Soviet reforms, 26; impact of
    survival crisis, 277; new economic model,
    134; reinventing Cuban, 16, 43–44, 45;
    religiosity and social concern, 253; risk to
    system, 102; stance on religion, 254. See
    also European socialism
socialist property, 115
socialization, 287, 378n. 12
social science studies, 96
social security, 111
social services sector, 58
social stratification. See dollar/peso social
    divide
social welfare state, 134, 304
Societa Finanziara Telefonica (STET, Italy),
    13, 154
Sodano, Angelo Cardinal, 222
Solás, Humberto, 289
South Africa, 292. See also Mandela, Nelson
South Korea, 292
sovereignty issues, 4, 179, 223, 301, 304
Soviet bloc: foreign debt, 169–70; formation,
    24; implosion, 24; reforms, 24
Soviet-Yugoslav Statement of Principles, 24
Spain: attitude toward Cuba, 243–47; Helms-
    Burton Act, 212–13; Ibero-American
    summit, 233; joint ventures, 153; pope's
    visit, 256; tourism, 158; trade, 244
special period in peacetime, 44–45;
    beginnings, 59; corruption, 96–99;
    economic reform, 138–40; foreign

investment, 153–55; Latin American left understanding process, 304; as military contingency, 21; political reform, 100; previous Soviet collaboration, 34–35; rectification process, 55; social effects summarized, 99; social implications, 69; social indicators, 40–41; women, effects on, 85, 88, 89f4.5; worst year, 140

speculation, free farmers' markets, 63

squatter evictions, 148

Stalinism, 283

standard of living: during economic downfall, 7; GDP share, 74; Latin America, 73–74; prostitution, 80; special period, 69; U.S. disparities, 73

state, new economic role, 134, 135. *See also* economic policy

state enterprises, 111, 152; tourism, 155–56

statistical system, 62

STET. *See* Societa Finanziara Telefonica

Stewart, Christine, 236

stress therapy workshops, 75

Suárez, Raúl, 253

subjective conditions, 51

subsidy policy, 34, 152

sugar economy: Basic Units of Cooperative Production, 144–46; burden on economy, 168–69, 174; capital accumulation, 129; early 1990s, 132; early problems, 50; exports to Russia, 36, 352n7; GDP contribution, 130, 130t6.1; imports for, 171–72; industrialization drive, 129; investor financing, 169; labor reserve of unemployed, 92; recovery, 157, 158f7.2; Soviet need for, 27, 28f2.1; sugar barter, 169

support for the revolution, 4

survival crisis: change potential, 289; people's goodwill, 53; people's reactions, 30; redefining core values, 277; will to resist, 43

Sustainable Development, Summit Conference on (Bolivia), 233

Switzerland, 30

syphilis, 81

System of Direction and Planning of the Economy (SDPE), 24–25; problems, 57

taxation, 150–52; income scale, 151t6.2

Temas journal, 283–84, 286

terrorist attacks: Cuban tourist industry, 158–

60, 232; Israeli, admired by Más Canosa, 185–86

theme of book, 5

Thiessen, Marc, 215

Third World, 29, 227

Torres-Dodd bill, 196, 216, 250

Torres, Esteban, 196, 216

Torres, Nelson, 145, 171–72

Torricelli-Graham bill: Clinton's support, 10; migration issues, 248; provisions, 186–87; signed into law, 186–88; two-track policy, 189

Torricelli, Robert, 183, 219, 323n. 13

tourism: Caribbean, 243; defending from saboteurs, 158–60, 349n. 23, 354–55n. 42; described, 155–58; exemptions from special period, 76; highly qualified workers, 74; joint ventures, 155; labor costs, 156; prostitution, 45, 78–80; rectification process, 67; rentals of rooms, 148; revenues, 157, 157f7.1; significance, 157; special period, 75; taxis, 76; terrorism, 158–60, 349n. 23, 354–55n. 42; veneral disease, 45

trade: Canada, 236–37, 235t10.3; CARICOM, 242; China, 36, 38–39, 38t2.1; Communist Party, 107; deficits, 132, 174t7.9; early 1990s, 132; France, 238–39; gains and deficits, 1995–1997, 173–74; Helms-Burton Act, 211; international structure transformed, 31; Japan, 227; with market economies, 31–32, 32f2.2; merchandise deficit, 66; Mexico, 240; post-Cold War, 35–36; Russia, 6, 38, 180–81; socialist countries, 31, 33; socialist crisis effects, 21; Soviet, 75; Spain, 244; top partners (1996), 38t2.3; USSR 1989–1996, 37t2.1

trade unions, 135

travel to Cuba, restrictions, 202, 203, 205

travel permits, 247

Treaty of Friendship and Cooperation (Cuba and USSR, 1989), 28

Trinidad and Tobago, 241

Trudeau, Pierre, 236

Trujillo Izquierdo, Elizabeth, 322n. 8

Tupac Amaru, 22

TV Martí, 116, 202, 207

two-class system, 137, 280

UBPCs (Basic Units of Cooperative Production). *See* agricultural cooperatives

unemployment, 66; self-employment, 146, 147; youth, 92–93
Union of Communist Youth (UJC), 92, 123, 156
United Methodist Church, 272
United Nations: Castro defending poor, 227; Cuban diplomacy, 225; Human Rights Commission, 29, 290, 291t12.1, 293–94; investigating Brothers to the Rescue incident, 197–99, 202; Mexico on coercion, 239; resolutions against embargo, 225–26, 226t10.1; Security Council, 197–99; Social Subcommittee of Economic and Social Council, 290–91
United Party of the Socialist Revolution (PURS), 50
United States: Brothers to the Rescue (BTTR) planes downed, 191–95; Caribbean tourism, 157–58; civil religion, 381n. 49; elections, Cuba role, 181, 183; GDP share, 73; health care, 81; infant mortality, 82; investment in Cuba, 6; investment group, 154; life expectancy, 82; obsession with Castro, 188–90, 194–95; political parties, 104; standard of living disparities, 73
Uruguay, 234
U.S.-Cuban relations: Helms-Burton Act effects, 204; sovereignty issue, 179
U.S. policy to Cuba: assessed, 18; assumptions, 4; biological warfare, 354–56n. 42; calls for change, 219; Clinton administration, 10; early years, 351–52n. 3; human rights issue, 290–91, 292–94; opposing signals, 12; pope's visit, 256, 257–58; reform potential related, 306–7; visa bans, 209–10, 240; website on Cuba, 369n. 70
USSR: Afghanistan, 23; benefits from Cuba, 27; commercial imbalance, 32; on Cuba, 27, 327n. 19, 327–28n. 20; development assistance, 32; financial assistance, 33; glasnost, Cuban reaction, 24–26; perestroika, 23–24; policy priorities, 20; post-Cold War trade, 35–36; reform process, 22<n. 24, 327n. 17; restructuring, 26; socialist realism, 297; special relationship questioned, 345n9; trade, 1989–1996, 37t2.1

Valdés, Dagoberto, 253, 375–76n. 48
Valdés, Nelson P., 203, 299, 301
Valdés Paz, Juan, 302
Varadero, 155, 158, 160
Varela, Félix, 262
venereal disease, 81
Venezuela, 230, 231–32; on embargo, 266; exiles, 231–32
Verba, Sidney, 286, 378n. 11
Vietnam, 227
Vietnamese model, 108
visa bans, U.S., 209–10, 240
voluntarism, revolutionary, 49, 51, 61
voting, 115–19

Walker, Lucius, 301
women: daily schedules, special period, 88, 89f4.5; education, 87, 87f4.3; electoral candidates, 117; employment and child-care centers, 58; Japan, 73; labor force, 85, 87–88; labor and marital status, 87–88, 88f4.4; legislative power, 124, 125t5.1; life expectancy, 82; magazines analyzed, 86, 335n. 31; public health, 81–84; special period, 85–88. See also prostitution (jineterismo)
World Health Organization (WHO), 84, 188; Helms-Burton Act, 213, 214, 237–38
World Trade Organization (WTO): Castro at, 228; Helms-Burton Act, 11

Yeltsin, Boris, 179, 352n. 7
youth: career opportunities, 90; Festival of Youth and Students, 301–2; frustration, 279; higher education, 92–96; history studies, 93–6, 94f4.6, 95f4.8; Marxism, 96; negative attitudes, 91–92; special period, 88–92; teaching methods, 95f4.7; unemployment, 92–93; Union of Communist Youth (UJC), 92, 123
yummies, 125–27

Zapatista rebellion, 22
Zimbalist, Andrew, 340n. 33

Max Azicri is professor of political science at Edinboro University of Pennsylvania. He is the author of *Cuba: Politics, Economics and Society* and numerous studies on Cuban politics, society, culture, the legal system, immigration, international relations, women, and the Cuban-American community.